Beyond the World Bank Agenda

Beyond the World Bank Agenda

An Institutional Approach to Development

HOWARD STEIN

THE UNIVERSITY OF CHICAGO PRESS   CHICAGO AND LONDON

HOWARD STEIN is a professor at the University of Michigan's Center for Afroamerican and African Studies.

The University of Chicago Press, Chicago 60637
The University of Chicago Press, Ltd., London
© 2008 by The University of Chicago
All rights reserved. Published 2008
Printed in the United States of America
17 16 15 14 13 12 11 10 09 08   1 2 3 4 5

ISBN-13: 978-0-226-77167-0 (cloth)
ISBN-10: 0-226-77167-9 (cloth)

Library of Congress Cataloging-in-Publication Data

Stein, Howard, 1952–
  Beyond the World Bank agenda : an institutional approach to development / Howard Stein.
     p. cm.
  Includes bibliographical references and index.
  ISBN-13: 978-0-226-77167-0 (cloth : alk. paper)
  ISBN-10: 0-226-77167-9 (cloth : alk. paper) 1. World Bank. 2. Economic development—Developing countries. 3. Institutional economics. I. Title.
  HG3881.5 .W57S74 2008
  338.9009172'4—dc22

                                                            2007049302

♾ The paper used in this publication meets the minimum requirements of the American National Standard for Information Sciences—Permanence of Paper for Printed Library Materials, ANSI Z39.48-1992.

TO ALISA, JOSHUA, AND DANIEL

Contents

List of Illustrations

Abbreviations

ABCDE	Annual Bank Conference on Development Economics
AIDS	Acquired Immunodeficiency Syndrome
ARV	antiretroviral drugs
BIS	Bank for International Settlements
CBN	Central Bank of Nigeria
CFAF	Communauté Française d'Afrique Franc
CGE	computational general equilibrium
CIBN	Chartered Institute of Bankers of Nigeria
CRED	Center for Research on Economic Development
DAC	Development Assistance Committee of OECD
DALY	disability-adjusted life year
DFID	Department for International Development (U.K.)
DI	distortion index
DPL	development policy loan
ECA	Economic Commission for Africa
EFF	extended fund facility
ESAF	enhanced structural adjustment facility
ETHNIC	a Soviet study of ethnic diversity
FAO	Food and Agriculture Organization of the United Nations
FIL	financial intermediary loan
FSAL	financial sector adjustment loan
FSLC	financial sector liaison committee
GDP	gross domestic product

GNP	gross national product
HIPC	Heavily indebted poor countries
HIV	Human Immunodeficiency Virus
HNP	Health, Nutrition and Population
IBRD	International Bank for Reconstruction and Development
ICOR	incremental capital-output ratio
IDA	International Development Association
IFC	International Finance Corporation
ILO	International Labor Organization
IMF	International Monetary Fund
IRIS	Institutional Reform and the Informal Sector
ITN	insecticide-treated net
MIGA	Multinational investment guarantee agency
MITI	Ministry of International Trade and Industry (Japan)
MOH	Ministry of Health
NBFO	nonbank financial organization
NDIC	Nigerian Deposit Insurance Corporation
NGO	nongovernmental organization
NIE	new institutional economics
NPM	new public management theory
NTP	National Tuberculosis Program (Zambia)
OECD	Organization for Economic Cooperation and Development
OED	Operations Evaluation Department
OIE	original institutional economics
OPEC	Organization of the Petroleum Exporting Countries
PHC	primary health care
PRBS	poverty reduction budget support
PRGF	Poverty reduction and growth facility
PRSP	Poverty reduction strategy papers
PSAC	Programmatic structural adjustment credit
PSI	Population Services International
SAL	structural adjustment loan
SAM	social accounting matrix
SAP	structural adjustment program

SCI   Social Capital Initiative (of the World Bank)
SDR   special drawing rights
SECAL   sectoral adjustment loan
SEIPR   Stanford Institute of Economic Policy Research
SFA   Special facility for sub-Saharan Africa
SIDA   Swedish International Development Agency
SUNFED   Special United Nations Fund for Economic Development
SWAPs   sector-wide action programs
TANU   Tanzania African National Union
UNCTAD   United Nations Conference on Trade and Development
UNDP   United Nations Development Programme
UNICEF   United Nations Children's Fund
USAID   United States Agency for International Development
WDR   World Development Report
WHO   World Health Organization
WTO   World Trade Organization

Preface

This volume represents the culmination of a number of years of research in structural adjustment and its impact on Africa and elsewhere. My early post-dissertation work in the mid-1980s focused on economic and policy transformation in Tanzania, which became particularly interesting after the country, contrary to its stated socialist principles, reached a settlement with the International Monetary Fund and the World Bank in 1986. The changes in Tanzania led me to look more broadly at structural adjustment, which was rapidly becoming ubiquitous throughout Africa. By the late 1980s, it was becoming quite apparent that Africa and other regions were doing rather poorly under this new policy regime. I began to investigate the reasons for this by critically evaluating the theoretical underpinnings of adjustment. My initial working hypothesis was that the problem arose from a fundamental disconnect between the reality of African economies and the economic world assumed by the adjustment-related theories. I was also very interested in the way in which adjustment had become the dominant policy paradigm in the World Bank. One of the first areas I investigated was the impact of adjustment on manufacturing and industry, which had not performed well during the 1980s. I carefully contrasted the world of manufacturing depicted in the structural adjustment literature with the reality in African countries and predicted that adjustment would deindustrialize African countries.

A common reaction voiced in seminars critical of structural adjustment was that, despite the weaknesses, there were no alternatives. Partly in response, I began to investigate the route to development undertaken in East and Southeast Asia; my aim was to contrast their historical experiences to strategies being adopted in Africa during the 1980s. At about the same time, I started thinking about the nature of institutions and their relation to the reform agenda. Structural adjustment is based on neoclassical economic theories that focus on individual agents exchanging goods and services to maximize utility goals relative to a set of price vectors. There are no institutions in this world, yet it would seem that institutions are vitally important to generating development.

The World Bank also began to consider institutions, particularly after the awarding of the Nobel Prize in economics to Douglass North and Ronald Coase. The Bank mainly focused on the New Institutional Economics variant, which I felt was a poor guide to development, in part because of its close linkage to the same theory that underlies adjustment and in part because it was focused on developed countries. At that point, I also began to reread the work of such original institutionalists as Thorstein Veblen and Gunnar Myrdal and came across a new generation of writers working in this tradition that included Geoff Hodgson and Ha-Joon Chang. I became convinced that institutional theory, which had its origins among economists drawing on research in social psychology, could provide a powerful set of tools with which to understand the socioeconomic transformation at the heart of the development process. In particular, development is all about altering the manner in which people interact to produce goods and services and to generate their standard of living. At the core of this transformation are new behavioral norms, new common mental constructs, and new capabilities to interpret and apply these constructs for purposes of coordinated development. This book tries to explain the origins, genesis, and failures of the World Bank development agenda while pointing to alternatives based on institutional economic theory.

Acknowledgments

Many kind people have provided me with critical feedback in seminars, in conversations, or by patiently reading earlier drafts of this work. I am particularly indebted to Ha-Joon Chang, Philip Arestis, Jeanne Koopman, John Weeks, Ajit Singh, Machiko Nissanke, the late Sanjaya Lall, Bill Dugger, Ulf Engel, Pam Cohen, Cathy Boone, Ian Gough, Steven Rosefielde, E. Wayne Nafziger, K. S. Jomo, Kelly Tzoumis, Peter Lewis, Juro Teranishi, Konosuke Odaka, Olu Ajakaiye, Jonathan Low, Holger Hansen, Dylan Sutherland, Jochen Oppenheimer, Stefano Ponte, Morten Boas, and Chris Cramer.

Many friends and colleagues at the University of Michigan have provided me with encouragement and intellectual and moral support through many months of researching and writing this book. I am particularly grateful to Mamadou Diouf, David William Cohen, James Jackson, Mark Wilson, Hal Morgenstern, George Kaplan, David Bloom, Sean Jacobs, Amal Fadlalla, Kelly Askew, Richard Turits, Frieda Ekotto, Elisha Renne, David Fox, Ray Silverman, Kevin Gaines, Don Sims, and Jose Tapia. I was very fortunate to have a series of research assistants dedicated to this project. Philip Carls worked with me in the early stages by gathering research material, undertaking interviews, and providing critical feedback about first drafts of chapters. Natalie Orpett was very helpful in gathering empirical material for the health chapter, in drafting the index, and in meticulously editing every sentence in the volume. Jennifer Lee Johnson and Theodore Lawrence worked with me to prepare the final manuscript for the publisher. I am grateful for the flexibility, professionalism, and support of the editors at the University of Chicago Press, including J. Alex Schwartz, Robert Devens, David Pervin, and Parker Smathers.

Finally, I am indebted to a number of key current and retired members of the World Bank staff who carefully responded to my questions in telephone interviews and email exchanges or in person. The vast majority prefer to remain anonymous. Two, however, agreed to be quoted by name: Pierre Landell-Mills and Ram Agarwala. Both were extremely generous with their time and were instrumental in providing important details in mapping out the evolution of the World Bank agenda.

PART I

Reflections on the History of the World Bank Agenda

CHAPTER ONE

The Ascendancy of Economics in the World Bank, 1944–1979

From Infrastructure to Structural Adjustment

The most fundamental thought that holds institutional economists together . . . is our recognition that even if we focus attention on specific economic problems our study must take into account the entire social system.—Gunnar Myrdal, 1978

[I]nstitutional economics . . . is destined to gain ground at the expense of conventional economics in the near future . . . because it will be needed for dealing effectively with practical and political problems that are now towering over and threatening to overwhelm us. Much of present establishment economics and in particular, those very abstract theoretical constructs enjoying up till now the highest prestige among economist will, I believe, be left by the wayside as irrelevant and uninteresting.—Gunnar Myrdal, 1978

[I]f orthodox economics is at fault the error is to be found not in the superstructure, which has been erected with great care for logical consistency, but in a lack of clearness and generality in the premises . . . the characteristics of the special case assumed by the . . . theory happen not to be those of the economic society in which we actually live, with the result that its teaching is misleading and disastrous if we attempt to apply it.—John Maynard Keynes, 1936

Introduction

The development strategies of the international financial institutions (IFIs) over the course of the past two decades have been a profound failure. A majority of the developing countries that participated in IFI programs have experienced lower growth and rising inequality during the period of IFI intervention than in previous periods. In some countries there has also been a noticeable increase in poverty rates. The most pernicious regional impact has been in sub-Saharan Africa, which has seen per capita GNP decline by 41 percent between 1980 and 2002 (World Bank 2004a). Between 1981 and 2001 the number of people living on less than $1 per day in sub-Saharan Africa—a common measure of poverty— increased from 164 to 313 million, or approximately 46 percent of the total population (World Bank 2005a).

The crisis in developing countries reflects a crisis in the economic theory that has driven the policies implemented since 1980. The challenge is not unlike the one faced in the 1930s, the last period in which the reigning policy had so little to offer to a population replete with despair, hopelessness, and a paucity of opportunities. Not surprisingly, there is also considerable overlap on a theoretical level between the orthodoxy of the depression era, which Keynes so heavily criticized, and the theory embedded in the neoliberal packages promoted by the IFIs since the 1980s.

Since the Great Depression, there has not been a more pressing moment for a fresh theoretical approach to design new pathways to development. Owing in part to dissatisfaction with the state of the theory in mainstream economics, there has been a plethora of new ideas challenging the fundamental premises and methodology of neoclassical approaches.

Perhaps the richest and most extensive new vein of thinking is found in a subdiscipline of economics called institutional economics, which is notable for its recognition of the complex relations between economic problems and other parts of the social system. As seen above, Myrdal clairvoyantly predicted that the turn to institutional economics would be driven by the fundamental inability of mainstream economics to deal with "towering" practical and political problems. This book attempts not only to deal with the theoretical and practical problems currently at hand but also to recommend an alternative policymaking agenda that builds on these alternative economic theories.

Parts I and II investigate the anatomy of World Bank (often known simply as the Bank) policy failures and the extent to which developments in institutional economics have been used to address the underlying weaknesses of the Bank's agenda. Chapters 1 and 2 investigate the origin, nature, and evolution of policies in the Bank. More precisely, I focus on how the increasing domination of economists within the Bank occurred in tandem with a theoretical narrowing of the economics profession and its gradual disconnection from its older institutional traditions. Chapter 1 examines the period from 1944 to 1980; the second concentrates on the particularly troublesome recent years, from 1980 to the present, during which structural adjustment and other related policies emerged and evolved. Chapter 3 shifts from a historical view of structural adjustment to a theoretical one by critically examining the theory underlying structural adjustment in order to explain its failures. Chapter 4 examines the origin and impact of the Bank's "discovery" of institutional economics in the 1990s, which was used not to rethink and reevaluate its policies but rather to attempt to justify the continuation of the orthodox agenda.

Part III develops an alternative policy framework based on the premise that an institutional matrix of norms, organizations, regulations, capacities, and incentives can transform economies. For development purposes, institutional transformation should focus on generating new forms of socially prescribed correlated behavior aimed at increasing the standard of living of a target population. Chapter 5 builds on the work of Gunnar Myrdal, the last economist to systematically apply original institutional economic theory to development, as well as forty years' worth of new research in organizational theory, sociology, social psychology, and institutional and behavioral economics. Chapters 6, 7, and 8 contrast the World Bank agenda and its underlying theory to the institutional approach in three vital areas: state formation, financial development, and health care policy. Chapter 9 provides a summary and conclusions.

I begin with a brief investigation of some of the competing theories about the nature of international organizations in international relations. Policy transformation in any large organization such as the Bank results from a confluence of factors interacting with an array of existing structures and interests. Hence, this section investigates a variety of elements influencing policy: the power of the Bank's constituent members, the ways in which the United States has asserted its dominance in the Bank, and the relation between American interests, organizational changes, and the ascendancy of economists.

Dynamics of Policy Transformation:
The Confluence of Ideology, Power, and Theory

The International Bank for Reconstruction and Development (IBRD), the original unit of the World Bank, was created at the Bretton Woods Conference in 1944. Purportedly, its aim was to help rebuild war-devastated countries and support development in poorer regions of the world. Yet the IBRD has proved to be a much more complicated entity. Literature

investigating the nature of international organizations such as the World
Bank has drawn from a wide body of writing within international relations. Generally, theories about international organizations can be sub-
divided into two opposing camps. Neo-realists such as Robert Keohane
(1986), see multilateral agencies as a product of the interaction and relative power of the participating states.

In contrast, new realists such as Robert Cox (1997) take a post-
Westphalian view that envisions an international system influenced by
global and antiglobal forces that lead to outcomes greater than the sum
of the interests of participating states.[1] Similarly, Boas and McNeill (2003)
see multilateral organizations such as the World Bank as structures of governance that establish a new social order. This new social order is then embedded in the "nexus between material conditions, ideas, and interests"
(5). According to this view, policy outcomes are products of the struggle
between international institutions operating within certain institutionalized rules. In this context, the actions of the hegemonic power (these days,
the United States) are modified and tempered by the confluence of other
international actors.

Robert Wade (2002), in an adaptation of the new realist perspective,
sees the American hegemony over the Bank as constrained less by the dynamics of multiple actors than by the need to maintain the appearance that
it is operating according to its own rules. This view is in accordance with
the Gramscian understanding of hegemony,[2] in which dominance is best
achieved by convincing subordinates that they are also the beneficiaries of
the actions (substantive) and convincing them that the rules are imposed
equally on both the hegemonic power and the subordinates (procedural).[3]

The construction of institutionalized rules that gave the illusion of
mutual benefit to all partners has increasingly allowed economists to
dominate the operational and research domain of the Bank. Mainstream
economic theory, with its pretensions to scientific objectivity and its usage
of increasingly abstruse methods and terminology, has provided an important legitimizing veneer for the realization of U.S. priorities inside the
World Bank.[4] Yet organizations are complex entities, subject to high degrees of path-determinacy as they change over time.[5] The apparent instrumentality of operating norms and principles says nothing of their origins
or their original purpose. Although the ascendancy of economists inside
the Bank reached its peak after 1980, the foundation that allowed it was
put in place over a number of decades. I first turn to the relation between
U.S. priorities and the structure of the Bank.

U.S. Dominance in the Bank: Structure and Voting Power

The utilization of the concept of hegemony to describe the relation between the Bank and American interests implies one of dominance, not of domination. In other words, explaining every Bank decision simply as an instrument of American priorities is overly simplistic.

The United States has, however, worked hard to ensure that any major alterations in the organization, procedures, and programs of the Bank have been in its best interests. Theoretically, the Bank's structures and policies are supposed to reflect the will of the membership, but in practice, the Bank has never worked on the principle of "one member, one vote" but rather has functioned according to a more complicated formula linked to the importance of a country's economy.

Take the example of African representation. In mid-1947, forty countries had become members of the World Bank. Only two were from Africa: Ethiopia and South Africa. As African countries gained their independence, their membership in the Bank rapidly expanded to eight by 1962, thirty-four by 1967, and forty by 1971. In that year African countries constituted 35 percent of the total membership but had only 8.6 percent of the voting power. In contrast, the developed countries in Europe and North America, plus Japan, controlled almost two-thirds of the votes despite representing only 20 percent of the membership (Mason and Asher 1973, 65). Today, little has changed. On the twenty-four-member executive board of the IBRD, for example, the United States had one seat in 2003, European nations had eight, and the forty-seven countries of sub-Saharan Africa had only two seats.[6]

In principle, the distribution of votes is based on measurements of national income, foreign reserves, and contributions to international trade. In practice, the process is highly political; the United States deliberately maintains its proportion of more than 15 percent of the voting power in order to maintain veto power over major decisions, which require an 85 percent special majority. In 2003, for example, when developing nations were pushing for an increase in their allocation of votes, the United States was able to block the proposal because it might have threatened its share.[7]

As seen in table 1.1, the United States has had by far the largest share of the voting power, around 24.5 percent, in 1970. Its share fell to a low of 15.1 percent in 1990 before rebounding to 16.38 percent in 2007. Note that no other country has veto power; the next largest share (7.86 percent) belongs to Japan (World Bank 2007).

TABLE 1.1 **U.S. voting shares in the World Bank, 1950–2007**

1950	1960	1970	1980	1990	2007
34.1	30.3	24.5	21.1	15.1	16.38

Source: Boas and McNeill 2003, 26; World Bank 2007.

Although the Executive Board of the IBRD mostly operates via consensus, the hegemonic veto power of the United States is omnipresent. If a loan does not have American approval, it is unlikely to be proposed to the board (Woods 2000, 133–34). Furthermore, as a recent empirical study has illustrated, the countries selected to receive loans frequently mirror American interests. Faini and Grilli (2004), for example, run a series of regressions testing the relationship between World Bank and International Monetary Fund (IMF) loans and the regional trading and financial interests of the United States, Japan, and the European Union (EU). The United States was the only country in which World Bank and IMF loans coincided with the trading interests and financial exposure of its own banks.

Moreover, since the World Bank's inception, the United States has always selected its president. Not surprisingly, many of the major shifts in World Bank structure and policy making have also tended to reflect shifting U.S. political priorities. For example, beginning in the late Eisenhower years, aid was seen as a vehicle to build up support in nations as a bulwark against Soviet expansion (Gwin 1994, 14).[8]

American politicians, however, believed that this strategic aid would be more effective if it were kept institutionally separate from U.S. foreign policy mechanisms. The United States therefore pushed for the creation of a new arm of the World Bank that would provide loans to the poorer developing countries at more generous terms than those offered by the IBRD. It was called the International Development Association, or IDA.

The idea of creating a new agency to support the least developed countries was actually proposed as early as 1951 by a U.S. presidential commission led by Nelson Rockefeller. But it took the events of the late 1950s, especially the Soviet success story, the launching of *Sputnik,* and the creation of the Special United Nations Fund for Economic Development, or SUNFED (Oliver 1995, 44) to finally spur its creation.[9] When the United States formally submitted the IDA proposal in July 1959, the organization was a fait accompli—it had already been cleared through Treasury discussions with World Bank officials and other donors.

Thus, the debate among the members was focused on the sectors to be covered by the IDA, not the loan terms, or eligibility criteria. At the Bank's annual meeting in the fall of 1959, World Bank president Eugene Black and the senior management, supported by such countries as West Germany and the Netherlands, opposed the idea of lending for social programming. Yet Douglas Dillon, the undersecretary of state for the United States, supported IDA lending for social overhead. Although the formal IDA Charter was vague regarding social spending, the "Accompanying Report of the Executive Directors" made it clear that the IDA was to lend to traditional Bank projects and development areas that were not directly revenue-producing, such as sanitation, water supply, and housing. Political events quickly pushed the IDA in this new direction. Although Jordan was turned down for a loan by the IBRD in 1958 because it was determined to have insufficient creditworthiness, the IDA quickly disbursed a loan in 1960 for a water project to help stabilize the pro-Western Hussein regime in Jordan following the pro-Nassar coup in neighboring Iraq. In the wake of the Cuban revolution and Cuba's nationalization of U.S.-owned property, the IDA rapidly disbursed loans to a host of pro-American regimes in Latin America, including some for projects that had been turned down by the IBRD on commercial grounds (Kapur et al. 1997, 154–65).

One of the lasting effects of the creation of the IDA arose from its financial structure. Unlike the IBRD, which was largely self-financed, the IDA loaned money at less than the market rate and needed replenishment from member states' contributions every three years. This gave the U.S. Congress, which voted on the American contribution, a mechanism with which to impose conditions on the American allocation, thereby influencing the World Bank agenda (Wade 2002, 203–4). For example, during negotiations among member nations in IDA 6 (1981–84) in 1979, World Bank president Robert McNamara was warned by key members of Congress that replenishment would be voted down unless he agreed to block all loans to Vietnam. McNamara had little choice but to comply (Kapur et al. 1997, 1150).

Nongovernmental organizations (NGOs) based in the United States, frustrated with direct appeals to the World Bank, have taken advantage of American hegemony and Congress's funding approval mechanism (via IDA replenishments and foreign appropriations bills) to change parts of the World Bank agenda. The two most prominent cases have been environmental policy, richly documented by Wade (1997), and the removal of user fees in 2000.[10]

Two other major units of the Bank were similarly shaped by American priorities. The International Finance Corporation (IFC) was finally established in 1956, after long negotiations with the U.S. government regarding its organization and responsibilities caused considerable delays. Simply put, the IFC's mission was to extend loans to private companies in developing countries. Yet the details of this mission were contentious; the modifications made during the negotiations were significant and clearly reflected pressures from a conservative U.S. administration, which felt that the Bank should not compete with the private sector. For example, changes were made regarding both the size of the IFC (which was reduced from a proposed capitalization of $400 million to $100 million) and its operating principles (which initially allowed for raising money on capital markets and investing in stock; these abilities were later removed). Likewise, the Reagan administration's skepticism delayed the creation of the Multinational Investment Guarantee Agency (MIGA), which was organized in 1988 to provide insurance for foreign investment and support for developing countries interested in formulating foreign investment policies.

U.S. Interests, the Shifting Policy Agenda, and Economists' Ascent

Eugene Meyer, the former chairman of the Federal Reserve, was the first president of the World Bank when it opened in June 1946. He abruptly resigned in December of the same year owing to a constant struggle with the executive directors over his role in the Bank. President Truman looked for a replacement for two months before persuading the lawyer John McCloy, former assistant secretary of war, to take the job. He agreed on the condition that he be allowed to choose the American executive director. He selected Eugene Black, who subsequently served as the president of the World Bank from 1949 to 1962 (Oliver 1995, 39). Black was a conservative; he limited the scope of the Bank to loans for infrastructure projects that could clearly demonstrate a capacity to expand GDP and generate the income to repay the loans. Eighty-three percent of all pre-IDA loans to poor countries went to power and transportation projects; not a single loan was for education, health, or other social sectors (Kapur et al. 1997, 109–10). Overall, as shown in table 1.2, more than 60 percent of all loans went to infrastructure in the 1950s and 1960s.

TABLE 1.2 **World Bank lending by sector**

Sector	1950–59	1960–69	1970–79	1980–89	1990–94	1995–99
Agriculture	4	13	28	24	15	11
Finance and industry	13	12	16	18	10	13
Infrastructure*	61	64	36	29	26	21
Social**	0	4	13	15	27	26
Other***	22	8	8	15	22	28

Source: Kapur et al. 1997, 6; World Bank 1999b.
Note: Figures in columns are percentages.
*Infrastructure includes transportation, telecommunications, and electricity
**Social spending includes education, environment, population, water and sanitation, social protection, and urban development.
***Other includes oil and gas, mining, public sector management, tourism, multisector, and unclassified. After 1980, multisector lending was by far the largest type of lending in this category (for example 14% in 1990–94 and 16% in 1995–99).

A former bond seller, Black was interested in securing the viability of the World Bank with a conservative portfolio. For the United States and other developed countries, he was an excellent choice for leading the Bank in the 1950s, especially given its capital structure. From its inception, only 3 percent to 5 percent of member country subscriptions—the portion of the capital base that was the responsibility of each country—were actually paid into the Bank. The rest was in the form of "guarantees" promised by the states. Yet under Black's tutelage, the World Bank was able to maintain an AAA rating by Moody's, the highest credit rating possible (Oliver 1995, 41). This rating was central to the Bank's operation: it required bonds to be floated at the lowest possible interest rates because profits to finance Bank operations came from the difference between the interest rate charged and the rate paid by the borrowing country. Moreover, the fact that interest rates on loans were kept lower than any available to developing countries from private credit markets ensured the Bank's primacy as lender to the developing world. By the early 1960s this approach had proved so successful that the Bank was saddled with significant excess earnings, in spite of decreasing investment opportunities from its traditional clients. Black's intransigence with regard to expanding the Bank into new areas was, however, becoming an increasingly annoying impediment to American interest in broadening spending to new social areas. In Black's view, the purpose of the IDA would be to fulfill the same functions as the IBRD but with better repayment terms.[11] Under Black's successor to the Bank presidency, however, priorities would begin to change.

Former First Boston Corporation executive George Woods began his term as president of the World Bank in 1963 at the urging of President

Kennedy. In accordance with Kennedy's argument that the increasing gap between rich and poor countries was a threat to global stability, Woods began rethinking the Bank's lending strategies for developing countries (Oliver 1995, 63). Despite some initial resistance, Woods soon realized that expanding IBRD loans into "riskier" areas would simultaneously solve the problem of excess profits (now justified by higher risk) and the desire for alternative avenues of investment. The new lending focused mostly on agriculture, with some additional commitment to social spending such as education and water supply and to "technical assistance,"[12] which aimed to build technical capacity in the newly independent states where it was particularly weak. By 1965, 15 percent of overall spending was going to agriculture (compared to 9 percent in 1960) and 5 percent to social spending (compared to 0 percent in 1960) (Mason and Asher 1973, 200). Overall, as shown in table 1.2, social and agricultural spending amounted to about 19 percent of the total, compared to 4 percent in the 1950s.

In the 1960s, the recipients who most benefited from the new commitment to social spending were not the newly emerging African nations but India and Pakistan. This concentration was not incidental; it represented a concerted effort to counter Chinese and Soviet influence. These two countries received 86 percent of all IDA loans to the poorest countries[13] between 1961 and 1968 (Kapur et al. 1997, 193). Yet despite the disproportionate increases in lending to India and Pakistan, overall Bank loans to Africa still increased from 5.7 percent in 1960–61 to 14.7 percent in 1966–67. In addition, African nations received more than half the technical assistance projects awarded in that year (Oliver 1995, 188).

Perhaps a more important legacy of the Woods period, however, was the expansion of the number, power, and influence of economists in the World Bank, as well as a tightening linkage between the Fund and the Bank. Prior to the Woods era, engineers and bankers had tended to dominate the technical departments of the Bank (Kapur et al. 457). There were some economists on the staff prior to the Woods era, but most were loan officers focusing on creditworthiness. In all there were only about twenty practicing economists on staff when Woods arrived in 1963 (Oliver 1995, 99–100, 119–20).

Woods felt that greater economic knowledge about individual countries was important if the World Bank was to truly focus on broadly defined development issues. He therefore decided to hire Irving Friedman, an IMF economist who, before joining the Fund, had worked for the division of monetary research in the U.S. Treasury from 1941 to 1946. From

1950 to 1964, Friedman served as director of the exchange restrictions department. In this context, he introduced economic studies to determine the preconditions for currency convertibility. By the late 1950s, country-specific reviews had become commonplace in the Fund and were included with all policy recommendations.

In 1964 Friedman joined the World Bank in the new position of economic advisor to the president. The position had a high profile, with daily access to George Woods and a membership equivalent to a vice-presidency on the president's council. Friedman was instrumental in raising the profile of economists, who had been previously looked down on by other World Bank officials.[14] He hired nearly two hundred economists, thus increasing the Bank's staff by 25 percent. He organized an economics department that became the second-largest department in the Bank and set up an economics committee, which evaluated all potential loan proposals to individual countries prior to being sent to the loan committee. Finally, Friedman conducted annual reviews of development and development finance. These initiatives were the precursors to the World Development Report, which was introduced in 1978. In accordance with IMF policies, he strongly believed in conservative monetary and fiscal policies whereby governments avoid trade or payments restrictions, multiple currency regimes, and inflation. Friedman also started the practice of IMF representation in country-specific meetings of the World Bank economic committee.[15] This IMF presence would prove to be an enduring and very influential one.

Moreover, Friedman's reforms—especially the growing presence of economists in the Bank—would prove instrumental to advancing American interests. With the previous focus on infrastructure within the confines of its very narrow "commercial" criteria, there had been little need for economists inside the organization. As the agenda began to expand, however, economists would provide the technical veneer for justifying new targets and priorities while maintaining substantive and procedural appearances. This also opened the Bank to the influence of changing fashions and developments within the economics profession.

Friedman and the economists quickly proved valuable in helping maintain procedural appearances. Although the Bank's Articles of Agreement prohibited tying its loans to the exports of any member, U.S. exports purchased via Bank loans always exceeded the U.S. contribution to the World Bank. During the negotiations for the second replenishment of IDA (1969–71), it became apparent that the IDA's costs would exceed the likely purchase of U.S. exports from associated loans. Consequently, the U.S. Treasury demanded a two-pool approach: if the exports generated were not as large as the IDA contribution, the amount allocated would be reduced accordingly. This proposition was a flagrant violation of the Articles of Agreement, but Friedman worked out a proposal whereby the amount of the contribution not offset by exports would be drawn upon last. Moreover, the United States would not need to allocate a third replenishment until all funds were used. In the end, the United States was able to delay its payment until the end of the replenishment period (1971) at a rate that was well below its earlier commitments (38 percent as opposed to 42 percent).

Although George Woods laid a foundation for a new agenda with U.S. backing, his overall effect on the direction of lending was nonetheless moderate. Infrastructure still accounted for 64 percent of the total loan program of the Bank from 1960 to 1969 (see table 1.2). It was the appointment of Robert McNamara in April 1968 that really changed the Bank's spending patterns. McNamara's candidacy had been heavily endorsed by Woods,[16] but his eventual appointment was probably due more to U.S. domestic politics: his growing opposition to the escalation of the Vietnam War had caused trouble in the Johnson administration, and it seemed wise to quietly relocate him (Oliver 1995, 228).

McNamara and the Bank Interest in Poverty Reduction

Given his role as secretary of defense and the failed military solution in Vietnam, it is not surprising that McNamara's early concerns with poverty focused on security issues.[17] He was clearly affected by the domestic war on poverty begun by Presidents Johnson and Kennedy, having served under both. In a speech delivered at the first annual meeting of his presidency, he explicitly pointed to a lack of correspondence between economic growth and poverty reduction. As we will see, this argument echoed that of the academic literature in economics.

Moreover, this turn toward poverty issues was largely in consonance with shifts in American foreign policy. In the 1960s the American government sponsored the Alliance for Progress in Latin America, which proposed policies to improve income distribution and accessibility to health, education, and housing. In addition, in 1973 Congress passed the U.S. Foreign Assistance Act, which called for a new approach to development that would focus on bilateral assistance—food, nutrition, health, and education (Ayres 1983, 9).

The Bank's spending reflected this new legislation. Spending on agriculture and areas of social concern such as education and water supply increased to 31 percent of the total amount lent to low- and middle-income countries during the first McNamara term (1968–73). Between 1974 and 1982 it increased to 40 percent (Kapur et al. 1997, 235). As seen in table 1.2, these two areas obtained an average of 41 percent of lending during the 1970s. The allocation to infrastructure fell to only 36 percent. The trend of deemphasizing infrastructure would continue throughout the structural adjustment period and would diminish to only 21 percent by the latter half of the 1990s.

The period of McNamara's first term can be characterized as a search for policy alternatives and strategies aimed at reducing poverty in developing countries. Various proposals put forward during Bank meetings—such as population control and the use of distributional weights in project appraisal—proved to be nonstarters. Two-thirds of spending in the first five years was still in areas that had long been targeted by the Bank, and even the policy modifications that had been made were slow to create real change because much of the increased spending in agriculture and social areas was still missing the poor.

The Bank dabbled in such issues as health, nutrition, and employment, some of which were discussed in the annual country program papers introduced in 1968, but the major shift occurred in the wake of McNamara's 1973 speech in Nairobi to the Board of Governors. In it, he argued that the backbone of a successful strategy for reducing poverty should be rural development that emphasized smallholder agriculture.[18]

During the McNamara period, lending for rural development rapidly expanded from eight projects per annum in the period 1968–70 to forty-nine projects in 1979–80 and forty-four projects in 1980–82. By 1980–82, rural development constituted 61 percent of total agricultural lending, an increase from 28 percent in 1968–70, and had increased to $2.039 billion from $83 million in the same period. In constant-dollar terms, the increase was a remarkable 700 percent.

The most dominant form of rural development lending with a consistent poverty focus was the area development approach, a type of multisector lending strategy focused on the social and economic progress of a particular region. For example, from 1974 to 1982, 59 percent of all rural projects in East Africa and 63 percent in West Africa were in area development

(World Bank 1988b, 11, 24, 116–17). In some African countries, the shift to area development strategies went beyond the World Bank to influence the priorities of other donors. In Tanzania, for example, four donors in four integrated rural development schemes joined the three area development programs of the World Bank. In total, between 1972 and 1984, $136.5 million from various donors was committed to these projects (Kleemeier 1984, 43).

Yet by the World Bank's own measurements, the area development approach was a major disappointment. In eastern and southern Africa, twelve of fifteen projects failed, and in West Africa, 43 percent of area development projects failed (World Bank 1988b).[19] Although a variety of technical factors were cited in the report, Bank officials in the early 1980s tended to place the blame on poor state policies and weak institutions rather than on problems of design inherent in the development strategies themselves.[20] This antistate rhetoric set the tone for the shift toward liberalization and privatization in rural areas after 1980.

After the Nairobi speech, the Bank also considered ways to launch a comparable agenda with regard to urban poverty. In 1974–75, the Bank released numerous studies of housing, services, and urban transport. It also drew up a policy paper concerning urban poverty. At the September 1974 annual meeting, McNamara's speech focused on this subject. A task force organized to address the subject quickly concluded that there was no urban group comparable to small rural farmers, the focus of rural poverty strategies. The policy response was reduced to a hodgepodge of less comprehensive projects such as water supply, which had—at best—only indirect benefits to the urban poor.

Prodded by International Labor Organization (ILO) studies (International Labor Organization 1976) to realize that employment generation and growth were insufficient to guarantee basic needs, the World Bank generated a series of country- and sector-specific evaluations of these dimensions. There was strong resistance to these studies by some senior Bank economists, who demanded that "basic needs" proposals be justified in strictly cost-benefit economic terms. Fierce opposition by chief economist Hollis Chenery and his assistant, Ernie Stern, who was chief of operations after 1978, ensured that the proposals did not go beyond the study stage. They argued that the basic needs approach created too many growth opportunity costs, or, in other words, that growth that would be impeded or prevented by a focus on basic needs (Kapur et al. 1997, 263–68).

With McNamara's departure in 1981, the basic needs agenda, which had developed alongside his poverty interests, was abruptly dropped. Given the poor performance of rural projects and the rather negative reaction to the basic needs agenda, the Bank's economists were clearly eager to pursue a shift in direction. As Ayres (1983) has pointed out, during the McNamara era "[t]he dominant ideology, widely shared, throughout the Bank, may be identified as that of neoliberalism. . . . The technocratic neoliberalism is tenacious and was certainly far from totally discarded as a result of the reorientations, real and proposed, of Bank activities since 1973. . . . Poverty-oriented emphases sometimes seemed to have been passed on the prevalent ideology without, however, altering its fundamental slant" (74–75).

There is little doubt that many Bank economists were happy to see this ideological shift toward neoliberalism because it was central to their core beliefs as classically trained economists. There was a great deal of enthusiasm when Washington pushed its new set of like-minded policy priorities in the early 1980s. It was from this context that the well-known policy package of structural adjustment arose. Although a confluence of events led to adjustment, it is clear that Bank economists played a major part in its creation. Their increasing prominence in the organization left it even more susceptible to the latest trends in the field of development economics, including critiques of state-led strategies.

The Shifting World Bank Policy Agenda and Development Economics

Although the Bank played a major role in shaping the development economics agenda with its influence and resources, it was almost never the originator of new ideas, and in fact it was often quite slow in adopting new techniques introduced by economists in academia (Gavin and Rodrick 1995). A brief summary of the shifts in development economics over time will provide a useful background for better understanding these dynamics.

The roots of development theory are often associated with the work of Georg Hegel and Karl Marx. Hegel saw world history as one of progression that arises from the dialectical process of contradictions, whereby evolving freedom leads to greater self-realization and a higher conceptualization of the spirit. The universe then has purpose in which process has not only immediate cause but also an ultimate design. Basing his conceptualization on Christian theology, Hegel believed that the natural order is not accidental but proves the existence of God. This basic teleological premise heavily influenced Marx's concept of development, but he omitted Hegel's religious implications.[21]

Marx rejected the notion of a world spirit but accepted a progression through dialectics that would lead to improvements in the level of material or social well-being through increasingly higher modes of production (Leys 1996).[22] Ultimately, improving material well-being and the satisfaction of human physical needs leads to the abolition of private property, complete self-actualization, and the emancipation of humanity.[23]

As the independence of former colonies loomed, the teleological notion of development as progress became the dominant ethos in economic and political circles. Some ignored the complex notion of human emancipation embedded in Marx and Hegel and focused instead on the reproduction of an idealized understanding of Western countries' route to development. The most egregious example was found in the work of W. W. Rostow (1960), which proposed a linear historical progression toward the Age of High Mass Consumption. This age was considered the apotheosis of human fulfillment and was embodied by Rostow's stylized version of the United States in the 1950s. Happily, few attempts to define development as progress were as crude as that of Rostow.

More generally, the emphasis was on using simple mathematical models to identify conditions that would lead to the sustainability of economic growth. In the classic approach of Harrod (1939) and Domar (1946), which was also inspired by Keynes,[24] the sustainable or "warranted growth" rate was linked to the rate of savings and incremental capital-output ratio (ICOR). In this model sustainability was narrowly defined along a "knife's edge": if the rate of growth varied from the ratio of savings to ICOR, the economy could expand at a rate that would ignite either inflation (when the growth rate exceeded the ratio of savings to ICOR) or unemployment (when it fell below this ratio).

Such a model, which predicted instability in market economies, left neoclassical economists in a rather disturbed state because their core assumption was that the market, left to its own devices, would always create equilibrium and stability. Solow (1956) therefore broadened the conditions for steady-state growth or sustainability by removing the Harrod-Domar assumption of fixed technical relations and instead allowing for capital and labor to be completely interchangeable. According to this model, if technical change and income shares are held constant, income per capita should be a product of the rate of savings divided by the rate of expansion of the fully employed labor force. The growth rate would thus be sustainable until it is overwhelmed by diminishing returns.

The Solow and Harrod-Domar models fell into the broad genre of capital-centered models of sustainable growth, which dominated much of the literature through the 1960s. Two somewhat divergent approaches came from this literature. According to the Harrod-Domar approach, the market alone would not be able to maintain the warranted growth rate and government planning and ownership were necessary to mobilize the resources necessary for high levels of sustainable growth. The second approach, inspired by Solow, argued that sustainable growth would arise from the mobilization of savings and investment via the market system. The latter approach, which became dominant in Bank policy strategies after 1980, is discussed further in chapters 2 and 3.

But it was the former approach, built on the Harrod-Domar model, that inspired many of the earlier studies in development economics. In the work of Nurkse (1953), for example, a cause of underdevelopment was insufficient capital accumulation and growth due to the "vicious circle of poverty." In this theory, the supply of capital is connected to the willingness and ability to save and the demand for capital is connected to the incentive to invest. On the supply side, a low rate of saving arises from low income, which arises from low productivity, which arises from the low level of capital, which arises from inadequate savings. On the demand side, the motivation to invest is low owing to small incomes, which are linked to low productivity, which arises from the low inducement to invest. Relying on the work of Nurkse and others, many of the early policies in developing countries were aimed at raising savings rates, improving techniques to lower the capital-to-output ratio, or devising mechanisms to control the population growth rate.

Although there was debate about the exact strategy for growth (balanced or unbalanced growth)[25] and the degree of dualism in an economy (between a modern sector and a backward sector), there was a broad consensus that a state-sponsored minimum effort, or "big push," to invest in industry was necessary for the economy to achieve self-sustaining growth (Killick 1980). Beyond economic theory, the centrality of the state in development in the 1950s and 1960s was also driven by the norms of acceptable strategy tempered by the political economy of the global order.

Until its demise in 1973, the international financial system was managed by the fixed exchange system established at Bretton Woods that relied heavily on Keynesian-type state intervention in order to maximize growth and employment. Capital flows were restricted, and governments were allowed more freedom to set interest rates, influence currency rates, tax, and spend. National economic planning in developing countries, therefore, seemed a logical extension of the global system. The success of the Marshall Plan also had a demonstration effect; it seemed that the newly independent former colonies could follow a route to prosperity similar to that of war-torn Europe, namely, relying on the support of bilateral foreign aid flows funneled through state coffers. In addition, the priorities of development were driven by cold war politics. Developing countries were encouraged to generate a trajectory of sustainable growth and were supported by Western countries. This support, however, was not merely benevolent. It was also strategic: economic growth sponsored by state aid would connect the poor countries to the Western bloc (Leys 1996), and the World Bank could assist in this process by financing state-sponsored infrastructure.

Yet by the mid-1960s it became increasingly clear that the growth-oriented models, with their focus on savings, investment, and planning, were not having the desired effects. Most disconcerting was that large segments of the population in developing countries were experiencing no improvement in their quality of life. Hirschman (1981) felt that the most influential and definitive empirical study concerning worsening poverty and income distribution was a study of the 1970 Brazilian census undertaken by Albert Fishlow in 1972.[26] This work slightly predated McNamara's expression of alarm at worsening poverty and distribution statistics, which was first presented at his annual address at the Board of Governors meeting in Nairobi a year later. As we have seen, however, McNamara's concerns also predated this official speech; they were first expressed as early as 1968. Perhaps the most widely quoted statistical study of the period was that by Adelman and Morris (1973), who argued that economic growth was "accompanied by an absolute as well as relative decline in the average income of the poor" (189). But the literature regarding the perceived failures of the capital-centered models and their associated policies appeared before publication of the wider empirical studies. In development economics theory, there were four general reactions to the perceived failures of the capital-centered models.

First, the dependency literature linked the negative outcome of earlier policies to a global system whereby developed countries have grown at the expense of poorer countries. This theory became increasingly popular in the 1960s, particularly in Latin America, although there was little evidence of any influence on economists at the Bank.[27] Despite the early popularity of the dependency literature, it lost its luster in the 1970s and 1980s, when the successful growth of the East Asian Tigers brought a rising standard of living and improved income distribution in part because of the region's trade linkages to the global system. This case presented a powerful contradiction to the fundamental assumptions of dependency theory and thus discredited it.

The second reaction to the disappointing performance of the capital-centered models came from such neoclassical writers as Bela Balassa, Anne Krueger, Ian Little, Peter Bauer, Deepak Lal, and Jagdish Bagwati. Lal's (1983) dogmatic critique of development economics, *The Poverty of Development Economics*, published by Margaret Thatcher's Institute of Economic Affairs, is perhaps the most widely cited attempt to reassert neoclassical monoeconomics (a single approach to economics applied to all places and times) in development theory. There is actually very little originality in Lal's volume, however; most of his arguments had been proposed many years earlier by such authors as Peter Bauer, whose work was more nuanced and sophisticated.[28] It is worth returning to the original author for a description of this reaction.

In 1965 Peter Bauer published a lengthy critique of the concept and policy implications of the vicious circle of poverty. Over the course of several years, he systematically attacked most of the major components of development economics including planning, foreign aid, state-led industrialization, the Prebisch-Singer hypothesis (decline in the terms of trade—the price that countries get for exports relative to imports—for countries specializing in raw materials), protectionism, income redistribution, and meliorism.[29] These critiques were eventually published as the 1971 volume *Dissent on Development*. Echoing the growing conservatism and anti-Keynesianism of the economics profession at the time, the work was a clear shot across the bow of development economists.

As the Bank went through its flirtation with redistribution, basic needs, and greater support for agriculture, the impact of Bauer's critique would be an enduring one.[30] By February 1982 Bauer was recognized by the World Bank as one of the six greatest development economists and was invited to address the Bank during its prestigious Pioneer Lecture Series.[31]

In many ways, Bauer's comment about the role of government in 1971 presaged the Bank's eventual recognition (by the end of the 1990s) of the role of the state in developing countries, including the focus of the new institutional economics on institutions in the service of individual activities. His observations are worth quoting at length: "Preoccupation with central planning has, paradoxically, contributed to a serious neglect of essential governmental tasks in many underdeveloped countries. These tasks include the successful conduct of external affairs; the maintenance of law and order; the effective management of monetary and fiscal policy; the promotion of a suitable institutional framework for the activities of individuals; the provision of basic health and education services and of basic communications; and also agricultural extension work" (91). But before recognizing this expanded but essentially neoclassical vision, the Bank went through a decade of supporting an even more emasculated vision of the state. Drawing on authors such as Anne Krueger, Ronald McKinnon, Bela Balassa, and Jagdish Bhagwati, the Bank economists pointed to the inefficiencies caused by state intervention: distorted prices, rent-seeking, drained government revenue, and regulatory obstacles to employment and investment generated by the private sector.[32] Theoretically, the state could play a broad role in supporting markets, but in practice, inefficiencies would be best avoided by retracting the state by means of deregulation and privatization in order to focus on stabilization functions. I discuss this period further in chapter 6.

The third reaction to the failure of conventional development economics was the focus on employment generation, income distribution, and basic needs. The main critique of the capital-centered models evolved from the work of the ILO, which in 1969 launched the World Employment Program with the aim of finding new ways to stimulate job growth. In its World Employment Conference of 1976, the ILO explicitly acknowledged that dealing with the wide and growing poverty levels would take more than growth and job creation. It was also necessary to target requirements particular to private consumption, such as food and shelter, essential services such as drinking water, and broader participation in decision making.[33]

Work to formalize a basic needs alternative continued throughout the latter 1970s and 1980s. Frances Stewart, who had worked on the ILO's 1972 Kenya mission, as well as on a 1975 technology project, was brought into the World Bank in 1977–78 to work on a basic needs strategy. After her time at the Bank she published a series of highly influential volumes about basic needs and poverty (Stewart 1985, 1995). Paul Streeten (1979, 1981), too, played an important role in pushing the basic needs agenda. Even some economists who were associated with capital-centered models began to contribute to the literature about the subject (for example,

Ranis 1982).[34] The most influential publication for the institutionalization of basic needs, however, was the United Nations Human Development Report. Mahbub ul Haq, who had helped push McNamara and the World Bank toward this approach in the 1970s, was instrumental in launching the Human Development Report in 1990.[35]

The fourth and final reaction to the failure of the capital-centered models was the rediscovery of the central importance of institutional economics, which focused on the interaction of economic and other social indicators in determining economic performance. This rediscovery was accompanied by a corresponding attempt to apply institutional economics to developing countries.

Perhaps the most prominent development economist to be influenced by this theory was Gunnar Myrdal, who began to adopt institutional economics while writing his 1944 study of African Americans.[36] In the 1950s he used elements of his earlier work to criticize emerging theories within development economics. For example, Myrdal (1957) dismisses the vicious circle of poverty because it presents the social process as a self-stabilizing, static system. Instead, he posits a cumulative, more dynamic process of causation in which interacting factors, including noneconomic variables, lead to an ever-worsening situation. He also focuses on criticizing the tenets of monoeconomics, including the emphasis on harmony of interests, laissez-faire economics, equilibrium, and free trade.

His institutional economic approach was more fully expressed in 1968 with the publication of his three-volume work *Asian Drama*. In it, Myrdal lumped the capital-centered models together with the classical school and argued that this body of Western economics had little or no application for understanding the complexities of South Asian underdevelopment (1:26). Myrdal focused mainly on understanding the institutional constraints to successful planning in South Asia. Sadly, with the neoclassical counterrevolution in development economics, as well as the complete abandonment of economic planning in the of wake neoliberalism's predominance, much of Myrdal's rich contribution has been lost. In chapter five I return to some of his insight to rebuild an institutional approach to development.

These four reactions to the failure of the capital-centered models offered a wide variety of alternatives to which future policymaking initiatives could turn. Yet the field of development economics would be progressively narrowed because only one approach was institutionalized, at the expense of the others. The other three were not ignored because of inferiority, however, Rather, as we will see in chapter 2, the dominance of the

neoclassical economic approach to development was ensured by a confluence of factors.

In any case, the golden era of development economics had come and
gone. As Hirschman (1981) put it: "[D]evelopment economics started out
as the spearhead of an effort that was to bring all-around emancipation
from backwardness. . . . By now it has become quite clear that this cannot
be done by economics alone. It is for this reason that the decline of development economics cannot be fully reversed" (23). Ironically, the influence of
postwar development theory on the Bank did, indeed, wane. But contrary
to many of the critiques cited above, this decline was not because development theory was too narrow, but rather because it became too broad.

Conclusions

This chapter has documented the shifting agenda and structure of the
World Bank in the first three decades of its existence. The emphasis on infrastructure in the 1950s and 1960s gave way to an increasing focus on agriculture, social spending, and industry in the 1970s. In very broad terms,
the changing agenda and structure reflected the changing interests and
priorities of the United States.

Economists also helped maintain the pretense that the Bank was operating in strict accordance with institutionalized rules by using their
"technical" criteria and abstruse methods and terminology. This façade
protected the substantive and procedural dimensions of hegemony, which
have provided a legitimizing veneer for the realization of U.S. priorities
in the Bank.

The influence of economists within the Bank has left it open to the
influence of the shifting fashions and tendencies in this profession. During
the 1950s and 1960s, emphasis on infrastructure was consistent with state-
led models of planned development. In the 1970s, academic work concerning rural poverty, income distribution, and basic needs helped shape
the policy agenda of the McNamara era. By the late 1970s, the counter-
revolution and return to the monoeconomic principles of the neoclassical
approach laid much of the intellectual groundwork for structural adjustment. This influence continued for a number of years. As we will see in
chapter 4, "advances" in new institutional economics also were adopted
by the Bank in the 1990s, not in order to rethink its policies but to buttress
its existing strategies.

CHAPTER TWO

From Structural Adjustment to "Poverty Reduction"

Adjustment to the Crisis and the Crisis of Adjustment after 1980

This, indeed, is the last remaining argument of economic liberalism . . . today. Its apologists are repeating in endless variations that but for the policies advocated by its critics, liberalism would have delivered the goods; that not the competitive system and the self-regulating market but interference with that system and interventions with that market are responsible for our ills.—Karl Polanyi, 1957

Introduction

Since 1980, the most ubiquitous and consequential set of policies influencing the developing world has been a series of economic reforms sponsored by the World Bank, the International Monetary Fund, and other multilateral and bilateral donors. From their inception, these policy packages, known collectively as structural adjustment, were imposed as conditions for receiving loans from the World Bank and the IMF. Underlying these packages was the belief that growth and development would arise from the stabilization, liberalization, and privatization of economies.

Each component of the structural adjustment was justified by neoclassical theory. Stabilization efforts focused on macro goals and were aimed at reducing volatility and restoring balance in the economy. According to this logic, constraining monetary growth and cutting government spending should reduce inflation and imbalances in the current account of the balance of payments and government budgets. Liberalization, meanwhile, retracted state intervention in markets in order to reverse the price distortions that were believed to impede consumers and private producers from making optimal choices. In addition, liberalization often meant "freeing up" prices by removing government subsidies for goods such as food for consumers and discontinuing support for input commodities such as fertilizer for farmers. User fees or charges to individuals for utilizing public goods such as education and healthcare were introduced to promote "efficiency" in their allocation. Finally, privatization meant selling state assets to the private sector on the assumption that private property ownership would encourage greater efficiency, investment, and growth.

Despite more than two and a half decades of rather disappointing results, these policies still remain at the core of the Bank's strategy. As Polanyi incisively observed in an earlier era of dominant orthodoxy, blame is never placed on the policies themselves.

As a result, in 1989 the World Bank began to expand its developmental lexicon to include other issues, such as governance and capacity building, social capital, poverty reduction, sustainable development, decentralization, and country-level ownership of aid policies. In the view of Bank official the failure of the 1980s was the fault not of structural adjustment but external factors that limited the positive influence of neoliberal policies. In the context of this effort to revitalize structural adjustment, the Bank began to discuss the role of institutions, which I explore in greater detail in chapter 4. For now, I begin with an exploration of the origins of adjustment, including the history of conditionality.

The Origins of Adjustment

To fully understand the origins of structural adjustment and its centrality to the Bank, one must begin with the history of the International Monetary Fund. During the first few decades of its existence, the Bank focused almost exclusively on project aid, whereby money was disbursed on the basis of a prescribed sequence of steps in project implementation. The Fund, in contrast, had a history of lending for programs. Program aid was accompanied by policy conditionality, or lending that was contingent on changes in policy. Conditionality, by nature, was derived from a preconceived theoretical understanding of the presumed relation between policy adjustment and outcome.

The IMF and the World Bank were both created at the Bretton Woods Conference of 1944, and the Fund formally came into existence at the end of 1945. According to its Articles of Agreement, twelve executive directors formed a board responsible for daily operations of the IMF.[1] Five of the twelve were appointed by the countries with the largest quotas (that is, the largest contributions to the IMF), and from the beginning, the United States has always appointed one director. As in the case of the Bank, the board seldom voted, opting instead for an artificial consensus because the voting power reflected the size of each country's quota. Again, the United States has maintained an effective veto by controlling at least 15 percent of the votes; as with the Bank, an 85 percent vote is required for major decisions.

American hegemony in the Fund was present from its inception, and conditionality reflected its early priorities. In accordance with American domestic and foreign policy, the United States wanted a Bank that was selective in its loan disbursements. It also wanted a Bank situated in Washington that used the U.S. dollar as the reserve currency backed by gold. John Maynard Keynes, who was leading the U.K. delegation, suggested a new international currency (bancors) and wanted easy access to resources in order to maximize sovereignty in the choice of policies. Keynes argued that the Fund should be in New York or Europe, where it would be further removed from congressional politics. Yet the United States effectively vetoed Keynes's proposal, and the IMF was born in accordance with American priorities, a pattern that has continued to the present.[2] The debate about the question of loan conditionality was particularly protracted; the U.S. representative to the Bretton Wood negotiations, Harry Dexter White, pushed heavily for the Fund to be given the right to challenge any country's attempt to draw funds.[3] Although the language regarding this issue was fairly ambiguous in the final articles, the board, almost from the outset, interpreted the clauses in accordance with American preferences.

The IMF was not affected to the same extent by the shifting fashions of development theory and policy. The Fund had six purposes according to its Articles of Agreement, but in practice, the Fund's principal focus until 1971 was to manage the fixed exchange rate system established at Bretton Woods and to make foreign currency available, via revolving loans, to countries with balance-of-payments problems. Countries contributed to the Fund's capital reserves through a quota system based on the size of their national income, their reserves, and their contribution to international trade.

Twenty-five percent of each country's quota or 10 percent of its gold and dollar reserves if the latter figure was smaller, was initially held in the form of gold; the rest of the quota was to be deposited in the form of the country's national currency. Initially, governments could swap up to 25 percent per annum of their currency for up to five years for a total deposit of 200 percent of their quota.[4] Graduated charges were set on amounts of currencies held in excess of their gold tranche (article 5, section 8). Beyond this, there was no formal conditionality on the loans except for some rather vaguely worded provisions. Article 5, section 5 states that "if the Fund is of the opinion that any member is using the resources of the Fund contrary to the purpose of the Fund" it can "declare it ineligible to use the resources of the Fund." Article 20, section 4(i) of the final provision reiterates this option to postpone exchange transactions if resources use would be "prejudicial to the Fund or the members" (Horsefielde 1969, 3:192, 209).

The board was free to interpret these provisions, and it did so according to American preferences. The first attempt to draw funds came in April 1947 from Ethiopia, which requested $900,000.[5] The board turned it down because it was skeptical that so large an amount could be "presently needed," although it approved a request in 1948 for one-third of that amount. Nevertheless, in May 1947, a drawing by France of about 5 percent of the Fund's capital was rapidly approved. The bias against developing countries was being put in place. When Mexico applied for a drawing in August of the same year, it was only approved after a lengthy discussion of its economic position. In September 1947, conditionality was formally put in place. Chile was told that its drawing would only be approved if appropriate fiscal and monetary measures were undertaken.[6] The board debated whether it had the right to impose conditions and in the end decided that if it was permitted to declare a member ineligible under article 5, section 5 (discussed above), then it could certainly impose lesser constraints such as tying loans to specific policies (Horsefielde 1969, 1:187–92).

Conditionality became ubiquitous in the wake of the standby agreement system formally introduced in 1952. This system directly linked lines of credit from the IMF to certain policy targets. Gradually, standby arrangements became the most common mechanism for accessing IMF resources, along with the commitment to stabilization programs. From the beginning, stabilization programs focused on anti-inflationary policies.[7] This relation, formalized by Polak (1957), become known as the financial programming approach (discussed in chapter 3). The typical agreement called for a loan to be disbursed over the course of twelve to eighteen months, with repayment in three and one-quarter to five years. Credit was allocated in tranches (slices), with conditionality becoming stricter with each tranche.

Just after the end of the colonial era in Africa, standby agreements dominated the Fund's agenda in Africa and in developing countries elsewhere. Between 1960 and 1972, fifty-one standby agreements between the Fund and twelve African countries were signed, forty-three of them with ten sub-Saharan countries. In 1962 Egypt became the first African country to sign a standby accord with the IMF, followed closely by Liberia in 1962, Mali in 1963, and Somalia and Tunisia in 1964. Loan amounts were typically small: ten million special drawing rights (SDRs) or less.[8] Only Egypt, Ghana, Sudan, and Zaire had higher loans; they drew between twenty and forty million SDRs (Mohamed 1993, 92–93). Still, the role of the Fund in Africa and other developing regions was minor; Fund officials were largely preoccupied with managing the Bretton Woods system in the more advanced countries. Only 3.7 percent of Fund credit went to African countries during the 1960s (Ferguson 1988, 204), but as we will see, this proportion changed dramatically after 1980.

By 1973, most developed countries had abandoned the fixed exchange system. The IMF's purpose seemed to be unraveling. Consequently, it was informally given the rather ill-defined responsibility of surveying exchange rate policies. Yet until 1978, when a new set of Articles of Agreement was formulated, no IMF member was performing its obligations regarding the exchange rate (De Vries 1986, 117–18). The period was characterized by a series of disturbances, including the severe recession of 1974–75, the OPEC oil price boosts, and considerable discord among the Fund's members. Against this backdrop, the Fund gradually evolved from an exchange rate system manager into a broad lending institution.

Simultaneously, developing countries with membership in the Fund pushed for SDR allocations to be decided by development needs rather than by quota size. Compared to other facilities, SDRs were quite attractive in the 1970s because of their low interest rates (1½ percent per annum) and easy access, which granted use of 70 percent of cumulative allocation without repayment obligations. The United States, however, blocked the proposal, despite strong support from Italy and France (Ferguson, 1988, 130). Yet the possibility of enlarging the Fund's role in developing countries was a persistent one; it became increasingly central in the search for a functional redefinition. In 1974 the Boards of Governors of the Bank and the Fund created a new joint committee on the transfer of resources to developing countries. New facilities such as the Extended Fund Facility (EFF) and the Trust Fund were created with developing countries in mind (De Vries 1986, 133–34).[9]

In the 1970s, countries in sub-Saharan Africa began to use some of these new facilities. In 1975, 91 percent of their collective allocation of 262 million SDRs, their net borrowing from the Fund, came from the Oil Facility,[10] and in 1976, 73 percent of the allocation of 264 million SDRs came from the Compensatory Financing Facility and the Buffer Stock Financing Facility.[11] By 1978, however, standby agreements with tougher conditionality again dominated flows from the Fund. Ninety-two percent of the total net borrowings came from credit tranches in 1977, 71 percent in 1979, and 76 percent in 1980 (Mohamed 1993, 92–93). This pattern foreshadowed developments after 1980, when structural adjustment became the dominant policy agenda and standby agreements became prerequisites for foreign assistance in Africa. Although developing countries in the 1970s took an increasing portion of total IMF resources, from 46 percent in the 1960s to nearly 59 percent in the 1970s, no other region's share grew as rapidly. Overall credit allocation to Africa increased nearly tenfold in nominal terms from the 1960s onward, rising to 11.3 percent of the total awarded to all countries in the 1970s (Ferguson 1988, 204). The commitment to Africa rapidly accelerated in the early 1980s and was a quintessential part of the IMF's attempt to redefine its raison d'être.

World Bank and IMF Convergence after 1980

The World Bank Shift to Adjustment

The IMF's commitment to the neoliberal model was in place long before 1980, but the World Bank's shift in this new direction was more sudden. Boas and McNeill (2003) argue that the foundation for adjustment was present beginning in the 1970s. In particular, there was growing criticism of state-led development models by such neoliberals as Peter Bauer, as well as vocal criticism by the U.S. government. They specifically point to a 1976 speech by Treasury Secretary William Simon that opposed increasing the American contribution to Bank capital and called for greater recognition of the private sector's role in development. This was hardly a revelation for the Bank; it already had a branch (the IFC) whose sole purpose was to lend to the private sector.[12]

The appointment of Ernest Stern in July 1978 as the vice president in charge of operations and as chair of the Loan Committee was crucial to the introduction of these policies inside the Bank. Since his days as an economist at the United States Agency for International Development (USAID), Stern had been particularly interested in macrostabilization. He was also quite uncomfortable with the basic needs strategy, protesting repeatedly that it compromised growth and was therefore detrimental. For McNamara, issues such as good macro policies and trade liberalization were "matter of fact" but were not necessarily of greater consequence than other issues (Kapur et. al. 1997, 267).

In a May 1979 speech to the United Nations Conference on Trade and Development, McNamara was planning to urge the developed countries to open up their markets to exports from developing countries. Stern and others, however, saw an opportunity to raise their pet issues; they argued instead that in order to avoid being a "nonplayer bearing unsolicited advice," the Bank should add trade policy to its agenda. Thus on May 10, 1979, in Manila, McNamara stated: "In order to benefit fully from an improved trade environment the developing countries will need to carry out structural adjustments favoring their export sectors. I would urge that the international community consider sympathetically the possibility of additional assistance to developing countries that undertake the needed structural adjustment for export promotion in line with their long-term comparative advantage. I am prepared to recommend to the Executive Directors that the World Bank consider such requests for assistance and that it make available program lending in appropriate cases" (quoted in Kapur et al. 1997, 506–7).

Less than a week later, Stern generated a long memo outlining the new approach, and McNamara was favorably inclined toward the proposal. By midsummer, the process was accelerated by the second oil shock and the need for rapid balance-of-payments support. Whereas McNamara saw the opportunity to increase the loans and profile of the Bank, Stern saw an opportunity for his new policy framework. After considerable discussions, the directors approved a moderate allocation of Bank funds—roughly 5 to 6.5 percent of total IBRD-IDA loans.

Shortly thereafter, a series of changes quickly pushed adjustment to the center of the new agenda. In July 1981 the newly established administration of Ronald Reagan, a conservative, appointed Bank of America president A. W. Clausen, a staunch supporter of free markets, as the new head of the World Bank. In addition, Mahbub ul Huq, the Bank's biggest

proponent of antipoverty strategies, departed, and in 1982 the pragmatic
Hollis Chenery was replaced by the dogmatic neoliberal Anne Krueger
as chief economist (Kapur et al. 1997, 507–12). The new senior staff had
close ties to the Reagan presidency (intellectually and otherwise) which
ensured the embedded presence of American priorities. The new agenda
had the greatest impact on sub-Saharan Africa, which was increasingly
dependent on multilateral finance.

The First Decade of Adjustment

In 1981 the World Bank published a study laying out its new agenda in
Africa. *Accelerated Development in Sub-Saharan Africa*, also called the
Berg Report after its principal author, placed the blame for Africa's poor
performance on bad government policies (World Bank 1981a). Although
the report was undertaken in response to a request by African governors
of the Bank in the late 1970s for a special study of the region, there is little
doubt that the hiring of Elliot Berg, who was well known for his strongly
held views concerning the failures of governments, was no coincidence.[13]

According to Pierre Landell-Mills, a senior economist for the East
Africa region from 1973 to 1977, he was the first person approached by
Ernie Stern to write the Africa report. Landell-Mills was an obvious choice
because his résumé included a decade of experience in Tanzania and Botswana prior to his arrival at the Bank. Moreover, Stern preferred that
an insider write the report so that he could be guaranteed the results he
desired in a timely manner. But the request languished for many months,
until African members of the Board of Governors finally complained to
McNamara about the delay. McNamara then persuaded the latter to ask
Landell-Mills to finish the report in four months. Landell-Mills, however,
protested that he needed more time if he was to adequately incorporate
African input, and when more time was not granted, he refused the assignment. Despite these strong actions, Stern dismissed Landell-Mills's
concerns. He felt that the World Bank had sufficient expertise for writing a report about Africa and therefore did not need to be told what to
include by external actors. Stern then turned to Berg to write the report.
Landell-Mills indicated that Stern and Berg were good friends, that Stern
knew in advance the agenda he wanted for Africa, and that he was certain
Berg would provide it. In the end, Berg took eighteen months to complete
a draft, a period that never would have been acceptable to Stern if it had
been done by a staff member. The report, originally scheduled to appear

in 1979, was published two years later.[14] Ernie Stern quickly used the report to justify his new agenda; it appeared in a memo to McNamara as early as April 1981.

In order for African economies to grow, Stern argued, they would require "governments individually coming to grips with the distortion of prices and resource allocation and the operational responsibility assigned to the public sector and making necessary changes." In the same memo Stern also blamed donor policies, "which have supported domestic strategies which were inappropriate." In response, he called for much closer country-specific coordination of donor aid policy, in which the Bank should be prepared to "take a lead in assisting governments to undertake the changes indicated on the one hand and to raise the resources and strengthen donor coordination on the other" (quoted in Kapur et al. 1997, 716–17). Thus, the idea of the donor cartel pushing the structural adjustment agenda was born.

The IMF, which had a long history of conditional program aid, was given the role of lender to the developing world early in the process. When the structural adjustment lending was proposed to the Executive Board of the Bank in 1980, it was concerned about overlapping with the Fund's sphere of operation. It also faced the possibility of coordination problems, as well as the Bank's Articles of Agreement, which restricted program loans to "exceptional" cases only. The senior staff of the Bank successfully avoided this latter dilemma by arguing that exceptionality would simply be deemed to apply to countries that already had a Fund stabilization program (Mosley et al. 1991, 37). Bank management also ensured that its proposed policy changes would fall outside the core concerns of the Fund and that any policies related to the macro level would be carefully synchronized with the Fund's efforts. Thus, the IMF was also co-opted into Bank strategy. Moreover, the IMF was given most of the responsibility for generating the "jointly produced" Policy Framework Papers, which were intended to set out the major multiyear targets for the countries that were undertaking adjustment measures.

After 1980, the IMF turned its focus to Africa with enormous enthusiasm, while the Bank moved more cautiously in its new direction. As the Fund's role in the global system was being questioned, the IMF was scrambling to redefine itself in the wake of widespread criticism in the press (Kapur et al. 1997, 747). Lending money to the impoverished African continent and to developing countries elsewhere therefore seemed to provide a worthy new purpose. The statistics regarding lending by

TABLE 2.1 **Net transfers of the World Bank and IMF to sub-Saharan Africa**

Agency	1980–83	1984–87	1988–91	1992–95
IMF	4.39	(3.22)	(1.99)	(1.20)
World Bank	2.83	4.70	3.93	1.52

Source: Kapur et al. 1997, 748.
Note: Figures in parentheses are negative numbers. Figures in columns are stated in billions of U.S. dollars.

international financial institutions during the 1980s and early 1990s reflect this discrepancy between the aims of the Fund and the Bank. As seen in table 2.1, between 1980 and 1983, the net flow of Fund loans to sub-Saharan African countries reached $4.4 billion, compared to only $2.83 billion from the World Bank. By 1983 it was clear that the economic crisis was not resolved and that repayment to the IMF, which consisted of short-term money—the loans had to be repaid over a much shorter period of time than Bank loans—would threaten the sustainability of the new strategy.

A number of events combined to push the Bank to take the lead in adjustment lending. Within a few years of the introduction of the adjustment policy, it was apparent that the situation was still not improving in many of the countries that were implementing reforms. Yet from the Bank's perspective, the blame was not on the policies but on the "lack of external capital," which the Bank would need to mobilize.[15] The economic and social crisis embodied in the African famine of 1982 rapidly moved the continent to the fore of Bank priorities. Partly in preparation for a UN conference about Africa in the wake of the famine, Stern recalled retired Bank employee Stanley Please to write a report focusing on adjustment as it pertained to Africa. Ramgopal Agarwala, an economist who was rising within the Bank thanks to his work on price distortions for the World Development Report of 1983 (discussed further in chapter 6), was asked to work with Please. The result was the report *Towards Sustained Development in Sub-Saharan Africa* (World Bank 1984). According to Agarwala, the report was a major turning point in the institutionalization of the adjustment agenda in the Bank, and it had a large impact at the level of operations. It set out what was called at the time a "Dean's List" approach, which aimed to ensure that resources would flow only to the countries that best implemented reforms required by the Bank.[16]

The report carefully laid out the importance of getting prices right in agriculture via devaluation and deregulation of marketing. It also emphasized reducing the size and expenditures of the state and building up capacities to meet the financial targets of stabilization. The report also called for greater coordination of the efforts of the donors who were backing the reforms, including working closely with the IMF (World Bank 1984, 43). At the core of the coordination effort were the annual consultative country meetings, chaired by the World Bank; five such meetings took place between 1980 and 1982. By 1984, there were nine active consultative groups in African countries, and an another three were planned in other countries. By 1987 the total had reached sixteen. The number of donor sector meetings also increased. These meetings continuously emphasized the importance of annual donor pledges, which would effectively ensure the cartelization of aid behind the Bank's vision of transformation, exemplified by the policies of structural adjustment.

The report also identified the problematic outflow going to repay the IMF and the accompanying large declines in net inflow, which were occurring just when "donors must be willing to make available adequate financial assistance . . . to support those Sub-Saharan African countries which are implementing major programs of policy reform." For these purposes, the report called for the creation of a "special assistance facility" to support countries embarking on reform (World Bank 1984, 45–46). The release of the report in September 1984 thus led to the creation of a new Special Office for African Affairs, which was placed directly under Stern's purview.

The special facility for support of reforming countries rapidly became a reality. In the wake of the U.S. failure to meet its IDA 6 obligations, donors were permitted to reduce their payments proportionately (to make them comparable to those of the United States) in the first year of IDA 7 (1984).[17] Because most of the money was already allocated, Stern was able to encourage governments, especially those of European countries, to redirect financial support to the new $1.1 billion Special Facility for Sub-Saharan Africa (SFA) formed in January 1985.[18] The SFA was financed by France, Italy, the Netherlands, Japan, Germany, the United Kingdom, and IBRD money that had been transferred from the profits of its loan operations (Kapur et al. 1997, 733). The Bank also succeeded in encouraging countries to support adjustment through bilateral aid programs. For example, by 1990, Japan allocated 25 percent of its growing commitment to sub-Saharan Africa to structural adjustment.[19]

These new funds, coupled with the emphasis on structural adjustment, led to the Bank's takeover of the Fund's role of implementing and perpetuating the reform agenda. Its commitment to structural adjustment rose from $0.9 billion from 1980 to 1983 (13 percent of the total awarded to the

TABLE 2.2 **World Bank adjustment lending by region**

Region	1980–82	1983–86	1987–90	1991–93
Sub-Saharan Africa	320(23)	916(26)	1,305(23)	1,049(22)
East Asia	301(21)	389(11)	687(12)	147(3)
Europe and Central Asia	440(31)	572(16)	498(9)	924(19)
Latin America and Caribbean	95(7)	1,257(35)	2,284(41)	1,527(32)
Middle East and Northern Africa	0	229(6)	437(8)	474(10)
South Asia	256(18)	189(5)	386(7)	621(13)
Total adjustment	1,412	3,553	5,597	4,744
lending as percentage of total lending	(7)	(18)	(26)	(23)
SECAL/T. SAL	(13)	(60)	(59)	(49)

Source: Kapur et al. 1997, 521.
Note: All numbers in parentheses represent percentages of the total. Figures in columns are annual averages stated in millions of U.S. dollars.

region) to $3.3 billion (36 percent) from 1984 to 1987. Overall net inflows to sub-Saharan Africa reached $4.7 billion, whereas the negative outflow from the Fund was $3.22 billion. Table 2.2 provides information about overall adjustment lending from 1980 to 1993. The annual figures grew rapidly in both absolute and relative terms.

After 1982, two regions—sub-Saharan Africa, and Latin America and the Caribbean—took the bulk of the adjustment funds. The funds were of much greater importance in Africa, however. Private capital flows to Africa largely dried up in the 1980s as the continent become increasingly reliant on the official aid given primarily by the IMF and the World Bank. Donors increasingly demanded structural adjustment programs as prerequisites to bilateral aid.

In 1980 roughly 46 percent of long-term debt came from private sources. By 1993 the figure had fallen to 21 percent. Overall debt from the private sector fell to only 12 percent of the total by 2002 (excluding South Africa) from 34 percent in 1980, and this figure was less in nominal dollar terms in 2002 than in 1980. In contrast, the Bank's share rose from 11 percent to 25 percent of total African debt in the same period (World Bank 2003, 2004a). Conversely, in the case of Latin America, net private capital flows greatly exceeded official flows throughout the 1980s and early 1990s (Kapur et al. 1997, 662, 697).

Much of this new adjustment money was in the form of sectoral adjustment loans (SECALs). These loans provided assistance to countries undertaking reforms in specific sectors such as trade, finance, and agriculture. Many countries were having trouble implementing economy-wide adjustment programs. In 1982 SECALs were introduced to deal with burgeoning problems with balance of payments and to help focus reforms more narrowly. Six African countries received structural adjustment loans (SALs) and SECALs between 1980 and 1983; an additional twenty-one countries were added to the list between 1984 and 1989 (Kapur et al. 1997, 510–11, 519). Overall, as seen in table 2.2, SECALs quickly jumped to 60 percent of the total number of adjustment loans between 1983 and 1986.

The introduction of SECALs was only the beginning of a long history of innovations in adjustment policy. To protect the integrity, resources, and reputation of the Bank, which had invested so much in adjustment, it became necessary to find a way for its policies to work, especially in the face of the protracted African decline.[20] A key factor in the ardent commitment to adjustment came from the growing domination of the neoclassically trained economists in the Bank. Their ideology led them to create policy that was deductively posited from a set of core axioms; it also limited the domain of self-criticism. According to their logic, fault could not arise from the premises of the neoclassical model but must instead result from external factors, inadequate implementation, or insufficient resources.

The domination of neoclassical economists inside the Bank was enhanced still further by the hiring of Anne Krueger as the chief economist in 1982.[21] As discussed in chapter 1, economists had become increasingly important in the Bank after the arrival of George Woods. During the 1960s and 1970s, a diverse group of economists were hired; they were influenced by a spectrum of development economic theories. In virtually all of these theories other than the neoliberalism of Bauer and others, state planning and policy were central to development. Soon after her arrival, however, Krueger systematically altered the nature of the Bank staff.[22] She saw the research staff as too "statist" in their views and too deficient in "appropriate" technical skills. Three years after her arrival, 80 percent of the staff of the Development Research Department had left, to be replaced by people with what were deemed the appropriate skills. Between 1983 and 1986 the Economics Department set up an "intelligence system" to identify staff with positions diverging from the established views and to reward loyal followers (Kapur et al. 1997, 1193–94).[23] By 1991, 80 percent of all senior staff of the Policy, Research, and External Affairs Departments had been trained in economics or finance by British or American universities, which tended to focus on a very narrow neoclassical economic curriculum (Woods 2000, 152).

During the 1980s the Bank all but forgot the problems of poverty. Stern, Krueger, and other economists on staff, who had been hired mainly for their conformity, relied on neoclassical assumptions that the poor would automatically gain from adjustment.[24] The neoclassical argument went as follows: because overvalued currencies, export taxes, and protectionism favored the urban population, and because most of the poor were in rural areas, devaluation and liberalization would raise the income of the rural sector, thereby reducing poverty. Stern took it further, invoking an argument that would later be employed in support of shock therapy: for political reasons, rapid adjustment was best for the poor because if implemented slowly, there was a risk of growing resistance among elites that were hurt by adjustment (that is, those who had benefited from the status quo before the introduction of structural adjustment). Moreover, rapid adjustment would be the fastest way to increase economic growth, which would be of greater value for the poor, as well as the quickest way to lower the debt burden. Krueger also deliberately discouraged any work on the social cost of adjustment or debt, thereby discouraging alternative policy development in the Bank.

These views were quite consistent with those of the conservative U.S. Treasury, which clearly prioritized privatization, macroeconomic policies, and financial and management issues, rather than poverty or social spending. They also helped shield the Bank from criticism by liberal members of Congress. The view of poverty and adjustment was also consistent with the view of the IMF throughout the 1980s.[25]

Although the Krueger period (1982–87) was the most ideologically extreme, the commitment to neoliberalism and neoclassical economic methods had been institutionalized thanks to a system that allowed pro–free market results to be rapidly and unquestioningly disseminated while critical studies were challenged and sent back for restudy (Wade 2002, 219). The research and operations section of the Bank were thus fully supportive of the neoliberal agenda.

The Failure of Adjustment and the Broadening Agenda

Even with this additional funding, by the end of the 1980s it was apparent that the situation in developing countries was deteriorating, particularly in Africa. This is not surprising given that sub-Saharan countries received roughly 50 percent of all the adjustment loans made from 1980 to 1990 (Kapur et al. 1997, 520). In the 1980s investment declined at an annual rate of 3.9 percent, after having grown by 4.0 percent from 1973 to 1980. Exports fell by 0.6 percent per year. Real per capita income fell by 1.2 percent per annum from 1980 to 1989, after having grown by 0.6 percent between 1973 and 1980. Per capita food production fell by 6 percent during the decade. Meanwhile, Africa was taking on an enormous burden of additional debt but had nothing to show for it. Between 1980 and 1988, debt increased at an annual compound rate of 12 percent, and the debt-to-exports ratio rose at a rate of 17.7 percent per annum to a completely unmanageable 360 percent of gross domestic product. By 1989 debt relative to GNP was at 98.3 percent, up from 27.4 percent in 1980 (Stein and Nafziger 1991; Tarp 1993; United Nations Development Program 1992).

Debt levels were becoming unsustainable. In 1986 the Bank's African directors asked for a new study regarding ways to deal with the debt situation. There was considerable debate in the Bank, as well as opposition from the IMF, which considered the debt to be under its control. In the end, a new study was commissioned. Agarwala, who was working in the Special Office for African Affairs, and Stanley Please were asked to be the main authors. During Agarwala's presentation of the report's outline in 1987, the Executive Board raised many questions. All previous reports about Africa, including the Berg Report, had been undertaken without any direct input from Africans. Demonstrating their commitment to African participation, the Scandinavians funded Agarwala's trips to fifteen countries, where he spoke with between three hundred and four hundred Africans. This trip played an important role in changing Agarwala's perspective: although he had been instrumental in pushing the adjustment agenda, he was now becoming increasingly skeptical owing to the poor performance of African economies and the overwhelmingly critical response of the Africans he had interviewed. This shift was visible in the first draft of the 1988 report *SSA: From Crisis to Sustainable Development,* which was quite critical of adjustment. It was well received by African governments, but Ed Jaycox, who took over the Africa office in the reorganization of 1987,[26] was extremely unhappy with its content. He gave Pierre Landell-Mills the responsibility of toning down the report's criticisms. He was also asked to provide alternative explanations for the poor performance of African economies in the 1980s. According to Agarwala, Jaycox's memo stated that "Agarwala would become Mr. Outside and Pierre Landell-Mills Mr. Inside."[27]

In 1981 the Berg Report had indicated that African countries had accomplished three major objectives in the first two decades after independence: "political consolidation," "laying down of basic infrastructure," and "the development of human resources." The report had also identified an important shortcoming: too little attention to production. In order to generate growth, it emphasized, the keys were "(1) more suitable trade and exchange rate policies; (2) increased efficiency of resource use in the public sector and (3) improvement in agricultural policies" (World Bank 1981a, 4–5). By 1989, however, the Bank's study of Africa, *From Crisis to Sustainable Growth*, had introduced an entirely new set of policy considerations and explanations for the region's poor performance. African governments needed not only to "consolidate the progress made on their adjustment programs," this report argued, but also to "address the fundamental questions relating to human capacities, institutions, governance, the environment, population growth and distribution and technology" (World Bank 1989, 1). This became the explanation for African economies' failures: the newly identified areas of concern had previously been neglected.

As the agenda began to broaden in the 1990s, three elements were evident. First, there was an unwavering commitment to the core set of adjustment policies; new elements were simply used to justify the assumption that poor performance had been due to "external factors" rather than the adjustment policy itself. Second, each new policy was seen as a complement to adjustment, which would enhance or act as a catalyst for reform. Third, the theoretical core of each new element was in many cases based on neoclassical economic theory, despite all of its problematic implications. The issue of governance merits particular focus given its clear political overtones and its potential to disrupt the technical veneer created by an exclusive reliance on economically generated targets.

The Origins of Governance

Frustration over the continuing lack of progress, especially in Africa, pushed the Bank to investigate and pursue new avenues, some of which— such as politics—were prohibited by the Articles of Agreement.[28] In its 1989 report about Africa, the Bank announced that "underlying the litany of Africa's development problems is a crisis of governance" (World Bank 1989, 60). Agarwala, however, considered governance to be "an alibi for the failure of adjustment" and did not support its inclusion. Landell-Mills, on the other hand, was quite pleased; he was able to reintroduce the elements that he found important after they had spent a decade on the back burner.[29]

Landell-Mills indicated that the discussion of governance-related issues such as politics and corruption was circumscribed by two reports issued in the late 1970s, one written by Michael Carter concerning Mali, on the other concerning the Philippines. Carter, the representative in Mali, had been asked to examine how the country actually worked and to identify factors that impeded the Bank's programs. According to Landell-Mills, after reading the report, Ernie Stern dismissed it, saying that if it were to be taken seriously, it would mean that they would need to end loans to the country, asking, "How could we do business with a government like that?" The report on the Philippines was a scathing attack on the politics of corruption under Marcos. When the regime got a copy of the report, it was furious with the Bank. Meanwhile, the representatives of developing countries on the Executive Board voiced their opposition. Consequently, the report was buried; only twelve copies were ever printed. This sequence of events had helped cause governance to be deemphasized; it was not raised publicly again until Landell-Mills's 1989 Africa report was published (World Bank 1989). In general, economists in the Bank, led by Stern and Krueger, were rather skeptical about the "soft" nature of the discussions of institutions and governance. Landell-Mills said Stern dismissed the report, claiming that the field had "no robust underpinnings."[30]

In addition, the Executive Board had become concerned that considering governance might contradict article 4 section 10 of the Articles of Agreement.[31] A legal opinion by the Bank's general counsel introduced the new agenda by specifying which aspects of governance were considered acceptable for the Bank's development work. These included civil service reform, legal reform, support for greater participation, accountability in public spending, and budgetary responsibility,[32] which were supposed to improve government stability and predictability and enhance the rule of law. These new governance initiatives arose not from ideological or political preferences but rather from the assertion that they would improve efficiency.[33]

The implications of the new governance agenda were explored in the April 1991 Annual Bank Conference on Development Economics in a section titled "The Role of Governance in Development." Unlike his skeptical predecessors, the newly appointed chief economist Lawrence

Summers endorsed the new agenda in his keynote address at the conference, saying, "The question of what governments must do, what they can do and how we can help them do it better leads to the difficult problem of governance" (Summers 1991, 13).[34]

Whereas other papers explored cultural dimensions of governance in the ABCDE conference, Landell-Mills, in collaboration with Ismail Serageldin (1991), concentrated on identifying the core elements of governance and how they could be fostered by external agencies such as the Bank.[35] Their work was instrumental in the development of the Bank's governance agenda.[36] Aiming to identify what constituted good governance, it focused on freedom, transparency, participation, accountability, and the rule of law. The agenda was not theoretically constructed, but the authors posited that potential theoretical tools did exist which could generate a "renewed attempt . . . to link the roles played by political science, institutional economics, and neoclassical economics to create a coherent theory of development management" (303).[37] Following the conference, and in the wake of Chief Consul Shihata's ruling, a 1991 task force on governance investigated its relation to economic development.

Governance and Development: Transparency, Accountability, and the Rule of Law to the Rescue

Governance and Development (World Bank 1992a) examines the parameters of governance in four major areas: public-sector management, accountability, the legal framework for development, and information and transparency.[38] Bank policy measures of 1980–92 were reinterpreted in terms of governance and used as a foundation to construct the new agenda. Beginning in the early 1980s, the Bank's state-oriented agenda was focused on improving public-sector management and nonfinancial-sector reforms such as civil service reform and parastatal reform. These goals were absorbed into the governance and development agenda, for "when the capacity of the public sector to manage the economy and deliver public sectors is weak, the prospects for development are poor" (12). Rather than legitimizing the effort by invoking UN human rights principles (used by Landell-Mills and Serageldin 1991), the agenda is justified by neoclassical arguments that relate improved governance to market efficiency.

For instance, the legal framework for development focuses on generating the rule of law (World Bank 1992a). The emphasis on the role of law in development was not new; it was, in fact, a part of the Bank's policy agenda in the 1960s and 1970s. The framework, however, was based on academic works that emphasized law as a vehicle for social change. It was deemed a failure for a variety of reasons, including the exclusion of informal legal mechanisms and crude attempts to transplant American legal approaches. The new approach introduced in the 1992 report, however, had a rather different vision that supported a neoclassical conception of a market system. More specifically, this latter version relied on one of the major elements of neoclassical economics, which argues that property rights must be impartially guaranteed by means of a properly operating judicial system. This vision of a capitalist economy is based on the neoclassical view that markets are exchanges between self-seeking individuals which, ipso facto, involve the exchange of property rights. The role of guarantors of property rights is thus a key element of the rule of law. Another explicitly neoliberal element focused on constraining the state with the rule of law (Ginsburg 2000).

The Bank's formulation of the factors necessary for rule of law included five major elements. First, laws must be known in advance. For example, privatization was said to work best with clearly defined guarantees of private property rights (World Bank 1992a, 33). Second, the laws must be strictly enforced. For instance, banks must be able to enforce foreclosures via court actions on collateral pledges of private debtors if financial systems were to operate properly within the private sector (35). Third, the law must apply equally and consistently to state officials and private citizens. In concrete terms this meant that new legislation regarding privatization and the creation of competition would help the creation of market systems (36). Fourth, private contracts must be ensured and protected by an independent and credible judicial system. Enforceability of contracts is essential "for conducting efficient private economic activities" and to "shield against arbitrarily exercised executive power" (37). Fifth and finally, the rule of law is argued to be "the antithesis to government arbitrariness," meaning that laws should be only infrequently amended or repealed and only in accordance with clear procedures that are publicly known.

Note, however, that the World Bank's approach to building legal system is at variance with the successful development experienced in places such Asia. Unlike the neoclassical Bank agendas, laws in Asian countries were frequently aimed at enabling states rather than constraining them. Similarly, the Asian cases excluded some private-sector actors rather than indiscriminately encouraging them (Ginsburg 2000). Moreover, as we will see in chapter 5, the importance of a legal system in development is not due to its formal implementation, which is implied in the exercise of the rule of law, but rather to its influence on new forms of socially prescribed correlative behavior.[39]

The new governance agenda was given further impetus with the 1992 publication of the report of the Bank's task force on portfolio management. The so-called Wapenhans Report responded to the rising incidence of implementation problems with programs funded by World Bank loans. It pointed to an insufficient focus on political and institutional factors. It questioned whether support would naturally arise as adjustment progressed and urged the Bank to find ways to increase borrower ownership (Miller-Adams 1999, 108; Santiso 2002, 11–12).

Governance in Practice

With growing pressure to deal with the governance agenda, the Bank searched for an operational meaning of the term. The 1990 Annual Report was one attempt; it contained a new category of loans for public-sector management. Data from the 1980s were reclassified to incorporate this new category. Again, the impact of these changes in Africa, which was most heavily affected by Bank actions, is particularly telling. On average, between 1981 and 1985, African countries received $3.3 million dollars to improve public-sector management, which was less than 1 percent of the total lent to Africa. By 1988 this amount had risen to $165 million, or 5.6 percent of total Bank loans to Africa. The total peaked in 1996 with $592.2 million, or 21.8 percent of the total lent to Africa in this category, before falling to 5.3 percent in 1998 and 5.2 percent in fiscal year 2001. In most years, African countries received proportionately more lending for public-sector management than the overall averages for this category of lending. In the peak year, nearly one-third of all of this kind of lending was going to sub-Saharan African countries, while, in comparison, the average allocation for all countries was only 8.7 percent (World Bank 1990a, 1999a, 1999b).

In a similar way, much of the "new" governance agenda introduced in the early 1990s was actually a creative reclassification of existing strategies. For example, a 1994 evaluation of governance attempted to assess the proportion of selected existing operations that contained some element of governance. The study determined that between 1991 and 1993, 68 percent of capacity building, 68 percent of decentralization, 49 percent of economic management, 33 percent of state-owned enterprise reform, 30 percent of participation, and 6 percent of legal framework was governance-related (World Bank 1994a, xv).

Beginning in 2002, the governance agenda became more firmly established via the introduction of a new "thematic" system with eleven different categories. Two new categories, "public-sector governance" and "rule of law," had an explicit relation to governance; categories, with "management" in their titles had a more implicit relation. Other themes included development (both urban and rural), as well as social protection and risk management. The new system was used to reconfigure data reaching back to 1993. This revisionist sweep of the hand helped create the illusion that the Bank had been focusing all along on governance, development, and poverty reduction instead of focusing on neoliberalism (World Bank 2002a).

In spite of the new commitment to governance, adjustment continued to be an overwhelming part of the World Bank agenda until the late 1990s. The 1999 annual report, issued prior to the reclassifications, provided a fairly clear picture. In 1997, adjustment lending accounted for 40 percent of total Bank lending to Africa. In 1998 it fell to 28.5 percent before rising to 37.1 percent in 1999. In all regions, adjustment spiked up in 1999 after the Asian crisis (World Bank 1999a, 33, 97).[40] Despite the rhetoric emphasizing governance, if financial allocation is any indication, adjustment still dominated the agenda in the late 1990s. Although it is less clear in the annual reports issued since 1999, the World Bank itself estimated that one-third of its total loans in the fiscal year ending June 30, 2003 were for structural adjustment (World Bank 2004b).[41]

With its usual flair for cooperation, the IMF also joined in the new agenda. In a 1997 document,[42] the Fund indicated that it would weigh in on the economic side of governance, including the transparency of government accounts, effective public resource management, and regulatory stability of the private sector. These would be handled via monitoring, advice about policies, and technical aid. Corruption would be suspected in cases indicating interference with macroeconomic indicators (International Monetary Fund 1997a, 3, 5). In practice, governance-related conditionality has involved five general areas: fiscal and public-sector reform, legal and judicial reform, transparency and accountability in public management, banking and financial-sector reforms, and informational reforms.

In a manner similar to the Bank's approach, many of the areas labeled as governance were simply reclassifications of long-existing programs. For example, in its 2001 review of governance the Fund designated bank privatizations, reform of state enterprises, elimination of customs exemptions, improvement of the macroeconomic database, removal of extrabudgetary spending, and more as governance. Much of this was simply old wine in a new bottle.[43] Three changes, however, were evident. First was a growth in the codification of acceptable practices after 1997, developed for the most part in cooperation with the World Bank.[44] Second was the increase in frequency of the discussion of governance issues in Executive Board country consultations from 18 percent in 1994–95 to 62 percent in 1998–99. Third was the increase in the number of governance-related conditions from an average of 3.4 in 1994–1995 to 6.6 in 1998–99 (IMF 2001, 11).

African countries seem to have borne a disproportionately large amount of governance-related conditionality. One survey of thirteen African countries' letters of intent and policy framework papers between 1997 and 1999 found an average of nine governance-related conditions of a total of twenty-three or roughly 39 percent (Santiso 2002, 22). Moreover, this conditionality was influential not only because of the high proportion of loans that included it, but also because of the extent to which African countries were dependent on loans from international financial institutions. The end of the cold war had brought a sudden decline in the availability of bilateral aid, which had been provided as a reward for ideological and strategic alignment with one of the superpowers. The post–cold war coordination of bilateral and multilateral aid around structural adjustment ensured that almost any African country interested in accessing international finance was required to accept conditionality. With the Heavily Indebted Poor Countries (HIPC) initiative, the incentives for agreeing to new forms of conditionality became even stronger.

As argued above, much of the new governance agenda is still replete with the same problematic neoclassical microfoundations. The view of governance in both the Bank and the Fund draws on the very public choice theory used by neoclassical economists.[45] The Fund is quite explicit regarding this when it states that the aim of governance is to "eliminate the opportunity for rent-seeking, corruption, and fraudulent activity in the management of public resources" (International Monetary Fund 2001, 5). The goal is to support standard stabilization policies: "The Fund's involvement with governance derives from its mandate to promote macroeconomic stability and sustained non-inflationary growth" (8). Governance does not displace any of the standard adjustment conditions, but rather adds a new layer of compliance on already overburdened African states. The number of conditions simply increased over time from an average of six in the 1970s to ten in the 1980s and to twenty-six in the 1990s (Santiso 2002, 21).

Poverty Reduction, Ownership, and Empowerment

Although the focus on governance is aimed at ensuring that the state is allowed to focus only on its main neoclassically defined role as the guarantors of private property and the money supply,[46] other parts of the new agenda have been aimed at enhancing or acting as a catalyst for orthodox reform. Poverty reduction, ownership, stakeholder participation, and budget support in the form of donor funds going directly into the government budget have, for both the Fund and the Bank, become important parts of the new agenda since 1999.[47] Indeed, these priorities are embodied in the new Poverty Reduction Strategy Papers (PSRPs), which have become prerequisites for debt relief under the HIPC initiative. According to the Bank, PSRPs should empower stakeholders and encourage the country receiving them to feel some ownership of the reform policies being implemented. The ownership principle derived from one of the Bank's excuses for the failure of its strategies: recipients had perceived policies as imposed and extrinsic. It was believed that increased ownership—the perception that the countries themselves had helped define the terms of conditionality— would help reverse policy failures (World Bank 2000, 1) The reality has been quite different, however. The case of Tanzania, for example, is quite telling.

Tanzania's relationship with donors, including the World Bank, was at times rocky, particularly in the period from 1992 to 1995. But with the election of President Benjamin Mkapa in November 1995, and the corresponding decision to formulate a shadow IMF (a Fundlike program without IMF approval) in June and July 1996, the new government regained approval from donors. The IMF rewarded Tanzania with a three-year Enhanced Structural Adjustment Facility, which was followed by an accord with the Paris Club (an organization dealing with official debt) that cleared the way for Tanzania to join the HIPC initiative in April 2000. To reach the HIPC conclusion point, with higher levels of debt relief, Tanzania had to satisfy several conditions, including the completion of a PRSP, the implementation of its poverty strategy for at least a year, and the achievement of three successful years of agreed macroeconomic stabilization targets defined by the IMF's Poverty Reduction and Growth Facility (PRGF).

The pertinent questions, however, given the emphasis by both the Bank and the Fund on ownership, were how the PRSPs were drafted and whether they were actually country-driven, with genuine participation by stakeholders.[48] The answers are quite disturbing. Beyond a few hurried hours on a Saturday morning, there was no parliamentary participation in the writing of the PRSP. Meanwhile, the Fund and the Bank rejected two drafts presented by the Ministry of Finance before finally accepting the third. Interviews with parliamentary representatives affirmed time and again that absolutely none of their views had been reflected in the document. In fact, only two sentences in the entire fifty-three-page paper were devoted to the views of Parliament: one indicating simply that they "concurred with the reported findings of the Zonal Workshop" (Government of Tanzania 2000, 13), and one rather banal comment about the need to consider regional differences.

Of Tanzania's population of 30 million, only 804 people were consulted in zonal workshops, in only a two-day period. Beyond listing of some of the concerns expressed by the poor in Part IIIA of the paper, there is no evidence of any resulting changes to the poverty reduction strategies embedded in the report. In the Tanzanian PRSP, the concerns of the poor are lumped together under a subheading and then essentially dismissed (Government of Tanzania 2000, 17).

This was hardly the commitment to country-driven reform that the Bank had professed. The façade of participation was evident in other PRSPs as well. According to a recent survey by Stewart and Wang (2003) that considered fifty-two countries with full or interim PRSPs, the role of national Parliaments in formulating the papers has been minimal. Only five of Malawi's Members of Parliament were involved in formulating that country's PRSP, while in Kenya, less than 10 percent of members attended meetings concerning the PRSP. In Senegal and Mali, representatives were only involved in the final ratification of the paper, and only six of the eighty-three Members of Parliament in Benin participated in any PRSP-related discussions.

Moreover, participation in the formulation of PRSPs has frequently been highly selective; governments are able to choose which groups are allowed to provide input, thus allowing for political maneuvering. In Cameroon, for example, the government bypassed important societal institutions such as the Catholic Church, which had heavily campaigned for debt relief. Even where a large number of nongovernmental organizations (NGOs) have been consulted, they have very rarely been representative of the concerns of poor constituents. In the case of Ghana, many participating NGOs had links to donors rather than to broader domestic anti-poverty groups.

Expediency has frequently been the priority in the drafting of the PRSPs, because countries have strong incentives to complete the process rapidly. Thus participation has often been pro forma. For example, in Ethiopia the government completed its consultations with one hundred districts in only three days. In Cameroon, workshops were convened only once, with no possibilities for follow-up. In Senegal, groups were asked to comment on initial drafts of PRSPs without having seen them! Stewart and Wang (2003) conclude that "it appears that participation has had limited impact on the wider content of PSRPs. The perception among many civil society participants and third party observers has been that the recommendations made during consultations have largely not been incorporated in final documents" (17).

Moreover, in Tanzania there was strong evidence of the continued overriding centrality of the typical orthodox policies. Tanzania's PRGF targets, which predated the PRSPs, focused on concerns such as inflation rates and foreign exchange liberalization and were found in their Poverty Reduction Strategy Paper and in the Poverty Assessment Framework that specified the goals of the Poverty Reduction Budget Support.[49] The report also reflected the IMF's official line that macro-level stabilization reduces poverty. Indeed, the PRSP states that "the poverty reduction strategy is to a large extent an integral part of ongoing macroeconomic and structural reforms. . . . Some of these reforms, including those being supported under the PRGF and Programmatic Structural Adjustment Credit-1 (PSAC-1), are expected to have a significant impact on the welfare of the poor" (Government of Tanzania 2001, 17).

Tanzania is not the only country where IMF and Bank targets dominate PRSPs and promote the same orthodox policies as do structural adjustment programs. Dembele (2003), for example, compared the targets of the Senegalese PRSP to the Bank's Country Assistance Strategy for Senegal and finds that the two documents have nearly identical goals.

Stewart and Wang's (2003) examination of the macroeconomic and structural reform policy contents of the thirty completed PRSPs reveals

that there is no fundamental departure from the kind of policy advice provided in earlier structural adjustment programs. Current policies contain
all the elements of the first generation of policy reforms, which had been
designed to promote the role of the market and "get the prices right."
They also have a similar format and content involving all of the following: financial and trade liberalization, privatization, public-sector reform,
sectoral policies (for example, infrastructure, energy, and manufacturing),
and social-sector reform.

Ownership, an important part of the new lexicon of the international
financial institutions, and yet another term borrowed from neoclassical
notions of property rights, is a major aim of the PRSPs. It can be seen as
having two dimensions: one of possession and one of the perception of
ownership. By this rationale, true ownership requires both of these dimensions, as well as the empowerment that is associated with the construct.

In the title of their paper, Stewart and Wang (2003) ask whether PRSPs
empower countries or whether the reality is actually the other way around.
They conclude that "the PRSP process to date has not empowered developing countries and disempowered the World Bank. It may have changed
perceptions and consequently national ownership from this perspective. If
so it would appear to have actually helped empower the World Bank, by
increasing the effectiveness of programs through raising national enthusiasm for them and increasing the perception they are homegrown strategies" (27–28).

Conclusions

This chapter has traced the origins of structural adjustment, which has
dominated the World Bank and IMF agendas since 1980. Conditionality
had been central to the IMF program lending almost from its inception.
With the demise of the Bretton Woods system, the Fund had to reinvent
its role and began to focus on lending to developing countries. The World
Bank was largely prohibited by its Articles of Agreement from undertaking program lending but for exceptional circumstances. Conveniently, the
Bank deemed "exceptional' any country with an IMF-approved loan, thus
allowing the Bank, too, to expand lending to the developing world.

Structural adjustment lending in the Bank grew rapidly during the
1980s. Most donors of bilateral aid supported a similar agenda, thus plac-
ing enormous pressures on governments in developing countries to accept

the policy packages. But in that decade the performance of countries subject to the adjustment program was quite dismal. To protect the integrity, resources, and reputation of the Bank, which had invested so much—both theoretically and financially—in adjustment, it was necessary to find a way to make it work. In the Bank's view, the problem was not that the policies of structural adjustment per se had failed but that other factors had limited the positive influence of neoliberal policies. After 1989 the Bank began to expand the agenda to incorporate governance ownership, social capital, legal reform, institutions, participation, and poverty reduction, which in the main shared three elements. First, there was a continued commitment to the core set of adjustment policies, with the new elements used to rationalize the poor performance of adjustment. Second, each new policy was seen as a complement to adjustment, and third, the microfoundations of the new agenda were frequently based on neoclassical economic theory with all its problematic implications.

In chapter 3 I argue that the problem of structural adjustment is fundamentally a theoretical one. The theories underlying adjustment are incapable of either explicating the exigencies of development, especially in places such as Africa, or of generating policies that will lead to a sustained improvement in the standard of living for the population.

PART II

Economic Theory and the World Bank Agenda

A Critical Evaluation

CHAPTER THREE

Economic Theory and Orthodox Reform

Critical Reflections on Structural Adjustment

Economic rationalism appears to achieve both the systematic limitation of reason to scarcity situations and its systematic extension to all human ends and means, thus validating an economistic culture with all the appearances of irresistible logic. . . . To atomize society and make every atom behave according to the principle of economic rationalism . . . [is to] place the whole of human existence with all its depth and wealth, in the frame of reference of the market. . . .

The eclipse of political thinking was the intellectual deficiency of the age. It originated in the economic sphere, yet it destroyed any objective approach to the economy itself, insofar as the economy possessed an institutional background other than a supply-demand-price mechanism. Economists felt so safe within the confines of such a purely theoretical market system that they only grudgingly conceded to nations more than a nuisance value.—Karl Polanyi, 1977

Introduction

Despite the increasing types of conditionality introduced by the World Bank and the IMF during the 1990s, the core program of adjustment with its trinity of stabilization, liberalization, and privatization remained intact. Moreover, the same problematic economic microfoundations, or theoretical propositions, that underlie adjustment continued to be present in many of the new strategies added to the World Bank agenda in the 1990s—a disconcerting fact given adjustment's poor performance and noted failures.

This chapter explores the neoclassical economic roots of adjustment and includes a critical analysis of this strategy, focusing on errors generated by overreliance on the methodology and content of the economic theory embedded in structural adjustment policies. The latter part of this chapter examines the issues involved in empirical testing. More specifically, it argues that the strict adherence to neoclassical economics methodology is largely to blame for the Bank's failure to question, adapt, or abandon policies despite the overwhelming evidence of downward economic trends among adjusting countries. In this context, two issues are considered in depth: ethnicity and social capital.

The poor performance of the countries that have followed the dictates of structural adjustment can be tied to the flawed roots of neoclassical economic theory. Not unlike the pre-Depression economics described by Karl Polanyi in the epigraph, today's orthodox economists have had a powerful influence in policy spheres. This influence has had significant consequences that reverberate well beyond the intellectual realm. Similarly, the neoclassical economic formulations that underlie Bank policies and on which orthodox economists depend are capable neither of adequately assessing the problems of development nor of designing a viable strategy with which to promote development. This failure is largely attributable to the neoclassical economists' emphasis on equilibrium, their static and narrow notions of human behavior, and their misplaced focus on financial variables.

Moreover, the theories used to justify structural adjustment strategies utilize absurd assumptions such as full employment of resources, which are completely contrary to the actual conditions in most developing countries. It is therefore unsurprising that the predicted outcomes do not, in fact, result from the adjustment-inspired policy changes. In this chapter I concentrate on these theories, for if we are to adequately assess structural adjustment, we must first expose the assumptions and beliefs that underlie it.

Structural Adjustment: The Theory of the Core Components

The theoretical underpinnings of structural adjustment were, at least in part, products of historical context. Structural adjustment rests on a theoretical foundation inherited from the Bretton Woods period: that of the stabilization policies of the International Monetary Fund. Two key models created the base of these policies: the Polak model and the Swan-Salter model. The former, designed by Polak (1957), formalized the financial programming model, a monetarist approach to dealing with balance-of-payments stabilization initially intended for use in the fixed-exchange regime of the Bretton Woods era. Yet even after the demise of the Bretton Woods system in 1973, the IMF continued to use the same model of stabilization to generate the terms of its loan conditionality. The Swan-Salter model focuses on the impact of devaluations on tradeable commodities (Salter 1959; Swan 1960).

The Polak model relies on a monetarist formulation to tie credit growth to the balance of payments. Like the monetarists, it assumes full employment of resources, including labor. There are two key parts to the model: money supply and a fixed exchange rate. Money supply is defined as the domestic credit available to the private and public sectors plus a country's monetary reserves. Changes in reserves are tied to the country's balance of trade on goods and services and nontraded related currency flows. According to the model, money demand occurs only when needed for transactions and not for other reasons, as the work of Keynes suggests.[1] Prices are positively related to the nominal level of GDP. In other words, the money supply increases, but real production does not increase accordingly; thus, prices will increase with nominal GDP. Because the supply and demand for money are assumed to be in equilibrium, any increase in government borrowing would lead to an increase in prices and nominal income, which in turn would increase the demand for imports. This would occur because government borrowing is essentially an increase in the money supply, which must be met with an increase in money demand if equilibrium is to be maintained.

The nominal rise in income would lead to an increase in imports because domestic production of goods would not have changed. Imports would cause the terms of trade to worsen since the country would now move closer to a trade deficit. Likewise, reserves would also fall because the country's central bank would have to use its reserves to buy extra domestic currency in order to keep the exchange rate fixed. The subsequent lowering of reserves would eventually offset the rise in the money supply. Yet a country in this situation would be left with higher prices, worsening balance of payments, and lowered reserves. The decrease in reserves would encourage speculation against the currency and thereby threaten the stability of the fixed exchange rate of the country.

The IMF used this model in its lending practices. In exchange for access to IMF loans, countries were expected to reach financial targets aimed at improving the balance of payments, lowering prices, raising reserves, and thus ultimately maintaining the integrity of the fixed exchange system. Whether the causes of balance-of-payments instability were domestic or external, the model dictated austerity via contraction of domestic expenditures, which would be achieved by fiscal retrenchment and credit reductions. The real world of developing countries, however, is replete with large-scale unemployment. Employing such a model, which takes as given that all resources, including labor, are fully utilized, is therefore dubious in these cases. Indeed, policies based on this model have tended to contract economic activity and further exacerbate the already dismal standard of living. Recent empirical studies have confirmed the negative impact of IMF conditionality on economic growth.[2] Moreover, this climate of austerity and credit constraint is hardly conducive to the types of investment needed for altering the structures of economies—an important key to development.

The Fund's stabilization policies also relied on the Swan-Salter model of macroeconomic adjustment, which tried to map the linkage effects of exchange rate adjustments on traded and nontraded commodities in a small and open economy. In this model, significant currency devaluations are seen to increase the return, in domestic currency terms, to tradable commodities, which therefore would induce higher levels of exports. This is assumed to universally improve balance of payments because exports are stimulated while import levels are curtailed by the currency devaluation. This model has several drawbacks, however—again, especially in the case of its application to developing countries—including its dismissal of structural weaknesses such as high dependence on imports, which would raise the domestic cost of production and counter inducements to export.

In addition, a country's exports can be subject to a fallacy-of-composition effect arising from the simultaneous expansion of exports by a number of "adjusting" countries with a significant market share. When the exported goods have low elasticity, the dramatic increase in supply leads to a fall in price, which is not offset by sufficient demand stimulation; this leads to a decline in revenues.

For example, if five developing countries whose main export was coffee devalued their currencies simultaneously (and if this represented a significant amount of coffee produced in the world), the world market would be flooded with an abundant supply of coffee, thereby making coffee cheaper. These five countries would not experience a jump in their exports, however, because demand for coffee does not change much with respect to the price. In other words, consumers will not start to drink three cups of coffee a day instead of one just because the price of their coffee has decreased by 10 percent; more likely, they will consume the same amount of coffee that they always have. Yet this strategy of expanding exports while devaluing currency was and still is strongly promoted by World Bank and IMF policies. Combined with trade liberalization (discussed below), this strategy encourages countries to pursue their static comparative advantage, which for developing countries tends to be the export of unprocessed raw materials (which is not surprising given their colonial history). Thus, rather than focusing on developmentally enhancing exports, which might encourage reorientation of economies toward industry and manufacturing and in turn help stimulate their structural transformation,[3] developing countries are locked into the same problematic patterns.

Other components of structural adjustment have also discouraged strategies that would structurally transform developing economies. The introduction of measures aimed at inducing an increase in the supply of good and services via liberalization and privatization, along with the policies of demand constraint, have focused on improvements in static efficiency, not structural transformation. Liberalization policies are derived from standard neoclassical microeconomic models applied to areas such as trade and financial repression (discussed in chapter 7). For example, recommendations for trade liberalization arise from static comparative advantage theory and its neoclassical extensions (by Heckscher, Ohlin, and Samuelson).

According to this model, which was based for simplicity's sake on a two-country, two-good world, the developing country should specialize in the product it produces with *less* comparative *dis*advantage; in other words, because it is unlikely that a developing country would be better at producing anything than would a developed country, the developing country should produce that which it is *least* bad at producing. Likewise, the richer country should specialize in the product it could produce with greater comparative advantage. Because efficiency would be static in this kind of equilibrium, there would be no incentive for a developing country to change its strategy of production in order to try to gain a comparative advantage in more advanced goods. Therefore, in this model, the developing country would be locked into producing the same kind of good, which more than likely would be something akin to a low-elasticity beverage crop.

In the Heckscher-Ohlin model, comparative advantage is given a "natural" basis due to the differences between countries in terms of endowments of various factors of production. Specialization via free trade would be based on products that use more of the readily available input. In this model, even without capital or labor mobility, trade would lead inexorably to the equality of income between countries (Samuelson's factor-price equalization theorem). In other words, if a labor-endowed country switches from producing capital-intensive goods to producing more labor-intensive goods, the price of labor will rise. If that country trades with a relatively capital-abundant country that specializes in producing more capital-intensive goods, then returns to capital will rise. If both the labor-abundant country and the capital-abundant country are open to trade, the price of both labor and capital will fall, and the countries will trade to the point at which wages and the price of capital are equalized in both relative and absolute terms. Thus, according to the Heckscher-Ohlin model, in a world with only labor and capital as inputs, trade liberalization should lead to one world price for labor and one world price for capital. This conclusion was a powerful affirmation of the claim that free trade would enhance development and welfare; it served to underscore the World Bank's policy advice to developing countries, which aimed to push them toward their comparative advantages through trade liberalization. I now turn to the common neoclassical economic microfoundations of these theories in order to illustrate their problematic nature relative to the conditions and transformative needs of developing countries.

The Microfoundations of Adjustment

Five subcomponents are at the heart of the neoclassical theories embedded in structural adjustment: *Homo economicus*, methodological individualism, the acceptance of equilibrium as a natural state, rational deductivity, and axiomatic reasoning. These subcomponents are implicitly or explicitly assumed in every neoclassical theory, including the models outlined above. *Homo economicus* posits a rationally calculating individual who naturally seeks to maximize his or her welfare. This concept incorporates an instrumental mode of rationality in which an actor makes choices that will best satisfy his or her utility. In the strictest neoclassical version, *Homo economicus* is assumed to live in a world of perfect certainty, where the future is fully described and people completely grasp the potential consequences of their choices.

This model relies entirely on the second core subcomponent: methodological individualism. Decision making is believed to begin with choices at the individual level, and the end point is the maximization of the welfare of the individual. Markets are perceived as exchanges where goods and services are transferred from individual producers to individual consumers. Exchange in the neoclassical model arises spontaneously from the atomistic interaction of self-seeking individuals. Goods traded in every market are assumed to be homogenous so that prices provide the only information needed to make the decisions about production and purchasing. No individual has sufficient market power to affect the market price.

This line of reasoning leads to the third subcomponent of neoclassical theory. Equilibrium arises in the sense that the market is clearing—reaching optimal conditions and thereby maximizing society's welfare. Pareto optimality occurs when no one will be able to be better off without making someone worse off. In such an ideal world, unfettered markets will normally lead to indicators that reflect scarcity and choice. Decisions based on such markets will lead to efficient choices regarding what and how to produce; these choices are then indicative of the endowment of societal resources. Thus the outcome is consistent with the natural underlying conditions. In short, equilibrium is a natural state.[4]

The final two subcomponents of neoclassical theory relate to the manner in which the above assumptions are created; the thinking behind the models is rational deductive and axiomatic. It is rational deductive thinking because the behavior of agents is predetermined by a posited set of rules. It is axiomatic because rational, predictable behavior is simply assumed to arise from a set of market signals. No argument or explanation is put forth as proof. Consumers and private producers are presupposed to be utility and profit maximizers that rationally respond in an efficient manner, as long as the market signals are correct.

Following the outline of these microfoundations of neoclassical theory, at least six propositions are generated. These focal points are at the heart of adjustment and its underlying theories: a commitment to the principle of state neutrality or minimalism; preoccupation with static efficiency; a focus on distortions; a focus on marginality; a view that changes in relative prices lead to predictable outcomes; and development as a static equilibrium state.

The axiomatic presupposition of private actors' behavior in the economy leads neoclassical theorists to focus on other explanations for why economies are not operating at "optimal" levels. The public sector is often made the scapegoat. The public choice school of neoclassical thinking views the state as purely predatory. On the other hand, according to the rational choice school, the members of the state are seen as selecting politically rational policies that are economically irrational; for example, the state has an incentive to keep agricultural prices low to build urban coalitions, which is wise politically but foolish economically (see Bates 1981). Of course, both approaches draw on methodological individualistic explanations of the behavior of acquisitive *Homo economicus* using the vehicle of the state for predatory purposes.

According to this line of reasoning, the public sector must be the source of the distortions that create inefficiencies. According to this logic, the solution to the economic malaise would be to retract state intervention in markets via deregulation and privatization. Once the state retracts from direct intervention in economic activities and resource allocation, it is assumed that private agents would react favorably to changed incentives and a more competitive environment by investing in and producing internationally tradable goods and services, thereby earning more foreign exchange via increased exports. Thus, trade liberalization and the deregulation of goods and factor markets are supposed to result in a removal of the "structural" causes of macroeconomic imbalances.

So what role should states play? In its most orthodox form, neoclassical economics does not recognize any role for states. The view arises from the general equilibrium component of neoclassical economic theory. As seen above, economies are understood to be driven by exchanges, which arise from the spontaneous interaction of self-seeking individuals. In a more relaxed model, there is some recognition for states in that property rights are transferred through exchanges; therefore there is a need for some external guarantor, such as a judiciary. There is also some recognition that money is needed in exchanges as a means of payment, which sets the preconditions for monetary institutions such as a central bank, which can tightly control credit creation to avoid problems with balance of payments. Like the guarantor of property rights, this monetary institution should also remain neutral by using objective criteria such as the monetary rule, whereby money supply increases at the anticipated rate of real growth of the economy.

Much of adjustment is driven by the principle of creating state neutrality and minimalism in the belief that once prices reflect their scarcity values, the private sector will respond accordingly. This view of state behavior did not change with the introduction of governance and other "new" elements of conditionality in the 1990s.

Structural Adjustment: Toward a Critique

Problems with Static Comparative Advantage

Neoclassical theory asserts that enormous static efficiency gains can arise from liberalization, privatization, and stabilization, which remove government-produced distortions in exchange rates, interest rates, and commodity and labor prices. Instead of viewing development as a process of structural and institutional transformation, it focuses on the creation of a static equilibrium state in which rational private actors make marginal changes in reaction to undistorted prices.

The consequences of following this kind of policy advice have been particularly pernicious for resource-intensive exporters, which have been common among the poorer developing countries. World commodity prices have plummeted in the past two decades. Between 1980 and 2003 the price of food, including beverages, fell by 73.3 percent, agricultural raw materials prices declined by 60.7 percent, and prices of minerals, ores, and metals fell by 59.5 percent. Worse still, the key commodities of the least developed countries were the hardest hit. In 2003 the price of coffee was only 17 percent of its 1980 level; cotton 33 percent, and copper 42 percent (United Nations Conference on Trade and Development 2004, 156).

The reasons for the failure of static comparative advantage are not difficult to ascertain. In addition to the fallacy-of-composition problem, which is most acute among beverage commodities, the decline in prices of key commodities is also directly related to the shifting nature of global production. The emphasis on raw material and primary product exports is very problematic in an era when knowledge has become a larger proportion of the value added to commodities. Advances in biotechnology and material sciences are leading to synthetic substitutes for primary products such as vanilla and sugar. Nations that produce commodities such as palm oil are also being challenged by newly industrialized countries such as Malaysia, which uses highly advanced methods of production that drive prices down and cut into the competitive advantage of the poorer developing countries. On the demand side, products such as copper, long used for communications, are being replaced by fiber optical cables or microwaves. Yet as raw materials are processed, protection rises in export markets, creating disincentives to move up the value-added chain (Adesida 1998).

Subsidies in developed countries have also driven prices downward. In a recent submission to the World Trade Organization (WTO), Brazil argued that the United States paid subsidies of $12.4 billion to American cotton producers between August 1999 and July 2003. During this time, the subsidies helped raise cotton production by 20 percent, increased the American share of the world cotton market from 17 to 42 percent, and created a fall in world prices from 72 to 29 cents per pound. Based on its econometric study, Brazil estimated that without the subsidies, U.S. cotton exports would have fallen by 41 percent and the world price of cotton would have risen by 12.6 percent (Embassy of Brazil 2004). The implications of this statistic for poor cotton-producing countries, whose dependency on cotton is clearly more pronounced than is that of the United States, are obvious. The poorest African countries were hit the hardest. Four African countries—Benin, Mali, Burkina Faso, and Chad—relied on cotton for between 54 percent and 78 percent of their total exports. Oxfam (2004) estimates that annual losses in West and Central Africa due to U.S. and European cotton subsidies totaled roughly $250 million.

Unfortunately, this illustration from West Africa is only the tip of the iceberg. In the period 1997–99, the poorest forty-nine countries in the world relied on an average of only three commodities for 76 percent of their total exports, most of which were non-oil mineral and agricultural raw materials. Eighty-four percent of the total commodity exports of this group consisted of unprocessed materials, and these frequently competed against each other. The United Nations Conference on Trade and Development (2004) estimates that if prices for primary non-oil products had remained at 1980 levels and the least developed countries had maintained their 1980 market share, their exports would have brought in $7.4 billion, or roughly 80 percent, more, Yet even these dramatic figures, being merely static comparisons, underestimate the opportunities lost from structural stagnancy. According to UNCTAD, only 12 percent of the primary commodity exports of least developed countries (LDCs) were market-dynamic products for which import demand exceeded the average. In contrast, 70 percent of exports of manufactured goods fell within this category.

Overall, if the LDCs' exports had grown in accordance with those of other countries, and if they had maintained their 1980 share of the market, total exports would have been $20.8 billion higher, or 44 percent larger, in 2001. The immensity of this amount should be contrasted with aid dependence. In 2001, the LDCs received net official transfers of only $9.8 billion, or less than half of what they would have received with a strategy that was able to sustain their portion of global exports (United Nations Conference on Trade and Development 2004, 43, 154–58). By this measure, the inflow of resources from aid, with the concomitant conditionality, including the imposition of policies prioritizing static comparative advantage, does not come close to what could have been accomplished if they had taken an alternative path of transformation.

These results are not terribly surprising given that the assumptions underlying trade theory have no correspondence to the reality of developing countries. The static neoclassical model assumed no economies of scale, perfect certainty, pure competition, no externalities, no capital or labor movement, costless and equally available technology, and no unemployment. Perhaps most problematic, the model does not recognize any economic difference between a country that produces unprocessed cocoa and a country that produces the most sophisticated computers. According to the model's assumptions, both countries should gain equally. Yet this claim is absurd when realistically considered. As Eric Reinert (2000) puts it:

> Few economists tell their children to become shoe-shine boys rather than go to college because factor-price equalization is around the corner. Domestically, then, economists practice what they would professionally decry as mercantilism. At home they see important practical implications from their own children's choice of professions. . . . Early economic policy seems everywhere to have originated in a very simple notion: some economic activities produce higher standard of living than others and nations are sometimes in the "wrong" business. Perhaps the most remarkable feature of modern economic theory is the compete suppression of this common-sense instinct on the level of society. International trade theory has "proved" that a nation specializing in being the stockbrokers of the world will have the same wage level as a nation specializing in shining the shoes of the world. (22)

Errors Stemming from the Microfoundations of Adjustment

Several basic errors arise from the use of neoclassical economics as a guide for the development of economies: (1) behavioral and interactive failures, (2) problems of scope, (3) definitional errors, (4) mistakes in interpreting comparative studies, (5) difficulties in dealing with the temporal and spatial dimensions of development, and (6) failures associated with aggregation problems.

1. *Homo economicus* is a very problematic representation of the nature of human behavior in general and in developing countries in particular. The error is not in the assumption that individuals undertake activities aimed at enhancing their personal welfare but rather in the failure to recognize that people are foremost social beings interacting in a broad social and institutional context that greatly affects their economic activities. For example, more realistic notions of human behavior acknowledge that rationality is bounded by limits on the human ability to process information.[5] This formulation cannot, however, adequately account for the existence of other people in society, whose interactions create additional boundaries, nor can it help predict the behavior modifications that are made in decision making as a result of taking other people into consideration. Alternative concepts of behavior are explored in chapter 5.

It is not surprising that this conceptualization of the individual—and the failure to recognize the context within which the individual functions— has led to a flawed assessment of human behavior. Such an assessment, of course, is crucial to understanding the functionality of an economy; its inadequacy is therefore deeply troubling. Thus, introducing private property ownership in Africa, contrary to the model's expectations, has often failed to improve the efficiency of land usage because of the competing claims to property ownership based on clientage and kinship, which are part of the decision making of rural Africa.[6] Also important in such decision-making is consideration of what is socially acceptable. For instance, in some places, other forms of socially defined property rights are more legitimate than are the Western-style private property rights forms imposed by external authorities.

Before transforming property rights, one must understand the basis of legitimacy and the normative prerequisites for moving toward new forms of legitimacy (Stein 1995b). But in the narrower traditions of neoclassical economics, there is little discussion of noneconomic factors, and therefore no place for consideration of social factors. In rational choice theory, for example, noneconomic variables are products of the calculus of *Homo economicus*. Causality between that which is economic and that which is noneconomic is therefore unidirectional, and all noneconomic variables are purposive and instrumental. For instance, one rational choice theorist explains African social structure as a rational outcome of reducing uncertainty in a high-risk environment. Critics show that this assertion is empirically unfounded, because high-risk environments in rural Africa are ubiquitous but social outcomes vary dramatically.[7] These arguments exhibit the old functionalist error of mistaking correlation for causality; they also provide a good example of an interactive failure arising from neoclassical microfoundations.

2. The theories underlying structural adjustment are flawed because of their failure of scope, which arises from the neoclassical microfoundations' dependence on nominal variables or legally defined categories. The focus on enhancing efficient decision making through marginal changes in response to correct prices and legal recognition of private property rights has been the major preoccupation of orthodox reform policies. In developing economies, however, lumpy organizational and structural factors must be proactively transformed in order to promote economic growth.

3. Definitional problems arise from reliance on neoclassical economic theory for understanding key constructs. Public choice and rational choice theories have dominated the conceptualization of the state by proponents of adjustment. One of the great paradoxes of structural adjustment in the 1980s, observed by proponents and critics alike, was that the state was the primary focus of criticism by the Bank and the Fund and was heavily blamed for the problems, but nevertheless remained the major vehicle of policy delivery. In the 1980s, the pattern in Africa was to tie credit conditionally to civil service retrenchment targets. This was said to help reduce government budget deficits and allow the country to meet IMF credit targets. Implicit in this policy was the erroneous assumption that cutting back on "bloated" bureaucracies would somehow diminish the dysfunctional nature of state intervention while "freeing up" scarce human resources for the private sector.[8] This misconception of civil service reform is explored in considerable detail in chapter 6.

4. These policies suffer from flawed analyses of comparative studies. An important dimension of any development strategy is to learn from successful development strategies in other parts of the world. Unfortunately, the proponents of adjustment have employed rational deductive methods and relied on axioms to interpret these comparative experiences in a manner that predetermines the importance of certain variables and their direction of causality.[9] Instead, any comparative exercise should begin with an accurate historical account aimed at identifying the factors responsible for generating development.

5. The foundations of the theories underlying the policies are by nature both spatially and temporally static. Adjustment policy has focused on

removing distortions to create an economy that is optimal and in equilibrium. This objective, however, belies the realities of development: rather than a constant state of affairs, development is a dynamic process that involves significant change over time. Adjustment policies have been aimed at addressing certain symptoms of bad economic performance, such as the role of the state (which is deemed an interference and therefore must be restrained) and trade deficits (which are believed to be inherently instable and therefore must be treated with macroeconomic stabilization). Such a focus divulges an ultimate objective of achieving macrostability. It is assumed that price stability and government constraint are necessary because they will "naturally" lead to increased private investment and consequently a better standard of living. Yet macrostability focuses on generating a monetary equilibrium and bears no relation to a future point in time and space. Development, on the other hand, involves the transformation of polity, economy, and society over time and therefore cannot be properly addressed with such an approach.

6. Likewise, the neoclassical emphasis on methodological individualism seems to contradict some important aspects of development. The relation between individual decision making and higher outcome levels is not conceptually coherent. The social outcomes that are at the heart of development are not as simple as the sum of all decisions made by utility-maximizing individuals.

Methodological Errors: Toward an Explanation of the Fealty to Adjustment Policy and the Search for the "Missing" Factor

In addition to these errors, the unbridled commitment to the core policies of adjustment can be explained in part by the methodology of neoclassical economics embedded in the underlying theory. The literature about economic methodology has begun to widely recognize that neoclassical economics almost never practices Popperian falsification.[10] Rather, it relies on a core set of propositions that remain unaltered, even in the face of counterevidence. Some scholars have explained this phenomenon by invoking Lakatos's work concerning the methodology of scientific research. From his perspective, scientific research should consist of a hard core of irrefutable metaphysical propositions; positive heuristics, which generate a guide to which tools and questions should be selected and which should be avoided; and a protective belt of theories, empirical conventions, and auxiliary hypotheses. For example, Weintraub (1985) has interpreted general equilibrium theory in these terms. His core propositions are that agents optimize, have preferences, and act independently. Heuristics encourage researchers to focus on theories wherein agents optimize while avoiding those that involve disequilibrium. The protective belt of the neoclassical Walrasian program is found in the realm of applied microeconomics: theoretical progression occurs when the theory predicts some novel, unexpected facts, and empirical progression occurs when apparently extraneous content is finally corroborated. Thus, failure to pursue this mode of inquiry implies that research is degenerating both theoretically and empirically.

This depiction has been widely challenged. For instance, Hands (1993) argues that Lakatos's approach does not provide any guidance for the acceptance or rejection of economic theories. Knudsen (1993) argues that there is little evidence that economics is in a crisis because it has failed to meet the test of progression. Less convincingly, Hausman (1994) argues that using Lakatos's categories hides the fact that most neoclassicists have many aspects that are not shared by all neoclassical works. This is a definitional problem with relation to the exact meaning of the term *neoclassical*. Even Hausman admits that neoclassical works have common elements such as methodological individualism. For the purposes of this book, I stand by the neoclassical subcomponents of adjustment theories outlined above and associate them with Lakatos's core propositions.[11]

The reliance on an axiomatic approach, or the commitment to a core set of unchanging propositions, is particularly problematic in methodological terms. Economists working in this framework begin with a series of axioms and then generate policy initiatives, which are applied to concrete historical conditions. When policies have not worked, it is generally assumed that noneconomic variables have subverted the process. Policy variations are possible within a narrow realm, but since the basic body of theory arises from identical axioms, there is no alteration at the basic theoretical level. In essence, the theoretical level is cut off from actual experiences; the concrete can only be used to affirm the theory, not to reject it.

In the face of empirical studies whose conclusions challenge fundamental theories, neoclassical economists try to generate alternative studies to present countervailing evidence that will support their theories; if neither of these options is possible, they simply ignore the challenging papers. For example, the so-called Leontief paradox[12] spawned a huge literature aimed at rescuing the factor endowment theory of international trade (see, for instance, Robert Baldwin's (1971) introduction of natural resources and crude measurements of human capital to try to counter the paradox). In spite of its problematic empirical base, however, the Heckscher-Ohlin-Samuelson theory is still presented as the core theory of international trade. The literature concerning expected utility theory provides another example. Axioms underlying the theory of rational choice under conditions of uncertainty are needed to show that individuals acting on a preference ordering that satisfies them can be seen as acting in a manner that maximizes expected utility. The mode of human behavior implied by these axioms, which assumes that all decisions arise from a carefully calculated ranking of the options in a completely consistent manner, is absurd.

Moreover, many of the expected utility theorems are challenged by experimental observations such as Allais's paradox, Ellsberg's paradox, preference reversal theory, and Newcomb's problem. The Allais and Ellsberg paradoxes show that some of the basic assumptions of expected utility theory do not hold in reality. In order to maintain the theory, which is widely used in the mainstream journals, many economists simply dismiss the observations. Some argue that the theory is normative and therefore cannot be directly challenged. Such an argument, however, is not terribly cogent, not only because of the impossibility of cleanly dichotomizing the normative and the positive in economics, but also because it would imply that all the neoclassical models that use expected utility theory would be concerned with how the economy *ought* to be, rather than how it actually operates. Moreover, if this argument were consistent, it would suggest that some neoclassical theories are nothing but speculation or that the theories predict behavior in the aggregate so that variations cancel each other out. Yet even these explanations do not make sense; for example, there is no evidence that the paradoxes identified are random events. Alternatively, some economists deal with these studies by arguing that they have not been gathered from real-world choices, that the stakes in the experiments are not high enough, or that once the actions are repeated, people will become more rational and behave as the neoclassical model predicts they will behave. All of these positions arise from an adamant attachment to a core set of axioms that are needed to maintain the logical integrity of neoclassical economics.[13]

In the same way, this adherence to axiomatic reasoning has driven the nearly unwavering commitment to the core policies of adjustment in spite of widespread evidence of economic decline in regions that are subject to these policies.

Economic Trends and Empirical Testing: The Example of Africa

The preceding chapters briefly reviewed some of the negative economic trends that occurred in Africa in the 1980s. But a more holistic picture is even more telling. Table 3.1 presents some key economic indicators for sub-Saharan Africa for 1980, 1990, and 2002. Although these are only annual data points, they are fairly indicative of the direction of the trends during the intervening years.

The data reveal how badly sub-Saharan Africa deteriorated over the entire structural adjustment period. Food production was unable to keep up with population growth. Merchandise exports fell dramatically in nominal dollar terms in the 1980s; there was some recovery in the 1990s, however, particularly after 1998, when export prices recovered somewhat (rising 17.7 percent between 1998 and 2002). In a twenty-two-year period during which many regions of the world experienced phenomenal growth of international trade, sub-Saharan Africa was a mere 20 percent above the 1980 level. Once again, the lack of structural transformation of trade in sub-Saharan Africa is obvious: less than 10 percent of the economy was in manufacturing, there was a drop in the terms of trade, and the levels of international debt increased massively. After four years of debt relief, the debt-to-export ratio was still an onerous 2.5. Living standards, as measured by gross national product (GNP) per capita, plummeted by 31 percent

TABLE 3.1 **Economic indicators for Africa**

Year	GNP per capita ($)	Food production per capita	Merchandise exports ($M)	Mfg Exports as a percentage of total exports	Current accounts/ GDP	Terms of trade (95=100)	Debt ($M)	Debt/ exports*
1980	551	106	53,049		−1.9	181.2	60,612	1.1
1990	381	100	45,738	8.5	−5.2	113.9	177,052	3.43
2002	307	95	63,852	9.6	−5.1	117.5	185,644	2.54

Sources: World Bank 2001; 2004a.
Note: Figures exclude South Africa.
*This category includes exports of goods and nonfactor services.

in the 1980s and a further 20 percent between 1990 and 2002. During the period, income per capita fell by a horrifying 44 percent on average.

Although identifying trends in Africa says nothing about causal factors, the ubiquity of adjustment is undeniable. By 1995, thirty-seven sub-Saharan countries had received at least one World Bank adjustment loan, and thirty-three had two or more loans (Kapur et al. 1997, 798). But there has been considerable debate concerning the impact of lending and its role in some of the negative economic trends witnessed in Africa. It is particularly difficult to isolate the effects of adjustment policies from other factors in a region in which quality data are so scarce. Why are there such distinctive variations in the interpretation of adjustment's impact? The answer is partly linked to the complications of undertaking empirical exercises aimed at illustrating cause and effect.[14]

In general, there are five approaches to assessing the impact of structural adjustment: the before-and-after method; the control-group approach; the modified control group approach; the decomposition approach; and the "with and without" simulations, which are based on computational general equilibrium (CGE) models and social accounting matrices (SAM).

The first method compares the differences in the mean values of growth before and after adjustment to see if there are statistically significant changes. A good representation of this technique is the work of Bannaga (2002). Examining factors that were intended to raise the growth rate of the GDP, he finds that the Bank's policies have not been successful. Table 3.2 shows results of positive growth rates, but none of them are statistically different from 0 in any period. But his finding is robust according to other statistical tests such as Phillips-Perron and Dickey-Fuller tests. He concludes that this descriptive analysis did not find significant impact from the structural adjustment programs (SAPs) on the Sudanese growth rate.

The second approach compares macroeconomic performance variables for program and nonprogram countries. This approach dominated many

TABLE 3.2 **Simple descriptive statistics for GDP growth in Sudan, 1960–2000**

Period	Mean	SD	Eco. Era
1960–70	3.32	2.90	Ten-year plan
1960–80	3.95	6.46	Pre-SAP
1981–2000	3.46	5.33	Introduction of SAPs
1960–2000	3.71	5.94	Whole period

Source: Bannaga 2002.

TABLE 3.3 **World Bank studies of program and nonprogram countries**

Study	Country group	GDP growth 1982–87	1985–88	1986–90	Investments/GDP 1985–88	1986–90	Exports/GDP 1982–87	1985–88	1986–90
World Bank (1988a)	Intensive adjusters	4.7					8.5		
	Nonintensive adjusters	4.8					7.1		
World Bank (1990b)	Intensive adjusters		4.2		18.6			28.1	
	Nonintensive adjusters		2.7		20.0			24.6	
World Bank (1992b)	Intensive adjusters								
	All countries			4.2		17.9			28.4
	Sub-Saharan Africa			3.5		16.3			28.0
	Nonintensive adjusters								
	All countries			2.4		18.4			28.4
	Sub-Saharan Africa			3.9		15.6			31.7

Source: Mosley 1994.

World Bank studies of adjustment, including three important evaluations undertaken between 1988 and 1992. Mosley (1994) summarizes the studies. Some of these data are reproduced in table 3.3.

A rather mixed picture emerges from this presentation. Although in the 1990 and 1992 studies the all-country adjusters had higher growth rates than did nonintensive adjusters, this was not the case for the period between 1982 and 1987. Moreover, the nonintensive adjusters did better in sub-Saharan Africa in the 1992 study. Generally, nonadjusters did better with respect to investment rates than did adjusters, except sub-Saharan Africa. The picture regarding export performance also showed generally better performance for adjusters, again with the exception of sub-Saharan Africa.

Mosley (1994) reviews the methodology used in these studies and finds major underlying weakness in the classification of countries. First, there was enormous variation in the type of adjustment package prescribed. Some emphasized trade liberalization, others agricultural price reform. Second, there was diversity in the extent to which packages were actually implemented. Third, some countries accepted the advice of the international financial institutions and implemented reforms without being required to do so as a condition of receiving loans. One cannot say with certainty that countries in the "intense" category were implementing packages any more or less rigorously than were the nonintensive adjusters.

Although Mosley does not accuse the Bank of deliberately manipulating the list for its own purposes, other researchers have. Mihevc (1995) relates the rancorous debate about the performance of countries subject to adjustment policies between the Economic Commission for Africa and the World Bank/United Nations Development Programme (UNDP). According to his study, the choice of reference years, weighting schemes, and base years, and the careful exclusion or inclusion of certain strategic data in the studies, suggest a bias "geared to produce a pre-ordained conclusion" (114). For instance, his work illustrates that the results of these studies are quite sensitive to the weighting schemes given to different countries when aggregating variables. When aggregating GDP across reforming and nonreforming countries, Mihevc shows that if one weights GDP by relative importance, rather than using the simple weighting used by the World Bank, the Bank's statistics are overturned: nonreformers fared better than reformers.

The third approach—the use of modified control studies—attempts to control for differences in the external environment when comparing the countries that adopted structural adjustment programs to those that did not. An example of this type of work is Elbadawi (1992). His paper uses several methods to evaluate structural adjustment programs in Africa. First, it uses before-and-after analysis and concludes that the countries that undertook structural reforms suffered from exogenous shocks and were weaker, thus explaining the lack of economic improvement. Elbadawi then uses a modified control group analysis to determine other effects of structural adjustment. He finds a positive and statistically significant impact on exports, a negative and statistically significant impact on investment, and no statistically significant impact on economic growth. This work corroborates findings by Faini et al. (1990), who used the same technique for a sample of ninety-three developing countries. Several other authors, including Corbo and Rojas (1991), have also echoed the important finding that investment rates drop in countries that are undergoing adjustment.

Clearly, there have been enormous variations in the results, even in World Bank studies.[15] All three approaches nonetheless suffer from methodological weakness. The first does not adequately differentiate the impact of nonadjustment factors such as the terms of trade from the influence of adjustment. The second approach suffers from the same weakness, as well as the complexity of determining which countries fit in which category, since many countries have implemented some adjustment policies but not others. The third approach overcomes the first problem but not the second.

The decomposition approach avoids the problem of classifying countries into groups and factors out the impact of variables not related to adjustment policies. The approach econometrically tests the relation between specific policy changes and outcomes by pooling data of countries undertaking quantitatively similar measures. An example of the decomposition approach is seen in Bannaga (2002). He decomposes the effects of growth into the GDP growth rate, the gross domestic investment as percentage of GDP, the log of the inflation rate, the log of the degree of openness, the average GDP growth of sub-Saharan countries (excluding Nigeria), and the log of the rainfall. He finds that openness has a negative and statistically significant impact on growth, while the other terms have unsurprising results. He also runs a long analysis and finds that over time GDP growth is increased significantly by following policies that promote gross domestic investment and lower inflation. But the trade policies that have been pursued to increase the degree of openness in the economy have brought about a negative impact on economic growth.

Bannaga runs many more econometric tests, including regressions intended to disentangle long- and short-term effects, and finds that the factors that contribute significantly to the changes in growth rate are changes in investment, changes in inflation, the lagged value of the growth rate, the lagged value of investment, and the degree of openness. His results indicate that in the long run, following policies that promote gross domestic investment and lower inflation leads to a significant increase in GDP. Yet the very trade policies pursued in order to increase the degree of openness in the economy have also brought about a negative impact on economic growth. In sum, in the short run, economic growth is influenced positively by changes in investment and by rainfall (lagged one year) and negatively by changes in inflation and degree of openness.

The fifth method, the with-and-without method, often relies on very problematic CGE simulations utilizing static social accounting frameworks for parameter determination. The poorest example is in the work of David Sahn (Sahn et al. 1998) and his team at Cornell University, which aims to demonstrate that structural adjustment has reduced poverty in Africa. They utilize restrictive neoclassical assumptions (such as perfectly clearing labor markets) and circular reasoning (such as defining wealth in terms of accessibility to economic rents) to prove that Africa was better off after liberalization because rents, by definition, diminish. They argue that the poor are better off after adjustment because they have proportionately more access to income from tradeables, which will rise in price in a world with adjustment theory.[16]

Sahn et al. (1998) conclude with aplomb that "most of the poor in most of the countries examined are small net gainers when their governments implement the types of adjustment policies discussed in the book" (247). But very different results arise in CGE models using more structuralist assumptions (for example, De Maio et al. 1999).[17] In general, these kinds of generalizations, based on a stylized household in a hypothetical world, do little to allay the concerns caused by increasing poverty of regions under adjustment.

Overall, statistical testing has been unable to convincingly show that adjustment has improved the economies of Africa. Even the Bank has been unable to tell a consistent story. On the other hand, there is a preponderance of evidence demonstrating that regions which, like sub-Saharan Africa, have been heavily burdened by adjustment have done very poorly during the adjustment period.

Adjustment and Auxiliary Hypotheses: Ethnicity and Social Capital

The Search for the African Residual: Ethnicity

Increasingly, neoclassical economic writers—including those with a close association with the Bank—have recognized that even with all of their inventive statistical techniques, it is difficult to counter the overwhelming signs of economic and social deterioration in Africa and elsewhere during the adjustment period. Instead of denying these trends, they have attempted to explain these patterns not by challenging the neoliberal model but by running large-scale cross-country regressions and using variables outside of their models.

Take Easterly and Levine (1997), a widely quoted article that purportedly explains "Africa's growth tragedy." The authors, both of whom had a lengthy affiliation with the Bank, argue that the key factor behind the disparate levels of economic growth in Africa is the influence (direct and indirect) on policy choices of regional patterns of ethnic diversity. With confidence, the authors argue that "ethnic diversity alone explains between one-fourth and two-fifths of the East Asia–Africa growth differential and may fully account for some extreme country cases" (1237). This is perhaps an intriguing conclusion, but the real question is how Easterly and Levine achieved such results.

First, the authors examine a standard array of indicators, including financial depth, black market premiums, fiscal surpluses, schooling of the population, and incidence of telephones among workers. Dummies for Africa and Latin America and the Caribbean are included. The results, unsurprisingly, are typically orthodox. Countries with greater financial depth, larger fiscal surpluses, lower black market premiums, and higher density of telephones were associated with higher growth. These kinds of simple regressions, however, say nothing about the direction of causality, nor about the value of orthodox policies. Obviously, surpluses will be higher when growth is higher, since government revenue will rise. Yet the authors examine the differences in the means of the variables between East Asia and Africa. After mechanically multiplying them by the coefficients in their equations, they argue that Africa has foregone 44 percent of the growth differential by not following the "orthodox route"[18] of East Asia. In a typically neoliberal manner, they ask why it is, if the value of the standard recipe is so great, that Africa did not follow the "universally recognized" linear route to success. According to their findings, the answer is in the extent of ethnic heterogeneity. Ethnically diverse populations are assumed to be less likely to agree on policies for the public good such as macrostability and infrastructure, and are more likely to implement policies that guarantee rents for their constituents while punishing other ethnic groups. For example, the authors argue that in Ghana, when the Akan groups from the coastal regions took over in the 1950s, the new leaders increased the tax on cocoa in an explicit effort to punish the Ashanti and that the ethnically motivated action unintentionally created terrible consequences for cocoa production.

These kinds of rational choice positions, however, are nothing more than axiomatic statements in search of confirmation; facts are simply stylized to suit the argument. For instance, in considering this example, note that taxation of export crops was utilized by the colonial powers and was adopted on a broad scale throughout Africa on independence because it was a comparatively accessible source of revenue for new governments. In Tanzania, the government taxed many cash crops (almost as heavily as did Ghana at times) grown by tribes in many parts of the country. Could one seriously argue that it was motivated by President Julius Nyerere's desire to punish all other ethnic groups, who made up most of the country, for the benefit of his very tiny tribal group from the Lake District?[19]

To verify their assertion about the role of ethnicity, Easterly and Levine use a Soviet survey of ethnic diversity called ETHNIC from the early 1960s and add it to their equations. They look at the direct effect first and assert that "the coefficient . . . implies that if Nigeria had the sample mean value of ETHNIC (.42) instead of an actual value of .87, its per capita growth rate over the 1960–89 [period] would have been almost double its actual value of .7 percent per annum" (1124). This kind of simple-minded linear extrapolation is common in the growth-testing literature. In reality, patterns of growth are nonlinear and vary with the historical and geographical context. Kenny and Williams (2001) remind us that if a 26 percent reduction in inflation leads to a 1 percent increase in per capita growth, as Easterly (1997) asserts on the basis of econometric studies, then Brazil's per capita income would have gone from 5 percent growth in 1994, when inflation was 2,948 percent, to 118 percent in 1996, when inflation had dropped to only 16 percent (15–16)![20] This, of course, was not the case.

Easterly and Levine also examine indirect effects by attempting to show that ethnic diversity is linked to the inability of governments to increase public goods and implement sound policies. In particular, they show that ethnic diversity is significant and negatively correlated with school attainment, financial depth, and telephones per worker and positively correlated with black market premiums. Once again, by multiplying the coefficients against the differential between East Asia and Africa, they conclude that the indirect effect accounts for 28 percent of the 2.6 percent growth difference due to policy indicators.

The results of their exercise are highly suspicious and suffer from many of the weaknesses inherent to such broad cross-sectional approaches. First, there is little evidence that the African countries that were undergoing structural adjustment that implemented some of Easterly and Levine's "good" policies, such as deficit reductions and liberalization of foreign exchange, have seen much improvement to their growth. Should Easterly and Levine conclude that in the presence of ethnic diversity, otherwise universally applicable policies advocated by the neoclassical view do not work? If so, the relationship is not explained. Moreover, this conclusion raises a more pressing question, which also goes unaddressed: How could good policies be implemented at all in the face of such fractionalization?

Second, the coefficient for the dummy variable for Africa in their equations does not change as they add ethnicity-related variables. Thus,

Easterly and Levine's ethnicity-based argument has hardly resolved the problem of why Africa has done so poorly compared to other regions. Third, if the African sample is a significant portion of the total sample, and these countries have both low growth and high ethnicity, then the overall results might simply reflect this coincidental relationship. In fact, the authors run a simple regression for ethnicity and growth with the total sample and then run it for the sample without Africa. The coefficient for ethnicity drops appreciably but remains significant. Still, because the authors' intent was to compare Africa to Asia, a proper test would have been to look at the influence of ethnicity within the regions before universalizing the results across regions. They fail to do this.

Finally, Easterly and Levine's results are not robust. In their work, Africa has a variation of 0.04 to 0.93 in its index of ethno-linguistic fragmentation. Englebert (2000) reruns the results for Africa alone and finds that the ethnicity variable, as a predictor of economic performance, is in the opposite direction (meaning that greater ethnicity is associated with greater growth) of that shown in Easterly and Levine's study and that it is completely insignificant in the sample for Africa (69).

Kenny and Williams (2001) indicate that the problems manifest in Easterly and Levine's study are common to large-scale cross-country regressions: because they assume a common global system of causal relationships between variables and output, such assumptions cannot capture regional variations. Yet problems of consistency also arise at lower-level econometrics, and as Kenny and Williams argue, if these issues are to be avoided, econometric studies should perhaps not only be split by region, subregion, or country but also by time (11). This argument suggests the need to focus on the socioeconomic and historical specificity of countries in order to understand prerequisites for transformation. Yet other problems still arise from relying on neoclassical assumptions. For example, the neoclassical approach suffers from epistemological and ontological universalism, which implies that economic processes are knowable through the scientific principles of neoclassical economics, that all economies are comparable, and that all economies are affected by the same laws, regardless of time or space. This interpretation has allowed econometricians to undertake sweeping cross-country regressions by assuming a common global system of causal relationships. When the assumptions do not work out according to the model, they simply introduce other variables in order to generate auxiliary hypotheses, thereby rescuing core neoliberal policies.

In Search of the Missing Link: Social Capital

In recent years, economists have turned to a new explanation in order to support neoliberal policies: social capital. Beginning in 1998, the Social Capital Initiative (SCI) of the World Bank selected a dozen research projects (of forty submissions) for funding.[21] These twelve concentrated on three goals: to assess the impact of the initiatives intended to strengthen social capital on project effectiveness; to demonstrate the positive impact of aid on the process of social capital formation; and to develop indicators for monitoring and measuring social capital (World Bank 1998b). The initiative also complemented other Bank efforts, such as the capacity-building and governance projects designed to deal with the enormous shortcomings of the two-decade-old experiment with structural adjustment.

Fine (1999) argues that the role of social capital has been to complement the market imperfections heart of the post-Washington consensus.[22] Not only do they have the same theoretical roots, he argues, but they also allow the Bank to incorporate the language of its critics without acknowledging the substance of the criticisms. In other words, Fine believes that Bank theorists strategically used social capital, which addresses market imperfections, to replace the literature concerning the developmental state, whose focus on state intervention as a method of resolving market imperfections had been too direct a challenge to orthodox neoclassical thought.

There are some problems with this argument. First, as I have argued elsewhere (Stein 2000a), the developmental state should not be defined as a vehicle for countering market imperfections and creating perfect markets (which exist only in the minds of neoclassicists), but rather as an agency essential to institution building. This view should make it impervious to surrogates such as social capital.

Second, the existence of a post-Washington consensus, or even the pursuit of such a consensus, is subject to considerable debate. Fine is correct to point out that the Bank was under significant pressure to move away from its narrow neoliberal agenda. Indeed, the modifications the Bank made to its rhetoric about poverty, social capital, and governance, as well as its willingness to launch new projects sponsored by members such as the Danish government, have clearly been responses to some of these pressures. Fine overemphasizes this fact, however: the Bank does not seem to have made any real changes at the operational level. Rather, its response seems to be aimed at disarming internal critics. Despite the addition of a few new projects, there is little evidence that the Bank or the IMF has truly moved away from core neoliberal models, with their emphasis on liberalization, privatization, and stabilization. The battle over moderate protection for the sugar industry and taxes on raw cashew nut exports after 1995 in Mozambique is a good example.[23] The social capital project at the Bank was an attempt to undermine the enormous criticisms leveraged against the performance of structural adjustment—especially in reaction to the profound failures in Africa and elsewhere—by creating an alternative explanation: exceptionalism.

Arguments by Collier and Hoeffler (1998), Easterly and Levine (1997), and others that Africa and other regions have done poorly because of their social structure (high levels of ethnic diversity and lack of social capital) have the same purpose. The aim is not to challenge the post-Washington consensus but rather to preserve it in a manner that supports its neoclassical economic microfoundations. The effort has been bolstered by a series of econometric studies that purport to illustrate the link between these social dimensions and economic growth.

Social Capital, Missing Links, and Growth: Toward a Critique of the Methodology

Kenny and Williams (2001), in the trenchant essay discussed above, critically assesses the literature aimed at testing theories of growth. Social developments such as networks and trusts are simply the latest additions to a model that has already included physical capital, human capital, policy, and institutional reform along orthodox lines. Regardless of these numerous variations, however, the model has still been unable to explain the poor growth performance of some regions. Their review of an exhaustive list of econometric testing unfailingly shows inconsistent and weak results. This is due in part to poor statistics, bad econometrics, and problems specifying measurable proxies for pertinent but immeasurable variables. Yet even if all the limitations of these models were overcome, the whole exercise is flawed for theoretical reasons. First, most of the econometrics has been aimed at verification, not falsification (10). This issue arises from a more general problem with the axiomatic approach of neoclassical economics that is not peculiar to mainstream growth theory.

In Lakatos's terms, social capital theory not only acts as an auxiliary hypothesis aimed at reinforcing growth theory, but is also being constructed using the standard methodology. It relies on the same core axioms or metaphysical propositions, such as *Homo economicus* and positive heuristics (that is, the potential of social organization to improve individual welfare).

The econometric testing of social capital theory's relation with economic growth has been at best ambiguous and is hardly the "missing link" asserted by some Bank economists such as Gootaert (1998). Englebert's (2000) review of the literature finds rather contradictory results. Neither Inglehart (1997) nor Helliwell (1996) found any positive cross-sectional relations between trust and civic associations and GDP per capita. La Porta et al. (1997) found a weak relation between trust and growth. Keefer and Knack (1997) found a positive relation between trust and growth, but not between associational life and growth. Temple and Johnson (1998) show a positive relation between previous social relations and growth. As with the general literature concerning economic growth, the problem arises from a paucity of consistent and clearly conceptualized measurements, weak econometrics, and conceptual difficulties (discussed below), including questions of the direction of causality. For example, Keefer and Knack (1997) find a positive correlation between trust, on one hand, and bureaucratic efficiency and the stability of property rights, on the other. Ignoring for the moment the glaring problem of using largely subjective variables for numerous countries that are at radically different stages of development, one can plausibly argue the inverse of the direction of causality. For example, stability of property right and of state efficiency breeds trust. Englebert (2000) astutely points out that their data for trust are actually from a 1990–93 survey, whereas their data for factors such as the "efficiency of the judiciary" come from the period 1980–83, which would actually support a reverse causality argument.

Adding variables such as social capital and ethnicity to rescue purported universals does nothing to advance the ahistorical nature of the approach. "Economics has yet to come to grips with the idea that individual economic agents are active thinking persons not simply throughputs in working out of timeless and spaceless economic laws and relations" (Kenny and Williams 2001, 14). This deficiency causes doubts about the process; once we move away from seeing beings as "atoms in chemical reactions," changes in conditions can lead to new and unpredictable behavioral responses. Changes in policies that might improve growth in one situation can do the very opposite in other cases. Import liberalization might increase the competitiveness of manufacturing when it is equipped with financial accessibility, technological capacity, and market opportunities abroad, but the same action might permanently destroy the manufacturing base of an economy with few capacities, opportunities, or support (Stein 1992). Returns to insecticide spraying are highly dependent on availability of water, early planting, weeding, and fertilizer. African field studies indicate that returns are eight times higher with these factors in place (Kenny and Williams 2001, 13). In other words, factors interact in a manner that cannot be captured by linear relationships, including the existence of critical thresholds of fundamental prerequisites. Nonlinear thinking that takes into account temporally and spatially differentiated institutional and social settings is an absolute prerequisite for understanding whether policy changes will lead to a virtuous or a vicious circle of change. An institutional economic approach is much more conducive to understanding these complex relationships. This is the focus of Part III.

Conclusions

This chapter has presented and critically analyzed the major theories underlying structural adjustment, including those used to justify stabilization, trade, and financial liberalization. It has also explored the common microfoundations underlying these models. These tenets generate six focal propositions, which are at the heart of adjustment and its underlying theories.

A variety of problems with adjustment have been presented, including the emphasis on static comparative advantage, which—despite its detrimental outcomes—has continued to result in policies requiring increased specialization in fewer resources for export, most of which tended to perform poorly in the 1980s and 1990s. The chapter also explored the divergence between the assumed world of structural adjustment and the actual world. Axiomatic views of the nature of states have frequently led to the emasculation of the state and the dismantling of the very apparatus needed to help create development-enhancing growth. At the same time, there has been a misplaced emphasis on "getting the prices right" in order to generate gains in static efficiency. These microfoundations are riddled with errors and therefore have such problematic implications for development as behavioral and interactive failures, problems of scope, definitional inaccuracies, misconstruction of comparative studies, inadequate acknowledgment of the temporal and spatial dimensions of development, and aggregation problems.

The assessment included an investigation of the five different approaches used to test the relationship between the imposition of adjustment policies and the performance of economies. In general, there is little consistent evidence that adjustment has improved economies; instead, most indicators demonstrate that adjusting economies have suffered from poor economic performance. Even World Bank studies have often been in conflict, in many cases due to methodological weakness of the testing. Partly as a reaction, World Bank economists, eager to point to factors other than their policy strategies, have tried to come up with alternative explanations for the decline of economies under adjustment. Two of these, ethnicity and social capital, represented an attempt to generate auxiliary hypotheses in an effort to provide a protective belt around the core axioms of structural adjustment, thus shifting the blame for policy failure away from the neoclassical theoretical bases and onto external causes.

In conclusion, the poor performance of the countries that followed the dictates of structural adjustment can be tied to its neoclassical economic theoretical roots. With its emphasis on equilibrium, static and narrow notions of human behavior, and misplaced focus on financial variables, neoclassical economics is capable neither of assessing the problems of development nor of coming up with a viable strategy to set development in motion. The key to reversing the economic malaise of the countries that are suffering from such drastic decline is to turn to a different set of theoretical tools based on a very different set of microfoundations: an institutional matrix.

CHAPTER FOUR

Institutions and the "Missing Link" in the World Bank's Strategy

Toward a Critique

Subsequent experience has convincingly demonstrated that the policies prescribed by the Washington Consensus are paying off. . . . But with one exception (namely, the protection of property rights), the policy prescriptions of the "Washington Consensus" ignored the potential role that changes in institutions could play in accelerating the economic and social development of the region.—Burki and Perry, 1998

Introduction

Profound and seemingly perpetual economic crises in many developing countries in the past two decades have inspired international agencies to search ineluctably for a "missing link" in their development strategies. The Bank has widened its agenda, but it has done so while pursuing a strategy designed to disarm critics by addressing not the content of its policies but rather the general sphere of criticism and the language of its opponents, including arguments that it has ignored developing countries' institutions.

In an attempt to address the criticism of its policies, the Bank, in line with its broadening agenda has added new conditionality in areas such as governance. As discussed in chapter 2, this effort came as a response to the idea that government corruption was to blame for the failure of Bank policies. Yet governance-related conditionality largely predated a theoretical understanding of governance. As argued in this chapter, instead of drawing on institutional theory to rethink and re-evaluate its policies, the Bank used it selectively and strategically to justify its expanding agenda. First, beginning in the mid-1990s, the Bank used institutional theory to reconstruct agenda items, such as governance and the devolution of power, and to provide the ex post appearance of what Oliver Williamson has called the "bottom-up" or "microanalytical" approach to institutions. This tactic has arguably been made easier by the Bank's focus on the new institutional economic variant of the theory (NIE) with its reliance on central elements of neoclassical economics. Second, in line with issues such as social capital and ethnicity, the Bank used institutions to explain the exceptionalism of some regions that did poorly in the adjustment era. Third, by adopting the language of its critics, the Bank cleverly disarmed the opposition under the pretense of compromise.

According to the epigraph, which is from a World Bank–sponsored study, the tools of NIE attempt to fill the gaps in what is otherwise perceived as a sound approach. In the World Bank's view, adding this dimension can lead to better results than the ones already delivered under the narrower "Washington Consensus." Strictly speaking, NIE has had little practical significance at the operations level. Over time, however, it has allowed the broadened agenda to move forward more readily for all three reasons. Moreover, as pointed out by a number of staff people, the controversy surrounding the publication of some NIE-inspired documents has made it easier to openly discuss the politics of loan recipients, and corruption more generally, in daily Bank operations.

This chapter begins with a brief comment about the role of institutions in structural adjustment, followed by a short survey of the ideas underlying new institutional economics, the variant of institutional economics used by the Bank. It then examines the rise of the NIE in the World Bank, beginning with the contribution of Oliver Williamson. Much of the rest of the chapter critically examines how NIE has been used in a series of key documents to reinforce the orthodox agenda, including arguments made to counter criticisms of neoliberal policies. The final section critically evaluates the ways in which institutional constructs are used in the World Development Report 2002 and helps set the stage for developing an alternative in chapter 5.

Structural Adjustment and Institutions

The theoretical tradition that heavily influences the thinking of World Bank economists arises from relaxed versions of general equilibrium theory. As discussed in chapter 3, in its strictest form, markets are presented as neoclassical exchanges arising from the spontaneous interaction of self-seeking individuals, not as institutional constructs. A Walrasian auctioneer ensures that overall equilibrium is reached between supply and demand by gathering and processing the information from all markets. This allows individuals to "feel their way" (*tâtonner*) toward the removal of all excess supply and demand by adjusting their decisions in each market. The outcome will be maximization of social welfare through Pareto optimality, ending with a situation in which no person can be better off without making another person worse off. In this "ideal" world there simply are no reasons for institutions of almost any definition.

In a more relaxed version of the same theory, it is recognized that market transactions require a means of payment, which introduces the concept of money. Moreover, markets, by definition, involve the exchange of property rights. Both circumstances raise the need for external institutions to support the proper operations of markets. This viewpoint has greatly influenced the institution-building projects of the World Bank and the IMF from the inception of structural adjustment. In the orthodox world, stability of the money supply ensures the value of money; it requires independent, well-developed central banking institutions. Similarly, private property rights must be properly instituted and ownership on exchange must be guaranteed by legal institutions.

As discussed in chapter 2, much of the new agenda was driven by the failure of structural adjustment, particularly in sub-Saharan Africa during the 1980s. Institutional economics, especially the NIE variant, began to appear in World Bank documents shortly after these crises. What was perhaps most consequential to the adoption of this theory by the Bank was the first invitation of a prominent NIE economist to an ABCDE conference.[1] Before turning to this, however, I briefly review of some of the main ideas of NIE.

NIE: A Brief Review

The new institutional economics has been inspired by the work of Ronald Coase (1937, 1960), Oliver Williamson (1985), and Douglass North (1990), who share in large part the microfoundations and methodology of neoclassical economic theory. Their aim is to fill the perceived gaps in the standard theory that arise when strict assumptions such as that of perfect certainty are relaxed, and when observations conflict dramatically with the predictions of the theory. Linked to some degree with NIE are the so-called Austrian approaches to institutional theory arising in the tradition of Hayek, as well as evolutionary economists such as Langlois. Hayek and the Austrian school also share most of the microfoundations of neoclassical economics, such as methodological individualism, the concept of *Homo economicus*, and reliance on marginalism. They are somewhat critical of the neoclassical emphasis on equilibrium, however, and take a strong evolutionary approach to institutions that emphasizes that they are largely spontaneous and unintended consequences of individual choice and interaction (Rutherford 1996, 3, 83–86).

Coase, Williamson, and North have inspired an extensive literature about transitional and developing countries. At the heart of Coase's work is the concept of transaction costs, or the costs of searching for exchange opportunities, negotiating exchanges, and enforcing them. For example, before selling property, a company might pay for a credit check on the purchaser, or the person buying the property may hire a lawyer to see whether there are any liens on the land.

Coase's theorem states that when transaction costs are zero, the allocation of initial property rights does not change the efficiency of market transactions. For example, think of a toy factory beside a hospital. The factory makes noise as it uses its machines and molds to produce toys. The noise disturbs the physicians and patients. To resolve the dispute, the two parties bargain for the least-cost solution, which might be building stronger walls or limiting the hours of operation of the factory when crucial operations need to be undertaken or when patients are sleeping. The assignment of the rights (either to be noise-free or to run the factory without restriction) will in part determine who pays for the solution, but not the outcome, which will be Pareto efficient. For this outcome to occur, it is important to clearly define property rights. In contrast, when transaction costs are positive, market outcomes can differ from the outcome predicted by neoclassical economics. For instance, negotiations might too expensive to allow an agreement to be reached. In this case it might be simpler to outlaw all noise above a certain decibel level and to have the courts be held responsible for carefully enforcing this law.

Thus, at the heart of an efficient market system, according to NIE, is an effective legal structure. "If we move from a world of zero transaction costs to one of positive transaction costs, what becomes immediately clear is the crucial importance of the legal system in the new world . . . what are traded on the market are not, as often supposed by economists, physical entities, but the rights to perform certain actions and the rights which individuals possess by the legal system. . . . As a result, the legal system will have a profound effect on the working of the economic system and may in certain respects be said to control it" (Coase 1992, 717–18). Governments interested in fostering a market economy must ensure that property rights are unambiguously and securely allocated, with a clear right to use and dispose of property (Smyth 1998).

Williamson builds on Coase's concept of transaction costs by focusing his theoretical contributions to NIE on economic institutions as economizing units that minimize opportunism and recognize the cognitive limitations of individuals. Coase's theory of the firm originally focused on the means by which to reduce transaction costs when "at the margin the costs of organizing within the firm will be equal either to the costs of organizing in another firm or to the costs involved in leaving the transaction to be 'organized' by the price mechanism" (Coase 1937, 404). Williamson (1985), accordingly, proposes a theory to explain the elements responsible for variations in transaction costs. Because prices cannot reflect all the information pertinent to parties involved in a market exchange, if it is uncertain whether one participant is honest, transaction costs will arise. This potential cause of transaction costs, or "opportunism," provides the rationale for the existence of governance structures such as firms, which can contain opportunism and reduce transaction costs.

In order to argue that an additional source of transaction costs arises from the cognitive limitations of individuals, Williamson also borrows from Simon's concept of bounded rationality. Simon emphasizes that decision making is constrained by the computational capacity of the human brain and the incompleteness of knowledge related to each choice. Unlike the strictly neoclassical being, which maximizes choice using all possible information and options, Simon argues, decisions are based on a small set of prerogatives. These cognitive limitations also create transaction costs by limiting the ability of people to achieve objectives over the range of all possibilities.

Williamson makes a distinction between the governance and the measurement branches of transaction costs, that is, the ability of firms to respond to disturbances outside of the company versus their capacity to bring goods and services to the market at a reasonable cost. Both limited cognition and unforeseen disturbances create openings for one party in an exchange to gain an advantage over the other. Williamson offers an additional complication to creating efficient organizational structures by linking transaction costs to "asset specificity." Asset specificity ties physical and human assets to specific transactions in economic institutions. The greater the degree of asset specificity, the less the firm will be able to deal with the uncertainty embedded in opportunism and bounded rationality. According to this view, as transactions become more complex and have higher levels of asset specificity, there will be greater motivation to invest in more complex activities and governance structures, including more complicated and longer-term contracts or even the reacquisition of former employees. For example, in a frequently discussed case, General Motors merged with Fisher Body in 1926 after the demand for Fisher's product increased, but Fisher refused to relocate next to the General Motors assembly plant, which would have saved transportation and other costs (Williamson 1985). Another consequence is transaction frequency, which allows companies to better allocate fixed cost-governance over a larger number of exchanges.

North (1990), in contrast, is more concerned with the institutional environment than with specific governance structures. To North, institutions are "the rules of the game in a society or, more formally, are the humanly devised constraints that shape human interaction" (North 1990, 6). These are divided into informal constraints, such as taboos, customs, and traditions, and formal constraints, which include contracts, laws, property rights, and constitutions. With increasing complexity, there is a greater formalization of rules, which, in turn, can make informal constraints more effective by lowering the costs of information, monitoring, and enforcement. Still, institutional change does not necessarily enhance economic efficiency, and it is in fact greatly influenced by such elements as path-dependency and the distribution of power.

In North's terms, path-dependency occurs when the outcome of a process depends on its history. Institutional path-dependency arises from network externalities, economies of scope, and complementarities.[2] Owing to the interdependent nature of institutions, inefficient paths are difficult to alter even if economic stagnation arises. Moreover, since the polity defines and enforces property rights, efficient markets will be more the exception than the rule (North 1995), because policy makers are tempted to create institutions to serve their own interests. For example, in the African context, NIE writers have illustrated this position using Robert Bates's argument that agricultural policies and institutions were put in place for the personal gain of politicians, not to achieve economic or social efficiency

TABLE 4.1 **Summary of NIE and its influence on the World Bank**

Author	Key ideas and terms	Key institutions	How the World Bank has used each author's ideas in practice
Coase	The keys to this view of institutions are transaction costs (the costs in money and timed incurred in economic exchange such as a buyer-seller search, negotiation, and contract-enforcement activities) and property rights. The Coase Theorem states that zero transaction costs can lead to efficient market solutions, provided that property rights are assigned to one party and are enforceable. Positive transaction costs can lead to inefficient market solutions, such as excessive noise from a toy factory next to a hospital.	Property rights Legal system	The World Bank has employed references to transaction costs in many of its reports. It suggests, e.g., that transaction costs are increased by rent-seeking public employees; this limits the effectiveness of potential reforms in areas such as education. Regulatory systems should be kept simple and minimized because they create high transaction costs. Beyond justifying the existing agenda they have had little impact at the operations level.
Williamson	Prices alone cannot explain variation in transaction costs; rather, imperfect information leads to opportunism by economic actors. In other words, since some actors have information that others don't, they can exploit this situation for personal gain. A related idea is bounded rationality, which creates opportunities for people to take advantage of others owing to limited information. Hence, limiting opportunism leads to more efficient solutions. Potential obstacles to dealing with imperfect information include asset specificity and transaction frequency. Less asset specificity and greater frequency reduce chances for opportunism, and vice versa.	Property rights Legal system Firm governance structures	Bank reports use Williamson's ideas including opportunism, bounded rationality, and credible commitment to explain why privatization and regulation of firms are superior to management contracts in state-owned enterprises. For instance, the Bank claims that managers in state firms act opportunistically by negotiating readily achievable targets because as political appointees they are not influenced by rewards and penalties. Though used to justify the existing agenda, the main influence of Williamson's ideas at the operational level is in allowing bank officials to discuss politics and corruption.
North	North takes a broad view of institutions as the rules of the game that a society follows and humanly constructed constraints that govern their interactions. He is more concerned with the overall institutional environment facing an economy than with specific institutions. As the economy grows, institutions become more formalized, but not necessarily more efficient. For example, they can be formed to serve the interests of the elite. Institutional path-dependency arises because of network externalities, economies of scope, and complementarities. Path dependency is also difficult to alter.	Property rights Legal system Informal institutions Formal and informal governance structures Historical traditions	The Bank uses North's formal-informal institutional dichotomy to argue that laws and regulations should remain simple. Informal institutions are more important for developing countries. This provides an additional justification for the Bank's emphasis on deregulation. There is no evidence of any shift at the operational level arising from use of North's framework.

(Ensminger 1992, 22). In particular, governments controlled agricultural prices and subsidized food production in order to reward their constituents in urban areas at the expense of the income and production levels of rural producers.[3] With this background in mind, I turn to the impact of these ideas and thinkers on the World Bank agenda. The key ideas and terms of the contributions of these three authors to NIE are summarized in table 4.1.

NIE Messengers at the World Bank:
Mr. Williamson Goes to Washington

Like many other developments within the economics profession, the new institutional economics influenced individual researchers before becoming more widespread within the Bank.[4] Following the award of Nobel Prizes to Coase (1991) and North (1993), the 1994 annual World Bank Conference on Development Economics devoted one section to this theory.[5] Signals about the need to consider institutions in the formula were also coming from other sources. In 1990, USAID approached Mancur Olsen to organize the Center for Institutional Reform and the Informal Sector (IRIS) at the University of Maryland.[6] Although the question of the informal economy was a hot-button issue at that moment, it was understood from the beginning that the agenda of the new center was to encompass all types of institutional reform (Adams 2003).

Williamson, who was invited to present a paper about governance and institutions in developing and reforming countries at the 1994 conference, attempted to apply his formula to the World Bank agenda. Williamson (1994) argued that although North and others focused on the institutional environment, his main contribution concerned institutional arrangements, governance, and transaction costs, or the "bottom-up approach to economic organization" (175). In his view, NIE was the end product of a logical progression of reform. This process was understood to begin with a focus on macroanalytic issues, with their emphasis on macroeconomic aggregates, followed by the neoclassical approach, with its focus on getting the prices right. The next phase was the narrow institutional approach, which implied a desire to establish property rights. Finally, NIE would complete the process by "getting institutions right," that is, by ensuring that a broader array of suitable institutions was in place.

In a statement that must have appealed to his hosts, Williamson argued that "the stages are overlapping: the appearance of a new stage does not annihilate its predecessors" (173). In essence, he suggested moderately reforming the reformers, not fundamentally questioning their strategies. In particular, he felt that there had been too much interest in court ordering that arose from an overemphasis on legal reform. By contrast, he argued, the Bank should have dealt with private ordering, or the mitigation of nongovernmental institutions by limiting opportunism in transactions. Two issues were salient to his argument: "credible commitments" and "remediableness."

Credible commitments focus on the long-term guarantees affecting the parties to a transaction. They reduce contractual hazards, while encouraging investment in transaction-specific assets. The mechanisms of state guarantees of property rights could take many forms beyond simple legal guarantees. For example, in China, there are no formal, central, private property rights. De facto federalism has generated credible commitment, however, by limiting the confiscatory capacity of the state and relying on local government channels to express credible commitment to private investors. As is made clear by the China example, an understanding of the microanalytics of the situation is more important than are general formulations.

Remediableness, or the ability of something to be improved, rejects the notion that there is a hypothetical ideal among institutions that should be used for comparison. Williamson provided three reasons to justify this move from idealized institutions toward incremental change: in practice, all institutions are flawed; incumbency can be much more advantageous than introducing new institutions because of gains from historical relations; and politics might constrain the introduction of new institutions. The focus should be on a careful evaluation of the weaknesses and strengths of new forms of institutions or proposed reorganizations.

Given these arguments, it is not surprising that Williamson is critical of the Bank's report about the East Asian Miracle (1993) for its failure to analyze the ways in which credible commitment induced investment and contracting in Asia. By contrast, he supports the work of Brian Levy, a proponent of NIE in the Bank, and Pablo Spiller (discussed below), who carefully studied the way the British created credible commitment in the telecommunications industry. Overall, the way forward is his comparative institutional economic approach, which relies on a careful understanding of the microanalytical logic of economic organizations, focusing on a bottom-up approach. In a rather mild rebuke, Williamson states: "Many nod in agreement, but then return to business as usual. That will not suffice. If the World Bank . . . and others are really persuaded that institutions are important, staffing changes are implied. Not only are institutional economists needed to do the archaeology of development and reform, but they should be expressly included in the planning and the oversight" (193).

Having laid out the theoretical contributions of NIE, I use the remainder of the chapter to explore the influence of Williamson and NIE on important World Bank documents, beginning with *Bureaucrats in Business* before turning to a critical look at the 2002 World Development Report, "Building Institutions for Markets."

Opening the Door for NIE at the Bank: *Bureaucrats in Business*

The first systematic utilization of NIE in a published World Bank document with wide distribution was a book about the economics and politics of government ownership of state enterprises titled *Bureaucrats in Business* (World Bank 1995). Its aim was to explain why bureaucrats were still in business despite a decade of divestitures and the consensus view that governments perform more poorly than private sectors (1). As discussed below, the study proved highly contentious. Yet it was not the first Bank study to visit these issues.

The 1983 World Development Report examined state-owned enterprises in the context of development management. The report noted that "in theory it is possible to create the kind of incentives that will maximize efficiency under any type of ownership. But there is a great difference between what is theoretically feasible and what typically happens" (World Bank 1983b, 50). The report promoted alternatives to state-owned enterprises, including opening sectors to private enterprise to enhance competition, using stabilization funds instead of marketing boards, allocating management responsibilities to private contractors, and privatization of ownership. Regulations were discouraged in favor of market mechanisms to "lighten the administrative burden" and "reduce costly distortions" (53).

By 1989 the Bank was softening its tone, arguing that "the division of responsibilities between the state should be a matter of pragmatism—not dogma . . . there need be no preconceptions about the 'right' type of organization; appropriate incentives count for much more" (World Bank 1989). Central to this task was the need for institution-building, because "development takes place through institutions, including markets, whether private or public. Institution-building in the widest sense is essential and must for the most part be nurtured by governments . . . governments need an explicit strategy for institution-building for both the public and private sector" (55).

Still, with little or no institutional-theoretic analysis to explain why some state enterprises operate well and others do not, the report fell back on the same pronouncements used in 1983 regarding the practical problems of state ownership (55). What was needed was a more solid theoretical grounding to justify the agenda, which the Bank soon began to deliver with its study of state enterprises.

Bureaucrats in Business did not challenge the emphasis on the market and the push for privatization found in earlier Bank documents. Instead, it utilized Willamson's theory to provide a microanalytical basis that could replace the stylized facts, assertions, and simple empirical exercises that had been used to justify the Bank's agenda up to that point.[7]

The report begins with the Bank's axiomatic belief in privatization and a series of related conundrums: "Although the potential gains from privatization and other reforms are substantial, only a few countries have reformed their state owned enterprises successfully." Despite some evidence of sales, the report notes that the "state owned share of developing market countries has remained stubbornly high." The authors then ask: "Why haven't more countries reformed? What are the political obstacles to reform and how have these been overcome? How can leaders and policymakers in developing countries hasten reform and increase the likelihood of success?" (World Bank 1995, 2).

In order to answer these questions, the performance of both state and privatized companies is analyzed as a set of contractual relationships between government on one hand and public and private managers (in the state-owned case) or a regulatory contract (in the privatized case) on the other. Incentives in all three cases are believed to be generated by the interface of three dimensions of information: rewards, penalties, and commitment. Without explicitly citing them, the study clearly draws on NIE constructs. Information is limited, and each party has different sets of information that it attempts to use at the expense of the other party. Here we have Williamson's concepts of opportunism and the cognitive limitations created by bounded rationality. Rewards and penalties should be designed to ensure that contractual participants reveal information and abide by contracts. Again, this line of reasoning implicitly references Williamson's question of governance design in the face of behavioral uncertainty[8] arising from opportunism. Commitment is the third dimension, whereby each party is convinced that the other will fulfill the terms of the contract. This is a clear reference to Williamson's principle of credible commitment.

Predictably, given the Bank's commitment to private property rights, the report argues that the performance of public managers was least effective and that private management contracts worked a bit better, but that "regulatory contracts, when properly designed and implemented, worked well for enterprises in monopoly markets" (6). It concluded, "Overall, then, the greater the participation of private agents in ownership and management, the better enterprise performance . . . this was because private managers and owners, unlike government counterparts, could readily capture the benefits if performance improved; responding to these incentives, they worked harder than government managers and obtained better results" (6–7).

But this improvement in results was deceptive; it was achieved by carefully redefining the criteria for success. The report readily admits that enterprises that were under public management met most of their contractual goals. Most people would suggest that this is a pretty good indicator of success. The study, however, dismisses the criteria as too soft and meaningless. Instead, it erects a separate set of criteria, which included improvements in profitability of assets and various measures of productivity. Note that this kind of standard was largely absent from public management contracts but was more often present in private contracts (in rather different industries and countries). Similarly, the method of analysis reflects a bias toward the private sector. In evaluating regulatory contracts, the report focuses on the expansion of service, returns to capital, effects on consumers before and after privatization, and associated regulatory contracts, as showing generally positive results.

There are problems with this exercise. To begin with, the Bank report is carefully selective with respect to the sample and readily admits that it is "small and not random, so care must be used in generalizing the results" (113) before going on to (not so carefully) generalize the results. It looks at the performance of only twelve enterprises in six countries in evaluating the role of public management contracts but examines twenty companies in twelve countries in evaluating private management contracts. These evaluations are done in different sectors for each contract. Moreover, for regulatory contracts, the report's authors look at six countries in a single sector: telecommunications.

In almost every case, the comparison is made between performance before privatization and after it, without any consideration of the impact of government funds used to pump up enterprises just prior to privatization. In sum, the authors of the report use different sectors and different criteria to obtain their results. This is clearly an exercise for which the most appropriate allegory is the evaluation of an apple, an orange, and a plum in a situation in which the color orange is always preferred to green or red.

Once again, NIE is invoked to explain these results once the "superiority" of privatization and regulatory contracts is demonstrated. Information asymmetries are said to create incentives for managers to act opportunistically by negotiating for easily achievable targets. Because many public managers are political appointees, rewards and penalties have little impact on their careers; thus there is little incentive for them to comply with contractual obligations. Finally, a lack of independent, third-party enforcement creates a commitment problem, so there is little reason for parties to enter into the contract in order to fulfill their obligations. By contrast, successful regulatory contracts were possible because competitive bidding reduced information disadvantages, price regulations were designed to improve performance, and legislatures passed laws defining procedures for arbitration and appeal of any disputes. Commitment could therefore be more readily achieved.[9]

The pertinent question, then, is how this particular use of NIE relates to Williamson's framework. The Bank clearly uses a comparative institutional approach as well as many parts of Williamson's theoretical toolbox. What is not as carefully addressed, however, is his principle of remediableness. In particular, the notion of incumbency is never incorporated into the evaluation of the costs of institutional change.[10] In places such as Tanzania, where state divestment often has meant the liquidation of enterprises,[11] the foregone opportunity costs of incumbency have been large, in addition to the huge social costs of rendering still more people jobless when the unemployment rate in the largest urban area is nearly 50 percent. Beyond neglecting this important concept, it is clearly evident that the World Bank, in spite of Williamson's warning, is working with an institutionalized ideal in which the results of any study are predetermined.

By means of the selective use of NIE, the World Bank has been able to reconstruct theoretically a fifteen-year-old agenda that has focused on the privatization of public-sector firms and management contracts. Yet the biggest impact of *Bureaucrats in Business* was less in its theoretical insights than in its open discussion of areas long forbidden by the Bank. Initially, the report was deemed too overtly political. Yet Vice-President and Chief Economist Michael Bruno threatened to resign if the study was not published. The Bank agreed to publish the report only after the chief counsel wrote a memo justifying the discussion of politics in the context of its impact on development as long as the issue of democracy was not raised. Some operations economists felt the report was pioneering, not for its theoretical contribution but for its explicit discussion of politics and corruption. Following the issuance of the report and the associated ruling of the chief counsel, the authors of the report were able to openly discuss politics and corruption with recipient governments. They also were able to specify these issue more clearly within governance-related conditionality.[12] The publication of *Bureaucrats in Business* emboldened proponents of NIE in the Bank and opened the door for its wider use after 1995.

NIE Enters the WDR

The 1997 World Development Report, *State in a Changing World*, was the first WDR to incorporate NIE theory into the analysis. It was also the first to have Douglass North on the panel of external experts and Brian Levy as a principal author.[13] The new institutional economics appears throughout the report, but as is the case with *Bureaucrats in Business*, it is used not to alter the agenda but to buttress existing policy priorities.

The report reaffirms the focal points about the role of the state— foundation of law, nondistortionary policy environment, basic social services and infrastructure, protecting the vulnerable and the environment (4)—that are justified by standard neoclassical microeconomic theory: market failures, pubic goods, externalities, and no on (26). Yet NIE comes into play almost immediately when the authors use a Northian definition of the state as "a set of institutions that possess the means of legitimate coercion."[14] Moreover, the report, at least on the surface, seems to identify new functions for states: "The state is essential for putting in place the appropriate institutional foundations for markets" (4). This would become the main theme of the 2002 World Development Report (*Building Institutions for Markets*), discussed below.

Chapter 2 of the WDR uses North's dichotomy between formal and informal rules and norms to define institutional structure.[15] In accordance with North, the report states that the informal rules come from culture and history. Formal rules arise from the legislative, executive, and judicial branches of the state. The state can influence transaction costs directly through the behavior of state agents or influence them indirectly via their impact on institutional structures. These structures influence incentive structures, including property rights, which have a direct bearing on transaction costs.

Although chapter 3 makes some vague references to information and opportunism à la Williamson, it really is a restatement of the standard primary role for states as envisioned by adjustment theory: as guarantor of property rights and macrostability. The chapter that draws most heavily on NIE is chapter 4, which focuses on liberalization, regulation, and industrial policy. The chapter can be described as a defense of the neoliberal terrain in these three core areas. The chapter largely dismisses critiques concerned with the neoliberal overemphasis on deregulation or the absence of regulatory structures prior to liberalization, the overreliance on privatization, and the continual opposition to state-sponsored industrial policy (despite the evidence of its success in Asian countries).[16]

How is NIE used to defend the World Bank's neoliberal agenda? The story begins a few years before the appearance of WDR 1997 with Levy and Spiller's paper for the 1993 ABCDE conference. Levy and Spiller (1994) utilize a North-type analysis of a country's institutional endowment in order to analyze a Williamson-inspired comparison of the ways in which countries fashion regulatory systems in the telecommunications industry. The focus is on how to restrain opportunism while permitting sufficient flexibility to allow companies to adapt to changing circumstances. In a comment on the paper in the 1993 ABCDE conference, David Sappington noted that Levy and Spiller deliver an important message that "the best policy for any country depends on the country's institutions and its standard methods of operation" (Sappington 1994, 253), which implies flexibility.

Yet, contrary to an implied flexibility, Levy and Spiller promote the dictum that when administrative capability is weak (which, they argue, is almost always the case in developing countries), regulatory rules must remain simple, light on information, and market-like so that governments can deliver a credible commitment to refrain from arbitrary administrative action. Thus, regulations are not determined by need—which would seem to be greater in developing countries—but by capacity, which means that developing countries with low capabilities should avoid highly interventionist or information-heavy regulatory regimes. Paradoxically, developing countries are asked to focus on fewer regulations and more market-like mechanisms even though they have the most poorly formed markets. Nevertheless, the authors recognize the importance of regulatory enforcement in richer countries with more well-formed markets.

A similarly dismissive stance is taken toward industrial policy and regulations in WDR 1997 after its authors recognize its potentially positive impact. For example, they state that "in the United Kingdom . . . price-cap regulation gives the utility an incentive to be efficient and can encourage innovation" (World Bank 1997, 69) and that "post-war Japan's development of its steel, coal machinery and shipbuilding industries illustrates this [industrial policy] rationale for intervention" (72). Moreover, the authors argue that "the theoretical case for industrial policy rests on the proposition that . . . information and coordination problems . . . can be pervasive" (72). The argument would seem to point to the exigencies of industrial policy. The authors quickly dismiss this argument, however, since "pursuing this style of investment coordination presupposes levels of public and private institutional capability that are beyond the reach of most developing countries" (73).

Ironically, the authors use NIE both to explain industrial policy needs and to reject them. In particular, they utilize a Williamson-type argument that people are, for opportunistic reasons, proprietary in their use of information. This would suggest a greater policy need for information and coordination, but the authors reject industrial policy by invoking a Northian argument that the institutional framework is too weak. Once again, exigencies are driven not by what is required but by the presupposed capacity. So, without the institutional capability, it is business as usual: "Until institutions can be strengthened the first challenge is to focus on the essentials—establishing a lawful state and setting sound economic policy" (Levy 1997, 23).

NIE and the Reconstitution of Governance

In line with the 1997 World Development Report, the executive directors of the Bank, in March 1997, endorsed a strategic compact aimed at helping poor countries "build their institutions to fight poverty." According to Wolfensohn, "More than ever the role of institutions is central to development effectiveness. Efforts to reshape the development assistance business are also putting pressure on evaluators to upgrade their work on capacity building in poor countries" (Wolfensohn 1998, ix). In response, a conference was organized and a volume published concerning institutions for development and program evaluation.[17]

The tone was set immediately. This work was not going to be based on Original Institutional Economics (OIE), or what the Bank referred to as the historical school, but on NIE, or what they referred to as neo-institutionalism. To Picciotto and Wiesner, the editors of the Bank study, what differentiates the new institutional approach from previous ones is that "variable admixtures of competition, cooperation, and hierarchy are needed to achieve positive societal outcomes . . . and a belief that getting incentives right is critical to overcome the restrictions that arise from the neoclassical model." They insist that their approach is "not tantamount to a rejection of the neoclassical model" but is aimed at broadening it to incorporate institutional constraints. The tone is heavily influenced by Williamson's version of NIE and reflects many of the themes discussed above. Following Williamson, they state that "the challenge is to focus on micro-analytical issues." Although not explicitly invoking Williamson's principle of remediableness, they recognize that "inefficient economic institutions and dysfunctional collective rules are the norm, not the exception" and that a "normative policy approach" should be replaced by a public choice and a "contractarian" framework to design feasible strategies for institutional development (Picciotto and Wiesner 1998, xi–xiii).

As Wiesner indicates in the same volume, neoinstitutional economics can be understood in Lakotos's terms. Recall Lakatos's work concerning the methodology of scientific research programs, outlined in chapter 3. It consisted of three propositions: a hard core of metaphysical, irrefutable propositions; positive heuristics that provide instructions as to which tools and questions should be selected and which should be avoided; and finally, a protective belt of theories, empirical conventions, and auxiliary hypotheses. Neoinstitutional economics is part of the protective belt around the hard core of the neoclassical model. It does not reject competition or rational choice assumptions but attempts to bolster them by dealing with the conceptual constraints related to information, incentives, property rights, rent-seeking in political and economic markets, and transaction costs (Wiesner 1998, 114). This, I argue, is precisely the problem. By sharing many microfoundations with neoclassical economics, NIE suffers from many of the same errors and flaws. Moreover, because the two systems share many core propositions, NIE can be used conceptually to qualify and contextualize neoliberal policies without rejecting their basic validity.

In essence we have a logical statement of conditionality, or "if only" (that is, the neoclassical vision would work if only there were certain preconditions) and the need to consider and create institutional design palliatives, or "only ifs." The new institutional economics must be used to build these conditions.

The most interesting part of the Picciotto and Wiesner volume is the section titled "Institutions and Governance Structures," which presents a clear attempt to provide a theoretical core for the rather ambiguous concept of governance, including constraints on the effectiveness of decentralization.[18] This was written as the Bank was expanding its governance agenda and was searching for a practical operational meaning. To deal with this, the Bank "reconstructed" its operational history via the ex post reclassification of strategies and projects under the rubric of governance. A 1994 evaluation of governance attempted to assess the proportion of selected operations with governance content between 1991 and 1993 including capacity building, at 68 percent; decentralization, at 68 percent; economic management, at 49 percent; state-owned enterprise reform, at 33 percent; participation, at 30 percent; and legal framework, at 6 percent (World Bank 1994a, xv).

In a similar manner, papers by Mary Shirley (1998) and Levy (1998) about creating "credible" regulatory policy both use NIE theoretical tools to bolster the governance concept. From the opposite perspective, Wiesner (1998) applies arguments regarding transaction costs to explain how rent-seeking by public employees limits the externality effect of public goods, thereby creating inefficiencies in governance. Wiesner's paper is particularly interesting because it is consciously aimed both at making the World Bank agenda work and explaining why reforms have failed.

Among other things, Wiesner examines the role of unions as rent-seekers inside public entities. In NIE terms, public-sector rent-seekers operate in stealth with a set of priorities that negatively influence the operation and purpose of public organizations. Institutions are created when the price system is unable to deal with externalities and other market failures. The rent-seekers are able to shape and influence institutions and the institutional climate by encouraging the creation of operating rules that work to their advantage, such as obtaining legislation to limit competition. Public-sector rent-seeking institutions, such as unions, are hybrid entities interested not in profit but in creating conditions under which information is diffuse and ambiguous, thereby allowing them to further increase quasi rents. Because these institutions are not operating within market forces, they have advantages over private rent-seekers because there is little competition, information is asymmetrical, and evaluations of performance can be influenced or even controlled.

Wiesner's analysis further focuses on why the Bank's decentralization strategy, which is "the right one" (Wiesner 1998, 112), did not work as designed. For example, in the area of education, decentralization in Colombia should have led to improvements in education via sharing of revenue with local governments. The blame for its failure to do so, however, was attributed to the teachers' union. The union was able to encourage the passage of central government legislation which ensured that there would be no competition with public schools and that the teacher's union would maintain monopoly control over the supply of inputs (teachers). No independent evaluations were permitted, and the private sector was not allowed to compete with the public sector. Wiesner (1998) emphasizes the need for local governments to assume greater fiscal responsibility (and supposedly restrict rent-seeking), to decentralize or denationalize public unions, and to increase political decentralization. Again, there is nothing wrong with decentralization, "if only" the pesky unions were absent. Of course all this is a reconstruction of the World Bank agenda using the tools of NIE to support its axiomatic belief that decentralization "matches services with local preferences" and is thereby "bringing the state back to the people" (World Bank 1997, 97).

As pointed out in the literature, the reality can be quite different, with widespread evidence of unaccountable local bodies, insufficient funds, poor guidelines, and weak local capacities. Instead of enhancing democratic accountability, decentralization can result in the opposite.[19] By 2002, sufficient interest was generated in the role of institutions that the Bank devoted a full World Development Report to the application of NIE to development issues.

NIE and Markets: Critical Reflections on WDR 2002

World Development Report 2002 represents a formal statement of the exigencies of expanding the agenda for institution-building in support of markets. In theoretical terms, institutions arise from a relaxation of the unrealistic assumptions underlying the neoclassical economic formulation of the operation of markets. According to WDR 2002, agricultural markets in rural areas "suffer from problems of information, inadequate competition, and weak enforcement of contracts. Building institutions that reduce transaction costs for farms, therefore, can greatly improve the way agricultural markets operate." Such institutions are "important for poverty reduction" and lead to improvements in productivity that "encourages farmers [to] leave agriculture for more productive employment in industry and services promoting overall growth" (World Bank 2002b, 31).

By implication, the performance of agriculture has nothing to do with the failure of the adjustment strategy but, rather, is linked to the absence of conditions such as perfect information and adequate competition, which, according to the neoclassical vision, lead to optimality and maximization of social welfare. Creation of institutional constructs in support of markets promises not only operational improvements, economic growth, and poverty reduction but also a transformation of the structure of the economy!

World Development Report 2002 largely draws on new institutional economic constructs and sees institutions as "rules, enforcement mechanisms, and organizations" (World Bank 2002b, 4). Enforcement mechanisms, which are major features of the NIE approach to institutions, have many of the neoclassical economic microfoundations discussed in chapter 3. As discussed above, in Williamson's world, individuals are opportunistic and utility-maximizing. This leads to collective action problems, in which the costs of behavior that are contrary to the rules must be sufficiently high to ensure that individuals conform to the rules after carefully calculating the costs and benefits of each marginal decision. Following the NIE approach, according to the World Bank, *Homo economicus* is ubiquitous and must be carefully influenced by the design of institutions: "Informal institutions and private formal mechanisms generally rely on their own members for enforcement. . . . Institutions with internal enforcement mechanisms are effective because there is a mutually recognized system of rewards and penalties. An important issue in the design of public institutions is ensuring that the incentives that are created actually lead to desired behavior" (6).

This kind of rational choice argument is problematic. Sanctions can explain obedience to rules only if an individual's behavior can be observed by others who might be in a position to impose sanctions. Moreover, in the *Homo economicus* world of neoclassical economics, there is no reason why individuals should impose penalties when their own material rewards are not at stake. Yet people often follow rules even when they cannot be monitored (Rutherford 1996, 72–73). As we see will see in chapter 5, transforming institutions in order to foster development is much more complex and involves a great deal more than merely constraining opportunistic behavior.

The reliance on a static view of human behavior, the extraneous definition of institutions and the failure to connect factors that can lead to institutional transformation–all lead to a series of false dichotomies and predefined hierarchies. Consider the role of social norms. Within the World Bank framework, norms are largely relegated to the realm of informal institutions. Formal institutions, in their view, focus on rules that are codified or written into law, whereas informal institutions are outside the formal legal system and reflect "unwritten codes of social conduct" (World Bank 2002b, 6). In order to overcome the tendency of *Homo economicus* to be opportunistic, informal institutions will have close religious or ethnic ties because they provide greater potential for mechanisms of punishment such as ostracism. By definition, these groups can only "support a less diverse set of activities than do formal legal institutions. As countries develop, the number and range of partners that market participants deal with increases and market transactions become more complicated, demanding more formal institutions" (ibid.).

The distinction between formal and informal institutions arises from the work of Douglass North (1990). North presents a hierarchy of market development, beginning with personalized exchange focusing on small enterprise and localized trading, moving to exchanges that are more impersonal, involving long-range trading including exchanges between groups with cultural ties, and culminating in the impersonal exchanges of the modern market systems. Institutions of the first two types rely on more informal arrangements such as common culture, kinship relations, or even the exchange of hostages when dealing with intercultural trade. Modern economies, however, require formal institutions that permit outside enforcement, "since the returns on opportunism, cheating and shirking rise in complex societies" (North 1990, 35). Informal institutions, according to this view, largely act as fetters on the development process.

The problem with this approach is that the formal-informal dichotomy is problematic as a guide for development. To begin with, the line between the formal and informal is rather arbitrary. If a scribe is hired to record the conditions of hostage exchanges, does this mean we now have a written code of conduct? Is it now formal? On the other hand, if two mega corporations shake hands on a multimillion-dollar transaction is this informal? The key is not the distinction between formal and informal but the degree to which common social norms have been internalized to form a common understanding and purpose. Beginning with the work of nineteenth-century psychologists such as William James (1893), it has long been recognized that habituation is absolutely central to the internalization of social norms. In the development context, it is norms that must change, not the degree of informality. A theory that focuses on institutions should focus on mechanisms that generate new common correlative patterns of behavior to enhance development. This topic is explored in chapter 5.

Faulty foundations create other false dichotomies. Consider the distinction between the public and the private roles in building institutions in support of markets. The domains of the state and the private sectors in the institutional context are predefined, with the state generally assumed to work against private markets. The role of the state simply is posited deductively from the theoretical propositions given above, including the enforcement of property rights: "Governments have an important role in providing public goods, such as laws that delineate property rights and the judicial institutions that enforce these rights and establish the rule of law" (World Bank 2002b, 7).

Any intervention beyond the narrow principles arising from their theoretical model will lead to problems because "governments have been known to impede the development of markets through arbitrary exercise of state power, overtaxation, corruption, short time horizons, cronyism, and the inability to uphold public order" (World Bank 2002b, 7). As discussed above, markets in developing countries generally are seen as poorly developed. Markets would seem to require both greater regulation and greater amounts of state support. According to the World Development Report 2002, overregulation is defined not by the state of the markets but by the extent of state capacity because "the limited capacity of developing country governments to implement regulations means that many activities in poor countries are overregulated . . . one solution is to write simple rules and have fewer of them" (12).

By contrast, an institution-based approach recognizes the hollowness of the state-market dichotomy. According to this view, the policy focus should not be on state retraction from markets in the hope of creating some ideal Pareto optimal exchange but on transforming the state-private institutional nexus to better serve the developmental process.

As Chang (2002a, 2002b) argues, markets are political constructs. The boundaries and operating principles of markets have always been the product of state decisions. Establishing and distributing property rights (witness the rise of the oligarchs in Russia as the latest episode), generating prices (immigration policies, minimum wages, interest rates), determining the acceptable constitution of products (drugs, child labor), stipulating who can participate (banking licenses, foreign ownership restrictions, the rights of slaves in earlier times), defining the rights and obligations of participants (environmental laws, zoning laws, fire restrictions), and establishing the rules of operation of the exchange process (fraud, contracts, consumer rights)—all are political decisions. Thus, neoliberal calls for "depoliticizing" the market are nothing more than political statements attempting to redefine the boundaries between states and markets.

Markets should be seen as institutional constructs. If we see institutions as habits of thought or socially prescribed correlated behaviors, then markets reflect a set of correlated behavioral patterns that structure and support the exchange process. Exchanges do not arise spontaneously from self-seeking behavior but rather stem from a confluence of factors and forces, often including significant forms of state support and intervention. Their operation is characterized by institutionalized or habitual patterns of behavior of customary, legal, economic, and political origin. The focal point of development should be transforming human behavior by altering what I refer to as the institutional matrix.

Conclusions

This chapter has illustrated the origins, nature, and impact of the rise of the new institutional economics at the World Bank. Although work on NIE had been done by Bank economists in the early 1990s, an important turning point was the presentation of a paper by Oliver Williamson in 1994 (following the awarding of North's Nobel Prize in 1993) at the annual ABCDE conference.

This chapter has analyzed critically the way in which NIE is used in *Bureaucrats in Business* and WDR 1997 to support the overall World Bank policy agenda and has examined the institutional constructs in WDR 2002.

Instead of using institutional economic theory to actually rethink and reevaluate its policies, which would have seemed especially appealing given the overwhelming evidence of the failures of its earlier programs, the Bank used institutional economic theory to buttress its orthodox agenda. This task has been made easier by referring to common neoclassical economic constructs that underlie both structural adjustment and new institutional economics. Overall, NIE has not had a major influence on the World Bank at the operational level. As noted by some Bank staff, however, the controversial nature of some NIE-influenced reports has helped clear the way to raise the issues of politics and corruption with recipient governments.

By contrast, institutional economic theory, using other traditions, points to a rather different policy agenda, which will be explored in the remainder of this volume.

PART III

Beyond the World Bank Agenda

An Institutional Approach to Development

CHAPTER FIVE

Building on Lost Foundations

The Institutional Matrix and Socioeconomic Development

The main hope must be that the economic profession will gradually turn to remodeling our framework of theories and concepts in the direction characterized as institutional. . . . With strong ideological influences and vested interests working to retain the Western approach to economic analysis . . . attempts to change it will meet resistance from the producers and consumers of economic research in South Asia, as well as the West.—Gunnar Myrdal, 1968

Introduction

In the prologue to *Asian Drama* Gunnar Myrdal reminds us that the problems of living are complex and that they cannot be fit into the "pigeonholes of our inherited disciplines." On the basis of advances in the social sciences, he argues that no one could possibly "draw inferences about social reality from the concepts of economics alone" (Myrdal 1968, 1:5). Yet he also recognizes the tendency of economic theorists more than any other social scientists to arrive at broad propositions and "then postulate [them] as valid for every time, place and culture" (1:16).

As presented in previous chapters, the World Bank agenda of the past two decades has done precisely this: it has projected a narrow economic doctrine onto a complex social and economic reality without regard to "time, place and culture," with disastrous consequences. It is time to return to the foundations put in place by institutional economists such as Gunnar Myrdal that have been lost to a discipline that has broadened its application while narrowing its thinking. Building on the contribution of Myrdal, this chapter draws on a large body of theory from sociology, economics, management studies, and psychology to map out an institutional approach to development.

The chapter begins with a discussion of the bias inherent in the orthodoxy of Myrdal's era and in today's. I then turn to an investigation of Myrdal's institutionalist view of development based largely on his *Asian Drama*. I examine the concept of institutions in the works of Myrdal and others and explore the five dimensions of the institutional matrix along with the relation between institutional change and development.

At the core of the institutional matrix are the habits of thought common to the generality of men and women. For purposes of development, institutional transformation should focus on generating new forms of correlated behavior aimed at increasing the generalized standard of living of the population of a country. Each subcomponent of the matrix interacts with each other subcomponent and, in turn, has the potential to alter the human behavior that is at the center of the matrix. Institutional change implies the creation of a new set of institutions that provides the basis for a new economic and social order. To truly understand the roots of these ideas, it is necessary to go back to the pioneering work of Gunnar Myrdal.

Bias in Constructs and Policies: Orthodoxy Then and Now

According to Myrdal, attitudes and institutions are firmly embedded in analytical constructs. The study of regions cannot be separated from the study's context and implied bias. In the 1960s, Myrdal pointed to the labels and analytical categories that were projected onto developing countries depending on their alignment during the cold war. The degree of freedom of a country was determined not by any objective measure but by the degree of allegiance to the West or to the Communist bloc. These categories spilled into the realm of economic policy, with an associated set of preferences regarding foreign trade, exchange rates, and public and private activity.

To a degree, conceptual categories spawned during the cold war period have continued to influence the theoretical framework. Emphasis on free markets and free elections continues to be a driving force in the analytical constructs of Western researchers long after the collapse of the Soviet bloc.[1] Yet a new set of constructs also emerged as the priorities shifted from cold war politics in poorer countries to "transitional" economies and former members of Comecon (the Soviet-era trading bloc of socialist nations that was abolished in 1991).

Instead of developing countries we now have "emerging" markets, which include lucrative assets with the potential for acquisition, a large, well-educated labor force, sophisticated infrastructure, and previously inaccessible populations to provide export markets. Resources in the World Bank and other agencies shifted toward the newly emerging countries. With the complete breakdown of barriers, globalization became the rage, and "openness" the means to access globalization. Every emerging country now needed a stock market in order to access the proliferation of financial flows from sources other than foreign direct investment (FDI). In 1990, development of stock markets was a rather low priority in sub-Saharan Africa. There were only seven exchanges, most dating back to colonial times. By 1998 the number had almost tripled to twenty (Stein 2003). The macrostabilization of the structural adjustment era took on new meaning. Non-FDI flows would reward countries that had low inflation and stable currencies. Researchers invented exercises in risk assessment, indexes of corruption, degrees of openness, and measures of competitiveness to evaluate the potential for FDI and non-FDI flows. Once again analytical categories were set not by an understanding of the intrinsic functioning of these economies but by constructs reflecting the needs and priorities of the Western world.[2]

As we have seen in the case of the World Bank agenda and in Myrdal's prescient statement (quoted in the epigraph), ideology and vested interests have worked to perpetuate the dominant approach to economic policy in recent decades. Alternatives are resisted not only in Western countries but in the developing world, precisely because the training of the elite in these countries is combined with penalties for taking an independent course and rewards for conforming (such as lucrative consultancies from donors). Constructs and theories become internalized and are difficult to reorder.[3] Vested interests should be seen not only at the national level, but also at the individual level. It is rare for an educated person to denounce all that he or she has learned, even when daily experience is in conflict with these principles. Rationality and explanation are likely to be used to dismiss any conflict, given all that has been invested.[4]

Moreover, the "appearance of superiority" of mainstream economic theory arises not from its powers of explanation but from the ease of generalization from a set of simple principles (Myrdal 1968, 1:25–27). The objectification of value judgments through the pretentious use of "universal" welfare principles (such as Pareto optimality) also has enhanced the air of prestige and superiority.[5] For all these reasons, changing the approach to policy formulation in developing countries will meet resistance not only in the Western countries but also in the developing world. When projected into new contexts, Western social sciences are "no different than the magical thinking of primitive man" since "they have no existence outside the framework of preconceptions" (1:25–26). When preconceptions are axiomatic (as with the neoclassical model), their application even to the realities of Western countries is subject to question.

In the world of the twenty-first century, constraints on charting a new course of research and on generating new strategies are greater than Myrdal could have imagined in 1968. Not only has the neoclassical vision captured academia, but it also has permeated markets and influenced the perceptions of actors in the private sector. The domain of acceptable policy has dramatically narrowed. Moreover, a singular concatenated vision of economic rationality has forced countries to dismantle regulatory bodies and alter policies in an attempt to meet an ideal concept. Mechanisms that could be used to mediate global flows in a manner which might be structurally enhancing have disappeared.[6] International organizations such as the World Bank and the IMF have followed the dual process of ignoring or even encouraging new vehicles of global finance (see chapter 7) while using their leverage to dismantle mechanisms of control at the level of the nation-state.

What is needed is not a grand singular theory of transformation. An institutional approach is, foremost, an analytical framework. The aim is to generate new sets of constructs and theories stemming from a contextualized understanding of reality. Theory always has an a priori dimension, but it must be adjusted as new observations arise from the phenomena being examined. As Myrdal pointed out in 1968, theory, more than anything, should be seen as a "correlated set of questions to the social reality under study." He continues, "All knowledge, and all ignorance, tends to be opportunistic," and it becomes more so when it is not continually adjusted to the research directed at empirical understanding (Myrdal 1968, 1:25).

Although the constraints are greater today than in Myrdal's time, so, too, is the need for a fresh approach as the life expectancy of millions of people in Africa and elsewhere is falling in the wake of failed economic strategies, growing poverty, and associated disease. The last economist to generate an alternative development vision based on original institutional theory was Gunnar Myrdal. I return to his lost foundations to build an institutional theory of development applicable to the challenges of the early twenty-first century and beyond.

Building on Lost Foundations: The Institutionalism of Gunnar Myrdal and Its Current Relevance

Myrdal focused on understanding the complexity of human behavior, its motivation, and how to change it when necessary. Even in economic pursuits Myrdal emphasized that people do not follow the "the single-mindedness of the 'economic man' of classical economic theory." In their economic choices they are influenced by their "total mental make-up" and "by the community in which they live" (Myrdal 1968, 1:7).

To Myrdal, underdevelopment is "a constellation of numerous undesirable conditions for work and life" and is linked to the nature of the social system, or the social and economic matrix (see below) (Myrdal 1968, 3:1840). Development will arise from policy-induced "changes in the social and institutional structure," not from spontaneous means (1:26). His approach, in particular, and an institutional one, in general, are not teleological.

As discussed in chapter 1, teleology is based on the principle that the universe has design and purpose. In Aristotelian terms, the explanation of a phenomenon has not only immediate purpose but also a final cause. Development is seen as following a singular route to progress. For Myrdal, the teleological approach has three major elements: "inevitability," "unintended purposiveness," and "implicit valuation." Inevitability delimits the options available in the present and rules out hypothetical alternatives in the past. Policies are not products of the choices made in the past but are products of an inevitable process and thus serve unintended purposes. They are caused by and arise from development itself. Values hidden in teleological intentionality lead to the specification of what constitutes good policies and bad policies. In addition, historical description is laden with implicit values because causal events are deductively specified as logical antecedents to the unraveling of historical process (Myrdal 1968, 3:1852–54). The teleological approach to development tends to be tautological (involving circular reasoning). For example, in the world of Rostow (1960), stages are characterized by shifts in leading sectors.

Without the stages of Rostow's work, the World Bank agenda has largely been driven by a teleological approach in which "good" policies are always assumed to lead inevitably to progress, as measured by high levels of economic growth. Tautologies abound. The countries that have done well are presumably those with the correct policies, which must be correct precisely because they have done well. Implicit values and bias also are ubiquitous. Because the Bank is in the business only of helping countries develop, it follows that the policies it has encouraged must be the ones responsible for positive outcomes. History is carefully rewritten to reflect implicit values. Countries that have done well in Africa after 1980 are the ones that have been the most subject to adjustment. If they are not doing well, it is because they are no longer so. The continually shifting subset of "successful" countries in Africa mentioned in World Bank studies always consists of the countries with the best policies. The good policies are deductively posited from neoclassical models and reflect the values arising from the ideology and priorities discussed in chapter 1.

Consider the teleology implicit in the IMF's comment about the inevitable pressures of globalization and its guaranteed path to success with "good" policies:

A key lesson seems to be that the *pressures* of globalization, especially in the past decade or so, have served to accentuate the benefits of good policies and the costs of bad policies. Countries that *align* themselves with the forces of globalization and embrace the reforms needed to do so, liberalizing markets and pursuing disciplined macroeconomic policies, are likely to put themselves on a path of convergence with the advanced economies, following the successful newly industrialized economies. These countries may expect to benefit from trade, gain global market share, and be increasingly rewarded with large private capital flows. Countries that do not adopt such policies are likely to face declining shares of world trade and private capital flows, and to find themselves falling behind in relative terms. (International Monetary Fund 1997b, 72, emphasis added)

Globalization acts as a deus ex machina, creating an unwavering set of opportunities and a final higher purpose (convergence with advanced countries). Fulfillment will arise from the inevitable sequence of events and good policies that align a country with globalization. In this case, *pressures* refers to an independent force much like a strong wind, with states simply putting in place the correct navigational course and setting their sails in order to gain the benefits in speed and time. From the IMF's perspective, any rational captain will choose the correct course. Countries following this route inevitably will converge with the advanced countries.

In contrast to the linearity and teleology of orthodoxy, Myrdal posits a framework of factors that interact to create a self-supporting and reproducing system of circular causation in which induced changes in one factor can alter the direction of other factors, setting off a process of cumulative change. When considering development there are no problems that are uniquely economic. The distinction between economic and noneconomic factors is artificial, given the socially embedded character of the economy and the interactive nature of the components of a social system. What should be studied are relevant elements, determined from a careful understanding of the specificity of the subject matter (Myrdal 1968, 1:42). By nature, the approach is antiteleological, because values are made explicit (defining what and what is not important), and inevitability is nonexistent because circular causation says nothing about the direction of movement. Policy choice serves intended purposes since it stems from a careful analysis of the matrix of social and economic relations. Each change in a condition has both independent value and instrumental value. For example, education is both an end and a means to induce cumulative change in other factors such as raising productivity.

Myrdal posits six broad categories of interacting dimensions of a social system. These are presented in table 5.1 with examples. First is output, as measured by average labor productivity and per capita income. The second dimension, which is the conditions of production, points to the structure of the economy, including the level of technology, the sectoral allocation of production, and its associated level of intensity. "Standard of living" refers to the quantity and quality of food, housing conditions, medical care availability and accessibility, education, provision of public goods, and so on. The fourth dimension, attitudes toward life and work, covers the degree of discipline, extent of superstitions, punctuality, levels of cooperation, personal hygiene, ambition, adaptability, and so on. "Attitudes" refers to the "totality of the beliefs and valuations that cause behavior to be what it is . . . that have been molded by a long spiritual and material history and that are causally related to levels and modes of living and working and to the entire framework of institutions" (Myrdal 1968, 1:102).

The fifth dimension, what Myrdal refers to as institutions, is largely composed of organizational entities and systems. He is interested in focusing on the state of institutions. Underdevelopment is due in part to

TABLE 5.1 **Mydral's social system matrix**

Category	Examples of measures
Output and income	• Average labor productivity • Per capita income levels
Conditions of production	• Level of technology in production • Adoption of new technology • Diversity of industries in the economy • Sectoral allocation and production
Level of living	• Quality of food and housing • Quality and accessibility of medical care • Education • Provision of public goods
Attitudes toward life and work	• Superstitions • Punctuality • Personal hygiene • Ambition • Degree of discipline
Institutions	• Efficiency of the civil service • Strength of judicial systems • Efficacy of regulatory systems • National ethos
Policies	• Export promotion programs • Poverty reduction programs • Literacy programs • Universal health care • Technology policy • Industrial policy

unfavorable institutional conditions and includes attributes such as low standards in the efficiency of public administrations, land tenure systems that impede agriculture, a weak base for voluntary organizations, insufficient national consolidation, and so on. A major cause of enfeebled institutions (what Myrdal refers to as "soft states") is that governments require too little of the populace. Just as weak institutions interact to perpetuate themselves, attitudes support institutions and in turn are supported by institutions. Both interact with output, conditions of production, and standard of living.

The final dimension of the matrix is policies, which are induced changes in any of the factors in conditions of production, standard of living, attitudes toward life and work, and institutions. Policies only indirectly affect output via changes in the other factors. The "coordination of policies in order to attain or speed up development" is referred to as planning, a main focal point of Myrdal's formulation (Myrdal 1968, 2:896, 3:1859–64).

Belief systems play a critical role in altering or perpetuating attitudes and institutions, and can influence the effectiveness of policies.[7] Myrdal is particularly critical of the impact of religion, which creates rigidities and inertia and often justifies social stratification and inequality. Religion is "a ritualized and stratified complex of highly emotional beliefs and valuations that give the sanction of sacredness, taboo, and immutability to inherited institutional arrangements, modes of living and attitudes" (Myrdal 1968, 1:103). Religion provides the "emotional container of this whole way of life and work and by its sanction has rendered it rigid and resistant to change" (1:112). By contrast, some forms of nationalism or "a feeling of solidarity with a group of people" can counteract the constraints created by feelings of "exclusiveness, separateness and particularism and can convert them into allegiance to the entire entity of peoples" (1:122–23). This psychological transformation can generate unity and inclusion that can increase the range and effectiveness of government policies.

In presenting an understanding of the social system, Myrdal emphasizes that the focal point of differentiation is neither ethical nor a priori as described in neoclassical welfare economics. Critical reflection, which is value laden, should be driven by reflecting on the priorities of the country. Historical analysis is important to understanding the origins and nature of this social system and should be a central component of national evaluation. History is "not a source of generalizing rationalization" (frequently the preoccupation of mainstream theoretical approaches), but rather a "long sequence of ramifying causation" that creates the social system (Myrdal 1968, 1:103). The social system is perpetuated by the interactive and self-supporting nature of its components, a process which Myrdal refers to as "unidirectional causal interdependence." The interactions among the components of Myrdal's system are illustrated in figure 5.1.

The dynamic interplay is wholly nonlinear. For example, consider the expansion of an industry using modern technology. The effects will be multifaceted. In addition to the direct employment impact, if the industry competes with more traditional enterprises, it could have a "backwash" effect on the older enterprises, leading to a net loss of employment. The backwash effect is not likely to appear in import-substituting or export-oriented industries.

In addition, there are "spread" effects. Myrdal divides these into demand, supply, and externality dimensions. Demand effects work through

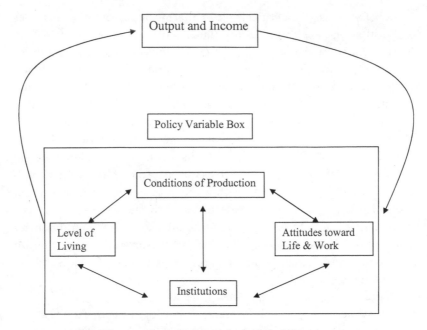

FIGURE 5.1. Myrdal's framework: Circular causation and development

both the expansion in the demand for inputs and the increase in income to newly employed workers. These are more widely known in the literature as backward and demand linkages. On the supply side, the focus is largely on the externality effects of spreading higher overheads for infrastructure among higher production levels and general improvements in labor skills, with the potential to influence the rest of the economy (Myrdal 1968, 2:1172–99).

Moreover, there are other likely spillovers from new technology into attitudes and institutions, including a "new spirit of rationalism, enterprise, discipline, punctuality, mobility, and efficiency" (Myrdal 1968, 2:1196). Industrial transformation can be constrained by points of inertia, which create critical thresholds that must be overcome if the cumulative process is to take off. These points of inertia can include rigidities in the social structure that could reduce these effects in important areas such as primary education.

Changes such as land reform may be necessary to break down the critical rigidities and encourage a more positive effect on education (Myrdal 1968, 3:1874–75). Although many of Myrdal's insights are helpful, there are also problems with his idea of institutions that limit the usefulness of his framework for understanding institutional development.

Myrdal and the Concept of Institutions:
Exploring Alternatives in the Literature

To begin with, Myrdal conceptualizes modes of human behavior largely as attitudes, and these compose but one of five dimensions of cumulative change. In contrast, the aim of this volume is to demonstrate the usefulness of a new framework to improve our understanding of the way new and correlated constructs can alter the ways people interact to improve their standard of living. The transformation of human behavior is at the center of the institutional matrix in which humans are both subjects and objects. To understand development we must go beyond the typical discussions of prices, savings, markets as exchanges, investment, and output to incorporate an array of economic and noneconomic factors, which determine the nature of institutions and institutional constructs.

Myrdal, however, seems to place output, income, and the conditions of production on an equal footing with standard of living, attitudes, and institutions (or, really, organizational entities and systems). This is conceptually problematic. Output and income are rather flawed representations of standard of living, which should be seen as both input and output in an institution-based theory of development focused on cumulative and circular causal relationships. The conditions of production should be embedded in the matrix as mechanisms for increasing capacities and organizations that enable human transformation and new forms of human interaction. For example, technology greatly enhances the capacity of organizations to induce new forms of worker interaction to increase output and standard of living. Conditions of production are not conceptually equivalent to standard of living, which is both a means to an end and an end in itself and should be used as a measure of progress in the development process. As indicated in figure 5.2 (page 143), standard of living should be placed outside the institutional matrix.

An additional problem with Myrdal's work is his concept of institutions as organizational entities and systems. Organizations and organizational change are salient to development. They are not institutions, however, but institutional constructs. The lack of clarity in the concept of institutions is common in all branches of institutional economics. We saw in chapter 4 that the World Bank defined institutions as "rules, enforcement mechanisms, and organizations." In addition to conflating three conceptually distinct but overlapping concepts, this definition also reflects the NIE-inspired emphasis on institutions as mechanisms of constraint. Williamson (1985), for example, sees institutions as structures of governance that constrain opportunism and reduce transaction costs.

Even authors writing in the OIE tradition, who have provided incisive and seminal contributions to institutional economics, sometimes provide a less-than-clear conceptualization of institutions. Chang (2002a) lumps together entities such as law, state regulations, markets, and self-regulatory organizations such as professional associations as "formal" institutions, and defines social conventions as "informal" institutions. Although all entities interact and are parts of the totality of a social system (in Myrdal's terms), each has both shared and autonomous dimensions. Lumping them into one category diminishes the analytical clarity needed to understand how they are formed and how they interact. Moreover, human beings both constitute and are constituted by these entities. They are also the products and producers of development. Some kind of common, underlying element connecting shifts in institutional constructs is needed for conceptual clarity. The key is in delineating the relations among institutional constructs, habits, and the transformations of behavior that are at the core of development.

Institution, Habits, and Behavior

North (1990) recognizes the importance of a common construct and defines institutions as "rules of the game in a society" or, more formally, "humanly devised constraints that shape human interaction" (3). This definition, however, places too much emphasis on institutions as constraining human behavior. As Sjostrand (1995, 38–41) points out, one cannot conceptualize a realistic theory of entrepreneurship or institutional change if institutions only constrain. Entrepreneurship arises from the underlying human essence, which differentiates individual humans' perception (of, for example, institutions), imagination, mobility (taking one set of institutions from one organizational context to another, leading to innovation), limitations (inability to fully comprehend all, leading to innovation) and commitment (frequency with which norms are used).

Following North, Hodgson (2004) focuses on rules, or to be more precise, "durable systems of established and embedded social rules that structure social interaction."[8] Yet he sees institutions as singularly focused not on constraining human behavior but on altering it in fundamental ways. Institutional durability arises from the ability to increase certainty in the expectations of the behavior of others. Constraint itself can open up new possibilities. Without traffic rules, transportation and its associated economic and social benefits would not exist. Institutions contribute "form and consistency" to human action and generate "ordered thought, expectation and action" (Hodgson 2004, 656). Institutions also go beyond constraining and enabling behavior to transforming or molding human behavior.

The key to transforming behavior is in altering habits; this creates new perspectives, intentions, and preferences, or what Hodgson refers to as "reconstitutive downward causation." Institutional structures act to alter existing habits, which in turn influence behavior. Habits are "submerged repertoires of potential behavior that can be triggered or reinforced by an appropriate stimulus or context" that creates a propensity for different forms of context-specific behavior (Hodgson 2004, 652). Although they might arise from social sanction or an understanding of legal boundaries or constraints, habits, once internalized, tend toward self-perpetuation, even if the boundaries are removed.

In this case we have persistence of habits that are increasingly being recognized by the rapidly growing branch of mainstream theory known as behavioral economics. Along these lines, experiments have indicated that individual consumption is heavily affected by reference points. For example, loss aversion is common, because for most people modest losses have an impact that greatly exceeds that of large gains. Thaler (1980), one of the leading proponents of behavioral economics, presents a related phenomenon known as an "endowment effect." Once a person comes into possession of an item, he or she will immediately value it at a level that exceeds the value assigned by the individual prior to possession. A related concept is the "status quo bias." Experiments have shown that people prefer the status quo rather than absorbing the loss of some goods offset by gains of other items (Rabin 1998).

These arguments, however, are abstracted from the key question of why people behave in this manner. Is it instinctive, learned, or a product of pressures from a society that values possession more than the process that creates possession? For purposes of transforming behavior (the focal point of an institutional approach to development) one must understand the cognitive processes that are not explained by behavioral economics.

Moreover, the field still is mired in the methodology of neoclassical economics. For example, behavioral economics still relies on methodological individualism. Reference point kinks in individual utility functions are used to reflect status quo bias or loss aversion. Overall, the main review of behavioral economics in the *Journal of Economic Literature* argues: "Mainstream economics employs a powerful combination of methods [such as methodological individualism]. . . . I believe these methods are tremendously useful . . . 'tractability' and 'parsimony' should be guiding principles in our efforts to make our research more realistic. . . . As it now stands, some important psychological findings seem tractable and parsimonious enough that we should begin the process of integrating them into economics" (Rabin 1998, 12). In other words, absorb what you can without challenging the fundamental core of neoclassical economic theory.

Still, the nuances implied in behavioral economics have yet to funnel to the World Bank agenda, which still is driven by the vision of constant calculating, not habituated *Homo economicus*. To this organization, behavior is simply a product of a rational being reacting in a predictable way to the information embedded in particular circumstances. Thus, price vectors lead to choices about what to produce and what to consume.

The challenge of development is not just in putting the correct information in place. The aim is not only to change the context of human behavior, but to create new institutional constructs which can alter the habits that underlie human behavior so that we can deal with these new contexts. In a dynamic, cumulative world of circular change, new contexts are supported by institutions and habits, which are in turn perpetuated by the new contexts. Veblen's (1919) definition of institutions as "habits of thought common to the generality of men [and women]" points to two elements vital to understanding the role of institutions in a dynamic setting.

First is his focus on "habits of thought," not simply "habits."[9] Thought implies process and activity and is kinetic. Habits, as we saw above, emphasize potential behavior that can be triggered by certain stimuli. Habits of thought are not passive entities, however, but constructs that are continuously and often repetitively invoked in response to contextualized stimuli as perceived during the thought process. They are integral to the human dynamic that connects thought to process and allows people to transform their activities. For development purposes, the focus is on habituating new mental constructs that allow people to better interact in newly created contexts. The second part of the definition says that these habits are "common to the generality of men and women." For mental constructs to be effective they must not be idiosyncratic and individualized but must be connected to other individuals to increase coordination, unity of purpose, and certainty of behavior. This is perhaps a good measure of an institution that is embedded within the matrix.

The common conflation of institutions and organizations (as is present even in Hodgson 2004, 655) is problematic, particularly in a developing country. Organizations are entities that require common habits of thought in order to operate, but they also have a host of other dimensions (such as structure, purpose, internal laws, and power relations). They therefore form an institutional construct that transforms institutions and that, in turn, is transformed by institutions. They form part of the institutional matrix, which consists of norms, organizations, regulations, capacities, and incentives. Each component of the matrix has an effect and in turn is affected by correlated behavior. The remainder of this chapter examines the nature of these vital institutional constructs. I begin with the concept of norms.

The Institutional Matrix: Toward a Theory of Institutional Development

Norms

Norms are socially derived behavioral guidelines concerning what is expected, required, or accepted. As we will see below, they are conceptually distinct and yet have an important influence on institutions. How does the World Bank understand norms in its work concerning institutions?

World Development Report 2002, *Building Institutions for Markets*, discusses norms largely as an afterthought in chapter 9;[10] they are minimally integrated into the first eight chapters, where they are simply part of the definition of institutions, rather than being conceptually distinct. Thus, "institutions are the rules, including behavioral norms, by which agents interact and the organizations that implement rules and codes of conduct to achieve desired outcomes" (World Bank 2002b, 6). Norms are primarily linked to informal structures such as the Maghribi trading networks of eleventh-century North Africa. In contrast, rules such as laws written by governments largely influence the operation of the formal sector, such as the modern corporate sector.

There are problems with this conceptualization of norms. First, the conflation of norms with rules is problematic. Rules can often be pro forma, or put
in place as a result of a legal or regulatory mechanism. They are "formally
recognized ways in which things should be done," in contrast to routines,
which are the way "things are actually done" (Burns and Scapens 2000, 6).

Second, the argument that informal entities are products of norms and
formal structures are products of formal rules such as laws is a false bifurcation. Clearly, norms are at the core of the functioning of every organizational entity. The ability of laws to influence corporate behavior arises
not only from the penalties and incentives associated with the law but also
from the legitimacy of law-based behavior. Norms make up a critical dimension of the operationalization of legal statutes and help internalize
legal guides to behavior (Etzioni 2000). Similarly, no informal sector is
entirely above the law. Part of the problem is a conceptual one.

In separating conceptual categories from empirical reality we often
choose different types of abstraction. Various definitions have been used
conceptually to differentiate the formal from the informal sector. The
definition given above reflects more of a neoclassical interpretation of informality that focuses on barriers created by state regulations and the lack
of legal recognition of producing entities. By nature, an implied hierarchy
is embedded in the process of formalization in which "as market transactions become more complicated [and] countries develop" they will be
"demanding more formal institutions" (World Bank 2002b, 6). From this
perspective, formalization can only arise in the early stages of development, when state regulation is minimal.

Yet a richer depiction of the informal sector would focus on companies
that fail to meet minimum socially acceptable standards or have limited
linkages to markets and therefore fewer economic linkages and limited
access to public goods. In Africa and other places, informal sectors have
grown rapidly, not because of a proliferation of regulations but as a means
for survival following the loss of formal-sector employment opportunities
under structural adjustment.[11]

The challenge is to find ways to increase the social benefit of the informal sector so that it contributes better to the development process.
Changing regulatory stipulations including licensing methods would have
little impact on the way these firms operate because public goods still are
largely absent or inaccessible, credit still is largely unobtainable, technological capacities and knowledge that would allow expansion often are not
available, and transaction costs of wider market participation are still very

high. Although many of these deficiencies need to be addressed, changing norms to increase the social benefit of the informal sector should be an important policy focus. For example, organizing free classes about hygiene for food producers and consumers in the informal sector can introduce new norms of hygienic standards and reduce the incidence of food poisoning. Changing norms in the formal sector could also be good for the development process by, for example, increasing a sense of social responsibility among company managers.

So, what is an institutional approach to understanding norms, and how do norms relate to correlated patterns of behavior? As discussed above, norms, from an institutional perspective, are guidelines that represent what is expected, required, or accepted. Norms are generally binding on groups and directly influence their behavior in particular contexts. Norms tend to be buttressed by social sanctions and lead to the socialization of individuals as they are internalized. A test of internalization occurs when "the actor learns to follow rules of behavior in situations that arouse impulses to transgress and there is no surveillance or sanction" (Etzioni 2000, 167). Norms, in Veblen's terms, may provide such economic benefits as coordination or cooperation, but they are primarily concerned with group identification, social position, and self-worth. Adherence to norms is driven by the threat of ostracism and disesteem (Rutherford 1996, 62–67).

There is little doubt that individuals can weigh the relative costs of adhering to norms, although certainly not in the marginal, calculating manner of *Homo economicus*. What makes norms so powerful is that they become internalized and are followed according to a process of what Etzioni (2000) refers to as "intrinsic affirmation," or a positive sense arising from acting in a manner consistent with a person's moral code or signaling. When one's behavior is inconsistent with this code, it can create a sense of disquiet or guilt leading to an adjustment of the behavior, not the creation of a new norm. Norms can become guides to the relative merit of rules and routines. Once norms are internalized they can become the "proximate end of endeavor," or goals (Rutherford 1996, 62–67).

Norms become habits of thought when internalized and become institutions once a sufficient number of people have internalized them. More broadly, institutionalization occurs when the practices expected in various social settings are widely developed and learned. In these conditions the behavior of individuals is heavily influenced by the "imperatives of legitimacy-seeking behavior" linked to the nature of socially determined norms (Dillard et al. 2004, 508).

The deep-seated nature of norms can make them difficult to alter. Norms can be repositories of power, and political and economic forces influence which norms will be deemed acceptable and legitimate. These forces determine norms that will shape and guide behavior (legitimation function) and circumscribe or define the parameters of appropriate models of structure and policy (signification). The outcome will reflect the relative power of the actors who support, oppose, or attempt to influence the process. The process can be recursive. Power creates and then is established by institutions, often via the selection and substantiation of norms (Dillard et al. 2004).

Yet norms form a major element in the constitution and normative evaluation of habits of thought. They allow us to measure the social connection and validity of our behavior and can act as a fetter or facilitator of development. The challenge in a development context is both how to change norms and how to deepen norms to better connect to and alter existing habits of thought. What type of norms will enhance development? The answer will depend on history, level of development, and sector. As discussed in chapter 7, countries in the early stages of building a banking system should try to instill norms such as trust, probity, social responsibility, professional standards for auditors, accountants and loan officers, new priorities for loans that finance investment, employment generation and entrepreneurship, and saving for the future.[12]

A shift in norms generally will not arise from the simple volition of an individual but will be the product of a process set in motion by cumulative change. Modifications in ideology, significant shocks, or major shifts in the technical or economic environment can change the pattern of life and alter existing norms. As we will see in later chapters, incentives can play an important role in deepening the impact of new systems of norms. Still, the habituation of new norms requires an interactive process that relates thought and intelligence to changing material conditions (Rutherford 1996, 62–67). Norms also play an important role in the formation and operation of organizations.

Organizations

Organizations are conceptually (and often legally) recognized entities that combine groups of people with defined common rules and purposes. World Development Report 2002 is heavily informed by a Williamson-type concept of organizations as structures of governance aimed at con-

straining opportunistic behavior. Thus, effective organizations, according
to the World Bank, are those that are "incentive-compatible institutions
with internal enforcement mechanisms" and a "mutually recognized system of rewards and penalties" (6). Effective organizations are not ones
that constantly exercise enforcement but rather those with institutionalized patterns of behavior with roles, rules, relations, and goals that are
clearly defined and largely internalized. Organizations are central elements in the social and economic transformation of developing countries,
although they are by no means the easiest to change.

Of the five areas of the matrix, organizational theory is by far the most
exhaustively analyzed, because for decades it has been a focal point of
such disciplines as sociology and business management studies. On the
basis of reviews by authors such as Hage and Finsterbusch (1987), Tayeb
(1988), and Oru et al. (1997) one can identify six different approaches in
the literature: universal, contingent, political economy, culture, market,
and institutional.

To begin with, much of the first half of the twentieth century focused
on a universal approach to organizations, which resulted in a "single best
practice" model of a rational and efficient structure, irrespective of the
underlying conditions. Weber (1968), for example, emphasized the advantages of a bureaucratic approach regardless of output, technology, market,
or societal context.[13]

The singularity of the approach was challenged in the 1960s by Burns
and Stalker (1961) and by Lawrence and Lorsch (1967). Based on a study
of the Scottish electronics industry, Burns and Stalker argued that the
bureaucratic approach was useful in a mass-production setting, such as
a television factory, whereas a more adaptive or "organic" approach was
needed in an innovative setting that emphasized small markets and new
products and services. Lawrence and Lorsch examined a range of companies in three industries and discovered that in more unpredictable or
complicated environments, the organizational structure needed to be
more complex, with a greater number of subunits and better communication among the components of the structure. These and other authors
argued for a more contingent relation between organizational design
and its operating environment, which can include a host of other factors
such as technology.[14] The contingent approach focuses too narrowly on
the specificity of organizational form, however, and not enough on the
broader climate that influences the overall direction of organizational
transformation.

The third way of looking at the topic is the political economy approach. A broad array of political and economic factors is seen as shaping the structure and nature of organizations. Here the character of the process of industrialization (Harbison and Myers 1959), the logic of the economic system of production, for example, socialism (Child and Tayeb 1983), the general pattern of labor market or management strategies (Piore 1972; Friedman 1977), and the character of the state (Alford and Friedland 1985) have an important impact on the nature of organizations. The approach is good at the systemic level. Yet it fails to capture the array of variations that exist at the micro level or the role of a host of noneconomic and political factors such as culture, ideology, and religion. As we will see, an institutional approach can overcome some of these weaknesses by capturing both a systemic dimension via the concept of path-determinacy and noneconomic variables via the impact of norms.

A cultural approach sees organizational structures as products of values that are embedded in society. For example, Confucianism influenced modern Chinese business by encouraging paternalistic power structures with a high degree of loyalty on the part of subordinates and highly personalized exchanges with an emphasis on family linkages (Hu 1984; Silin 1976; Redding and Tam 1995). Cultural approaches point to the importance of socially derived norms in influencing the structure and practices of organizations. Yet they provide little explanation of how the culture becomes embedded in organizations, they understate the importance of an array of noncultural norms (for example, economic and political norms), and are too unidirectional (organizations also greatly influence norms). Moreover, the approach is often too idiosyncratic to allow careful comparative analyses, and because culture is often slow to change, this approach cannot explain organizational shifts, which tend to be much more rapid and frequent (Orru et al. 1997, 18, 19). As we will see, an institutional approach addresses many of these weaknesses.

The fifth approach is what some have termed the market approach, in which organizations adapt to the conditions of markets. Thus, new forms of enterprise arise owing to new technologies in production and transportation and the supply of new managers (Chandler 1977). New governance structures arise in response to shifting transaction costs (Williamson 1985), and as rational-strategic responses to shifting opportunities and impediments (Porter 1980). This approach, however, is far too mechanical; it treats organizations as products of instrumental rationality. Although there is little doubt that organizations devise strategies for specific purposes, the goals, means, and boundaries of acceptable behavior are never universally defined but reflect an array of social norms and generalized habits of thought.

The final way at looking at organizations is based on institutional theory.[15] (All the approaches are summarized in table 5.2.) An institutional approach sees organizations as socially constituted entities embedded within and interacting with a web of norms, rules, and beliefs. Organizations frequently undertake behavior that is acceptable to constituents in their environment. In this approach norms are indicators of acceptable behavior and guides to attaining legitimacy.

Variations in institutionalized patterns of organizational behavior challenge the universal and contingent models. Orru et al. (1997), for example, point to the differences in logic between Japanese firms and Korean and Taiwanese companies, which leads to different reactions to the factors cited in contingent theory. In a country that emphasizes interlocking ownership and communitarian principles, differences in industries have a much smaller effect on the type of organizational structures.

Political economy approaches also often point to similarities, at the abstract level, in the organizational form as a reflection of broader forces. An institutional approach begins with this recognition but goes beyond it to focus on the process by which this occurs. Dimaggio and Powell (1983), in a frequently cited article, point to a mechanism of organizational transformation that they refer to as "institutional isomorphism," or a one-to-one correspondence between a perceived object and its internal representation. Isomorphism affects the process of organizational adaptation by three mechanisms: coercive pressures, mimetic design, and normative influences. Coercive isomorphism arises from the degree of dependence on other organizations and the more generalized social expectations of an institution's operational environment. Mimetic isomorphism is a reflection of a generalized process of learning that is frequently a product of reproducing what is perceived as successful in other organizations. Normative isomorphism arises from the process of professionalization, in which standards evolve from the interaction of members of an occupation found in different organizations (accountants, lawyers, and so on). Isomorphism is a useful concept for understanding the operation of the institutional matrix. Regulations, for example, and associated incentives can play a large role in changing the nature of organizational constructs and structures via coercive isomorphism. Once the effectiveness is demonstrated, cumulative change can arise by means of mimetic isomorphism.

TABLE 5.2 **Six types of organizational theory**

Type of theory	Description	Weakness
Universal	This is a "one size fits all" idea that there is one unique efficient organizational structure irrespective of different contexts or settings.	This theory fails to account for diversity in organizations.
Contingent	Variations in technology and market size drive organizational design and change. It is especially used to study organizations in developing countries.	This approach ignores other noneconomic factors such as norms and culture that affect organizations as well.
Political economy	This branch examines the political and economic factors that shape organizations and their evolution.	This approach ignores noneconomic factors such as norms.
Culture	Organizational change and design result from values and culture embedded in a society.	The cultural approach takes culture as exogenous and does not say how it becomes embedded in society.
Market	Markets and transaction costs influence organizational design and change. In other words, organizations constitute themselves in response to market pressures to operate most efficiently.	A key assumption is rationality of organizations and actors in those organizations. In reality, actors are not necessarily rational, as experiments have shown, nor do markets operate as the theory suggests.
Institutional	This approach views organizations as entities formed by actors within a society that are shaped by forces in their social environment. These forces include norms, regulations, and cultural beliefs.	This approach fails to include capacities and incentives.

Isomorphism also assists in the creation of the shared interpretations of behavior that allow organizations to interact for the exchange and coordination of activities. From an institutional economic perspective, shared interpretations and expectations are the generalized habits of thought that are the heart of the functioning of an economic system. From the standpoint of economic development, organizations are the cauldrons of socialization. They are entities of containment linked spatially and temporally to the localized environment, and yet they have their own internal dynamic. They have the power, through new correlated patterns of human behavior, to transform the human condition. They play a special role in the institutional matrix and therefore are heavily emphasized in the sectoral strategies of the remainder of this volume. Regulations also are of great importance because, more than any other parts of the matrix, they contain the power of deliberated institutional transformation.

Regulations

Regulations constitute the legal boundaries that help set the rules of operation in economies. They are part of the legal order that defines both norms and rules and a system of sanctions that enforces them. Institutions are products and constitutive parts of the support mechanism that perpetuates regulations.

Generally speaking, regulations are instrumental in defining, initiating, supporting, and transforming institutions. How do regulations influence socially prescribed correlative behavior? Quite clearly, people respond to the guidance of the rule itself, the likely behavior of the regulatory implementing agency, the resources, abilities, and constraints influencing the capacity of individuals to respond to new regulations, and the feedback effect of the participant in the process. An additional dimension is the intrinsic motivation of individuals, groups, or organizations to change their behavior in response to a new regulation.

There are two competing perspectives in the literature. The sociological school argues that people obey regulations because they are consistent with their values.[16] This argument raises a serious question: why pass new laws if they are simply consistent with people's behavior? Moreover, the argument delimits the instrumentality of regulations to alter behavior that is simply taken as given. The second approach, inspired by neoclassical economics, sees self-interest as the motivating factor behind following a regulation or new law.[17] Because the motivation is predictable, along Coasean lines, the law should be designed to maximize social welfare in the face of such market imperfections as transaction costs. In addition to the weaknesses of neoclassical approaches discussed in chapter 3, the notion that there is some optimal regulation with a predictable outcome seems rather mechanical and inconsistent with the wide variations in behavior observed in response to the same regulations. Requiring farmers to sell rice in exchange for fertilizer might work where private markets for inputs and outputs are poorly formed, but it is likely to be less successful when relations between farmers and the market are well established.

Seidman and Seidman (1994) provide a useful framework for understanding the likely impact of laws and regulations on the behavior of what they refer to as role occupants, or individuals who are potentially affected by these laws. The mnemonic for it is ROCCIPI, or rules, opportunity, capacity, communication, interest, process, and ideology. The rules must be clearly specified in order to spur the desired behavior, including well- designed implementation procedures and adequate authority and resources to implementing agencies. Role occupants must have the opportunity and capacity to obey the regulation. The regulation must be clearly communicated. Interests of the implementation agency must be in line with the regulations. The process of formulating and implementing regulations should include role occupants. Finally, new regulations must take into account the ideology of the role occupants, in terms of their beliefs, interpretation, and ultimate impact on their behavioral response.

For example, if a new regulation was passed pertaining to the sale of tuberculin-free milk in Dar- Es Salaam (cows can be carriers of tuberculin), adequate resources would be necessary to test the milk. Sellers would need to understand the meaning of the regulation; this goal would be assisted by involving them in the formulation of the legislation. Education about the origins and pathogenesis of the disease could counter myths and ignorance about tuberculosis, leading to a greater commitment to the regulation. Testing results should be communicated to sellers before penalties are imposed. Implementing officers should be professional and free of influence by the milk industry, affording them an opportunity to confront the source. Testing should be done free of charge and should provide sellers with the capacity to obey the regulation. Protection could be provided to those willing to identify the source of milk found to contain the tuberculin.

Although the ROCCIPI framework points to a series of elements that are essential for understanding the relationship between the legal plain and its aim of transforming human behavior, the framework has some limitations. First, the authors do not present a clear theoretical evaluation of its components. Second, the components are largely taken as given and regarded as unidirectional in their effect on the ways in which laws translate into behavioral change. Third, the components are presented as independent entities, with little exploration of the nature of their linkages. The result is an overemphasis on explanation by example.

For instance, ideology is the structure of related values and beliefs that shape people's understanding of themselves and the world around them. Ideologies provide mental models of what ought to be done and how best to achieve it. They are flawed owing to cognitive limitations, inadequate information, and the inherent bias of any belief structure (Ensminger 1992). Regulations must go through the filtering process of ideology before they can influence behavior. Yet ideology is not like a coffee filter that is simply rinsed and used again. The process of interpreting the regulations can al-

ter the ideology itself, particularly if one takes into account the impact of
other components of ROCCIPI. In the example above, the involvement
of sellers of milk in drafting the legislation (process) or using education
as part of communication could begin to change the structure governing
people's beliefs about disease.

Finally, elements seem to be missing. For example, in another presentation of their theory, Seidman and Seidman argue, "Laws constitute norms.
Like all norms they purport to address behaviors" (Seidman and Seidman
1999, 258). Laws, indeed, can constitute norms. Yet there is no discussion
of how this process transpires, how laws interact with other norms, or how
norms relate to behavior. Norms, in contrast, are theoretically derived and
form an important component of the matrix presented in this chapter.
The ROCCIPI framework points to the importance of incorporating other
aspects of the matrix into our understanding of the likely impact of new
regulations on the institutional context of development.

Capacities

In an organizational context, capacities are related to the underlying capabilities of the constitutive members (individuals and other subunits) to
operate in an effective manner to achieve its goals within the confines of
its rules and purposes. More generally, changing capacity for development
should focus on enhancing or transforming the ability of actors (individuals, groups, organizations, and countries) to set and achieve their goals in
an effective, efficient, and sustainable manner relative to their accepted
norms and rules (Malik 2002, 23).

The notion that there is some unified set of technical capacities that
merely needs to be absorbed by a developing country has driven technical
assistance for decades. Western experts would simply impart their knowledge and experience to local populations on the assumption that doing so
would help spur economic development. As we saw in chapter 2, during
the 1990s technical aid from the World Bank was largely repackaged and
reconstituted as "capacity building" under the broader rubric of building
governance in developing countries.

The 2002 World Development Report shows that little has changed. A
single, universal model continues to be the central focal point of capacity-
building for governance: "Good governance includes the creation, protection, and enforcement of [a] property rights... regulatory regime that works
with the market to promote competition. And it includes the provision

of sound macroeconomic policies. Good governance also includes the absence of corruption" (99).

Since the 1991 DAC critique of technical assistance appeared, the consequence of importing systems from abroad according to some preconceived approach has led to an undermining of local capacities, because they are frequently displaced by new ones brought by technical assistance. Embedded in donor-driven capacity-building has been a series of "perverse incentives." Donors can be driven by the commercial needs of enterprises in home countries, disbursement pressures, ideology, and political and strategic targets. Recipients are eager to meet the donors' conditions in order to ensure rapid approval and large financial disbursements.

Technical exports that accompany projects are seldom vetted and are taken as part of the package. The psychology of expertise can create lasting cognitive dissonance since locals feel disdained and subservient. Projects tend to bypass normal budgetary procedures, creating parallel organizations, procedures, and structures, fragmenting management as recipients try to respond to multiple donors, creating enclaves of locals who are ideationally more attuned to donor or global discourse, and undermining local goals and aspirations (Fukuda-Parr et al. 2002, 8–10; Mkandawire 2002; Lopes and Theison 2003, 92–93). Outside expertise is not the only problem.

One of the most distressing developments in capacity-building has been the subversion of indigenous capabilities in the name of localization by the latest donor fashions. In African countries there has been a wholesale departure of scarce social scientists from universities to donor-supported consultancies.[18] In terms of the state, the capacity-building project of the adjustment period was focused on enhancing the macroeconomic abilities of the government (for example, the Ministry of Finance and the central bank) while retracting more spending-oriented ministries (Mkandawire 2002). The result was a rather distempered state that has been bloated in the service of the short-term outlook of misconceived conditionality and emasculated with regard to longer-term developmental exigencies. The approach followed the neoclassical economic logic that perceived the public sector as the major impediment to the operation of markets. Once the state retracted, private agents would react favorably to undistorted prices by producing competitive goods and services.

In this largely neoclassically inspired world, there was little concern about the abilities of the private sector. According to this vision, competitive firms, operating with complete knowledge and accessibility to all technologies, select the most efficient process, given undistorted market-generated prices of inputs and outputs. The international technology market is assumed to work perfectly, with firms purchasing the optimal technology without costs or barriers. Capital and technology should also flow freely without state interference such as protectionism. The new incentives and opportunities created by deregulation and privatization would be sufficient to induce increases in production and investment.

Ironically, the anemic behavior of the private sector was not only a product of its intrinsically weak capacity (low technological capacities, poor management and labor skills, barriers to finance, high information costs and other transaction-related costs), which did not disappear under structural adjustment; it was also hampered by the emaciation of the state.[19] In order for capacities to improve, they must be perceived not as technical phenomena but as institutional ones. Not only must new skills be acquired; they must also be usable. Just as ideology acts to filter regulations and rules, capacities influence interpretation, action, and ultimately correlative behavior. As new capacities are created they alter human cognizance and the people's conceptual constructs. They change the range or scope of what can be perceived and create new interpretations of information and contexts. Think of a violin player. Learning to play his or her instrument can be done through instruction (for example, where to place one's fingers to get a particular sound). Learning to read musical notes and to alter movement in response to a mental construct of that sound, however, generates an entirely new level of proficiency. At aggregated levels, expanded capacities increase the sphere of cooperation between organizational entities and in turn the diversity of economic and social activities. Returning to the musical metaphor, without individual player fluency in a common instrumental language, the mellifluous sounds of the coordinated orchestration of the different instrument groups would be difficult to produce.

Capacity-building in a developing country should not be seen as building a new edifice based on extrinsic drawings but as understanding existing structures so they can be retrofitted, rehabilitated, and expanded. Salient to the effort is improving the efficiency of absorptive capacities (static improvements), enabling existing capacities to absorb new types of capacities (innovative improvements), and creating capacities to generate new capacities (sustainable improvements) (Malik 2002, 31; Kifle 1998, 82). Clearly, other aspects of the matrix, such as new norms and organizations, are needed to better embed capacity. Moving away from the perverse patterns of donor rewards and sanctions toward a host of new moral and material incentives is a major component of the strategy to generate new cumulative change.

Incentives

Incentives focus on the rewards and penalties that arise from different modes of behavior. An institution-based theory of incentives is both formative and reactive. In polar cases, such as the extremes of reward and punishment, there are some shared human commonalities. For humans, proximity to a burning candle is likely to elicit general measures of avoidance, although the speed of reaction is subject to experience (some young children might burn themselves the first time). In a variety of less extreme cases, reactions to incentives are gradually formed and highly contextualized. The process involves a high degree of cognition and can be highly differentiated until the reaction becomes more institutionalized.

This can best be understood in a situation generating an institutional hiatus. Such a hiatus occurs when the existing habits of thought are no longer capable of coordinating economic activity owing to a shift in the rules or organizations or an erosion of capacities. The breakup of the former Soviet bloc countries has provided an excellent opportunity to examine how new incentives are formed. Because of the ubiquity of neoclassical economics in institutions of higher learning, even in Eastern and Central Europe, there is a paucity of economists studying transitional countries who can understand the idea of an institutional hiatus. In their universalistic world, which lays out a singular vision of human behavior,[20] the key is ensuring a correct set of signals.[21] The World Bank believed firmly in this formulation in spite of the economic collapse of the early 1990s.[22]

Partly in reaction to the unevenness of the response in transitional countries, some authors have transcended the universalism of orthodoxy to try to examine variations in the psychology of people in transitional countries. Lawson and Saltmarshe (2002) looked at the behavior of households in northern Albanian villages following the collapse of Communist Party control. Based on detailed sampling of households eight years after reforms were instituted, they examined indicators of wealth and status at the village level. Although membership in a political party moved from first place to last as a measure of status, most other characteristics, including wealth, have not changed. Poverty, in fact, was associated with honesty. As in many transitional countries, where the expediency of the reforms was of primary importance, wealth is associated with ill-gotten gains due to corruption in contacts between the state and the private sector and in privatization efforts. These perceptions represent constraints on strategies to encourage private investment and entrepreneurship. The potential reaction to incentives is not universal but is learned, contextual, and a product of historical experience.

A more nuanced view of what motivates humans to act has emerged from an empirical investigation of the psychology of incentives. Fehr and Falk (2002) provide a review of the literature to indicate that, contrary to the usual orthodox view, material penalties and rewards can lead to entirely different outcomes in the face of variations in such nonpecuniary motives as reciprocity, a wish to avoid social disapprobation, and a desire for an interesting task. For example, in multiple-player games, people greatly augment their contribution to the public good at the expense of their private gain when their practices are being observed by others. An investigation of the concept of motivation is one way of understanding the potential role of incentives in an institutional context.

One of the first economists to examine economic motivation and its relation to findings in social psychology was Z. Clark Dickinson (1919, 1922). Motive, in Dickinson's view, is the "spring to human action," or "what induces the human agent to work, to contrive, to save, to part with his goods." The role of psychology was to be restricted, however: "It is only by adding significantly to our knowledge of motives that the psychologist can help us with our own theory; and here only so far as our explanations do imply certain incentives to economic conduct—not throughout the whole of economic theory " (1919, 387). In the end, Dickinson dismisses broader views of motivation such as "the power of instincts and customs" and falls back on narrow monetary incentives: "[P]art of the supply society wants, either of work or of saving, would doubtless be forthcoming if there were less reward than at present. . . . But the output of these enthusiasts would not go far toward supplying the whole community; in order to get the full amount desired, it is necessary to pay all producers or all savers the rate which we have to pay the most reluctant one" (402–3). With this we are back to the neoclassical view of the price as the main incentive and as equal to the value of the marginal product.

In contrast, an institutional view of motivation sees price as only one possible material incentive that must be carefully viewed in the context of nonmaterial incentives and motivations. Most wages are not paid via markets but are paid within organizational entities and must be weighed against the internal and external culture. For example, paying a higher salary to the most productive workers might be an affront to people with greater seniority in a society that puts a high priority on respect based on age (such as Japan). The incentive might then lead to a loss of productivity due to disaffection among other employees.

The design of incentives to improve correlative behavior in organizations to better meet development objectives must take into account other dimensions of the institutional matrix. For example, building confidence is linked not only to psychological change via nonmaterial incentives such as recognition and praise but also to real improvements in capacities so that people feel they can achieve more. Incentives must be provided in a manner that is consistent with articulated norms and standards of behavior or the organizational culture. If the culture is hierarchical and authoritarian, then rewarding individuals for initiative and entrepreneurship will send a rather mixed message leading to inconsistent behavior. Subcultures also can arise in organizations, particularly when subgroups have a shared work or training-level experience. Professional subcultures can be particularly important where positions are technical, where there are high levels of professional norms and standards, and where there is outside enforcement via peer pressure. In some cases, regulatory or statutory standards can lead to potential penalties to professionals within organizations (for example, accredited auditors). Organizational structures and incentives should be designed to reflect and reward greater autonomy of groups concatenated by self-enforcing norms and standards. The organizational culture must also be in consonance with more general societal norms. The definition, relation to the institutional matrix, goals, and rate of change of each component of the matrix are summarized in table 5.3.

Institutional Change and Development

For development purposes, institutional transformation should focus on generating new forms of correlated behavior aimed at increasing the generalized standard of living of the population of a country. Each subcomponent of the matrix interacts with each other component and in turn has the potential to alter human behavior, which is at the center of the matrix. Institutional change implies the creation of a new set of institutions that provide the basis for a new economic and social order. The relations among the components are illustrated in figure 5.2. As discussed above, standard of living is both an input and an output of the matrix.

TABLE 5.3 **Components of the institutional matrix**

Category	Definition	Relation to the institutional matrix	Institutional goal	Rate of change
Norms	Norms are the formal and informal rules that govern what is expected, required, and accepted in a society. They are especially important in determining behavior in groups.	They affect correlated behavior by changing what is acceptable or required; likewise, correlated behavior can change norms by making acceptable what was once unacceptable.	The goal is to internalize development enhancing norms in a society.	The part of the matrix governing norms is the hardest to change.
Organizations	Organizations are conceptually recognized entities that combine groups of people who follow defined common rules and purposes. There are 6 approaches to viewing forces that affect organizational change and design.	They can affect correlated behavior by changing how people interpret behavior and by altering rules governing behavior. They can, e.g., change how an accountant feels about new accounting regulations and cause him or her to internalize them. This allows organizations to interact better than before.	The aim is to design organizations that can promote the internalization of norms and improve goals and rules by changing how actors feel about them, thus changing correlated behavior.	Organizations are difficult to change.
Regulations	Regulations are the legal boundaries that set the rules of operation in economies.	Regulations affect correlated behavior by changing what kind of behavior is legally accepted. It can affect organizations and then affect individuals or influence them directly. Correlated behavior can also affect regulations. If a practice becomes widely adopted or internalized by the populace or organizations, it may well be written into law.	The goal is to design and implement regulations that are easy to understand, are accessible, and provide consistency between formal regulations and rules of operation.	Regulations are relatively easy to change in writing. It is more difficult to design regulations that are readily internalized, especially in developing countries.
Capacities	In an organizational context, capacities are the abilities of members to operate effectively to achieve the organization's goal within its rules and purposes.	Capacities affect correlated behavior by determining the scope of behavior. In other words, the greater the capacities, the greater the possible interactions and range of activities between individuals or organizations.	What is needed in development is to understand existing capacities and then retrofit or change them to meet new developmental goals.	Capacities are rather difficult to change because it takes time to build up capacity (e.g., training).
Incentives	Incentives are the rewards and penalties that arise from different modes of behavior. They can be material or nonmaterial in nature and are often highly contextualized. When considering incentives, one must consider goals and values, self-evaluation, and cognitive anticipation.	Incentives affect correlated behavior by motivating individuals or organizations to act differently. Incentives also rely on other parts of the matrix; e.g., sufficient capacity is needed to enforce incentives, and it must have the regulations to back it up. Capacities apply to organizations and can change organizational behavior and design and thus can feed back to norms.	Incentives need to be designed to be consistent with and complement capacities and regulations in order to help effect internalization of new habits of thought. These in turn alter correlated behavior.	Incentives can change rather quickly when enacted by law or policy change. The effects of incentives, particularly nonpecuniary ones, can be quite slow since there are barriers to understanding new signals.

How is change to come about? Myrdal emphasized economic planning that arose from two propositions. He was "rationalist in approach and interventionist in conclusions" (1968, 2:709). First, human agency is at the heart of institutions, which reflect the human thought process. Like institutions in general, planning is a product of reflection, formulation, and election. "The strategy for these policies would emerge as a set of practical inferences from rational analysis of the facts in country's situation and the positing of certain development goals" (2:710).

The second proposition is recognition of the centrality of the state in the transformation and that "state intervention . . . is needed to bring about economic development" (Myrdal 1968, 2:15). The remainder of this volume, without invoking an overreaching conceptualization of planning, builds on these two basic notions concerning human thought and state transformation.

New patterns of correlated behavior that underlie development must be conceptualized before they can emerge. Although these new patterns can originate with an individual or a group of individuals, any new structure will arise from some conjoint (often legal or legislative) mechanism. One can conceptualize three types of institutional change: path-independent, path-dependent, and path-determinant. Path-independent change arises deductively from a logical set of propositions and is free of any locally generated pattern of culture, ideation, or behavioral regularity. Inspired by the neoclassical vision, the approach has dominated reform in the developing and transitional world in recent decades.

In contrast, the path-dependent approach has minimal scope for discretion and is largely informed by existing arrangements. According this view, there is room for only moderate change that largely reflects prior correlations. New approaches that are introduced are largely ceremonial. The status quo defines any adjustment. Think of structural adjustment in Zaire in the 1980s under the dictator Mobutu. Supporters of path-dependency would suggest that institutional reform was not possible because the state was too deeply embedded in the system of personalized rule.[23]

Path-determinant change implies significant discretionary intervention, wherein design is fairly open but is also linked to the past. New insights are offered, and doubts about the existing pattern of circular causation are raised. Although the ideas might appear to be path-independent, they are well grounded and aim to be self-sustaining and self-correcting. New ideas arise from a causal understanding of historical patterns and rela-

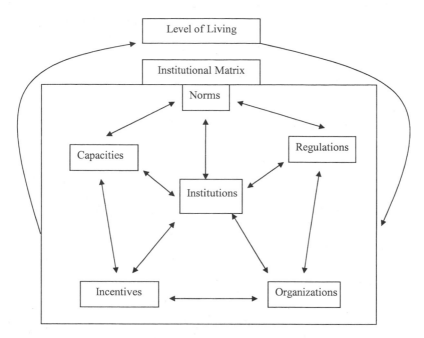

FIGURE 5.2. The institutional matrix: Circular causation and development

tionships with ideational influences. Yet the approach is not contained by the past but builds on and is an instrument of transformation. The path-determinant approach is aimed at not only understanding what is transpiring but what could transpire. Cognition is both expansive and continuous (Tool 1995). This is the basis of the circular causation and cumulative change that leads to the transformation of the institutional matrix. Institutions transform and are transformed by the elements of the matrix in a continuous fashion. This approach is used in the remainder of this volume.

I apply the institutional matrix to the transformation of the state, to health, and to the financial sector, with a focus on analyzing the existing institutional matrix in each sector and developing clear strategies for a homologous and coordinated process of transformation. The aim is not to generate new empirical studies but to interpret existing studies in new ways using inductive reasoning (from facts to principles), deductive reasoning (from the general principles to the particular situations), and abductive reasoning (the generation of hypotheses from logical processes for unforeseen evidence) (Kilpinen 1998). In the latter case, to stimulate new ways of examining the challenges of development, it might be necessary to posit logical arguments, or what Myrdal called "conjectural reasoning."[24]

Conclusions

This chapter began with an examination of the methodology and constructs of Gunnar Myrdal. Among other things, Myrdal reminds us that an institutional approach to development is not a grand singular theory of transformation, but an analytical framework that needs to generate new constructs and theories arising from a contextualized understanding of development. The institutional matrix approach determines not the specific content of factors to be studied but rather the scope of analysis.

The meaning of institutions and the relations among habits, rules, and behavior were carefully explored. The five dimensions of the institutional matrix were presented along with discussion of how they relate to changing institutions to encourage development. Norms generally provide behavioral guides and are most effective when they are internalized.

Organizations are entities that combine groups of people with common rules and purposes. Organizational theory encompasses the universal, contingent, culture, market political economy, and institutional approaches to understanding organizations. The first five provide insights but reveal weaknesses that are largely overcome by an institutional approach. The last views organizations as vessels of containment linked spatially and temporally to the localized environment, yet having their own internal dynamic. They have the power, via new correlated patterns of human behavior, to transform the human condition. From the standpoint of economic development, organizations are the cauldrons of socialization.

Regulations, more than any other parts of the matrix, contain the power of deliberated institutional transformation. Regulations constitute the legal boundaries that help set the rules of operation in economies. They form part of the legal order that defines norms and rules and represent a system of sanctions that enforces them. Institutions are products of and constitutive parts of the support mechanism that perpetuates legal order.

Capacity is the ability of actors (individuals, groups, organizations, and even countries) to set and achieve their goals in an effective, efficient, and sustainable manner relative to their accepted norms and rules. For capacities to improve, they must be perceived not as technical but as institutional phenomena. Capacities influence interpretation, action, and, ultimately, correlative behavior. As new capacities are created they alter human cognizance and the conceptual constructs of people. They change the range or scope of what can be perceived and create new interpretations of information and contexts. At the aggregate level, expanded capacities increase the linkages between organizational entities and in turn the diversity of economic and social activities at the heart of development.

An institutional approach recognizes that a variety of incentives exist and that the response to incentives is formed gradually and is highly contextualized, unlike the universalities of the *Homo economicus* of neoclassical economics. The response involves a high degree of cognition and can be highly differentiated until the reaction becomes more institutionalized.

. In the remainder of this volume I apply the matrix to state transformation, health, finance, and development. In each application of the matrix, after critically assessing the theory and policy underlying the World Bank agenda, I attempt to generate an alternative framework and policies. The aim is to both overcome the weaknesses of the Bank's approach and to deal with the challenges of transforming institutions for development in each sector.

CHAPTER SIX

State Formation as an Institutional Phenomenon

If the pattern of individual preferences was such as to produce economic growth, we would have it now. The present situation in underdeveloped countries is the result of somebody's decision. And no government can launch economic growth where it does not exist without "interfering in the market" in a sense quite different from the intervention involved in the nostrums of welfare economics.—B. H. Higgins, 1959

Reasons for state intervention . . . are present in any economy, but they are of course, much more important in an underdeveloped economy bent on rapid economic development. To the list must be added: the relative lack of entrepreneurial talent and training in the private sector; the disinclination of most of those who are wealthy to risk their funds in productive investment and their preferences for speculation, quick profit and conspicuous consumption and investment; and finally the tendency in underdeveloped countries for any large-scale enterprises to acquire an extraordinary degree of monopoly or oligopoly.— Gunnar Myrdal, 1968

Countries are "soft states" both in that policies decided on are not enforced, if they are enacted at all, and in that the authorities, even when framing policies, are reluctant to place obligations on people. . . . The problem . . . is how to induce people to participate and cooperate in remedying all the less satisfactory conditions that make a country underdeveloped. —Gunnar Myrdal, 1968

Introduction: From Planning to Anti-Planning

As with other elements of the Bank's development strategy, the perceived role of the state in shaping and possibly reversing economic underdevelopment was subject to theoretical shifts within the economics profession. For much of the postwar period through the end of the 1960s, the dominant view was that states were facilitators of growth and economic transformation. Thus, to reverse underdevelopment, the central task was seen to be development planning, which aimed at coordinating the effort of states to intervene in the market economy. At this time, largely because of the memory of the Great Depression, it was believed that the market system could not guarantee a social optimum. So the need for planning and state intervention was inversely related to the level of development, because "the more difficult . . . the problems confronting development, the less adequate will be a policy of nonintervention, and the greater will be the need for planning" (Griffin and Enos 1970, 21). Hagen (1963) also pointed to planning as an "integrating force drawing the people of the country toward national unity as they are drawn into the development efforts" (18).

By the 1970s, a series of writers including Waterston (1972), Seers (1972), Mehmet (1978), Roemer (1976), and Leys (1969) began to question the conventional view of planning. These authors pointed to methodological shortcomings; the plans used techniques from developed countries that misrepresented Third World conditions and required data that frequently were unavailable. Development plans were often rendered irrelevant by political instability and the shifting vagaries of the global economy, which vitiated the plans' underlying assumptions. The shortage of foreign exchange also left countries overly reliant on foreign aid. Projects were seldom coordinated and often reflected the priorities of donors rather than development needs. Planning typically was undertaken by a handful of foreign experts in a foreign language, usually English, thus precluding the possibility of broader citizen participation at any stage of its development. The objectives were narrowly focused on growth in aggregate targets, such as the expansion of GNP, per capita income, and savings levels, with little or no mention of social objectives associated with broader views of development.

There were two reactions to these criticisms. One was to consider ways to improve planning by broadening its goals to include basic needs and equity, decentralizing planning by shifting it to the regional and local levels—in an attempt to make it more participatory—and focusing on short-term policies and budgeting instead of formal planning in line with long-term planning goals. This approach was, for the most part, consistent with the expanding agenda of the Bank in the 1970s, during Robert McNamara's tenure. The approach was also a focal point of Gunnar Myrdal's recommendations for improving planning in Asian countries.[1]

The second reaction was to use the criticisms as an excuse to entirely reject development planning in favor of a neoclassically inspired call for the retraction of state intervention in the economy. This approach became important for theoretically justifying the neoliberal agenda, especially with the arrival of one of its most ardent supporters, Anne Krueger, as the Bank's chief economist in 1982. This chapter investigates the way in which the Bank began to reconceptualize the nature and role of states and push a neoclassical vision of the part they play in development. The main focus is on civil service reform, an important element of the World Bank agenda after 1980. Moreover, when considering the major development success stories of our time, it is quite clear that consistency in the quality and capacities of the civil service was a key factor (Stein 1995a). Other elements of state-transforming policies including governance, legal reform, and privatization are covered in previous chapters.

I also attempt to generate a vision of state formation as an agent of development, in opposition to the views underlying neoliberal reforms. I argue, following Myrdal and Higgins (as quoted in the epigraphs) and contrary to the position of the World Bank, that conditions in developing countries justify greater—not less—state responsibility for development. The approach is not intended to justify a certain quantity of intervention, nor a particular size for states, but rather is aimed at transforming states to endow them with the ability to set in motion a cumulative process of development. Following the framework developed in chapter 5, I focus on conceptualizing the state as an institutional construct and on altering the various components of the institutional matrix related to state formation.

Background of WDR 1983: From "Managing Development" to "Management in Development"

In the early 1980s, the Bank's commitment to structural adjustment led it to rely heavily on neoclassical economists in order to build the case for these neoliberal policies. The conservative economist Bela Balassa, who had consulted for the Bank since 1968, played an increasingly central role in providing intellectual support for the Bank's new agenda. The analysis contained in WDR 1981, for instance, is based almost exclusively on Balassa's series of World Bank working papers presenting very orthodox interpretations of how countries best adjusted to the economic shocks of the 1970s. The WDR is highly critical of any country that would not undertake orthodox macro-level stabilization adjustments in response to a worsening external situation.[2]

Still, the 1981 report was overseen by chief economist Hollis Chenery and therefore continued to reflect to a degree the priorities of the McNamara-Chenery years. For example, its final chapter, titled "Human Development: A Continuing Imperative," is largely a warning against relying exclusively on economic growth as a means for resolving poverty. The report also warns against cutbacks in government spending on social needs, arguing that they could have disastrous effects. With the arrival of Anne Krueger in 1982, these concerns disappeared from the Bank.[3]

The first complete WDR produced during Krueger's tenure (World Bank 1983b) represented an unwavering commitment to the neoliberal agenda and its associated focus on state retraction and state minimalism. Krueger, according to the principal author, Pierre Landell-Mills, "went over drafts of the report line by line" and provided continual feedback concerning the content. Her main input, according to Landell-Mills, dealt with what should be included in the report, not what should be excluded. Most important, she wanted to send a clear message about "why the state was not needed" in developing countries. The anti-statist content of the report also reflected the "growing sentiment in the Bank at the time"[4] that state-centered strategies and planning had failed.

The topic of the report, according to Landell-Mills, was based on the recommendation of the 1978 Wright Task Force on public administration.[5] The preceding series of background papers and the WDR were to be titled "Managing Development." Krueger, however, considered the subject matter to be the equivalent of "teaching the state to kill efficiently" and demanded that the title be changed to "Management in Development."[6] Although the working papers are fairly diverse on a theoretical level (in part a reflection of their pre-Krueger origin), the report itself selected only the elements of the papers that would emphasize the static inefficiencies created by past policies owing to corruption, price distortions, rent-seeking, poor planning, and badly run state enterprises. The report also presented new strategies intended to curtail the functions and size of the civil service, reform and privatize parastatals (state-owned companies), decentralize government, and introduce new sources of financing public goods such as user fees.

From Distortions and Growth to Getting the Prices Right: Toward a Critique

Perhaps the most critical background paper was the one titled "Price Distortions and Growth in Developing Countries" by Ramgopal Agarwala (1983), which provided much of the empirical and theoretical justification for the agenda of the 1980s.[7]

Agarwala was an econometrician who came to the Bank in 1971 to work in the Comparative Analysis and Projections unit. He had worked on econometric models of the Indian, British, and Canadian economies before arriving at the Bank, where he developed models for Korea and Kenya. He was quite friendly with and had a high regard on both a personal and a professional level for some of the major contributors to the neoclassical counterrevolution against development economics, including Arthur D. Little and Bela Balassa. Like them, he had become increasingly skeptical of the predictive power of the models and their role in planning and had developed strong sentiments about the centrality of the role of prices in economies. For Anne Krueger, Agarwala instantly became the "blue-eyed wonder" who would convey the exact message she wanted in her first WDR. Other members of the WDR team felt that he had "saved" their effort with his paper.[8] Given the enormous praise lavished on Agarwala's work, as well as its centrality to the Bank's new agenda, it is worth reviewing the details of this important background paper.

Agarwala identifies four standard market failures, including monopolies, externalities, public goods, and income distribution, but argues that they are "not sufficient ground for government intervention." His outright dismissal of state intervention leads him to a question at the heart of the epistemology of structural adjustment: "Are market failures more damaging than government failures?" His axiomatic answer is embodied in a quotation from Frank Hahn (1982): "In the early stages of a market economy, most people are concerned with eminently reproducible necessities of life. The invisible hand works in harmony with expectations and leads to the growth in the output of goods which people desire" (quoted in Agarwala 1983, 3). According to Agarwala, increasing returns, externalities, and the need for public goods are more important to technologically advanced economies. Agarwala's proposition seems rather counterintuitive because it would seem that markets are less well formed in poorer countries and have greater levels of market failure, which is one of the reasons why these economies have not developed. To Agarwala, "patterns of growth depend on relative prices" (Agarwala 1983, 4), and disruptions in growth must be due to distortions in the price signals.

According to Agarwala, distortions occur when the prices of goods and services do not reflect their scarcity value.[9] Although distortions can have their origins in the private sector, he argues that "in most instances, however, government—sometimes deliberately, sometimes inadvertently—introduces price distortions in pursuit of some social or economic objective" (Agarwala 1983, 7). A great deal of attention is thus given to the measurement of price distortions. Yet Agarwala's method relies on an array of crude and subjective measures to come up with proxies of price distortions. In a sample of thirty-one countries, he examines foreign exchange, labor, capital, manufactured goods, agricultural goods, public utilities, and inflation levels. He then classifies countries into categories according to level of distortion, high, medium, and low, depending on their deviation from some "nondistortionary level."

The economic meanings of this level, as well as the significance and determination of the degree of deviation, are certainly subject to question. In the case of labor markets, for instance, instead of examining wage growth relative to productivity, Agarwala looks at real wage growth in manufacturing against per capita incomes adjusted for external terms of trade in the 1970s.[10] To this he adds subjective impressions about government intervention and carries forward effects of rapid increases in wages from the 1960s. He concludes that labor market distortions explain 10 percent of the variance of growth. The explanation is circular: if, by definition, distortions occur when GNP per capita is lower relative to wages, then lower growth will obviously be associated with these distortions.

Agarwala's other measures for distortion do not offer much improvement. The rate of return on power utilities is taken as the measure of distortions of infrastructural services, with high distortions associated with returns of less than 4 percent and low returns with those greater than 8 percent. He assumes that the weaker rates of return reflect administrative intervention that leads to excess demand, rationing, and inefficiencies. By failing to consider a host of other possibilities such as low economic growth, he neglects to see that a low return may be the result of foreign exchange, spare parts shortages, or revenue collection problems caused by high transaction costs and declining incomes. If that were the case, the direction of causation would be reversed: weak growth would lead to low returns, not vice-versa.

Despite the questionable methodology used to reach its conclusions, Agarwala's paper became a crucial dimension of WDR 1983.[11] It was used as the core empirical justification for the reconfiguration of the structure, functions, and policy of the state. After discussing the relation between distortions and growth in chapter 6, WDR 1983 links the new functions of the state to the promised benefits: "On average those countries where adjustment led to low price distortions have managed a significantly better growth performance . . . than have those with high distortions. . . . The elements of these programs usually include a lower exchange rate, more export incentives, less industrial protection, tighter monetary policy, higher real interest rates less direction of credit, higher energy prices, and smaller consumer subsidies. In addition, programs usually try to restrain public sector spending and increase the scope for the private sector and market forces" (World Bank 1983b, 65). Other background papers were interesting not because of their influence on WDR 1983 but rather because of the way their recommendations were ignored in writing the report.

Civil Service Reform and WDR 1983

A core component of the neoliberal agenda pointed to the exigencies of civil service reform. The background paper by Ozgediz (1983) provides a complex understanding of the challenges of improving the performance of public sectors. His analysis draws on sociology, social psychology, and organizational theory and includes warnings against overgeneralization and the imposition of models from one cultural setting on another. While reviewing empirical evidence about oversized bureaucracies, excessive growth rates, and administrative overstaffing, Ozgediz concludes, "The evidence reviewed above does not provide clear-cut support for any of the three common views about the public service in developing countries. Public service employment is not relatively bigger in developing countries compared with industrialized countries. . . . [I]t cannot be stated categorically that the growth of public service employment in developing countries is unproductive. . . . Finally, there does not seem to be too much 'fat' in administration in developing countries when the composition of public service employment in developed countries is used as a yardstick" (4).

The 1983 World Development Report, of course, dissects this very nuanced presentation and extracts only the elements that can be used to support its neoclassical claims. It completely ignores the paper's call for greater recognition of the complexity of the civil service's role in developing countries. Indeed, the report twists Ozgediz's arguments to ensure compliance with Bank theories inspired by neoclassicism. For instance, the report downplays Ozgediz's concern that the civil service is so small compared the rest of the population by switching the comparison of the civil service's size to that of the nonagricultural population alone: "A different picture emerges when agriculture is excluded. In a sample of 28 developing countries, an average of 27 percent of salaried jobs in the non-agricultural sectors were in government, compared with 20 percent in industrial countries" (World Bank 1983b, 102).

Ignoring the central conclusion of the background paper—that there was no evidence that the civil service was unproductive—WDR 1983 argues that "overstaffing imposes a financial burden on the state, undermines morale, and obstructs efficient management" (World Bank 1983b, 103). Similarly, although the background paper emphasizes the problematic social dislocation caused by firing staff and the need to use early retirement or transfers, the WDR makes no mention of it.

Both WDR 1983 and the background paper point to shortages of highly skilled individuals in the civil service caused by the flight of civil servants to the private sector. But though Ozgediz (1983, 24–25) is concerned that civil service problems are "compounded" by this flight, the report's main worry is "balanc[ing] the needs of the public and private sector" since "highly successful government recruitment may risk choking off the supply of skills to the private sector" (World Bank 1983b, 106).

Ozgediz (1983) challenges the thesis that all Western management practices are universally applicable, emphasizing instead that "each model is a byproduct of the history and tradition of administration in a given society" and that "an indigenously established system may be more appropriate for a developing country" (50, 66). Yet WDR 1983 barely references these strong conclusions, and even then it waters them down in a brief closing note on the role of culture. The report argues that transferring "qualitative management practices" is problematic owing to cultural differences and therefore favors quantitative ones (World Bank 1983b, 114). That "quantitative" management practices exist in reality or that such practices would be automatically acultural is simply assumed without forethought.

"Reorienting Government," Decentralization, Corruption, and WDR 1983

Perhaps the epitome of the neoclassical reconceptualization of the state is contained in chapter 11 of WDR 1983, titled "Reorienting Government." This chapter focuses primarily on corruption and argues that there is a need for greater decentralization. The arguments are derived from a working paper by Gould and Amaro-Reyes (1983) that examines five basic sources: first, the functional role of government in the economy and the opportunities for rent-seeking à la Anne Krueger (Krueger 1974); second, the nature of the political system (this factor drawing heavily on Myrdal's view of "soft states" that do not sufficiently promote the public interest); third, the social and economic conditions (for example, poverty, inequality, and patronage systems) that encourage corruption; fourth, cultural factors such as traditional norms that might erode professional standards; and finally, the organizational structure of the state, including rigid decision-making structures that encourage the use of bribes. The authors insist that "none by itself is a sufficient condition for corruption to take place" (16).

In a purely Kruger-like interpretation, WDR 1983 ignores issues of endemic poverty and inequality, the nature of the political system, and the cultural context, choosing instead to focus on administrative and functional causes of corruption. The key to reducing corruption, the report argues, is not an anticorruption campaign, but "designing interventions so as to minimize the opportunities or incentives for corruption . . . by avoiding administratively created scarcities . . . ; by reducing controls on international trade and payments; and by improving the incentives and accountability of officials in areas where regulations or administrative discretion remain" (World Bank 1983b, 116). The report outlines several strategies for curtailing corruption. First, management should be made more efficient by "rationalization," which means that government interventions in markets should be minimized in order to "improve their economic performance"; and rationalization should lead to managerial benefits, "since officials would have fewer economic instruments to administer" (117). Second, the state can be better coordinated for budgeting to meet adjustment targets; it must, however, guard against planning and "over-centralization" (120). Finally, the state can be "economized" by decentralizing government activities.

The emphasis on decentralization has been ubiquitous in World Bank programs since the early 1980s. The report and its supporting background paper by Cochrane explain this infatuation. Cochrane (1983) focuses on significant "comparative advantages" over central government, including increasing participation, better allocation of services to local populations, better collection of revenue including user fees, and encouragement of a higher overall level of democracy. World Development Report 1983 takes it one step further. Where there are limits to the state transfer of ownership to the private sector, decentralization can be a viable alternative: "Decentralization should . . . be seen as part of a broader market-surrogate strategy, designed to make public enterprises and bureaucracies more responsive . . . to their clientele and to achieve a closer connection between inputs and outputs" (123). A convenient exception to this rule is suggested, however: "[g]overnments . . . need greater central control over some activities—as they do today over budgets and foreign debt" (123). In other words, important functions such as repaying loans and meeting Bank conditionality should remain centralized.

The World Bank's preoccupation with decentralization is hardly surprising. In the market fetishistic world of neoclassical economists, the real appeal of decentralization is that it seems market-like and therefore will ipso facto act with greater efficiency than will central governments. Services can, so to speak, be best provided by local government sellers to be purchased by local buyers; in other words, the government creates a market-like environment by charging user fees, which mimic prices as in a market: "They should be employed more often by local authorities, since those who consume services and have the necessary resources are, in principle, those who should pay" (Cochrane 1983, 13). The focus on user fees ignores what was once a staple of introductory economics classes: that there is no efficient way of pricing public goods and that charging fees is likely to exclude large elements of the population from gaining the benefits of those goods. This is precisely what happened in education and health care, with dire welfare consequences to poorer segments of the population, as discussed in chapter 8. Although WDR 1983 and its associated background papers were important for rethinking the role of states, the literature known as new public management (NPM) theory also played a role.

NPM, World Bank Policy, and State Formation in Practice

New public management has its theoretical origins in public choice theory. It was born of the conservative regimes of Thatcher's Britain and the right-wing governments of New Zealand and Australia in the early 1980s. Like the neoliberal agenda embodied by structural adjustment, NPM emphasized decentralization, contracting out goods and services, imposing user charges for government services, introducing performance measurement, separating politics from administration, and rationalizing administrative structures.

In line with public choice theory and its neoclassical economic roots, NPM conceptualizes the state as an aggregate of individuals pursuing their utility-maximizing interests without the discipline of the market. The theory emphasizes the need to create a polycentric system where individuals can make the best decisions based on market-simulating signals (user fees), where the provision and production of services are separated via contracting, and where governments can be closer to the consumers of products through decentralization (Gruening 2001). Despite the problematic nature of these arguments and papers, they had a significant impact on the formation of the World Bank's agenda.

World Development Report 1983, its associated background papers, and NPM secured the rationale for transforming the state in the neoclassical image. During the first decade of adjustment, two general types of state reforms were implemented. The first focused on building up the state's organizational and procedural capacities in order to enable it to implement structural adjustment policies. The second was linked to the reforms focused on the state itself, rather than as a means of accommodating other reforms.[12] The first category signified changes in support of macroeconomic and financial management, nonfinancial sectoral reform, and trade and policy administration reform; the second addressed the perceived ills of public administration by advocating retrenchment of the state. In total, the efforts were supported by forty-three technical assistance loans as well as components of all fifty-nine of the structural adjustment loans granted between 1979 and June 1988 (Nunberg 1990, 3).

Likewise, all countries that received SALs during that period were granted assistance only on condition that they reform the state in the neoclassical image. Four subgroups of loans were granted with that aim. The first subgroup involved public sector investment program management, which attempted to more carefully control outlays in order to curtail overall state spending. To ensure that budget targets were met, new monitoring units were set up within Ministries of Finance. In the case of Ghana, the new unit was actually housed inside the World Bank resident mission during the early phases of the first structural adjustment credit (Nunberg

1990, 4), demonstrating the Bank's preeminent influence in budgetary matters. This brought a whole new dimension to the idea of Bank-sponsored capacity- building projects.

The second type of loan was based on strengthening economic policy-making bodies that would be responsible for improving macroeconomic control. For example, in Côte D'Ivoire, the Comité de Suivi et Reflexion was organized to monitor progress toward SAL targets and to report regularly to the Bank team. The third kind of loan was based on new debt management systems, which monitored and controlled debt levels and coordinated payments with budgeting efforts. The final type of loan aimed at improving the efficiency of tax administrations by simplifying procedures and introducing ways to lower "distortionary" taxes. Togo, for example, was provided loans to develop a new tax code.

Reforms apart from those aimed at macroeconomic management capacities focused on new state structures for liberalizing prices and reorganizing state entities involved with sectoral policies. All in all, there were state reform components in fifty-six structural adjustment loans until June 1988. These components emphasized transforming the government bodies that affected agriculture, industry, and trade. In agriculture, the focus was on strengthening capacities to liberalize pricing, reduce input subsidies, and retract the role of the state in marketing. In Jamaica, for example, major commodity boards were divested of all nonmarketing functions, and private-sector external marketing was promoted. In industry, the focus was on streamlining bureaucratic procedures and retracting industrial regulatory capacities. In Thailand, for instance, reforms were supposed to simplify investment approval criteria to reduce discretionary intervention. Finally, in trade, a high priority was placed on liberalization policies. The key was to abolish quantitative restrictions and to lower tariffs while adjusting exchange rates and establishing a neutral incentive structure (for example, removing other barriers such as export taxes) for importing and exporting. In Côte d'Ivoire, for example, new streamlining procedures were developed for the trade administration, and in Gabon and Senegal, new tariff codes were drafted.

The final area of state-based reform initiatives was directed at the civil service. Between 1981 and February 1987, civil service reform was a part of forty-five Bank lending operations in twenty-four countries throughout the developing world. The goals were to reduce "excessive public sector wage bills" and "surplus public servants" while dealing with the erosion of public service salaries[13] and the compression of wages between the higher and lower grades of the civil service. The Bank, along with the IMF, overwhelmingly focused on the first two areas. Between 1981 and March 1987, sixteen countries with actual or proposed Bank support for civil service reform arrangements were diagnosed with excessive wage bills. In the Bank's view, a total of nineteen countries needed to reduce their surplus of civil servants. In contrast, only six programs were aimed at wage erosion, and six more were aimed at wage compression (Nunberg 1988).

Nunberg (1988) provides a systematic review of Bank efforts between 1981 and 1987 in this area. What is quite apparent from her depiction is the rather ill-conceived and often contradictory nature of the entire enterprise, including the obvious conflict between raising wages and reducing the wage bill. Guyana was diagnosed with both an excessive wage bill and a surplus of civil servants. In 1981–82, there was a dramatic retrenchment of public employees: thirteen thousand workers—a full 24 percent of the public service—were deemed redundant. Their severance payments actually led to an increase in the wage bill, however, and therefore contributed to a large increase in government loans and debt servicing (9). Such large layoffs were not unusual. In Guinea, the civil service was cut by nearly forty thousand employees. The net impact was a 21 percent reduction in the total between 1985 and 1989 (Das 1998). Despite the huge number of layoffs, Nunberg makes it quite clear that the Bank never "assessed the capacity of specific sectors to take on surplus civil servants, or the mechanisms whereby such redeployment could take place" (Nunberg 1988, 21). In the Central African Republic the decline in the purchasing power of public employees had a dramatic impact on the economy of the capital between 1982 and 1985 (6).

One would think that data about the number and functions of employees would be vital to any serious reform effort, particularly one aimed at retracting the state to reduce perceived distortions in markets. Yet only 18 percent of all civil service reform loans included census or functional surveys (Nunberg 1998, 33). In a rather understated comment, Nunberg admits that "poor or inaccessible information has sometimes forced Bank staff to make judgments that are more instinctual than empirical" (22). The IMF's approaches to civil service reform were little better. According to Nunberg, "the IMF . . . appears generally to have prescribed wholesale wage reduction without significant attention to the detailed mechanism by which this reduction might take place" (5).

Partly in reaction to critiques such as Nunberg's, the IMF began to expand civil service reform beyond what it termed "first generation" or "quantitative adjustments" aimed at macrostabilization. While not abandoning its initial set of priorities, the new focus was a "second generation" of changes intended to raise the "quality" of the remaining civil service to "improve efficiency and boost economic growth" (Lienert and Modi 1997, 9). The strategies included more emphasis on performance criteria, restructuring remuneration to minimize the loss of skilled staff, ensuring rewards based on merit, and reassessing the mix between wage and nonwage spending. In practice, the expanded focus was intended to increase the wages of selected groups, limit automatic increments by replacing them with merit increases and performance-related promotions, reverse wage decompression, and improve civil service management with better record-keeping, training to upgrade skills, and improved staff audits (Lienert and Modi 1997).

Although most of these measures were not terribly new, they nevertheless represented a shift in emphasis for the IMF; it was beginning to intentionally align itself with the Bank agenda. Yet the Bank was having troubles of its own; as its Operations Evaluation Department (OED) judged, the strategies it had employed throughout the 1980s had been anything but successful.

The OED's evaluations of individual civil service reform projects completed between 1987 and 1998 indicated an unsatisfactory rating of 38 percent (Nunberg 1999). Most of the projects, however, belonged to adjustment packages and were separately evaluated. The OED's first systematic comparative evaluation of completed and ongoing civil service initiatives—including those disaggregated from larger programs—indicated far worse performance.[14] The review covered 123 loans in thirty-two countries, as well as components of sector loans from eleven countries from the period 1980–97. The reviews examined three areas: downsizing, which focused on fiscal discipline; capacity-building, which focused on operational efficiency; and reforming of institutions, which focused on policymaking abilities and improving governance.

Even on the basis of the rather narrow criteria of whether the civil service reform projects met their stated objectives, only 33 percent of completed and 38 percent of ongoing projects were deemed satisfactory. Projects that had attempted to reform institutions were the least effective; only 22 percent of completed projects and 19 percent of ongoing interventions were given satisfactory ratings. The success rates for downsizing were only 46 percent for completed projects and 31 percent for ongoing projects, and the rates were 30 percent and 47 percent, respectively, for capacity-building. The report also expands this rather limited choice of evaluation options, which it refers to as a "low threshold" (Operations Evaluation Department 1999, 3), to deal with a more qualitative understanding of the relevance and efficacy of the projects.

Relevance relates to the relation between policy content (in the three areas discussed), country context (macroeconomic performance, labor market trends, and institutional endowment), and upstream instruments and processes, which arise from policy dialogue and diagnostic assessments of the state of the civil services. Efficacy focuses on policy content, country context, and downstream factors associated with supervision, monitoring, and evaluation.

According to the OED report, relevance was greatly affected by the policy environment, which focused on the "fiscal imperatives of adjustment," the "compelling examples of NPM (New Public Management) in the OECD," and "conceptual advances in NIE, public choice and managerial economics" (Operations Evaluation Department 1999, 15). This is a rather clear statement of the intellectual roots of civil service reform and all of its associated theoretical baggage, which helps explain the failure of the approach.

Moreover, there were large problems in the upstream process. The OED review found a very high number of interventions that were not based on any diagnosis. Overall, 40 percent of interventions supported by adjustment lending were considered to be "shots in the dark" (Operations Evaluation Department 1999, 16). Part of the problem was the usage of a "blueprint" approach. "There was little in the CSR strategy for either Eastern and Central Asia or Latin America and the Caribbean that distinguished it from the approach used in Africa" (19).

Efficacy was little better. Downsizing and capacity-building frequently did not produce permanent reductions in the size of the civil service, nor did they reveal any meaningful commitment to new formal rules. The main reason for this failure was the continued focus on a technocratic approach as a unilateral policy. Interventions were aimed at implementing discrete improvements such as wage bills and bureaucratic skills. What was needed instead, in their view, was a systems approach, one which conceptualizes the bureaucracy as a dynamic set of principle-agent relationships between managers and civil servants, on one hand, and senior bureaucrats and politicians, on the other. Reflecting the authorship of pro-

NIE individuals like Robert Picciotto and Brian Levy, the report stated that the way forward was to draw on the insights of "modern" institutional economics to deal with the underlying information and incentive problems: "Even in the 1990s, the Bank only sparingly assessed checks and balances on the interaction between bureaucrats and their principles–that is politicians and citizens." Moreover, "P-A [principal-agent] problems were often rooted in information asymmetries because managers lacked accurate information about the performance of civil servants" (Operations Evaluation Department 1999, 7). Yet, they argued, the Bank continued to rely on a technocratic approach, which, in their view, limited the effectiveness and ownership of reforms. The "relevance and ownership of reforms was . . . weakened by a technocratic approach that failed to mainstream institutional analysis and develop a coherent framework for intervening in administrative systems." Once again NIE was used not to rethink policies but rather to buttress the same orthodoxies. The Bank concluded the report by stating its commitment to a greater adherence to the NPM strategies: "The development community urgently requires an empirical basis for supporting NPM reforms. . . . The Bank should help pilot comprehensive NPM reforms in three to five countries that are committed to developing results-based civil services" (26).

The continued commitment to a neoliberal core theory and its associated vision of the state has precluded the possibility of a state-led strategy of growth and development that could raise the standard of living in developing countries. The remainder of this chapter lays out a different vision of state transformation based on the institutional matrix developed in chapter 5.

The State and the Institutional Matrix

In 1968 Myrdal made a cogent case for state-led development. He reasoned that underdevelopment arises from a series of noneconomic conditions that not only are regarded as undesirable in themselves but also are believed to act as "obstacles and inhibitions to economic development" (Myrdal 1968, 2:710–11). These conditions include poor nutrition, insufficient housing, bad health, lack of education, rigid social stratification, lack of citizen participation, and poorly performing organizations. In a world where causation is circular and cumulative, development is contingent on both transforming these areas and in turn being transformed by them.

The state-led approach is promoted in order to address certain conditions of underdevelopment. These include a lack of entrepreneurial talent and training in the private sector, a preference among the wealthy for quick, speculative profit and conspicuous consumption rather than productive investment, and the high degree of monopoly among large-scale private enterprise in developing countries (2:717–18). For Myrdal, the main goal was to establish a planning system that could deal with these endemic weaknesses.[15]

According to Myrdal's logic, irrespective of whether a state organizes formal planning systems, the state is the only agent capable of altering the components of the institutional matrix to set in motion the cumulative process of development. He generalizes the potential role of states based on his observations of conditions in various Asian countries, but the nature of intervention is likely to vary enormously in practice. The scope and structure of states should not be preconceived or deductively posited, as in the work of neoclassical economists, but rather should be based on an understanding of the interstices between private economic activities and of the lacunae in the broad elements affecting all economic activities. An institutional matrix approach provides a guide to identifying the intrinsic sources of weaknesses in sectors (diagnostic assessment), constructing a homologous set of state formations to deal with perceived interstices (formative assessment), and finally, beginning to set in motion a cumulative process of transformation to deal with the gaps in the development process (transformative assessment). Before I examine ways to apply the matrix for these purposes, a quick review of some of the literature concerning the role of states in development will illustrate the added value of the theoretical framework developed in chapter 5.

The seminal work regarding the state's role in development was presented in the final chapter of Chalmers Johnson's 1982 book about Japan's Ministry of International Trade and Industry, *MITI and the Japanese Miracle*. Johnson's model of the developmental state has four components:

1. The existence of a small, inexpensive, but elite state bureaucracy staffed by the best managerial talent available in the system;
2. A political system in which the bureaucracy is given sufficient scope to take the initiative and operate effectively;
3. The perfection of market-conforming methods of state intervention in the economy;
4. A pilot organization like MITI.

The concept of a market-conforming state was not meant to convey simply a "market-friendly" approach in the sense of the World Bank's East Asian Miracle, in which governments "ensure adequate investment in people, provide a competitive climate for private enterprise, keep the economy open to international trade and maintain a stable macroeconomy" (World Bank 1993a, 10). In hindsight, Johnson would consider this to be a "regulatory" or "market rational" state where "the state concerns itself with the forms and procedures—the rules, if you will—of economic competition, but it does not concern itself with substantive matters" (C. Johnson 1982, 19).[16] In contrast, he sees the market as being deliberately used by a developmental state to achieve broader developmental goals. Johnson makes this opinion quite explicit in an article criticizing the dichotomization of states and markets: "Industrial policy is not an alternative to the market, but what the state does when it intentionally alters incentives within markets in order to influence the behavior of civilian producers, consumers and investors. . . . Altering market incentives, reducing risks, offering entrepreneurial visions and managing conflicts are some of the functions of the developmental state" (C. Johnson 1999, 48).

Much of Johnson's work intended to establish the instrumentality of the development state within the institutional context of Japanese economic history from 1925 to 1975. Some authors responding to Johnson have raised questions about the specificity of the conditions surrounding the developmental state, in terms of the both uniqueness of the social and political setting and the peculiarity of the historical conjuncture which was conducive to the success of the developmental state. In addition, others have pointed out that identifying the instruments of state intervention in a period of high growth says nothing of the causal linkage between industrial policy and industrial expansion.[17] The evolution of the strategic state in other Asian countries such as South Korea has clearly illustrated that similar policies and institutions have also been associated with high growth periods. Yet critics of the viability of the development state still argue (a) that because interventionist states have not worked in places such as Latin America, the success is linked to either the uniqueness of the region or the historical period concerned or (b) that development has occurred in spite of the role of the state. For example, if the neoclassical literature concerning Asia is to be believed, success has come from openness, an orientation toward exports, macrostability, and keeping prices right, in spite of the intervention.

Evans (1995) begins to answer some of these criticisms by positing a more theoretical understanding of developmental states; his analysis is based primarily on the introduction of institutional theory. According to Evans, Johnson has provided an explanation that fits nicely into a model of what Evans refers to as "embedded autonomy," that is, the combination of the professional Weberian state with an apparent autonomy belied by thick ties binding the state to society.

Evans starts with a fundamental challenge to the literature that attempts to differentiate states by degree of intervention. Contrasts between *dirigiste* and liberal states erroneously focus on the extent of departure from some ideal competitive market. The key is not the quantity of intervention but the type and impact. To understand the role of states in a developmental context, one needs to understand the connection between the impact of state policies and the structural characteristics of states, including the way they are organized and their relation to society. To Evans, the contrast between predatory and developmental states is clearly delineated. In predatory states, officials pursue their own goals by using personalized connections to individuals in the private sector. Developmental states, in contrast, are driven by collective goals and display Weberian-type attributes such as merit-based appointments and a long-term professional commitment to employment. The combination creates a sense of organizational coherence that in turn generates a degree of state autonomy. To be an effective development-generating force, however, the state must be connected to society in order to ensure clear channels of communication and negotiation.

The pairing of thick ties to society and professional autonomy creates what Evans considers the sine qua non of a developmental state: embedded autonomy. In the context of industrial development, the state takes on four basic roles: it is "custodian," or regulator; "demiurge," or producer of infrastructure or goods where gaps exist in private sectors; "midwife," or promoter of the emergence of new entrepreneurs or existing venture capitalists into new areas; and finally, "husband," or supporter of existing private-sector groups (Evans 1995, 13–14).

The concept of embedded autonomy is very much in the spirit of the institutional matrix approach discussed above. The instrumentality of the state is not predefined or deductively posited. Successful developmental states are designed to fill the interstices between areas of private activity and are closely connected and integrated into broader social structures.

The notion of four general roles of states is indeed a useful way to divide their functions in developing countries, and these roles are clearly best undertaken with a Weberian sense of autonomy driven by professionals. Evans begins to run into problems, however, when he presents his analytical framework.

He identifies his methodology as a "comparative institutional approach." States, in his view, are historically rooted, and state-society relations are "constrained by institutionalized sets of relations." Moreover, "economic outcomes are the products of social and political institutions, not just responses to prevailing market conditions." These concepts are thick with meaning and beg to be theoretically constructed. But he elides this central issue with the following comment: "[H]aving become fashionable again, 'institutionalism' has also become a term with many meanings, but in the analysis of the state's role in the economic development, the comparative institutional approach can be defined concretely" (Evans 1995, 18). Most of the rest of the volume is aimed at illustrating professionalism, its linkages to the private sector, and the resulting roles the state played in building industrial development in Korea, India, and Brazil according to his four functional categories.

Although it provides a fascinating ex post interpretation of the histories in these important countries, Evans's approach unfortunately limits this important work by envisioning it as a guide for generating state-led development in other countries and regions. He gives a plethora of examples of policies, organizations, regulations, network structures, and shifting incentives, but he provides no theoretical connection between these somewhat disparately presented elements. His work would benefit from categories for assessing and measuring the developmental ability of states and private actors and how to transform them. Also needed is a common understanding of the meaning of institutions and how they can be altered for development. The five components of the institutional matrix, with its associated aim of shifting socially prescribed correlative behavior or institutions for development, can begin to address the theoretical questions left unanswered by Evan's important book. The remainder of this chapter utilizes the matrix to describe an institutional approach to the World Bank strategy of civil service reform. The key is not only in properly defining the scope of state activity but also in generating new institutional forms conducive to a coordinated application of the instruments of the state for developmental purposes.

The Institutional Matrix and the Civil Service:
Beyond Weber and Evans

Perhaps the most influential and enduring characterization of a civil service in support of capitalist economies is by Max Weber. Weber (1968,
vol. 3) specified six attributes of "modern bureaucracy." First, each office
has a jurisdiction, which includes assigned official duties along with the
authority and resources to fulfill these duties. Second, offices are placed in
hierarchical order with clear authority at higher levels in a monocratically
organized system. Third, is a clear separation of the official activities from
the private affairs of officials. Fourth, individuals hired by the bureaucracy
should be thoroughly trained in their field of specialization. Fifth, employment inside bureaucracies should be deemed full-time work. Finally, offices of bureaucracies should follow stable and exhaustive rules that are
known among officials. Rules should involve matters of jurisprudence,
administration, and business management.

The enduring nature of Weber's depiction of well-operating bureaucracies is easy to understand. What we have is a quintessential representation of a professional civil service in the abstract. Who could argue
with the notion that civil servants must be well-trained, fully occupied, focused on public matters as opposed to private business, and operating by
a stable set of rules? Yet the approach is presented in rather ideal terms
as a polar opposite of what Weber refers to as the "patrimonial state"; it
lacks context. There is no discussion of how to create professionalism, of
the extent of transformation necessary for civil services to be effective,
and of how the character of the bureaucracy needs to be tied to the shifting nature of the exigencies of development. An institutional approach
to building states can begin to deal with some of these important issues.
Because an institutional transformation is, first and foremost, one that is
path-determinant (open to design but linked to the past), any reconfigur-
ing of states for the purposes of development must build on existing foundations. Unlike a path-independent approach, which has largely driven
civil service reform under the guidance of the World Bank, this approach
requires a detailed understanding of the operations and context of transformation within a specific country.

The five elements of the institutional matrix—norms, organizations,
regulations, capacities, and incentives—can help us reconceptualize development in these terms. In the context of states, norms are not simply
rules, which can be pro forma; rather, they are typically supported by in-

ternal and external sanctions and rewards and can provide some understanding of the merit or legitimacy of rules.

The World Bank's conception of the state prevents norms from being transformative. The Bank's approach to civil service reform assumes that all individuals, by nature, are acquisitive. According to this view, individuals will be opportunistic and therefore create inefficiencies within the state, which lacks market constraints and the associated rewards and penalties. Moreover, this view assumes that individuals will use any form of intervention to extract rents from the private sector. The Bank prescribes the retraction of the state as the remedy for corruption and inefficiencies; it believes that the state must operate in market-like conditions by introducing user fees for services and by decentralizing operations. In this neoclassically inspired world, norms cannot be transformative because human behavior is fundamentally inherent and intractable. The focus must be on constraining the bureaucracy and altering its operational context so that punishment and rewards channel the behavior of individuals toward the efficient provision of a limited number of public goods that are absolutely needed.

A more complex understanding of the potential range of human motivation and action, however, allows for norms to play a powerful role in generating the socially prescribed correlative behavior underlying state-supported development. Similarly, norms can play a powerful role in undermining the development process. The issue of corruption is a case in point. There is little doubt that a pervasive climate of corrupt practices in the civil service can have a debilitating impact on the functioning of economies. Yet there is no natural propensity to corruption. It becomes endemic when it becomes expected, accepted, and sometimes even required. Myrdal (1968) refers to such a situation as the "climate of corruption," in which, if it "is taken for granted, resentment amounts essentially to envy of those who have opportunities for private gain by dishonest dealings." Norms then legitimize corrupt practices such that "if everybody seems corrupt, why shouldn't I be corrupt?" (2:941).

In contrast, norms can also generate habits of thought that deem corruption an anathema to the normal operations of the government. At the heart of a well-functioning civil service are Weberian bureaucratic norms, which generate a firm commitment to procedure and process, as well as a technical base for generating decisions. Bureaucratic norms are important for institutionalizing professionalism as a guiding principle for civil servants. For states to be developmentally oriented, however, much more than a professional commitment to the civil service is needed.

The bureaucracy must foster other attitudes as well, including a common commitment to the ethos of development and an associated belief in the enabling capacity of states to promote the private sector's transformation. The commitment to the concept of *Homo faber*[18] and the human capacity to be creative are foremost. The organizational structure of states is also central to the task of development.

A state is not really a single organizational entity but rather a cluster of interconnected organizational constructs. Organizations are important vehicles of socialization because they are able to focus incentives, rules, purposes, and norms aimed at transforming behavior within a single entity. Relationships between the various elements of the bureaucracy provide ideal settings for the operationalized effects of isomorphism. The close proximity of and interactions between elements of the civil service are conducive to both mimetic and coercive elements of isomorphism. In developing countries, where resources are scarce, the focus should be on transforming one or two organizational entities to develop best practices for the civil service while allowing isomorphic processes to help transform other elements of the state.

Because organizations often have distinct purposes, they can be designed to deal with diagnostic, formative, and transformative assessments. For instance, if an organization must align with private-sector groups, it will create specific entities to deal with the logistics of alignment. These new organizational entities will focus on transformative assessments and will develop associated instrumentality to deal with the weaknesses of private-sector production, accumulation, and employment-generating activities.

A major element of the state's organization should therefore deal with the exchange of information and the creation of linkages between the state and the private sector. Such a framework can be used to identify potential areas of growth, resources, factors, and constraints and can also help inform the strategies necessary for supporting the creation of new industry. In many places, particularly in Africa, collaboration between the state and the private sector is practically nonexistent, with disastrous effects for various countries' developmental status. A transparent process of dialogue and participation is necessary to remedy this problem; the focal point of the dialogue should be to choose strategic industrial needs and to develop programs to meet those needs. The starting point would be to identify a minimum of three priority areas in industry and manufacturing with the potential for domestic and foreign investment, generation of employment, development of internal and external markets, and significant backward and forward linkages.

Regulations are seen as the legal boundaries that help set the rules of operation in economies. They are both defined by and help to define the state, since they are part of the legal order specifying the boundaries of organizations, the rules of their operation, and the sanctions and rewards that enforce them. Regulations have a highly privileged role in the institutional matrix because they can be rapidly altered by legislative statutes, bureaucratic edicts, and new interpretations by legal bodies. In contrast to the principle of regulatory minimalism pursued by the World Bank (as discussed in chapter 4), states should focus on regulatory necessity. Regulations should not be constrained and defined by the capacities of the civil service. In a development context, this idea inverts the subject and the object. The abilities of the civil service should be altered according to the regulatory requirements of development and its associated management of the economy.

In the context of states, capacities are related to the underlying abilities of the members of the civil service to operate in an effective manner to achieve the goals of a state within the confines of its rules and purposes. But programs meant to augment a state's capacities should also focus on increasing its ability to create capacities or to enhance or transform the ability of actors to set and achieve their goals in an effective, efficient, and sustainable manner relative to their accepted norms and rules. In association with civil service reform, capacity-building has largely focused on enhancing the state's ability to manage macrostabilization and to meet the financial targets of the World Bank and the IMF. The result has been a state that has been deprived of its capacity to intervene in support of development.

Finally, incentives are the rewards and penalties that arise from different modes of behavior. In the context of states, incentives are important for enhancing the impact of rules as civil services are transformed. They are major components of the internalization of common habits of thought that are at the heart of the effective exercise of state functions. The World Bank approach notwithstanding, there is no single set of incentives that can lead to a predictable alteration in the behavior of civil servants in all places and times. Incentives must be understood in relation to motivation. An institutional view of motivation sees a wage as only one possible material incentive that must be carefully viewed in the context of nonmaterial incentives and motivations. Motivation in an organizational setting such as the state is a product of goals and values, self-evaluation, and cognitive anticipation. Although individual civil servants can be motivated by material incentives, higher-level goals—such as the nature of work, the extent of one's responsibility, and the potential for increasing stature—can be equally important. Moreover, organizational and cultural norms can have an impact on the effectiveness of basic material incentives such as wages. For instance, the World Bank's focus on reversing wage compression in African countries might not have the desired effect where the commitment to equity is the norm. A salary increase for senior civil servants might be seen as an affront to those in the middle and lower ranks, leading to resentment and declines in the quality of job performance. In this case, raising all salaries might have a more positive impact.

Self-evaluation is also important. Individuals weigh their basic ability and competency to handle tasks in specific domains in response to incentives. In the context of the civil service and other organizations, capacity-building becomes central to increasing the effectiveness of incentives. A very simple example can illustrate this point: civil servants with low self-esteem will probably be less successful in performing difficult organizational tasks because they are likely to feel rapidly overwhelmed. Training can help raise confidence and increase the response to new incentives while building a common set of constructs with which to increase the coordination and unity of purpose of the civil service members.

Equally important are cognitive expectations, which shape an agent's understanding of the causal sequence and consequences of a particular action. The civil service needs to be designed along Weberian lines to provide sufficient resources, clear responsibilities, and sufficient authority for individuals to complete tasks. Within the state, information feedback mechanisms are necessary so that civil servants can assess the accuracy of their cognitive expectations and adjust them as needed. Where possible, incentives need to be nondiscretionary; they must have clearly stated rewards for particular actions or the attainment of specific goals and penalties for inaction or for irresponsible behavior.

The principle of nondiscretionary intervention is also important as the state designs incentives for the development of private sectors. Whereas in Krueger's time the World Bank linked corruption to the degree of state intervention and consequently encouraged minimalism, retraction, and deregulation as regarded the state, an institutional analysis suggests that the key to fighting corruption is the transformation of all aspects of the

institutional matrix, including a commitment to the principle of nondiscretionary intervention.

According to Myrdal, the principle of nondiscretionary rewards and
penalties is in operation where "the application follows automatically
from the laying down of a definite rule." Myrdal was adamant about the
importance of what he called "nondiscretionary controls," whether positive or negative, over the private sector. Positive controls were aimed at
"stimulating, facilitating, or inducing production or consumption" and
included subsidies, tax holidays, and price controls. Negative controls including the denial of foreign exchange and the raising of costs to some
operations, were intended to prevent production or impose limits on it.
Whether discretion was involved had nothing to do with the degree of
intervention, nor did "it imply that the one is more in accord with a laissez-
faire philosophy than the other" (Myrdal 1968, 2:903–4). Where states are
rife with corruption and there is a shortage of civil servants with competence and integrity, one might start by shifting the rules governing decision
making toward nondiscretionary principles. Over time, as civil services
build up organizational structures, norms of professionalism, technical
capacities, and appropriate incentives, they will develop the commonly
defined correlative behavior that is at the heart of the coordinated effort
underlying the dynamics of state-led development.

Conclusion

The transformation of the civil service is central to developing country-
level strategies for generating development. The World Bank, however,
was driven mainly by a neoclassical economic vision of both how states
should operate and what states should do.

With the arrival of the conservative Anne Krueger as chief economist,
the Bank began to conceptualize the nature of the state according to the
theory of structural adjustment. The focus was on minimizing the state
and fostering neutrality, in line with her view that most state intervention generated price distortions, inefficiencies, and opportunities for rent-
seeking.

Many of the civil service reform efforts in practice were poorly conceived and badly implemented, even by the Bank's own standards, as set
by the Operations Evaluation Department. An initial focus on downsizing the state via layoffs and other means often led to the departure of

the most competent people and frequently generated few if any financial savings. There was no evidence that the remaining civil servants operated any more efficiently. Frequently civil service wages continued to decline in real terms as other elements of adjustment were implemented including cutbacks in government spending and the removal of subsidies for food. Moreover, the social and economic impact of layoffs of tens of thousands of workers was never evaluated.

Capacity-building frequently emphasized financial management and meeting IMF and World Bank targets as other development related capabilities eroded within the state. Other approaches including reversing wage compression were introduced with little effect. In general, after twenty-five years, states have been emasculated in terms of dealing with development while being bloated to adhere to the conditions of stabilization. If development is to occur, a fresh approach needs to be undertaken.

A rather different vision of development is based on a conceptualization of the state that can lead the process. In developing countries, the state is the only agent capable of altering the components of the institutional matrix to set in motion the cumulative process of development. The scope and structure of states should not be preconceived or deductively posited, as in neoclassical economics, but should arise from an understanding of the gaps in private economic activity and of the weaknesses in the broad elements affecting all economic activities. An approach using the institutional matrix provides a guide to generating diagnostic, formative, and transformative assessments aimed at identifying the exigencies of state formation and functions. This chapter provided some general guidelines as to how one applies the institutional matrix to begin to form a developmental state; chapter 7 discusses how one can apply the matrix in order to transform financial sectors.

CHAPTER SEVEN

An Institutional Approach to Financial Development

Speculators may do no harm as bubbles on a steady stream of enterprise. But the position is serious when enterprise becomes the bubbles on a whirlpool of speculation. When the capital development of a country becomes the by-product of the activities of a casino, the job is likely to be ill done.—John Maynard Keynes, 1936

Introduction

The main argument of this chapter is that the World Bank reform agenda for the financial sector has been driven largely by financial repression theory, despite its rather shaky theoretical premises. As Keynes comments in the epigraph, we have witnessed far too many episodes of enterprises becoming "the bubbles on a whirlpool of speculation" following exercises of financial liberalization. The financial crises in developing and transitional economies at such times have not been the fault of inappropriate implementation. Rather, these practices, which are often embedded in World Bank loan conditionality, have engendered widespread banking crises precisely because of the problematic foundations of the theory. It is not surprising that weak theory generates policies that frequently lead to crises. Perhaps most problematic, the virtually exclusive focus on price formation has rendered orthodox financial repression theory largely independent of institutions. Yet this is a serious misstep; it is critical to understand existing institutional relationships in the financial sector and to design a path of institutional transformation in order to generate the causal linkages between finance and development.

This chapter begins with a critical review of the theory underlying orthodox financial liberalization. I then discuss the way in which the theory has influenced the World Bank and the way the Bank has explained the failure of financial sector loans (even in Operations Evaluation Department reports), while adhering to the same core orthodox policies. Next I examine the influence of NIE on the Bank's approach to financial liberalization. The latter part of the chapter considers an institutional approach to finance and attempts to generate an alternative strategy based on the institutional matrix developed in chapter 5.

Financial Liberalization Theory: The Original Formulation

The origins of financial liberalization theory are usually traced to the work of McKinnon (1973) and Shaw (1973), often referred to as the McKinnon-Shaw or financial repression theory. The truly seminal work introducing this theory, however, was published by Patrick in 1966. It argued that there are two ways to evaluate the relationship between development and finance. One of them is "demand-following" and occurs when finance deepens as the economy grows (Robinson 1952); the other is "supply-leading" and occurs when the expansion of financial institutions leads to growth. Patrick's work is based on that of Bagehot (1873) and Schumpeter (1912), and is typically known as the financial liberalization school; it adopts a supply-leading argument. The school's central argument assumes a highly simplified world in which capital purchases arise only from self-finance. Without financial intermediaries, when an individual wishes to "purchase physical capital of a type that is different from his own output . . . he may store inventories of his own output for eventual sale when the capital assets are acquired or he may steadily accumulate cash balances for the same purpose" (McKinnon 1993, 57).

This orthodox approach is premised on the pre-Keynesian notion that prior saving is needed for financial development and that interest rates provide the return, or reward, for postponing consumption.[1] Thus, if interest rates are artificially low, finance will be rather shallow. In contrast to Keynes's (1936) focus on the influence of interest rates on the demand and supply of money, Shaw (1973) argues along strictly classical lines, insisting that interest rates determine the equilibrium between savings and investment. A rise in real interest rates would therefore generate increased savings and reduce the excess demand for savings.

The demand for money, according to the McKinnon-Shaw world, is also positively related to the rate of return on capital. This runs contrary to the negative relationship assumed by the portfolio approach (since investment is self-financed). McKinnon-Shaw also argues that a higher interest rate improves the quality of investment and creates a rise in the proportion of savings allocated through the market. By extension, the claim is that rationing of credit is "expensive to administer" and "vulnerable to corruption and conspiracy. . . . The rationing process discriminates poorly among investment opportunities . . . and the social cost of this misallocation is suggested by the high incremental ratios of investment to output that lagging economies report." (86)

According to this logic, competition via private bank ownership can shrink interest rate margins, thereby improving the efficiency of intermediation. Fragmentation in developing countries, "in the sense that firms and households face . . . different effective prices for land, labor, capital, and produced commodities . . . has been largely the result of government policy" (McKinnon 1973, 5–7). Reversing fragmentation by creating a unified capital market via the retraction of state intervention is therefore considered the sine qua non of development: "Arbitrary measures to introduce modern technology via tariffs, or to increase the rate of capital accumulation . . . by relying on foreign aid or domestic forced saving, will not necessarily lead to economic development. Thus it is hypothesized that unification of the capital market, which sharply increases rates of return to domestic savers by widening exploitable investment opportunities, is essential for eliminating other forms of fragmentation" (9). By implication, McKinnon (1973) and Shaw (1973) support the liberalization of the capital account[2] in order to provide an unimpeded, unified capital market for private sector players to pursue utility-maximizing intertemporal choice (that is, choice between investing now or in the future).[3]

To summarize, in the orthodox world of finance of McKinnon-Shaw, the low rates of savings and investment that characterize developing economies are assumed to be the results of government intervention in the financial sector. The theory argues that investment and savings have been repressed by a combination of controlled and negative interest rates, insufficient competition, high reserve requirements, and government allocation of credit. Pursuing economic development therefore means that countries need to deregulate interest rates, privatize, and liberalize bank licensing in order to increase competition, lower reserve requirements, and dismantle any credit allocation schemes. The rise in interest rates increases the incentive to save, and the resulting higher financial savings lead to an augmentation of investment levels. The increase in interest rates should also weed out less productive investment, thereby leading to an increase in the quality of investment. Discerning private bankers, without the constraints of credit controls, will allocate funds to the most productive users. Increased competition will lower the spread between savings and loan rates, thereby increasing the efficiency of the financial system. Overall, there will be a higher rate of savings, which generate more investment, thereby stimulating economic growth, which in turn augments savings—thus creating a virtuous circle. The key is to ensure that interest rates are market-determined and that banks are privately owned and operated so that bankers can make decisions without political constraints. A sufficient number of bank licenses must be made available to enhance competition while avoiding too much deposit insurance and its associated problems of moral hazard (encouraging risky behavior) and adverse selection (leading to poorly run banks).

Critical Reflections on Financial Liberalization Theory

There are a number of fundamental difficulties with the financial liberalization hypothesis. To begin with, it assumes that all investment is self-financed. This assumption is disconnected from the reality of money, which is a socially embedded construct. The holding of money, even within the simple rural setting discussed by McKinnon (1973), is subject to social obligations and constraints and is not simply the product of the intertemporal choice of individuals.[4] Moreover, McKinnon's presentation is inconsistent. One cannot talk of self-financing as if there were no other financial options present while simultaneously presenting a return to holding money as some "weighted average of nominal interest rates of all forms of deposits" (39). The latter concept presupposes the existence of a complex financial system.

McKinnon (1973) is determined to illustrate a positive correlation among rising interest rates, financial development, investment, and economic growth. His aim is to reject the neoclassical portfolio approach because it posits a negative relation between the demand for real money

balances and the return on nonfinancial assets. In reality, he is not departing from a portfolio approach but simply redefining it as a choice between
an asset that does not bear interest (for example, stocks of products) and
one that does (money). The portfolio is seen as a store of value that is a
reflection of the desired rate of future capital investment.[5] Capital investment is assumed to have a degree of indivisibility, and therefore it requires
the accumulation of "funds" prior to purchase. Real interest rates constitute the central determinant: higher interest rates motivate individuals
to save more and consume less, thus inducing them to hold more of their
"portfolio" in money balances.

But what if other sources of finance become available? Would not the
dynamics change, since there would be less inducement to undertake investment if interest rates were to rise? Not according to McKinnon; he
argues that higher interest rates induce higher holdings of money, which
provide collateral and consequently make increases of loans possible
(1973, 65–66).

McKinnon (1973) argues that it is possible to determine an "optimum
level" of monetization, which will be reached when the real return on
monetary holdings plus the marginal cost of supplying banking services
is equal to the marginal return on new investment. How would it be possible to devise some economy-wide "marginal efficiency of investment"
as well as a single rate of interest, given that rates of return and interest
are so widely dispersed?[6] He assumes that it is possible to determine some
"average" at each level of monetary balances. Economy-wide choices are
seen as some averaging of individual choices wherein there is a single representative interest rate.

The problem with this argument is that capital markets have never operated in this manner, not even in the most advanced economies. Markets
are always fragmented and replete with variations of risk and uncertainty.
Rates of return vary not only within similar asset types but also with different types of financial vehicles.[7] Moreover, this analysis relies on enormous
variations in perceptions, not only of the returns on investment projects,
but of interest rates. An individual who invests in a particular project will
always perceive interest rates paid by governments differently from those
paid by other organizations. Moreover, it is doubtful that any unifying
equilibrium between some anticipated future return and a single interest
rate exists.

The theory of financial liberalization also relies on the textbook world
of pure competition. Although the notion of markets for competitive

goods in the nonfinancial world is sufficiently suspect, the divergence between the world of finance and that of McKinnon-Shaw is more profound. As the imperfect-market theorists have argued, finance is more replete with the asymmetries of risk and information than are goods (Stiglitz 1989, 1994).

In the McKinnon-Shaw world, there are three types of actors (savers, lenders, and borrowers) in two markets (deposit and lending), balanced by interest rates. The difference in the price of the two exchanges reflects the cost of intermediation, which will supposedly diminish with privatization and competition. Financial liberalization is aimed at removing government-imposed barriers to self-seeking individuals to arrive at Pareto-efficient decisions. Finance is simply the sum of a multitude of individual actors making utility-, profit-, and investment-maximizing decisions. Governments need only generate sufficient money supply to accommodate the needs of these actors, while avoiding seigniorage and generating optimal interest rates.

Unfortunately, this position is abstracted from the complex web of factors that generates finance. McKinnon-Shaw would have us believe that there is simply no need for institutions.[8] Yet finance is profoundly institutional; interest rates are among many possible incentives that can influence behavior in financial systems. Financial transformation inspired by McKinnon-Shaw's view of finance has engendered widespread banking crises precisely because of the weak foundations of the theory. In response, McKinnon (1993) and his supporters, including World Bank economists, have argued that the problem is not with the theory or its policies but, rather, is a problem of sequencing.

The 1980s saw a rapid increase in financial liberalization policies, with enormous consequences for banking stability. Between 1981 and 1992, there were at least fifteen major financial crises. It cost the affected countries' treasuries between 5 percent and 40 percent of GDP to rescue the banking system (Honohan and Klingebiel 2000; Caprio and Klingebiel 1999).[9] How did McKinnon respond to the crises that invariably followed adherence to his recommended policies? He argued that the key is not in the content but in the sequence of policy implementation (McKinnon 1993, 4). The optimal plan would begin with bringing inflation under control, followed by interest rate deregulation, privatization, commercialization of banks, unification of foreign exchange rates from multitiered regimes, the liberalization of international trade, and, finally, liberalizing restrictions on capital flows.

Arguments that financial crises can be avoided with the proper sequencing or the correct pace have come under increasing challenge. In places such as Chile and Uruguay, where opposite sequences were used, the results were the same: banking crises followed financial liberalization. Irrespective of the order in which policies are implemented, there was a marked increase in the intensity and frequency of financial crises in the 1980s and 1990s (Lindgreen, Garcia, and Saal 1996; Grabel 1995; Demirguc-Kunt and Detragiache 1998, 1999; Arestis and Demetriades 1999; Arestis et al. 2003; Weller 2001).

Financial transformation in the image of McKinnon-Shaw has engendered widespread banking crises precisely because of its weak foundations. Despite these weaknesses, this theory has been at the core of World Bank strategy in the financial sector since the early 1980s. In fact, its supporters, including the Bank, see financial crises as somehow irrelevant to their theory and to the core strategy that it has inspired. This seems paradoxical; proponents argue that when crises occur, more of their policy prescriptions should be implemented to cure them, although it was precisely these policies that caused the crises in the first place.

Polanyi (1957), in a related context, explains this paradox well when he argues that orthodox apologists "are repeating in endless variations that but for the policies advocated by its critics, liberalism would have delivered the goods; that not the competitive system and the self-regulating market, but interference with that system and interventions with that market are responsible for our ills" (143). This same circular logic shaped the evolution of World Bank financial-sector policy.

Financial Repression and World Bank
Financial Sector Adjustment Loans

Prior to the adjustment era, support for the financial sector largely took the form of financial intermediary loans (FILs), which were loans made through the banking sector for on-lending to other borrowers. This type of loan had a long history; the first was granted to Chile in 1948. These were driven not by a McKinnon-Shaw vision of reform (which was embedded in later devices) but rather by the view that more finance would spur higher investment and growth.

The financial sector adjustment loan (FSAL) was a comparatively late addition to the sectoral adjustment loan (SECAL) program, although the orthodox view of finance was embedded in earlier country reports produced by the Bank (see the discussion below concerning the 1983 study of Nigeria). Until mid-1988 only four such loans—one to Argentina (1988), one to Ecuador (1988), and two to Turkey (1986 and 1988)—were so designated. A fifth FSAL was part of a trade and financial sector adjustment loan to Jamaica in 1987. Earlier structural adjustment packages were made conditional in part on financial reform in a number of countries, however.

The introduction of an explicit financial SECAL inspired a series of studies within the World Bank beginning in 1987. Many of these are referenced in Gelb and Honohan (1989), which laid out the theory underlying financial sector reform as a series of SECALs (those for Ghana, Nepal, Kenya, Hungary, and Nigeria) were in preparation. The working paper draws heavily on McKinnon-Shaw-type arguments in mapping out policies for financial transformation.[10] It states: "The recent upsurge of concerns with financial sector policy issues in developing countries . . . arises primarily . . . from excessive control over interest rates and the direction of credit, amounting to repression of financial systems" (1). The core of the strategy is reversing financial repression by "removal of all interest rate controls, . . . withdrawals of interest subsidies, . . . removal of overall credit ceilings, . . . ensuring that barriers to entry into banking are no more than is required for prudential reasons," and "liberalization of exchange controls" (12).

If spreads between deposit and lending rates are too large, Gelb and Honohan argue, the "ideal long-run solution in such circumstances is to encourage competition through liberal (though prudent) policies towards entry of new banks" (1989, 20) and might include "opening the system to foreign banks" (16). Along the lines of the McKinnon-Shaw theory, they argue that financial liberalization leads to "a causal chain from higher interest rates, through greater mobilization of saving through the financial system to increased efficiency of investment and thereby growth" (27). Unlike McKinnon (1993), who accepts overwhelming evidence that interest rates do not lead to higher savings rates, the authors argue that "higher deposit rates encourage additional saving (notably in Asia)," although they admit the effect is small (27).

The Gelb and Honohan paper goes to extraordinary lengths to dismiss any linkage between orthodox reform and financial crisis. For example, the well-documented financial crisis in Chile in the 1970s, which followed liberalization, is largely attributed to inadequate financial supervision and unsustainable exchange rate policies, along with the damaging decision to simultaneously liberalize both trade and capital accounts (Gelb and Honohan 1989, 18). They also argue, with a boldness seldom heard among proponents of orthodox liberalization, that "financial liberalization will have favorable effects on income distribution and on reducing the concentration of economic power" (24). By their logic, small savers should gain from higher deposit rates and lose nothing from the loss of subsidized credit, which mostly goes to more prosperous groups anyway. Reminiscent of the "getting the prices right" argument, small savers are said to gain by the improvement in growth and employment, both from the mobilization of finance and from the removal of the "artificial stimulus to capital-intensive production from severely negative interest rates" (24).[11]

Following the appearance of this working paper, a World Bank task force on the financial sector issued a 1989 report calling for a comprehensive approach to financial sector lending. The policy focused on financial-sector reform aimed at a greater reliance on market forces. The prerequisites to reform were other elements typically found in standard adjustment packages, including macrostability, removal of real-sector distortions, and the elimination of barriers to competition. The report was strongly opposed to the directed credit finance that characterized many of the Bank's FILs. Correspondingly, the task force emphasized the need for a new set of operational guidelines to support FSALs.

It took three years, but in 1992 the policies were formally embedded in a new set of guidelines known as Operational Directive 8.30 (OD 8.30). Although in many ways the directive reaffirmed the types of policies used in the 1980s in FSALs, the document provided more detailed guidelines concerning the macroeconomic and microeconomic factors that should be considered when lending.[12] It issued a strong word of caution against lending to economies with "distorted incentives," macroeconomic instability, and administered interest rates. The report's greatest impact was on the number of FILs—which fell from about twenty-five loans in 1991 to only ten in 1994—and a renewed emphasis on reform at the sectoral level. The report is also important because the OED has used it as a framework for evaluating the Bank's assistance with financial-sector reform (for example, Operations Evaluation Department 1998, 1:6–8). It was also instrumental in institutionalizing a completely orthodox approach to financial change, which continued to drive Bank policy during the subsequent decade.

The World Bank and Its Faith in Orthodoxy:
In Search of Explanations for Failure

By 1993 it was apparent to the Bank that the FSALs were not having
the predicted effect, and that the same problems kept appearing across
countries. The policies implemented had the same core strategy: a combination of standard macro stabilization in coordination with the IMF,
as well as financial liberalization focusing on interest rate deregulation,
positive real rates, and establishing a secondary market for government
securities.

The case of the Kenyan SECAL illustrates this point. All targets were
met and the three tranches were released, yet the FSAL was "not a successful or sustainable operation" (Operations Evaluation Department 1993,
vi). In accordance with the orthodox view discussed above, it was expected
that these measures would improve credit allocation by diminishing credit
flows to the government and weak enterprises and by "increasing credit
flows to an expanding number of high yielding private sector investments"
(4). Moreover, it was believed that interest rates would become market-
determined "by the establishment of a truly competitive . . . secondary
market for its longer term bond issues" (8). This statement exposes an
unstated assumption found in most IMF and World Bank financial sector
programs: that the U.S. financial system, with its "arm's-length" banking
and open-market operations, is the superior model (see below).[13] In the
end, the secondary market was not properly operationalized, and credit
constraints existed alongside reserve requirements. Thus, the system
could not operate via market-driven competition and efficiency. What was
needed was "at least one, truly competitive financial market" (11). Yet this
did not fully explain the failure.

The worst disappointment was that lending to quality actors in private
sector-investment, which would have been a major contributor to increasing the GDP, did not increase (Operations Evaluation Department 1993,
4). It is reasonable to assume that this failure had resulted from the high
interest rates, which increased from 17 percent to 30 percent between 1993
and 1994, combined with the austerity demanded by the stabilization policy (Johnson 2004, 253). Yet the report dismisses this explanation. Instead,
it contends that investment did not increase because of an "absence of
good investment opportunities" and the "incomplete real sector adjustment" of other parts of the economy, not their high cost relative to their
potential return. What was missing, the report argued, was an "interest

inelastic demand for 'quality' credit" caused largely by "price controls" not anticipated by the FSAL. Without citing any actual evidence, relying instead on some perfunctory comments from bankers, the report claimed that although the government had "de-Gazetted" price controls, they were still being enforced "on behalf of poor Kenyans." The difficulty, it said, was that private companies were unable to pass on to consumer increased costs such as those associated with devaluation (Operations Evaluation Department 1993, 5–7). These assertions were simply attempts to defend orthodoxy of the McKinnon-Shaw type and argue that the problem being witnessed could be blamed on the lack of sufficient deregulation in other sectors of the economy.

With this rather rosy assessment of the financial sector strategy, the World Bank pressed on, expanding the number as well as the scope of the FSALs during the 1990s. Between 1990 and 1996 sixteen FSALs were initiated. In addition, twenty-seven other World Bank loans contained financial reform conditionality of the kind found in FSALs (Cull 1997, 62). New policies inspired by McKinnon-Shaw, such as privatization, were added to the list of other conditions.[14]

After 1997, orthodox financial liberalization engendered financial chaos in a number of countries including Argentina, Ecuador, Thailand, Russia, Uruguay, Columbia, Indonesia, Kenya, and Korea. Much of this instability was associated with rapid financial liberalization. For example, the Korean crisis of November 1997 followed the deregulation of interest rates, the opening of the capital market, liberalization of foreign exchange, the granting of new banking licenses, and the dismantling of government monitoring mechanisms that were linked to policy loans (Chang et al. 2002).

The first evaluation of the Financial Sector Liaison Committees (FSLC) conducted after the Asian crisis created a conundrum for the Bank, because it was forced to recognize that even countries that had the fundamentals right, including "sustained macroeconomic performance, fiscal surpluses, high savings and investment rates, and strong trade performance," were "not immune to financial turbulence" (Operations Evaluation Department 1998, 1:5). Although some might conclude that these experiences proved that following orthodox policies was problematic, the Bank argued that the crisis was linked to "issues of economic governance, industrial policy, interlocking ownership of enterprises and banks, foreign investment regulations, and debt management" (1:8). In the literature, this reasoning is known as the Greenspan-Summers-IMF thesis (GSI), which uses cronyism and poor corporate governance to explain the Asian crisis.[15] By inventing a new, extraneous explanation—again—the Bank was able to justify adherence to orthodox policies in the face of overwhelming evidence of instability and crises resulting from these policies.[16]

NIE and Rescuing Financial Liberalization Theory at the Altar: Ms. NIE Marries Mr. McKinnon-Shaw

New Institutional Economics, too, was selectively used to rescue orthodoxy. World Development Report (2002), with its focus on institutions and development, devotes an entire chapter to a discussion of financial systems. Bank studies continued to point to problems with exercises in financial liberalization. For example, Demirguc-Kunt and Detragiache (1999) surveyed banking crises in fifty-three countries between 1980 and 1995 and found that 78 percent of all crises were linked to periods of financial liberalization. Despite the accumulation of evidence discrediting the Bank's previous initiatives, the report asserts the Bank's commitment to the same orthodox policies of privatization, competition, and deregulation (World Bank 2002b, 75–76).

Yet the Bank also recognized that "the recent spate of banking crises—whose severity was exacerbated by international financial linkages—has had severe economic consequences for growth and poverty reduction" (World Bank 2002b, 79). Rather than suggesting that these crises might be linked to financial liberalization, the report cites evidence that countries with a higher degree of state ownership of banks between 1980 and 1997 were associated with a greater probability of banking crises and higher associated fiscal costs.[17] This is completely disingenuous. In Asia, for example, countries with a high level of state ownership also went through much greater financial liberalization at the beginning of the crisis. The causality, then, would not be in the level of state ownership but rather in the extent to which financial liberalization was implemented. The literature linking liberalization to the financial crisis is quite cogent and extensive.[18]

These crises also occurred because of an absence of financial regulation and "renewed interest in improving financial regulation" (World Bank 2002b, 79). Regulation in this case does not mean intervening in markets to set interest rates, lending priorities, or ownership restrictions, but instead means "largely prudential regulation to promote an efficient, safe and stable financial system" (79). Governments should not worry about particular types of financial organizations such as development banks because "policymakers should consider improving the legal and regulatory environment rather than building a financial system. What is important is to have secure rights for outside investors and efficient contract enforcement mechanisms—central themes of the report. Openness to trade and greater competition contribute to the development of financial institutions regardless of a country's legal origin, colonial history, or political system. Financial regulation becomes a far easier task when it makes use of the monitoring and disciplining ability of market participants" (76). Such logic relies on the core principle of neoliberalism, which has now become not merely an end in itself but also a means for enhancing regulation.[19] But by invoking the benefits of trade and competition regardless of a country's history or political system, this view ignores elements of path-dependency that are at the heart of North's vision of institutional change. It is also in conflict with Williamson's warning that universals must be avoided when pondering remediableness (see chapter 4).

So how does NIE fit into the WDR 2002's chapter about finance? It is largely to be found in the way in which regulation is conceptualized. In simple terms, the chapter can be seen as an attempt to marry Ms. NIE to Mr. McKinnon-Shaw in the hope that they will commingle to produce poverty reduction, financial stability, and economic development—in other words, the effects neither of them had been able to produce on their own. As we will see, however, their progeny are more likely to be chaos, misery, and underdevelopment.

At the heart of the NIE conceptualization of the financial system is Williamson's opportunistic being. According to his plan, the key is to put in place governance structures and incentives that will limit the damage created by *Homo opportunicus*. Risk taking will be minimized on the ownership side by having sufficient amounts of capital invested by the owners of the banks. In NIE, financial institutions are conceptualized as "better able to collect, evaluate, and monitor information than individuals." These institutions are greatly affected by the risks people take and by the "perceptions of those risks by individual market participants" (World Bank 2002b, 79).

The chapter argues that incentives must be put in place to deal with the information asymmetries, and, by implication, Williamson's behavioral uncertainty, that are at the core of these perceptions. In order to create incentives for those who deposit funds in banks to seek out information, deposit insurance should be kept to a bare minimum. In the case of interbank lending markets, insurance should not be available; in this way, banks will have an incentive to monitor one another. On the regulatory side, agencies need the right incentives to battle opportunism. Regulatory supervisors should be banned from taking banking jobs after their departure. To insulate them from politics, these supervisors should come under the authority of the central bank, which is the most independent and detached from politics. This view argues that low capacity in developing countries means that rules should be simple and minimal, but it relies on a false assumption that poor countries will have private-sector capacity for monitoring. Once again, regulation is defined not by need but by perceived capacity.

Yet the Bank was quick to innovate in order to buttress its orthodox view. In order to ease pressure on the regulatory system, it would now recommend adding a new dimension to orthodox financial liberalization: selling off the banking sector to foreign owners. This was believed to extend the benefits of privatization and improve "sector efficiency and stability" (World Bank 2002b, 86).

Again, the negative consequences—this time, those of foreign ownership—are discussed but dismissed. For example, the report raises the possibility that foreign banks might reduce access to loans for small and medium enterprise because of information problems. Yet this possibility is dismissed with the assertion that the presence of foreign banks is likely to have the effect of pushing local banks into small and medium enterprise markets where they have a greater comparative advantage.

Apart from all of these clever rationalizations, what is the reality? Let us consider the example of the Czech Republic. In the early 1990s the Czech Republic went through the typical orthodox liberalization exercise. The number of private Czech-owned banks rose from zero to twenty-eight between 1990 and 1994. The financial crisis that ensued cost the government roughly 21 percent of the GDP to clean up (Honohan and Klingebiel 2000; Caprio and Klingebiel 1999). By 2000 most of these new Czech-owned banks were either liquidated or sold off to foreign banks. The number of foreign banks or branches rose to twenty-six, compared to only eight remaining local banks. By the end of 2000, nearly 60 percent of the equity of the banking sector was foreign-owned. Furthermore, the foreign banks were overwhelmingly larger and controlled 95 percent of the total assets by June 2002 (Die Bank 2003). How did the small and medium enterprise sector fare? In 2000, roughly 60 percent of total employment in the Czech

Republic was generated from this sector. Its share of GDP was roughly 40 percent. A survey of 656 such enterprises undertaken by the Chamber of Commerce of the Czech Republic found that only 6 percent felt they had no problems getting bank loans. The remaining 94 percent felt that banks had little or no interest in granting loans or that the requirements were too difficult (Pasekova and Hyblova 2003). Likewise, only about 2 percent of small and medium enterprises were able to obtain a loan in 2000.[20] Clearly, the hypothesis that foreign banks would induce local banks to fill a new role in such markets did not prove accurate.

Owing to the drying up of domestic sources of finance, the Czech government has turned increasingly to FDI. Yet unemployment has continued to rise; it increased from 8.1 percent to 11 percent between 2001 and 2004 (Czech National Bank 2005). Other countries, too, increasingly relied on selling banks to foreign owners. In Tanzania, where the national bank was sold to a single foreign buyer, private commercial banks were holding massive excess reserves (mostly in government paper) amounting to roughly 60 percent of the total available credit.[21] With such stark evidence of the failures of the orthodox approach and the damage it causes, it would seem reasonable to begin seeking new answers, but the Bank neglects to do so. The question then becomes, what are the theoretical and policy alternatives to orthodox financial liberalization strategies?

Going Beyond the Bank Agenda: An Institutional Approach to Finance

An Institutional View of Money and Credit

In contrast to the Bank's approach, I propose a more holistic approach in which institutional transformation is the focal point of the strategy. To start, it is important to clearly differentiate between an institutional approach and an orthodox one. How does each approach view the ways in which financial systems operate and the role they should play in developing countries?

The World Bank's orthodox view of money and credit in the context of stabilization theory is well summarized in chapter 3. An institutional theory of finance, on the other hand, rejects this view of money and banking and, more generally, of a financial system built on these premises. Rather, the institutional approach views money as an endogenous construct: loans generate deposits, deposits expand reserves, and the demand for money induces the supply of money. From the perspective of a company, the demand for money symbolizes the inducement to undertake a debt, and the supply arises from the loans it obtains. Conversely, the Bank's view is that demand for money represents a firm's willingness to enter into debt, and the supply of money is an indicator of the bank's acceptance of the note, which induces it to issue liabilities to purchase the firm's note. What we have, then, are two sides of the balance sheet. In the United States, for example, the banks find the reserves to cover any loan they deem profitable through asset and liability management, the Fed funds market, international sources, or the discount window (Wray 1990, 73–74). The central bank can influence the cost of loans by raising the discount rate, by affecting reserves via open market operations, or even by refusing loans through its discount window. It can hardly reach a specific target, however (as suggested by the monetarist concept of the exogenous money supply), and if interest rates get too high, it might need to flood the system with reserves as the lender of last resort.[22] Overall, there is not likely to be a clear and predictable relation between the supply of money and the level of prices.

From an institutional perspective, financial systems are important because debt-credit relations, which are denominated in money, are determinants of growth and development. The orthodox theory underlying the Bank's vision of financial transformation confuses money with the medium of exchange. In order to understand the centrality of finance, however, this distinction is important. As discussed above, money itself is created by the process of facilitating flows and is reflected in the conditions associated with the generation of debt. Medium of exchange, in contrast, allows an individual to spend without incurring a debt. When money is used as a medium of exchange, one person is utilizing another person's debt to facilitate a purchase. Further, money can be used for purposes other than spending, such as settling a debt, reducing balance sheet liabilities, and in turn destroying other money. Moreover, spending often has little to do with the broadly accepted medium of exchange (such as demand deposits and currency). For instance, credit card transactions generate debt, which may or may not be settled at the end of the month by the payment of demand deposits (Wray 1990, 14–15). There is no simple relation between a given stock of money as a medium of exchange and a particular level of prices and nominal spending.

Another focal point of the orthodox approach to finance is facilitating a rise in savings. This goal is based on the assumption that investment cannot expand without prior savings, which will only rise in response to positive real interest rates. This view implies that banks evolved to act as intermediaries between savers and investors. As discussed in chapter 5, however, such behavior is not inherent but is learned, which suggests a different historical process: "The true order of events shows that orthodoxy clearly has reversed the process through which investment is funded. Banks do not begin as intermediaries which accept the deposit of 'savers' and then make loans to 'investors,' for this would assume that the public has already developed the 'banking habit.' This habit is the end result of public experience with short term bank liabilities which have been created as banks extend short term credit to finance working capital expenses" (Wray 1990, 58).

In many developing countries, banks are poorly formed institutions and are often restricted to large urban centers. The orthodox argument that raising interest rates to real levels will lead to some predicted increase in savings is untenable. Empirical evidence discrediting this theory has been so overwhelming that even strong proponents of the orthodox view, after surveying the literature, have declared that "there is virtually no evidence that higher interest rates mobilize increased saving" (Dornbusch and Reynoso 1993, 71).[23]

Moreover, from an institutional perspective, the causal direction between savings and investment is reversed. Spending on investment goods financed by credit generates income, which becomes the root of savings (Wray 1990, 58). Central to this process is a well-developed financial system that can provide credit for growth and accumulation. Once again, empirical testing generally has confirmed the causal relation of growth to savings.[24]

Building an institutional matrix is critical for the construction of a system of endogenous money. At the core of successful credit creation for development is a common comprehension of the mechanisms, expectations, rules, information, rewards, and penalties associated with the issuing of new loans. These are contingent on a carefully constructed matrix of five interactive institutionally related components: norms, incentives, regulations, capacities, and organizations.

The Institutional Matrix and Financial Systems

Norms. As discussed in chapter 5, norms provide behavioral guides to what is expected, required, or accepted. Unlike rules, they are typically supported by social sanctions and provide some understanding of the merit or legitimacy of rules. Establishment of norms for banking is critical to transforming financial systems in developing countries. These norms involve not only rules of thumb, the generation of trust, and professional habits that encourage probity, but also proper banking conduct. Norms must go beyond issues of honesty to recognize that finance is central to achieving developmental goals such as investment, employment generation, and accommodation of entrepreneurship.

Norms associated with subcultures can also be important. Technical employees, for example, are subject to professional norms and standards as well as outside enforcement via membership in associations. Regulatory or statutory standards can generate penalties on professionals within organizations. In banking structures, this applies to a variety of groups (such as auditors, accountants, lawyers, and loan officers). In a developing country, these organizations should be fostered and supported by the state. Financial organizations should induce employee membership in these groups. Organizational structures and internal incentives should be adjusted to reflect and reward greater group autonomy when concatenated by self-enforcing norms and professional standards. The organizational culture should also be cognizant of the broader societal norms discussed above.

Incentives. Design of incentives for financial transformation should focus on delivering rewards and penalties for different forms of behavior. Unlike the behavior implied by *Homo economicus*, real individuals do not constantly react to each marginal change in prices. Incentives require a high degree of cognition and involve differentiated patterns of behavior until reactions become more consistent. They are highly contextualized and are not simply delivered via markets. Incentives can also arise within a variety of organizational constructs. In the orthodox world of finance, financial firms are simply black boxes, mere automatons reacting to market signals. In the real world, however, organizations have a filtering process that can cause numerous reactions to the same signals. Lowering interest rates on Treasury bills, for example, may not lead to more lending to the private sector if loan companies are risk-averse or if employees lack authority to seek out new loans or interest in doing so.

Moreover, humans are foremost social beings who are motivated by factors that transcend income or material needs. In the context of banking, financial variables such as interest rates are not the only things that shape behavior. Promotions, the loss of social esteem, threats of ostracism, social responsibility, legal repercussions, professionalism, pride, and so on are all important to generating incentives for expanding and operating banking systems in developing countries. Material and nonmaterial rewards are needed to change the goals of banking in order to accommodate development. States must create incentives to encourage private bankers to support the loans that will yield greater social and economic benefit. In the early stages, before bankers see that loans can be both socially beneficial and profitable, states will need to be involved with risk sharing. In addition, incentives must take into account other aspects of the matrix such as norms. The case of an Islamic society demonstrates the importance of this point: cultural codes and norms mean that emphasis on interest rates can be quite problematic, and focusing rewards at the individual level may alienate employees and reduce overall productivity in societies that emphasize group rewards or seniority based on age.

Regulations. Regulations are the legal parameters that set the operating rules for financial systems. Institutions are both the products and constitutive elements of the mechanism that perpetuates legal systems. In general, regulations are instrumental in constructing, initiating, supporting, and altering institutions. For instance, regulations create guidelines for generating the provisions for asset risk, standards for accounting, stipulations regard deposit insurance, requirements for capital, and rules and procedures for licensing. It is necessary to specify how different components of the economy interact, including ownership of the various segments of the financial system and their linkage to industrial, agricultural, and other companies in the service sector. A framework that conceptualizes development as a process of cumulative causation predicts that successful banking will arise when investment, production, and banking interact dynamically.

The issue of creating legal incentives to loan, monitor, and supervise activities that have higher risk but more developmental value becomes an important part of the juridical design of financial systems. An equally important issue is the promotion of mechanisms to institutionalize the legal system in an effort to encourage internalization of the rules of operation. Rewards as well as punitive measures may be necessary to enforce regulations in the initial phases. The ultimate aim, however, is a regulatory system in which monitoring is the prime function, rendering intervention the exception rather than the rule. Regulatory systems must become institutionalized; this occurs when they are internalized in the operating procedures of financial firms and as correlative mental constructs within organizations. Because regulations constitute the most modifiable part of the institutional matrix, I treat them as mechanisms for the transformation of institutions.

Capacities. Capacities are linked to the underlying capabilities of the constitutive members (individuals and other subunits) of organizations to effectively achieve the goals of the organization within the boundaries of its norms and rules. These capabilities must be developed in a balanced fashion. The banking sectors should not expand beyond the supply of capable bankers and regulators. In contrast, the capacity-building project of the adjustment period focused on enhancing the stabilization components of the government. Public agencies focused on orthodox stabilization (and its associated austerity), which dictated that central banks and ministries of finance would expand rapidly while the machinery of the state was truncated. The hope was that with retraction of the state, private agents would respond to the new vector of undistorted prices to produce goods and services competitively.

In the same vein, liberalization encouraged the asymmetric expansion of banking organizations rather than the auditing and other regulatory capacities of supervising agencies. There was little concern about the capacities of the private sector in financial markets; they were simply assumed to be intact. In a misconceived attempt to increase competition in the financial sector, banking licenses were frequently handed to new owners lacking both capital and banking experience. The financial sector was expanded far too rapidly relative to the availability of trained, professional, and capable employees (Stein et al. 2002).

Yet this is not a purely technical issue. Capacities must be perceived as institutional rather than simply technical if they are to expand. New skills must not merely be acquired; they must be internalized. Because capacities influence the nature of perceptions, conceptions, and even correlative behavior, new interpretations of the same information are created when capacities are altered. Gathering and interpreting information about potential loan recipients, understanding regulatory stipulations, developing strategies for financial markets, developing and comprehending company auditing stipulations—all are contingent on increasing the institutionalization of capacities.

Organizations. Organizations are legally recognized entities that combine groups of people with defined common rules and purposes. They include state regulatory bodies and financial intermediaries. When considering intermediaries, countries should focus on creating a variety of ownership and banking types to deal with the multileveled financial needs of a developing economy. The state will need to assume risk in all of these structures, both on the deposit side and on the loan side (given that the most development-oriented projects often have the higher risks). Where private risk is not socialized, it is difficult to see how private investment and accumulation can occur in developing countries. Options for ensuring that the criteria for subsidization are being realized and are consonant with developmental objectives include Korean-style policy loans, the Japanese main bank system, business-government councils, planning agencies, partial state ownership of banks, and developmental banks. To avoid instability, capital accounts must be carefully controlled; even the access of banking systems to international loans must be closely monitored.

Details of the five components of the matrix and how they relate to financial development are summarized in table 7.1. It presents criteria for evaluating the relation between the institutions and financial development along with goals and examples of ways to measure progress. The final part of this chapter discusses the utility of the institutional framework for explaining financial crises in developing countries and for generating new institutions for financial development. In each case, examples will be drawn from Nigeria.[25]

Application of the Institutional Framework to Crises and the Development of Financial Systems

Toward an Institutional Understanding of Financial Crises

The institutional framework can provide a different understanding of the crises that frequently follow liberalization, as well as a new set of guidelines concerning how to prevent them. At the heart of the World Bank's commitment to the orthodox view of financial liberalization is a belief in a singular mode of human behavior. In other words, individuals are believed to react in a predictable manner to a correct set of signals as long as these individuals are independent, unfettered, and compensated for their actions. The Bank's perspective implies that individuals' behavior is not affected by learning curves, variations in capacity, behavioral norms, extramarket communications between participants, organizational entities, or incentives. This view acknowledges neither the institutional context of a previous system nor the institutional transformation necessary to put in place a new system of finance. This is exactly the problem.

TABLE 7.1 **Financial development and the institutional matrix**

Category	Evaluation	Goal	Measures
Norms	• Formalism vs. internalization • Norms within subcultures: professional habits and standards • Time horizons • Degree of trust • Uniqueness • Stability	• Increase the internalization of development-enhancing norms • Improve and extend professional standards • Increase time horizons and trust of the financial system with norms that allow for more development-enhancing projects • Create unique norms to avoid competing norms that prevent internalization of ones that enhance development • Increase the stability of development-enhancing norms	• Number of prosecutions of individuals for breaking regulations; size and availability of training programs, including courses on professional ethics • Incidence of audits from regulators; number of investigations for financial wrongdoing per regulator • Degree of collateralization of loans; transactions in interbank lending markets, changes in duration of loans; number and size of credit agencies
Incentives	• Criteria for internal success • Criteria for external success • Penalties • Rewards	• Consistency of internal and external criteria and regulations that induce development-enhancing behavior • Creation or existence of a penalty-reward system that will reinforce development-enhancing behavior • Consideration of the context of incentives	• Consistency between government statements and actions in financial policy • Existence of a penal code for financial crimes including types of penalties • Existence of a system of rewards and punishments in banks and government regulatory bodies • Discrepancy between the official rewards and penalties and reality • The extent to which the financial sector (private and regulatory) is praised by the press and other external evaluating agencies (BIS, IMF, Moody)for providing a sound financial system • The extent to which bad financial behavior is publicized and criticized and how this affects behavior • Pay difference between regulators and private sectors
Regulations	• Degree of clarity • Enforcement mechanisms • Consistency between formal and informal regulations	• Ease of accessibility and understanding of regulatory climate • Consistency between formal regulation and the rules of operation	• Percentage of final transactions covered by regulations • Kind of transactions that are covered by regulations • Number of legal challenges about interpretation of regulations

Organizations	• Harmony of operation between the operational, judicial, and legislative levels • Harmony of regulation across sectors of the economy • Types • Ownership • Intermediaries between different sectors • State involvement through public regulatory and supervisory and monitoring bodies	• Consistency of the regulatory level to create a more consistent climate of regulations for the financial sector • Create an optimal mix of organizations consistent with the needs of the economy • Ensure consistency between regulatory and supervisory structures in financial organizations • Expanding and creating new state organizations for increasing information flows, improving monitoring, creating safety nets and socializing risks	• Extent of overlap between government agencies • Democratic accountability of regulators, lawmakers, and judges • Ease of bankruptcy and other legal procedures involving financial actors • Measure of how well a country's political system works • Breadth: number of sectors covered by financial firms (e.g., personal banking, investment banking, agriculture banks) • Depth: number of financial firms by sector • Percentage of financial firms that are foreign-owned • Number of financial regulatory organizations • Number of sectors that each organization regulates
Capacities	• Regulatory and other supervisory training • Labor force and management training in financial organizations • Effectiveness and efficiency of public intervention • Ability to stabilize the financial sector relative to financial shocks • Quantity and types of access to global financial flows — informational access to loan recipients	• Ensure a supply of well-trained regulators and bankers • Ensure that public-sector structures are adequate to support private-sector actors • Increase access to less volatile, long-term capital flows • Increase the depth of financial flows and new options to deal with them • New organizations to audit and evaluate accounting practices and procedures	• Number of hours and kinds and quality of training programs available per regulator • Number of private-sector employees per regulator • Number of years of experience per regulator vis à vis the number of years of experience per private-sector employee • Number of years of schooling per regulator vis à vis private-sector employees

When financial liberalization generates a new operating environment, an institutional hiatus emerges during which the players, organizations, and incentives change but new forms of correlative behavior have not yet been institutionalized. In such a climate regulations and regulatory structures are poorly developed and are seen as the causes of financial problems rather than the solutions, the virtues of unfettered private property rights are extolled because of ideology, the capacities of new banks are weak, the rules of operation of newly formed organizations are just being formulated, and professional norms are absent. Therefore one is likely to find the same rampant abuse, incompetence, and blatant fraud that has been witnessed in too many countries, with many dire consequences for other sectors of the economy.

Much of the literature has focused on the side of financial bubbles that deals with demand for loans. From the supply side, or banking side, however, asset inflation increases the value of collateral, which justifies high loan amounts and numbers. With no development-oriented norms or regulations to guide loans, new banks will seek avenues for rapid short-term profit accumulation. Typically, groups expecting rapid asset turnover will be willing to pay loftier interest rates. The McKinnon-Shaw view assumes that private actors make the most efficient choices. This assumption, combined with the demand for state retraction, means that there are likely to be few regulators or politicians questioning these lending patterns. Moreover, in the absence of well-formed organizational entities with their own operating principles and systems, mimetic isomorphism will encourage new banks to emulate other "successful" enterprises by reproducing structures designed to support loans that generate rapid profit. In this climate, lending in support of speculation is likely to become ubiquitous, leading to the financial fragility and ensuing crises that we have frequently seen. In this case, the behavior that develops in conjunction with financial system reforms is disastrous, costly, and ultimately unsustainable.

The institutional interpretation of financial crisis is quite useful in explaining the events following liberalization in a number of countries. Consider the example of Nigeria, where, in 1982, twenty-two commercial banks and eight merchant banks were operating.[26] The commercial banks had an average of forty-five branches each. The industry was dominated by four large banks with a mix of state and private ownership (First Bank, Union Bank, United Bank for Africa, and Afribank). The first three had originated in the colonial era and had prominent foreign partners: Standard Chartered of London, Barclays of London, and Bankers Trust of New York and Banque Nationale de Paris, respectively. The fourth, Afribank, was established in 1960. By 1986 the number of commercial banks had increased to twenty-nine and that of merchant banks to twelve, with about fifteen firms controlled by domestic private owners. Overall, about 80 percent of assets in the commercial banks and 45 percent of assets in the merchant banks were under federal control. In addition, state governments had equity in two dozen banks.

Meanwhile, the economy was troubled: it was far too dependent on oil revenues, it was not generating employment opportunities for a rapidly growing labor force, it had low savings rates and a very small manufacturing sector, and it was rife with government corruption and inefficiencies, particularly in the state-owned banks. An institutional approach would have started with a careful evaluation of the institutional matrix before working out a strategy to transform it.

The World Bank's approach, however, was completely different. In 1983 the Bank wrote a report urging Nigeria to deregulate its financial system. In classic McKinnon-Shaw terms, the report criticized government allocation of credit, public subsidies, the inadequate number of banks, and the complexity and rigidity of government regulations. These measures were said to encourage distortions, create inefficiencies, and discourage savings. To counter these perceived weaknesses, the Bank called for implementation of positive real interest rates, granting of more bank licenses, relaxation of credit allocation rules, secession of interest rate subsidization in preferred sectors, and deregulation of interest rate controls (World Bank 1983a).

Accordingly, between 1984 and 1986 the Central Bank of Nigeria (CBN) raised interest rates and committed itself to reforming the banking system. Additional measures including discontinuing credit to priority sectors, unifying interest rates, and ensuring real positive interest levels were promised as part of the 1986 adjustment program. Liberalization of financial instruments continued throughout the 1980s with the deregulation of lending and savings rates, the opening of an interbank foreign exchange market, and the freeing of price setting on interbank lending markets. The standards of the Bank for International Settlements (BIS) for capital (8 percent of its total risk-weighted assets) were not put in place until 1992.[27] Open market operations did not commence until mid-1993 after the first of three discount houses for government securities was established. To encourage greater competition, the CBN eased restrictions on bank licenses and stipulated very low capital requirements.[28]

By 1991 the number of banks in Nigeria had risen from 41 to 119.[29] In this deregulated climate, the orthodox belief was that increasing the number of financial organizations would create better efficiency and competition. The number of finance houses (largely unregulated private investment companies that often attracted funds by promising large up-front payments) rapidly proliferated. In 1992, when licensing (which brought financial organizations under the authority of the CBN) began, there were an estimated 666 organizations, although only half were ultimately licensed. In addition, the National Housing Fund, which promised matching funds for low-interest mortgages, inspired the creation of hundreds more nonbank financial organizations (NBFOs). When the matching funds were not forthcoming, these new ventures did not act as mortgage organizations but simply operated like finance houses. By 1993, about 250 were licensed. New insurance companies were initiated, and government insurance was privatized.

Using interlocking ownership, new bank owners used such organizations in their accumulation strategies. In 1993 there were 310 interlocking directorates among banks, insurance companies, and NBFOs. Banks used their control of NBFOs to evade regulatory authorities via round-tripping (shipping funds to unregulated affiliates between bank inspections). Potential depositors often were directed by bank workers to affiliated NBFOs, where they would receive large amounts of income up front after making their "investment" (a classic Ponzi scheme). Many of these outfits used deposits illegally for real estate purchases, foreign exchange deals, or personal consumption until the assets were bled dry. In the laissez-faire financial world of the 1980s and early 1990s, NBFOs simply disappeared overnight, sometimes resurfacing soon afterward as new firms.

The behavior of many of the new banks was not much better. There was widespread evidence of "kite flying" (floating checks on nonexistent funds to create liquidity by taking advantage of the writing-day clearance period), charge duplication, embezzlement, and bidding on official foreign exchange markets using dummy companies.[30] With rapid devaluation, high real interest levels, multiple foreign exchange rates, and import liberalization, banks gravitated toward financing speculation in foreign exchange and in importing, two areas with rapid turnover, which also encouraged deindustrialization. Even the more well-established banks were pulled into the frenzy via the liberalized interbank lending market, where rates exceeded 100 percent in some years. New banks hungry for additional sources of cash income were more than willing to pay the exorbitant rates.

By 1995, nearly half the banks were distressed, and thirty-three were eventually liquidated (the thirty-fourth was blocked from doing so by a court injunction). Nonperforming loans reached 57.8 billion naira, or roughly five times shareholders' equity (6.3 percent of 1994 GDP). The cost to the Nigerian economy to date has been very high.[31] As of December 2001, the Nigerian Deposit Insurance Corporation (NDIC) had recovered only 12 percent of the 31.6 billion naira owed in total to the liquidated bank. By the end of 2000, the top thirty banks with assets of more than 15 billion naira controlled 78.4 percent of the total. Moreover, asset quality was still poor: 22 percent of loans were nonperforming in 2000, and 17 percent were nonperforming in 2001. This amounted to 92 percent and 77 percent, respectively, of shareholder equity. In addition, there were still widespread problems throughout the industry. The total deposits in distressed banks amounted to 44.2 billion naira by the end of 2001. In 2002 twelve banks were having major liquidity problems and were bailed out by loans from the six largest banks.[32]

From a finance and development perspective, the result was disastrous. Between 1987 and 1996, real lending to the private sector declined by an astonishing 60 percent. Meanwhile, the finance sector's contribution to GDP more than tripled, from 3.1 percent to 9.9 percent. This was prima facie evidence of the way a McKinnon-Shaw–inspired expansion of finance led to disintermediation (a disruption in the flow from savings to investment).[33]

What happened? An institutional hiatus was created by deregulation, leading to modes of behavior that ultimately were unstable. The rapid pace of deregulation attracted a massive influx of people from other sectors with no banking experience. These individuals, motivated by a desire for access to foreign exchange rather than a desire to serve the profession, brought new norms to the banking sector: fraud and malfeasance. The speed of transformation outstripped the structures and legal stipulations of the regulatory system. New organizations were put in place not for social development but for the rapid accumulation of individual wealth. Mimetic isomorphism encouraged other financial organizations to emulate the structures and practices of companies making massive short-term profits. When failed firms were liquidated or reorganized in an effort to create stability and new correlative behavior for the purpose of generating profits, these financial organizations missed the opportunity to promote the kinds of behaviors that would have improved development—for instance, financing initiatives that would generate employment.

In contrast to the Bank's recommendations, an institutional approach would focus on analyzing the existing institutional matrix in the country in question and developing clear strategies for carefully coordinated change in each component of that matrix. It would employ an alternative sequence of steps for transforming financial systems. It therefore would reach different conclusions about what changes Nigeria could have made in the mid-1980s in order to avoid financial crisis.

Financial Transformation and Development: Beyond Orthodoxy

Unlike the orthodox approach to finance, the institutional approach emphatically rejects the possibility that policy formulations can be universally applied to all economies at all times. Nevertheless, within the institutional framework, it is possible to determine some broad guidelines to aid in transforming finance for purposes of development.

An institutional approach begins with a careful analysis of the institutionally related endowments of an economy: how the components of the institutional matrix interact to create existing forms of correlative behavior and how they can be changed to generate new generalized habits of thought. If development involves creating a sustained improvement in the standard of living of a population, then purposeful intermediation should aim at channeling finance into forms of production and accumulation that will lead to rising income and employment. How can this be accomplished in practice?

If the existing finance-related institutional matrix is inadequate, the first step must be to change the regulatory structure so that new legal stipulations promote the creation of new organizational entities to fill the gaps. The institutionalization of regulatory structures is a complicated but necessary component of financial transformation.

How do regulatory changes influence human behavior in practice? People respond to the rule itself, to the perceived behavior of the agency implementing the regulations, to the feedback of the participants in the process, and to the resources, capacities, and constraints that influence individuals' ability to respond to new regulations. Thus, in the context of reforming the finance, legally specified operating rules must include incentives for undertaking productive lending and penalties for financing speculative activities. Enforcement agencies must exist before new organizations are created. In the past, regulatory structures have tended to lag behind the creation of new organizations and have often arisen only in the face of financial disarray, rather than as a necessary counterpart to these new organizations.

In the countries where bank finance is used as a source of private investment, it is necessary to establish new banking organizations with charters for specific kinds of lending. The risky nature of crucial loans for such purposes as financing new market entrants and the acquisition of new technology means that the state must be responsible for risk sharing and subsidization. In addition, the state should enact aggressive auditing procedures to ensure the fulfillment of contingent criteria. In regimes prone to corruption, the approach should initially focus on nondiscretionary rewards and penalties. Once operating procedures become institutionalized within organizations, intrusive instruments will be increasingly unnecessary as new norms evolve and new forms of correlative behavior (for example, among loan recipients, lenders, and regulatory agencies) develop. As indicated above, speed is important, along with the state's initiation and fostering of a small number of new financial organizations.

To support organizational and regulatory transformation, a sufficient labor force must be trained in order to promote growth. Too often, new financial entities have been created without due consideration of manpower capacities, leading to ill-suited appointments and labor shortages; the operation of these organizations suffers as a result. Capacity should be continuously upgraded through on- and off-site training, as well as through the creation of incentives that will encourage the internalization of new techniques. Internalization of norms occurs when members of financial organizations are able to understand the rules, are responsible enough to act in accordance with the rules, and are aware of the potential consequences of not following the rules, even when they may be neither rewarded nor punished. In this way, new regulations and their associated incentives set in motion a process of transformation, eventually leading to new forms of correlated behavior.

What of the role of specific incentives such as interest rates? As previously discussed, free-floating interest rates will not send correct market signals in the poorly formed financial systems of developing countries. Instead, it is necessary to carefully set rates in accordance with development priorities or through mechanisms of subsidization. Moreover, countries need to move beyond the practice of inflation targeting, which is predicated solely on price stability and therefore excludes other important objectives such as output and employment generation.

Would an institutional approach to finance have created a different strategy for Nigeria in the mid-1980s? I argue in the affirmative. The first priority of the state should have been to allocate a portion of oil revenues to support manufacturing investment and exports to generate employment. Yet the model being followed at the time was that of the American-style banking system, which is typically promoted as the ideal organizational structure of financial liberalization (Stein 2002a). Nigeria should have looked to alternative approaches that were more accepting of the realities of developing countries.

The American-style banking system is problematic for many reasons. First, it relies on bond and stock markets, which tend to be poorly formed in most developing countries, rather than on bank loans for financing in-vestment. Given the frequent unreliability of information, stock markets have difficulty assessing the relative risk of share offerings, which leads to a high probability of fraud and malfeasance (Stiglitz 1989). Moreover, there is widespread evidence that corporate management strategies aimed at maximizing shareholder value will not lead to strategies that enhance investment in vital development-related areas, such as information and technology (Singh et al. 2005).

By contrast, certain financial systems, such as the main bank approach used in Japan, provide a more viable system for supporting bank financing for development. Under this system, a single bank acts as the main bank and takes the lead in arranging financing, owns a significant number of shares in enterprises to which it lends money (but does not own a control-ling interest), and is involved in gathering information about the usage of loans. Long-term lending banks, which raise funds from debentures on the markets, are made responsible for supporting industrial investment. The long-term industrial banks have the highest concentration of experts, who are able to perform the important task of assessing the worth of manu-facturing projects. They play a crucial role in reliably and realistically ex-tending the time horizons of lending; that has positive consequences for development.

In a main bank system, the government has a close relationship with private-sector banks.[34] It purchases debentures using money from a trust fund, which raises funds from postal savings (or oil revenue, in Nigeria's case). Banks can then purchase debentures for use as collateral on loans from the central bank. Interest rates are tightly controlled. On the lending side, once the government bond rate is determined, the bank debenture rate (interest rate paid on industrial bank bonds) is set slightly higher than the bond rate, and the long-term prime rate is fixed at nearly 1 percent above the debenture rate, thus providing profitability to the industrial banks. Likewise, the short-term prime is kept slightly higher than the official discount rate, and the maximum deposit rate is set according to guidelines issued by the central bank. All rates are carefully manipulated to ensure bank profitability; that is, bank lending rates are sufficiently far above deposit rates and discount rates to generate net income flows. The level of subsidization is quite significant. For instance, in Japan's case, the implicit subsidy created by keeping deposit rates artificially low was estimated at between 20 and 25 percent of bank profits (Stein 2002a). The main bank system also had a dual auditing process in which officials from both the Ministry of Finance and the central bank were responsible, thereby creating a better system of checks and balances.

In 1986, instead of deregulating the financial system and handing out bank licenses to create some textbook ideal of competition, Nigeria should have introduced institutional building blocks of finance such as the main bank system. Nigeria organized four development banks between 1964 and 1977, but their appraisal system was political and often nonselective (Adeyemi 2002). The Nigerian Industrial Development Bank could have been resuscitated and reorganized with a focus on building its capacity with a more professional cadre of project assessors. New regulations should have created new rules, allocated new responsibilities to organizations, and generated new incentives.

New training institutes should have been organized to generate a sufficient number of professionals to administer the system and to ensure sufficient capacity on the private sector banking side. In 1977 the financial sector formed the Nigerian Institute of Bankers. Yet its status as a charter organization with the power to provide education and banking credentials, set professional norms, and undertake audits was not legally recognized until 1990 (Chartered Institute of Bankers of Nigeria 2005). The potential impact of the Nigerian Institute of Bankers was not recognized until after the banking crisis of the mid-90s took place. The charter should have been put in place before any transformation of the financial system so that it could play an effective role in building financial capabilities and in generating new norms in line with the changing priorities of the banking system.

Two of the four largest banks could have taken responsibility as the main banks. For the first two or three years, they could have acted as the principal banks to a handful of key companies in important manufacturing sectors with local and regional markets, such as food processing, textiles, and petroleum by-products. Once established, the system could have been extended by means of a mimetic process of organizational transformation. Expansion would only have occurred at the rate of capacity development on the regulatory and private banking side. The regulatory framework could have been extended to accommodate this new system on the basis of the procedures that were first put in place in the first two banks. The central bank and Nigerian Deposit Insurance Corporation should have formed a dual auditing process, perhaps with initial outside assistance from an organization such as the Bank for International Settlements.

The main banks should have been rewarded by the state (with tax write-offs, subsidies, access to international loans, and so on) for successful allocation of funds that were able to stimulate greater investment, output, exports of manufactured goods, and employment. Banks, in turn, could have provided pecuniary and nonpecuniary rewards (praise, recognition, rewards) for initiating, monitoring, and ultimately completing projects that expanded growth and development. Regulatory agencies such as the CBN and NDIC should also have set up definitive reward and punishment systems and ensured that internal auditors had both sufficient investigatory powers and the means to deal rapidly with cases of corruption. Even such nonfinancial actors as the media and the National Assembly could have played a significant role by, for example, publicly praising banks' efforts, thereby contributing to their prestige.

As discussed in chapter 5, the key to transforming behavior is altering habits to create new perspectives, intentions, and preferences. Slowly, over time, with the appropriate exercise of rewards and penalties, norms crucial to development—such as professional standards, honesty, and a sense of the importance of socioeconomic development—could have formed within the bank and regulatory system in Nigeria. The core of financial development's virtuous circle consists not of a predetermined level of savings but rather new forms of correlated behavioral patterns that increase coordination, unity of purpose, and certainty.

Conclusions

The McKinnon-Shaw theory relies on a pre-Keynesian notion that prior saving is needed for financial development. Higher interest rates are assumed to induce saving because they represent the main reward for postponing consumption. They also are believed to improve the quality of investment, whereas rationing and other forms of government intervention are believed to reduce the quality of intermediation. Competition and private ownership of banks are held to be preferable for improving efficiency of intermediation by shrinking the margin between rates of interest on deposits and on loans. Likewise, government deregulation is promoted because it is said to unify capital markets and, in turn, reduce the inefficiencies associated with fragmentation. McKinnon-Shaw emphasizes state retraction, increasing interest rates, and the introduction of greater competition in the banking sector as the means by which to achieve an idealized virtuous circle of higher savings, improvements in the quantity and quality of investment, and greater growth, in turn raising savings further.

The problem with this vision is that it is fundamentally flawed at a theoretical level. Among other things, the financial liberalization theory treats finance as if it were the kind of purely competitive market described in introductory economics textbooks. As the imperfect-information theorists have argued, however, finance is replete with asymmetries of risk and information. In finance, those who are willing to pay the most for a loan may not be those who provide the greatest return to the lender, because higher interest rates may increase the probability of default. At a more fundamental level, McKinnon-Shaw is essentially noninstitutional, despite the fact that finance is a profoundly institutional phenomenon.

The widespread nature of the banking crises that followed exercises in financial liberalization inspired McKinnon and others to argue that the problem lay not in the theory but in the sequence of reforms. On the contrary, there is widespread evidence that the order of the steps does not alter the outcome.

Despite its flaws, the McKinnon-Shaw view of finance has been the main theoretical inspiration behind the World Bank's adjustment loans to the financial sectors of various countries and the conditions imposed on financial sectors in adjustment packages. In the past, the Bank had issued a type of loan called the financial intermediary loan to banks for on-lending to other sectors. After 1987, however, orthodox financial sector adjustment loans replaced such loans. Despite their poor track record, the Bank adhered to the same core policies throughout the 1990s. The poor performance was dismissed, largely by adding new variables and using extrinsic explanations. In cases where macrostabilization was present, the Bank attempted to explain the crises by extraneous factors such as cronyism and poor corporate governance. In addition, the Bank began supplementing these recommendations with new ones, invoking NIE to explain why regulation should be minimized in financial sectors and encouraging foreign ownership of banks to help counter the instability created by selling off banks to local owners. In some countries, however this has had an adverse effect in that it has limited the financing available for small- and medium-sized enterprises.

According to the orthodox view, money is a means of payment in which price stability is the prime consideration, and this goal is best achieved by constraining the growth of the money supply. By contrast, the institutional theory of finance focuses on money as an endogenous construct. Loans generate deposits, deposits expand reserves, and the demand for money induces the supply of money.

The institutional matrix is critical to conceptualizing a system of endogenous money. At the core of successful credit creation for the purpose of development is a general comprehension of the mechanisms, expectations, rules, information, rewards, and penalties associated with the issuing of new loans. These are contingent on a carefully constructed matrix of five interactive components: norms, regulations, capacities, organizations, and incentives. This matrix can be used to understand why orthodox policies lead to banking crises. In the example of Nigeria, an alternative framework could have been used to build financial systems that would aid development.

CHAPTER EIGHT

Transcending Neoliberal Health Policies

[N]either definitional difficulties nor a lack of empirical data have ever deterred economists, and least of all the model builders among them, from tackling problems and presenting solutions [to health-care problems] that pretend knowledge.

From the planning point of view the effect of any particular measure in the health field depends on all other policy measures and is, by itself indeterminate. . . . A generalized model, in aggregate visualizing a sum of inputs in preventative and curative measures giving rise to an output of improved health conditions cannot be of any help . . . such a model . . . is premised on an optimum combination of all policy measures, which cannot be achieved without taking account with circular causation within the health field and in the whole social system . . . planning for better health conditions must proceed by an intuitive process, wherein segmented information is complemented by informed estimates and made to yield the outline of a strategy.

Doing everything possible to improve health conditions in all strata of the population stands . . . as a moral imperative. Besides having an independent value, health advances have an instrumental value in the development process in that they affect other social and economic conditions. . . . The other side of circular causation is that health itself is affected by socio-economic factors, notably income, level of living and particular nutrition.—Gunnar Myrdal, 1968

Introduction

Gunnar Myrdal's "moral imperative" to improve health conditions and the quality of human life is as pressing today as it was in 1968. In sub-Saharan Africa the life expectancy fell from fifty years to forty-six years between 1980 and 2003, and in the Russian Federation it fell from sixty-nine years to sixty-six years. In Russia, the decline is mainly among men, whose life expectancy dropped from seventy years in the mid-1980s to fifty-nine years in 2003 (United National Development Program 2005; World Bank 2005b).

The decrease in life expectancy in some African countries is nothing short of tragic. It fell from sixty-two to forty-six years in South Africa, from fifty-eight to thirty-seven years in Lesotho, from forty-five to thirty-eight years in Malawi, from fifty-six to thirty-nine years in Zimbabwe, from forty-nine to thirty-six years in Zambia, and from fifty-seven to thirty-eight years in Botswana. In areas outside of southern Africa, which is known to be the epicenter of the HIV/AIDS pandemic, declines have been significant, indicating that HIV/AIDS cannot be entirely to blame. In Nigeria, for example, the life expectancy declined from forty-nine to forty-five years from 1980 to 2004; in Côte D'Ivoire it fell from fifty to forty-five years; and in Central African Republic it fell from forty-eight to forty-two years. On the other hand, Sierra Leone, a country whose protracted civil war began to die down not long ago, has seen an increase in life expectancy—all the way to thirty-seven years from thirty-five (World Bank 2005b).

The high—and in some cases, rising—mortality rates stem from largely preventable diseases. On the basis of WHO categorizations, which determine the severity of mortality rates, in countries designated as having "high" child mortality rates and "very high" adult mortality rates (which are also the poorest countries in Africa), 74 percent of deaths in 2002 were from communicable diseases, maternal and perinatal conditions, or nutritional disorders. In contrast, in countries with low mortality rates (which also happen to be the richest nations in western Europe), only 6 percent of deaths were from these causes (World Health Organization 2003). In the poor countries, young children have been hit particularly hard. By 1990, nine African countries of the fifteen for which data are available had infant mortality rates higher than the 1978 level. In 2003, the rates in six of these countries were still above the 1978 level. Overall, in 2003, infant mortality rates were equal to or higher than the 1990 rates in twenty of forty-five sub-Saharan African countries; the regionwide average exceeded 10 percent of the population (Golladay and Liese 1980; World Bank 2005b).

In spite of these enormous health challenges and the preventable nature of many illnesses afflicting the poor in developing countries, the World Bank largely neglected health issues for many decades.[1] Moreover, as we will see, when the Bank finally began to focus on this area, strategies were designed by neoclassical economists rather than by health experts. In the manner observed by Myrdal, "neither definitional difficulties nor a lack of empirical data" stopped the economists from "tackling problems and presenting solutions that pretend[ed] knowledge." As a result, Bank policies in some cases actually exacerbated poor health conditions in developing countries.

The first part of this chapter documents the history of health policy at the World Bank, including the increasing influence of economic thinking during the 1980s. As we will see, Bank health economists not only influenced health policy within the organization but also greatly influenced the agendas of other donor agencies. This is followed by an empirical review of the impact of the reform policies. The latter part of the chapter develops an institutional approach to health care based not on some optimum level of health spending but rather on an intuitive approach that carefully applies the institutional matrix to concrete health problems.

Health Policy and the Bank: A Brief History to 1980

We saw in chapter 1 that the Bank was initially very reluctant to support "risky" social spending because of the potential impact on its bond ratings. As seen in table 1.2, the commitment of resources to social spending therefore grew rather slowly, reaching 4 percent of the total only in the 1960s (compared with 0 percent in the 1950s). During this period, there were no explicitly designated health projects but several projects had obvious health implications, including the expansion of water supply.

With McNamara's commitment to poverty reduction, the Bank began to fund work in social areas such as population control. The first loan for family planning was made to Jamaica in June 1970. Lending was very moderate during most of the 1970s, with an average of only three projects per year between 1971 and 1978 (World Bank 1975).

Following the organization of a USAID-sponsored program concerning international nutrition at the Massachusetts Institute of Technology in 1972, McNamara showed an increasing interest in poverty and nutrition. In 1972, the Bank published a report titled "Possible Bank Action on Malnutrition Problems" that signaled the movement toward lending for programs in this new area. The Bank did not approve the first formal loan for nutrition, however, until 1976 (it loaned $19 million to Brazil), and it only approved three loans in total in this area through 1978.

At this point Bank health policy in such areas as nutrition was developed not by economists but by scientists such as the biochemist James Lee, who was hired as a scientific advisor in late 1970. In June 1973, Mc-Namara requested a health policy paper from the Bank staff, which eventually produced its first comprehensive health sector policy paper in 1975. Meanwhile, in 1974, in cooperation with the Food and Agriculture Organization of the United Nations(FAO), the United Nations Development Programme (UNDP), and WHO, the Bank became directly involved in disease control with the initiation of the eleven-country West African effort to combat onchocerciasis (river blindness). The Bank coordinated the financing, successfully securing aid from a variety of bilateral donors, and WHO acted as the executing agency (World Bank 1975; Ruger 2005).

The 1975 Health Sector Policy Report drew heavily on WHO's work and on scientific sources relating to public health in order to explain the factors responsible for health outcomes. The section of the report concerning health policy focused on the social goals and productive investment dimensions of health that reflected the kinds of studies that were available in the development literature of the time.[2] The report warned about relying too narrowly on cost-benefit analysis and on the private sector to deliver health goods; both were said to be precluded by fundamental market failures. In particular, the report put forth four major points regarding the understanding of health care: first, consumers of health care will not have sufficient understanding to always make sensible choices. Second, there are too many externalities associated with disease for the responsibility for rational decision making to be given to the individual alone. Third, there is likely to be little competition in the health sector because hospitals require very large investment to provide any service and are therefore more like a public utility than a private good. Finally, maldistribution of income is also likely to limit the ability of the poor to gain access to health care through the market. As we will see below, by the mid-1980s these concerns had almost entirely disappeared with the rise of health economics and neoliberalism inside the Bank.

The policy focus of the report echoed much of the thinking in the UN system, where health care was seen as too top-heavy and focused on cities at the expense of primary care needs in rural areas. The report also carefully considered two options for future Bank strategies in health care: one in which the Bank would continue to fund health projects as part of initiatives in other sectors (for example, training health professionals as part of broader educational projects) and one in which it would begin to develop its own health-focused strategies. In 1975 the Bank felt it did not have the expertise to undertake a broad health-focused initiative and so it chose the first option (World Bank 1975). This approach continued through the 1970s; during this time health components were included in only about 5 percent of all Bank projects, particularly those focusing on agriculture, rural development, and urban areas (Golladay and Liese 1980). By 1979, with the formation of the Health, Nutrition, and Population Department (HNP), the Bank began to gradually move toward the second option (Ruger 2005).

In its earliest commitment to a coordinated health policy the Bank continued to be influenced by the movement toward primary health care, whose premises are best captured by the Alma-Ata Declaration of 1978. The declaration was the product of a meeting in Alma-Ata, U.S.S.R., of health representatives from 134 countries and 64 organizations, including UN agencies, and it set the tone for significant health-sector reforms. Until the early 1970s health care development had focused on the construction of medical and paramedical schools, hospitals, and other facilities. This was characterized as a "trickle down" approach in line with similar development strategies. Yet the trickle-down approach faced increasing criticism. In 1971, WHO and the United Nations Children's Fund (UNICEF) formed the Joint Committee on Alternative Approaches to Meeting Basic Health Needs of Populations in Developing Countries. The committee focused on barriers to access to health care in developing countries and drew on the experience of eleven countries that had overcome these impediments. The committee report was presented to the World Health Assembly in May 1975. In response, the assembly asked WHO to develop new approaches and proposed an international conference on primary health care, which was eventually held in 1978 in Alma-Ata. Its revolutionary declaration asserted that health care was a human right and that, as such, all governments should focus on policies that would make health care accessible, affordable, and more socially responsible (Golladay and Liese 1980).

The main background paper concerning health care for World Development Report 1980 identified six basic principles of primary health care (Golladay and Liese 1980). First, health is a basic human right. Second, achievement of health via the reduction of morbidity and mortality in the population is at the core of the development process and should not be seen as merely an instrument for decreasing morbidity. Third, community participation is an important dimension of low-cost health care; people have both the right and the duty to be involved with the planning and implementation of their care. Fourth, health care planning should incorporate all possible activities that can best improve health outcomes. Fifth, health interventions, such as those stemming from the relation between nutrition and infectious disease, are synergistic. Finally, primary health care focuses on affordability and social acceptability and moves away from highly technical solutions, opting instead for a greater utilization of less costly auxiliary workers and health solutions.

The major premises of the paper were quite contrary to the market-oriented strategy that the Bank would adopt only a few years later. First there were strong admonishments that "the use of prices and markets to allocate health care is generally not desirable" (Golladay and Liese 1980, 47). Echoing the 1975 health sector report, the authors argue that incomes are not distributed in a manner that corresponds to health care needs of the population; consumers are not well qualified to select the best health services and thus cost is not a sound basis for choice; many people may be too ill to make health care choices and may rely on family members instead; eradication of disease has many social benefits that exceed private benefits; and finally, because health crises are frequently random and catastrophic, individuals cannot budget adequately to protect themselves. Thus, risk-sharing or insurance is needed to ensure good health care. In the last case, the authors encourage either pooling risk by means of compulsory membership in insurance schemes or the direct provision of services by the public sector (Golladay and Liese 1980).

Health issues are incorporated into a broader strategy aimed at alleviating poverty and improving human development. Other background papers represent the final exertion of influence by proponents of basic needs in the Bank and are authored by writers such as Haq, Sen, and Hicks who were concerned with basic needs.[3] World Development Report 1980. which followed the background papers, shows a strong commitment to primary health care and its associated integration of health, education, food and nutrition, water, and sanitation. In contrast to the adjustment agenda that soon followed, the report is unequivocal about the importance of food subsidies to improving life expectancy: "few low income countries have come near to nutritional adequacy without some form of food subsidy" (World Bank 1980, 62).

The report expresses strong concerns about the impact of user fees and other related costs on access to health care, education, and water, although the following two decades would see wide promulgation of user fees. Citing a Malaysian study, WDR 1980 point to the strong disincentive effect of user fees on utilization of piped water for the poorest 40 percent of the population. With regard to health care, the same Malaysian study illustrated a strong positive relation between income and use of private health care but none between income and public care, which had no fees for public inpatient or outpatient treatment. The report concludes from this that "the need for medical care of the poorest and most of the rest of the population was met through the public system" (World Bank 1980, 79).[4]

From the perspective of the Bank circa 1980, the key to success in primary health care would be to mobilize political support, increase public expenditures, and improve public-sector administrative capacities. The last is deemed extremely important because "human development programs can rarely be put out to contract" (World Bank 1980, 76).

Only a few years later, however, the broad support for primary health care began to falter as continued shortages of available resources and a lack of a redirection of expenditures from modern high-tech approaches to less costly approaches began to chip away at political will to pursue the reforms. Primary health care had been heralded as a cheap means by which to meet necessary health demands, but the policymakers who were dealing with the messiness of trying to implement it apparently had not realized that the term *cheap* was relative and that the reforms would still require substantial commitments of resources (Lee and Goodman 2002). One reaction to the funding problem was to continue to focus on public-sector initiatives but to modify the approach in an effort to curtail expenses, for example, by moving from a comprehensive to a more selective approach. Along these lines, in 1980, UNICEF began to promote its program for the priority areas of growth monitoring, oral rehydration, breast feeding, immunization, food supplements, family spacing, and female literacy.

Another approach to the crisis in health care financing was to consider alternative methods of mobilizing funds. Not long afterward there was a consensus that the efficiency of the public health sector could be improved by the introduction of user fees, which would raise the revenues necessary to make the health sector financially viable. With the increasing influence of the neoliberal agenda, this latter approach began to drive health care policy in the early 1980s. The 1981 Berg Report, whose official title was "Accelerated Development in Sub-Saharan Africa," was the first to comprehensively lay out this future direction. In response to the shortage of funds and administrative personnel in support of primary health care it called for industrial insurance schemes, user fees for public health clinics, rationalization of staff, simplification of procedures, and freeing up of the trade in pharmaceuticals. The final recommendation was aimed at private distribution of water and at the training and contracting of private actors to build latrines and lay water pipes (World Bank 1981, 87–90).

With the rise of health economics and the arrival of economists such as David de Ferranti into HNP, the new approach gradually became institutionalized inside the Bank (Brugha and Zwi 2002; Lee and Goodman 2002). Given his role as champion of the neoliberal approach to health policy and his powerful influence inside the Bank, de Ferranti's work is worth examining in detail.

Neoliberalism and Health Policy

David de Ferranti was a Princeton-trained economist who arrived at the World Bank March 1981. He was well suited to the challenge of reformulating health policy along neoliberal lines: the topic of his dissertation was welfare dependence and family disintegration. Between 1981 and 1985, de Ferranti wrote ten reports for HNP, including reports about Malawi, Nigeria, Argentina, and Peru.[5]

De Ferranti played an important role in introducing neoclassical economic principles into health care decision making. In his view, until the early 1980s routine practices in health care were "extremely backward in relation to known methodologies." In accordance with standard economic approaches, he argued that the focus should be on improving efficiency in a marginal world by "achieving incremental improvement over existing analytical practice" on the basis of the principles of "affordability" and "effectiveness" (Prescott and de Ferranti 1985, 1235).

He defines affordability by reference to the voluntarism and equilibrium inherent in neoclassical economics: "a health program is affordable if and only if each of the parties that must contribute to financing its operation at its design scale are able and willing to do so"; moreover, "affordability is a necessary condition for achieving an efficient balance of resource use" (Prescott and de Ferranti 1985, 1237).[6] To ensure affordability according to this definition, two elements are necessary: an accurate estimate of the recurrent costs of programs that have tended to be insufficiently analyzed in the past and balancing of costs against available resources, including central and local governments, health insurers, NGOs, donors, and private households. He warns of the looming gap between resources and recurrent costs. Instead of finding ways to mobilize public expenditures, however, de Ferranti's strategy focuses on the need for policy adjustments that will restrain the public sector's involvement in health care while increasing nonfiscal resources such as user fees (ibid.).

Being true to the concept of affordability was not sufficient to guarantee the efficiency of health care investment; it would also be necessary to design policies focused on improvements to effectiveness. Such a focal point implies the neoclassical principle of optimality. An optimal investment program is one that maximizes objectives while adhering to budget constraints. Following standard economics, then, the "first best solution" for health care reform is to choose health projects "which maximize the health sector contribution to some agreed measure of social welfare" (Prescott and de Ferranti 1985, 1238). A tidy-sounding resolution, perhaps, but it is overwhelmingly simplistic; it falsely suggests that health sector contribution and social welfare are easily measurable and readily definable.

The second-best solution is "to identify through cost-effectiveness analysis those projects which would yield the greatest improvement in health status subject to the resource constraint" (Prescott and de Ferranti 1985, 1238). More precisely, he suggests moving beyond disease-specific analysis to analyzing multipurpose interventions to tackle a wide variety of health measurements. As we will see, this choice of theoretical framework presupposes some common measurement of the potential health outcomes of various interventions. Meanwhile, the Alma-Ata Declaration's commitment to health care as a universal human right was rapidly abandoned as the Bank focused on the retrenchment of the state, the privatization of health care, and the introduction of user fees to deal with resource gaps and reduce "needless" usage and waste in the system. An important contribution to the latter was de Ferranti's 1985 working paper "Paying for Health Services in Developing Countries: An Overview."

The arguments generated in the 1985 paper derive almost entirely from the same neoclassical economic microfoundations and related propositions that were embedded in structural adjustment, as presented in chapter 3. We will see that, as Myrdal put it "neither definitional difficulties nor a lack of empirical data" impeded de Ferranti from advocating user fees and privatization of health care. We will see that de Ferranti's paper is seminal both because it introduced neoclassical economics to health care analysis and because it lay the foundation of the World Bank's health policy in the structural adjustment era.

De Ferranti (1985) begins with the proposition that countries are cutting back on health care as a logical outcome of "the struggle to exercise fiscal restraint in the face of poor economic performance and burgeoning debt" (1). Yet throughout the entire paper there is not a single mention of the role of the IMF and the World Bank in imposing fiscal austerity, which often necessitated cutbacks in health care.

The starting point of the paper completely inverts the argument of the 1980 WDR background paper discussed above (Golladay and Liese 1980) that "[t]he use of prices and markets to allocate health cares is generally not desirable." De Ferranti begins instead with the basic neoclassical proposition that efficiency is maximized by competitive market prices, which equal the marginal private costs of production. Only then can one ask "whether there are good reasons for departing from that price level" (de Ferranti 1985, 5). The aim of the paper is to delimit the circumstances in which prices based on marginal costs are relaxed such that health care is allocated according to the principles of market efficiency. The setting of user fees, de Ferranti argues, has a triple benefit: it generates revenue, generates efficiency, and improves equity.

The first benefit follows from the arguments made above regarding the growing gap between health care needs and available revenue. Financial difficulties lead the author to conclude that the goals of universal primary health care must be abandoned as "overambitious"; resource gaps are enormous even if one has more limited ends in mind (de Ferranti 1985, 20). The second benefit addresses inefficiencies in allocation, which are believed to be created by poor pricing as well as the distortionary impact of social sector spending and its associated taxes; these issues were of increasing concern in the Bank.[7] The third benefit is said to focus on the improvements in supply made in response to the fees that will purportedly benefit the poor.

For purposes of analyzing the impact of user fees, de Ferranti divides health care into two categories: curative services and preventive services, the latter including such nonpatient services as vector eradication (for example, spraying against mosquitoes). The formulation of prices is based on the neoclassical principles of individual rationality. By this logic, nonpatient-related preventive services cannot be efficiently priced owing to the absence of exclusivity. This is because the fee policy would "collapse under the weight of unchecked free-ridership" (29).

In contrast, de Ferranti argues, private patient user fees can be assessed exclusively, allowing utility-maximizing decisions based on the quantity and quality of service relative to the price. User fees, he says, are not likely to have much impact on ability to pay because "existing fees are often small relative to wage levels" and "higher fees closer to providers' marginal cost would still be affordable to most households" (37). These assertions are made with little or no evidence.[8] He also cites studies of the sensitivity of health care utilization to charges for different services in order to largely dismiss any problems with willingness to pay. A proper approach to analyzing the effect of user fees would have been to actually observe the outcome of imposing them. This was never done before the World Bank pushed for user fees.[9]

With worries about the equity problems that accompany user fees behind him, de Ferranti goes on to search for possible exceptions to a policy of setting user fees equal to the marginal cost of patient-specific services. External factors in the transmission of infectious diseases, according to the author, provide a high level of justification for "subsidizing" fees. Yet this only applies to such preventive services as vaccinations, because with regard to curative services, "it is doubtful whether any reduction in transmission probabilities is achieved[;] . . . available technologies for treatment . . . rarely can be made effective before diseased individuals already have had maximal infectious impact on others around them" (44). As we will see below, this is precisely the kind of flawed reasoning that led to the imposition of fees in sexually transmitted disease (STD) clinics in such places as Kenya, with dire consequences to public health including the transmission of Human Immunodeficiency Virus/Acquired Immunodeficiency Syndrome (STDs constitute an important co-factor).

First-contact services rendered for curative purposes are not subject to reduced fees. The argument is a rationally deductive one with no evidence provided. Simply stated, rational individuals have all the information they need, such that "when an illness or injury occurs . . . one should seek medical help" (de Ferranti 1985, 55). This assertion that symptoms are universally understood, unambiguous, or unaffected by weighing the potential financial burden of seeking medical care shows no understanding of the vast literature about medical anthropology and the related cultural issues.

Users are "likely to know less about the nature and effects of referral," although "the patient's ignorance is compensated in part by the involvement in the provider in the decision making" (de Ferranti 1985, 56). This creates a problem of agency, however, because the incentives for providers may not be consistent with the interests of the patient, particularly if the provider receives income from additional services (such as kickbacks). For de Ferranti, "fees, while not a flawless means of signaling resource scarcity to both providers and users, can nonetheless curtail some excesses" (58). Still, since referrals are overly expensive, some pricing of services below their marginal cost might be justified "for some form of protection against high referral care costs" (60). Finally, preventive services provide a clear case for such pricing because patients do not exhibit symptoms and therefore cannot make rational decisions about seeking medical assistance.

To complete the full reversal of the 1975 *Health Sector Policy Paper,* de Ferranti needs to make an explicit statement about the preference for private sector health care development. He presents exactly this preference in the final section of the paper, stating that the role of the private sector is "a key one." While admitting that the evidence is "too anecdotal to support generalizable conclusions," he does not refrain from drawing strong conclusions in favor of the privatization of health care. The analysis simply follows from the arguments discussed above regarding charging full-cost marginal prices for patient care, since efficient private markets (in the neoclassical world) operate on this basis. Thus, "for patient related services . . . the arguments in favor of a strong public role in the provision of health care are, on close inspection, not very compelling" (de Ferranti 1985, 88). The first step is to foster the development of private institutions while restraining the growth of the public sector, with the eventual aim of handing ownership to the private sector. By 1985, all of the intellectual pieces needed to justify the allocation of health care via the market with the World Bank policy advice and conditionality were in place.

In 1987, de Ferranti joined with Nancy Birdsall and John Akin[10] to write and publish a new Bank policy study titled "Financing Health Services in Developing Countries."[11] They placed heavy emphasis on the decentralization of government health services for the reasons as discussed in chapter 6. The key is to "use market incentives where possible" and encourage the collection of revenues "as close as possible to the point of service" (World Bank 1987, 6). The study adds little to de Ferranti's theoretical arguments for the shift in the Bank's health agenda. It does, however, provide a simple, accessible statement of the new policy priorities of the Bank, which continue to influence the Bank's health care priorities.[12]

By 1987 the new dictum of the Bank had become "the use of prices and markets to allocate health cares is [highly] desirable." The policies that followed from this new strategy had enormous consequences for the health and welfare of the populations of affected countries.

Toward the Institutionalization of the Market in Health Care

The Bank clearly took the lead in developing the market approach to health care. But the approach was parallel to that of other organizations, thus ensuring its institutionalization across many influential organizations. The projects and priorities of USAID in the 1980s, for instance, reflected a similar approach to health care including prepayment schemes in Bolivia (1984), the $8 million Reach program, which included a health financing effort, in French West Africa (1985–89), and the Health Financing and Sustainability Program (1989–95). Washington-based consultancies and American universities cooperated in undertaking studies and promoting the new policies.[13]

Some international agencies, including UNICEF, added to the reform effort.[14] Others, such as WHO, did little to challenge the World Bank besides protesting that the organization had little expertise in health economics. The World Health Organization even joined the Bank in producing the important WDR 1993, "Investing in Health," although the degree of collaboration and accord with the final product is disputed (Lee and Goodman 2002).

The 1993 report was the first health-focused World Development Report published by the Bank, though it added little to the agenda already set by previous working papers and reports. The report shows the same commitment to promoting user fees, privatization, risk sharing, and decentralization of government services. It relies on an unrequited commitment to methodological individualism, an axiomatic belief in the superiority of the private sector to the state, and the view that the state is overextended in health care and needs to be retracted.[15] Instead of carefully weighing the empirical evidence concerning these assertions, the Bank dismisses any negative studies: "Studies on the effect of user fees are inconclusive and contradictory. One reason is that some researchers have failed to calculate the true cost to patients of treatment at government clinics. People often pay dearly for supposedly 'free' health care . . . the indirect costs such as transport and the opportunity cost of time spent seeking care are substantial. Since patients are already paying for supposedly free or low-cost health care, new user fees, when accompanied by a reduction in indirect costs and improvement in services, may increase utilization" (World Bank 1993b, 118). The argument that somehow imputed costs such as the cost of waiting are the equivalent of cash payments is of course ridiculous to anyone except a neoclassical economist. In cash-poor economies in rural Africa, individuals do not simply weigh the possibility of less time at the clinic against an increase in the payment for a health service. Instead, they are focused on the question of what essential goods will be foregone (often with health implications) to pay for a treatment. Often, as we will see, user fees have had a marked impact on the attendance of patients, and when they finally go to the clinic, they tend to be considerably sicker. Moreover, for a variety of reasons, the quality of the health services has seldom been improved after the introduction of costs to users.

Despite the continuity between WDR 1993 and earlier analysis, the report breaks new ground by developing an innovative framework. To finally fulfill the neoclassically inspired vision of improving the effectiveness of health outcomes by optimizing the health of individuals, subject to resource constraints, the report introduces disability-adjusted life years (DALY), a new common measurement of the burden of disease.

Recall the rather simple bifurcation of preventive and curative care in distinguishing the level of user fees and the extent to which the private sector is encouraged. This consideration was modified to focus on three criteria: cost-effectiveness, as measured by the cost per DALY; the size and distribution of the health problem; and the resources available. Curative interventions are now justified owing to the widespread nature of some problems and the comparatively inexpensive treatments used to deal with them (for example, STDs). The report defines a package of "essential" clinical services (both curative and preventive in nature) that should be guaranteed by the government. These include prenatal and delivery care, family planning services, treatment of childhood ailments such as malaria and measles, short-course treatments of tuberculosis (TB), and treatment for STDs (World Bank 1993, 112–16).

Although the DALY allows the Bank to finally analyze the kind of health care opportunity costs preferred by its staff economists without resorting to crude dollar measures, it is—to put it mildly—a very problematic tool. The DALY reflects the total amount of healthy life lost, to all causes, whether from premature mortality or from some degree of disability during a period of time. These disabilities can be physical or mental. Five key elements are embedded in DALYs. First is the duration of time lost due to premature death, which is considered in relation to the world's highest national life expectancy for men and women. Second is the use of disability weights, which are applied to adjust the value of life years. Weights ranging from 0 to 1 are assigned to different diseases. Some are fairly humorous. In some studies erectile dysfunction is assigned a severity weight higher than that accorded to severe anemia, perhaps reflecting the gender of the authors of the report (Murray and Acharya 1996). Sensitivity tests designed to measure the impact of varying these weights are never carried out though priorities can change dramatically when different measures are used (Arnesen and Kapiriri 2004). Moreover, values used in the weightings are universally applied and completely abstracted from the social context, which can significantly alter the severity of diseases (Allotey et al. 2003; Allotey and Reidpath 2002). Finally, the disability weights lead to overt discrimination and therefore cannot justifiably purport to be value-free. For example, assuming a disability weighting of one-half, an intervention to extend the life of a disabled person is assigned half the value of an intervention to extend the life of a healthy person (Anand and Hanson 1998).

The third dimension is the weighting of the age of individuals. This value rises from birth to age twenty-five and declines thereafter. Thus, a year lived at age two is valued at only 20 percent of a year lived at age twenty-five. At age seventy a person is valued at only 46 percent of the maximum. In an effort to avoid being accused of devaluing life by analyzing it the same way as one would income, age differentiation is justified on the basis of "social roles." This is presumably because middle-aged individuals are assumed to take care of the health of the young and the old. Yet social roles are highly variable in different contexts, and such a claim thus reflects a fundamental ignorance of other cultures and situations. Witness, for instance, the current role of grandmothers in taking care of AIDS orphans in Africa. Moreover, if age weights vary with social roles, then, by extension the highest value should be placed on health professionals such as nurses, doctors, and midwives, whose contributions to society are more valuable than those of other people. Varying the weight allocated to age again changes the priorities. For example, downgrading the disabilities of young people because of their lower weighting in DALY calculations leads to an underestimation of the communicable disease burden of children, which has serious implications for resource allocation

(Anand and Hanson 1998; Arnesen and Kapiriri 2004). Overall, age weighting is fundamentally inequitable and discriminatory because the health of the young and the old is deemed less valuable than that of people in the middle group.

The fourth dimension of DALYs is time discounting, in which the value of health gains made today is compared to the value of those made in the future. World Development Report 1993 uses a discount rate of 3 percent. Economists typically argue that because one can place a dollar today in an account and earn interest on it, future money should be discounted to make it equivalent to today's money. Of course, human health is not the equivalent of money. To justify the use of a discount rate on human life, the Bank rejects the investment argument to focus on a "pure social rate of time preference" which is assumed to be "of the order of 0–3 percent per year" (214). The idea is closely associated with the classical theory that interest on savings represents the reward for postponing consumption. For purposes of utility, *Homo economicus* then discounts the future relative to the present (see the discussion in chapter 7).

Although it does not want a higher rate that would "reduce the importance of premature deaths at young ages in relation to those at older ages" (which is exactly what the Bank does with its age weights and any positive discount rate), the Bank provides no further justification for a 3 percent rate (World Bank 1993b, 214). Yet any discounting of future human lives to benefit present ones has enormous implications. At a 3 percent time discount, one life saved today is the equivalent of five lives saved in fifty-five years.[16] If life fifty-five years from now is only worth one-fifth of life today, then environmental degradation such as global warming is totally justifiable. The approach is patently inequitable. Why should society place greater value on an ill person today than on someone else with the exact illness a year from now?

Finally, DALYs involve a simple linear summing of the adjusted values of all health-related losses for all individuals brought to the present using the discount rate. With this measure, the Bank boasts, not only can it compare the regional distribution of the global burden of disease to "track improvements in the nation's health over time" (World Bank 1993b, 27), but it can also determine the "most cost-effective interventions" (61). Others, however, are rather skeptical of an approach that "disregards the political, ethical, cultural, and symbolic aspects of health care" (Laurell and Arellano 1996, 5). Disability-adjusted life years treat individuals not as subjects but as dehumanized objects that are used as inputs in a statistical artifact pretentiously presented as value-free. The lives of one group of human beings are traded off against the lives of another group in the name of optimization, which itself is subject to the artificially created resource constraints imposed by the Bank's and the Fund's macroeconomic conditionality.

With these problems of reasoning in mind, I propose a very different set of priorities arising from an institutional analysis of health care. I begin with a return to the premise that health is a fundamental human right, not some commodity to be allocated to "maximize the health sector contribution to some agreed measure of social welfare." Before doing so, however, I review the nature and impact of the programs and policies of the Bank in the past two decades or so, including the experience with user fees. What happened when these rationally deductive theories were put into practice in developing countries?

World Bank Policy in Practice

The first set of systematic reviews of the Health, Nutrition, and Population sector was not published by the OED until 1998. The extent to which the Bank's lending strategy was influenced by the rethinking of health policy after 1985 was clear. The "first generation" of programs was aimed at increasing delivery of health services by establishing "physical infrastructure" and channeling "technical expertise toward easing constraints on the delivery of particular services such as family planning, nutrition, education and disease control programs" (World Bank 1998a, 15). The Bank refers to this as "non-systemic lending." Approximately 92 percent of projects funded between 1975 and 1979 were in this area, and 85 percent of those funded between 1980 and 1984. With the publication of the de Ferranti paper and the Bank study "Financing Health Services in Developing Countries," though, the priorities began to move toward "systemic" objectives consisting of organizational change or systemwide financial reform. Table 8.1 provides information arranged by interval and by region.

After 1985 the Bank increasingly committed its projects to neoliberal reforms both in absolute and relative terms. More than half of the projects were aimed at altering the organizational and financial dimensions of the health sector. The statistics underestimate the degree of financial commitment to neoliberal reforms. Between 1970 and 1997, the Bank lent roughly $12 billion to the HNP sector, but 75 percent of this lending came

TABLE 8.1 **Systemic and nonsystemic objectives in HNP projects**

	Systemic		Nonsystemic	
	Number	%	Number	%
Fiscal years				
1970–74	2	22	7	78
1975–79	1	7	12	92
1980–84	3	15	17	85
1985–89	14	33	29	67
1990–94	29	37	50	68
1995–97	31	52	29	48
Region				
Africa	26	38	43	62
East Asia and the Pacific	5	12	35	88
Europe and Central Asia	9	60	6	40
Latin America and the Caribbean	18	44	23	56
Middle East and North Africa	9	38	15	63
South Asia	11	31	24	69

Source: World Bank 1998a, 12.

after 1990, when it was increasingly oriented toward systemic change (9). Moreover, the financial inducements for recipients to pursue the reforms have increased over time. The average project size rose from $24 million in the early 1980s to $58 million in the 1991–95 period and to $87 million in the 1995–97 period. As we can see, for all regions except East Asia and the Pacific, 30 percent or more of loans are for projects in this area. Funding aimed at neoliberal reforms in Europe and Central Asia is much higher because most of these loans were made after 1990.

The component of reform that the Bank has supported most systematically has been decentralization. Roughly 40 percent of the projects in the HNP portfolio have included some form of decentralization, although 75 percent of them were begun after 1990 (World Bank 1998a, 12). The proportion of projects aimed at increasing the role of the private sector as a mechanism to build health institutions increased from 23 percent of all projects between 1970 and 1994 to 43 percent between 1995 and 1997 (33). In addition, the introduction of user fees as part of Bank projects was widespread. In 40 percent of all Bank projects, there were plans to establish or expand user fees. In sub-Saharan Africa the proportion was much higher; nearly 75 percent of all projects promoted user fees (28).

Despite the huge commitment to organizational development and reform, the OED considered the rate of success to be abysmally low. Only

21 percent of the completed projects in this area had a "substantial" impact, though 60 percent of all HNP projects received satisfactory ratings (1). As with other OED reports, there is no critical consideration of the intrinsic nature or logic of the reforms. Instead, the focus is on three possible sources of project failure: country context, borrower performance, and Bank performance. The Bank concludes that, "consistent with OED findings for the entire Bank portfolio, borrower performance is the most important determinant of project outcome with borrower implementation performance very highly correlated with project outcome" (23). In the country context, other "institutional" factors including corruption, institutional quality as measured by the views of those in the private sector of "government credibility," and "economic openness" had significance in the probit testing. In other words, borrowers are doubly at fault for both incompetent implementation and failure to put in place other Bank reforms relating to governance and neoliberalism.

Critiques of the Bank itself focused on its failure to properly use economic theory to justify state intervention in projects. For example, support for public-sector involvement was not sufficiently buttressed by evidence of "market failures, public goods, or externalities." The OED cited inadequate analysis of the consumer demand for projects, improper assessment of health inputs, especially from the private sector, and an lack of cost-effectiveness studies based on tools of the 1993 WDR such as DALYs (World Bank 1998a, 26–27).

A few of the other issues that were raised with regard to the strategies are interesting. Despite all the rhetoric contained in Bank documents of the 1990s regarding poverty, the OED admits that "project designs are typically silent regarding poverty impact" or "simply assert the poor will benefit due to the nature of the intervention" and acknowledges that "this claim has validity" (28). The consequences for the poor are discussed below. The Bank also admits that project ownership and participation have been quite low. Only 20 percent of all projects cited any form of consultation with the "beneficiaries." The OED could find only four projects of the 224 evaluated that showed evidence that beneficiaries were given any decision-making power (34). Still, the main hope was that participation would increase via the price mechanism, because "experience with cost recovery in the Niger health project . . . demonstrated that consumers demand higher levels of service quality and take greater interest in the management of local health activities as their financial participation increases" (28).

Toward a Critique of World Bank Health Policy

Health Expenditures

The degree to which public spending on health care was affected by IMF and World Bank austerity measures is subject to debate (Sahn 1992; World Bank 1994b). Some have argued that in the 1980s adjustment policy emphasized meeting spending targets with little regard to the implications for social spending on matters such as health care. Available information would seem to support the view that this was the case in sub-Saharan Africa. Sahn (1992) provides data about health expenditures as a proportion of total discretionary spending before (that is, in the initial year and two years prior to adjustment) and after (three years following the initial year) the first adjustment. In the majority of the fifteen countries surveyed, health expenditures fell to about 5.75 percent of discretionary spending from an already low level of around 6 percent. Under the supervision of the World Bank, an agency purportedly meant to promote development, nearly half of the countries surveyed allocated less than 5 percent of their budgets to health care three years after adjustment had started.

The data for actual expenditures paint an even more depressing picture. A survey of real health expenditures in twelve countries that undertook some adjustment in the 1980s indicated a decline in average real per capita spending on health care of nearly 20 percent. Only four countries kept per capita health expenditures in line with population growth.[17] Long-range data about public spending present a very dismal picture for many African countries. For instance, Ghana spent $10 per capita in 1976 but a mere $6 in the period from 1995 to 2000. In the same time period, spending in Côte d'Ivoire dropped from $9 to $6, in Zambia it fell from $14 to $11, and in Nigeria it fell from nearly $3 to $1.81. Liberia actually spent $7 per capita in 1976 compared to $1.50 in the most recent period (World Bank 1980; 2004). Excluding South Africa, spending on health care amounted to a mere 4.1 percent of GDP, which is roughly equivalent to $13 per capita, between 1995 and 2000. Compare this spending to the cost of a year's dosage of the cheapest antiretroviral drugs (ARVs), which is still set at about $40 to $50 per year. Similarly, at the end of 2004, only 4 percent of the four million people who were in desperate need of ARVs in Africa were receiving them. For people in the developing world, HIV/AIDS has largely been a death sentence, even as treatment in the developed world is prolonging life more than ever before.

These statistics about government expenditures, however, tell only a small part of story of Bank-influenced strategies. One must move beyond the public spending to see the impact the new health care policy, with its emphasis on user fees, decentralization, and privatization, has had on the quality and availability of health care.[18]

The Impact of World Bank Policies: User Fees

Recall that the arguments in support of user fees focused on improving revenue, efficiency, and equity. Unfortunately, user fees created few of these forecasted benefits but caused major problems in the accessibility and delivery of health care services.

To begin with, user fees generated negligible revenue. A study conducted in the mid-1980s found that fee revenues composed between 0 percent and 12 percent of total recurrent government expenditures on health, depending on the country (Vogel 1991, cited in Nyonator and Kutzin 1999). In Niger, between 1997 and 1999, a well-formulated and well-implemented cost recovery program failed not only to achieve its long-term objectives of durable improved quality and accessibility but also to realize its immediate objective of recovering the expenses of health facility operation. Although the cost recovery program was only intended to cover a small portion of operating costs (it excluded health workers' salaries, transport costs, and training for capacity building) only 85 percent of eligible costs were recovered at the district level. At the level of the individual facility, this number varied from 48 percent to 116 percent, indicating that cost recovery depends largely on the ability of a facility's clientele to pay for services (Meuwissen 2002). More specifically, it seems that cost recovery depends on the kind of fee charged: if it is service-based, it is more successful in generating revenue, whereas if it is registration-based, revenue generation is exceedingly difficult (Collins et al. 1996 and Okello et al. 1998, cited in Blas and Limbambala 2001).

Although a longer experience with cost recovery, as is the case in Ghana, can be associated with more successful collection and utilization of user fees, these instances are also reason for considerable concern with respect to equity, for although the health sector functions relatively well for its clientele, it also excludes a significant portion of the population (Nyonator and Kutzin 1999). An implicit value system is attached to the World Bank's approach: if Ghana's eleven-year experience is to be seen as a model, we must conclude that what is being advocated is a financially functional health system that is unresponsive to the health needs of the population. Indeed, this rhetoric is clear in early Bank reports: if the poor could not afford to "contribute measurably to cost recovery and are too numerous to be subsidized by the smaller number of those better able to pay for medical care, they should do without medical care" (Ruderman 1990, 484).

The devastating consequences of dismissing the health needs of the poor are abundantly documented in the literature. When user fees are imposed, they consistently cause a dramatic decline in attendance at health facilities. In Zambia, attendance declined by one-third over the course of two years (Blas and Limbambala 2001). In Ghana, outpatient attendance dropped by 40 percent (Biritwum 1994, cited in Blas and Limbambala 2001). In Niger the decline was 41 percent (Meuwissen 2002). In Kenya the introduction of user fees in a Nairobi STD clinic led to a 60 percent reduction in attendance by men and 35 percent reduction in attendance by women over a nine-month period, undoubtedly contributing to the spread of HIV (Moses et al. 1992). Still more disturbing, studies investigating the particular effect of user fees on poor people report more drastic declines in usage. Tanzania's government hospitals in Dar es Salaam, which were known to be heavily frequented by the poor, saw a decline of 50 percent when user fees were imposed (Blas and Limbambala 2001). Usage of health services among the poorest people in Cambodia, identified using the proxy of landlessness, decreased from 16 percent to 5 percent when fees were implemented. When user fees were increased by what authorities considered to be a marginal amount, the number of patients who reported being unable to pay all of their medical expenses increased from 40 percent to 60 percent (Jacobs and Price 2004).

A distribution analysis of the study carried out in Niger showed that although the decrease in new medical consultations among the total population was only 6.3 percent when user fees were introduced, the decline was an astonishing 32.4 percent for the poorest quarter of the population (Meuwissen 2002). Among the poorest two quintiles of the population in Tanzania, 25 percent said that they would not be able to pay for health services in any circumstances, regardless of the cost or the quality of service received in exchange (Bonu et al. 2001). Similarly, when user fees were abolished in Ghana, the increase in utilization was greater among the poor than among any other socioeconomic group (Nabyonga et al. 2005).

It is obvious that when user fees are implemented, then, many poor people stop seeking health care. Perhaps implicitly recognizing the absurdity

of arguing that the poor should go without medical care when they cannot afford the fees, the World Bank has proposed a solution to this problem: granting exemptions, or fee waivers, to the poor. Yet the evidence
concerning exemptions is disturbing, especially since they are presented
as the Bank's "cure-all" resolution to problems of equity. Seventy-eight
percent of health care workers surveyed in Ghana reported that exemptions were granted at their facilities, but the total number of exemptions
represented less than 1 percent of the patients in a region with a poverty
rate of 35 percent. Worse still, 71 percent of those granted exemptions
were health workers, not poor people (Nyonator and Kutzin 1999). According to a cross-country survey, 27 percent of developing countries have
no exemption policy for the poor (Russell and Gilson 1997). Numerous
studies cited the enormous difficulties of unambiguously determining who
was eligible for an exemption. In many cases this uncertainty discouraged
health practitioners from granting waivers for fear of being accused of
unfair treatment by other patients. Moreover, in facilities where user fees
were implemented as part of a cost recovery scheme, health practitioners
reported being hesitant to grant exemptions because of the priority of sus-
taining the facility. Many patients are unaware of exemption policies or of
the possibility of having fees waived because these rules are intentionally
unadvertised or ambiguous.[19]

Clearly, the World Bank strategy regarding user fees and exemption
policies is seriously flawed. Yet the consequences of having adamantly pursued it for the past twenty years are more distressing than the remarkable
declines in utilization and the failure to ensure accessibility of services for
the poor. Poor people adopt new methods of health-seeking behavior in the
private or the informal sector, with disastrous consequences for their health
and for the public interest (more on this below). Health practitioners consistently report that patients are more seriously ill when they first present
themselves at the hospital than they were before user fees were imposed;
this is attributed to having been deterred from seeking service because of
cost (Blas and Limbambala 2001; Jacobs and Price 2004; Russell and Gilson
1997). Sicker patients are not only more expensive to treat; they are also
much more likely to die. For example, in Cambodia, the mortality rate in
hospitals rose from 6.6 deaths per thousand patients to 13.6 per thousand
after user fees were implemented (Jacobs and Price 2004). Even a World
Bank economist would have to conclude that this is not an optimal health
outcome. The declines in utilization also have particularly disturbing effects in developing countries because of their particular epidemiological

profiles, which include a significant burden of contagious diseases. This corollary was apparently ignored by the neoclassical theorists, despite the abundance of information and warnings from disease control experts (Alubo 2001; Bosman 2000).

Other studies have questioned the World Bank's presumption that quality will improve. A study carried out in Zambia showed that although the goal of user fee implementation was to improve the quality of care, patients did not perceive that quality had improved and were correspondingly very angry about being charged for services, although many indicated their willingness to pay as long as improvements were tangible (van der Geest et al. 2000).

The most dramatic and most consistent finding, however, was that usage dropped off significantly when user fees were introduced. The decline was particularly pernicious among the poor. In addition, some studies noted that usage did not increase to previous levels once fees were removed (for example, Moses et al. 1992). This final observation could indicate any number of things: increasing reliance on alternative medical treatment among the poor, loss of faith in the system among the poor, discriminatory practices among health practitioners, corruption due to charging user fees after they were officially removed, and so on. Even after user fees have been removed, their impact on the health of populations is likely to be an enduring one.

Privatization

The reforms recommended by the World Bank and the IMF have included increasing the proportion of health care facilities in developing countries that are privately run to improve efficiency, quality, and accessibility. The assumption is that private owners best respond to market signals. As discussed above, the Bank insisted that its reforms would help increase accessibility of care and equity of coverage by making health care more cost-efficient.

Yet the results of the empirical studies of privatization have proved just the opposite. Although the objective of privatizing care was met in some places, the impact of doing so was contrary to expectations. This should not be terribly surprising. The simple proposition that market incentives would likely lead to the concentration of health care facilities in higher-income urban areas and the neglect of poorer rural areas seems to have entirely escaped the promoters of this policy.

In Tanzania, the number of health facilities almost doubled during the early period of structural adjustment (which was accompanied by conditionality relating to health policy reforms). Eighty-eight percent of the new facilities were private. A study by Benson (2001) of their distribution indicated that private facilities were consistently located in places where the need (measured using well-established demographic proxies) for health care was the lowest. Benson found that the proportion of private facilities was significantly higher where they could cater to a population of working-age males living in rural areas. Conversely, the proportion of free government-run facilities was much higher in areas where women, children, and the elderly were more numerous. Given that only six of the fifty new facilities built during this period were government-run, this finding essentially indicates that those who needed health care most were neglected by the private sector and, more generally, by the enormous increase in healthcare facilities. Without studying the distributional effects of their policies, the Bank and the IMF would conclude, based on appearances, that their recommendations concerning privatization actually did increase accessibility. This would be true if accessibility were defined in terms of the number of health facilities per capita. Clearly, however, such a measure has no significance when considering whether real people—especially those who need it the most—are benefiting from improved access to health care.

The cost-efficiency logic of the World Bank and the IMF would suggest that these findings are appropriate. After all, numerous studies confirm that women, children, the poor, and the elderly are the least likely to be willing to pay for health services (for example, Bonu, Rani, and Bishai 2001; Blas and Limbambala 2001), and when health care is considered a commodity, it should be "sold" where people can afford it and will choose to "buy" it. We must wonder whether strategists at the Bank are familiar with vulnerability theory, which concludes that these population groups are also those that are most vulnerable to disease and poor health and are therefore most in need of care. This theory is well developed in the work of social scientists such as Watts and Bohle, Mead, Packard and Epstein, and Kalipeni and Craddock (Kalipeni 2000).

Moreover, privatization has had some troubling effects on health. In Cambodia, the attempt to shift the burden of health care costs to the private sector by imposing user fees in two incremental stages was enormously successful from a policy standpoint: the proportion of patients who had sought care in the private sector before coming to the hospital increased from 20 percent prior to 2001, when the program began, to 73 percent in 2002. But from a health standpoint, the consequences were disastrous. Health workers in the hospitals reported that patients were much more seriously ill on presentation, and the mortality rate in the hospitals more than doubled. The obvious ineffectiveness of private health care was blamed on Cambodia's weak government oversight of the private sector, where healthcare practitioners and drug administration go unmonitored (Jacobs and Price 2004).

Similarly, in Niger, privatization occurred as a by-product of the implementation of user fees. Patients no longer sought professional care for relatively minor diseases such as conjunctivitis and therefore sought alternative treatments. The private sector responded with a rapid increase in the number of nonformal drug vendors and fostered a greater reliance on self-medication through the illegal drug trade (Meuwissen 2002). Both responses, although perfectly in line with the neoclassical vision of private sector responsiveness, had negative health consequences: because of the lack of oversight, patients often received drugs that had passed their expiration date, were prohibited, or incorrectly prescribed. Critics of privatization also argue that although privatization may be beneficial in ensuring availability of health care to those who are wealthy enough to afford it, it is very unlikely to provide any solutions to large-scale health problems such as high morbidity and mortality rates or to disease burdens such as that of HIV/AIDS (Alubo 2001).

Finally, privatization has serious negative implications for equity. In Nigeria, where privatization strategies were quite successful in shifting the patient burden to the private sector, health care rapidly became profit-oriented. Pharmacies and other health-related businesses followed the concentration of private health care facilities, which were strategically located close to target populations of wealthier people. Not only are the fees at these private facilities significantly higher than those at government facilities, but so, too, are the costs of the nontreatment-related services offered by businesses, which set their prices in tandem with the private facilities and with the wealthy target population in mind. Moreover, the quality of public sector care, on which the poor are totally dependent, has been further eroded by the enormous shift of resources and personnel to the private sector (Alubo 2001). Likewise, in Cambodia, the private sector increased its prices in response to the implementation of user fees in public hospitals (Jacobs and Price 2004).

Decentralization

Decentralization has been ubiquitous in World Bank programs since the early 1980s. It is promoted as a "market-surrogate strategy" designed to make bureaucracies more responsive to their clientele and to achieve a closer connection between inputs and outputs.

Yet again, however, the empirical reviews of this strategy contradict the optimistic predictions of its creators. Decentralization does not have the same immediate effects on the patient population that user fees have, but as with privatization, it causes certain systemic changes that are closely associated with the performance delivery of health care. Influential work by Bossert (1998, 2002, 2003) argues that researchers' understanding of decentralization may be overly superficial. In proposing an alternative, Bossert has created an innovative analytical tool called the "decision space" approach that allows a better perspective on the extent to which local authorities actually have the ability to make decisions regarding financing, policies, organization, payment mechanisms, and human resources. This framework, however, only allows us to see whether decentralization is really being implemented and in which areas. It does not offer much insight into the effects of decentralization on the performance of health care institutions. While maintaining that data are scarce, Bossert nevertheless concedes that the scant existing evidence points largely toward negative health outcomes (Bossert 2002, 2003).

The most common finding in the literature is that decentralization causes a decay of regulatory mechanisms. Policies set at the national level by, for example, the Ministry of Health, may not be known or may simply be ignored at the local level. In several studies health workers reported being uncertain about which policies they were supposed to be following, although they were set by the central government (Schuler et al. 2002; Blas 2001). In Ghana, the national policy regarding drug pricing indicated that drugs were to be sold at a 33 percent markup; in practice, however, patients were paying markups that were anywhere from 11 percent to 275 percent (Nyonator and Kutzin 1999).

Such a discrepancy brings to mind another potential consequence of decentralization: a complete lack of oversight, which enables corruption and the pursuit of local interests. There is ample evidence to suggest that the practice of taking bribes to obtain faster service is still prevalent, and numerous studies expressed concern about the inherent disincentive to grant waivers of user fees when the objective of the fees was cost recovery at the local level (Meuwissen 2002; Schuler et al. 2002). As is the case with the evidence regarding privatization, when the capacities of the central state are weakened, it may not be able to act as a monitor to ensure that standards of quality are met. Likewise, the central government may not be able to guarantee implementation of its own policies. This is because, in accordance with neoclassical views, decentralization has been envisioned as an alternative to, rather than a complement to, the central state. In the Bank's formula, it is a component of the effort to retract the state.

Yet decentralization without the accompanying strengthening of local capacities can lead to disastrous health outcomes (Collins and Green 1994). As we will see below, when introduced as part of World Bank conditionality in Zambia, it led to the dismantling of a highly effective national tuberculosis control program and its substitution with an incoherent, unplanned, and unsuccessful strategy (Bosman 2000). Decentralization caused "ongoing" problems with the health service's quality and civil servants' morale in the Philippines (Bossert and Beauvais 2002, 27). In particular, however, the failure to strengthen local capacities has had consistently negative effects on equity. In Uganda, changes in human resource management that were made in conjunction with the decentralization strategy created significant equity and quality issues: "[A]s the MOH [Ministry of Health] was no longer nationally unified, district health professionals no longer had the same geographic mobility and access to promotion, making it significantly more difficult for poorer, rural districts to attract qualified personnel" (ibid.). Similarly, a study of health facilities in Zambia found that rural facilities were severely understaffed after implementation of the government's structural adjustment–inspired reform strategy. A site serving ten thousand people had a staff of only four people, the most highly qualified of whom was a nurse; patient health status was worse in rural areas than in urban areas (van der Geest et al. 2000).

Even more disconcerting, it seems that other aspects of decentralization are also responsible for negatively affecting the equity of health care. A study of geographic patterns of deprivation in South Africa confirms that the health care infrastructure is worse in the poorer regions of the country (McIntyre et al. 2002) Similarly, Miller (1998) found that per capita disbursements to the Internal Revenue Allotment fund for health care varied by a factor of twenty-three between the provinces that were receiving the most and the least funding in the Philippines (cited in

Bossert and Beauvais 2002). In addition, a cross-country survey found that 89 percent of countries which had a specific policy to exempt the poor from user fees were vague about eligibility and intentionally gave a great deal of discretion to local administrators (Russell and Gilson 1996). As discussed above and elsewhere (Russell and Gilson 1996; Scheuler et al. 2002; van der Geest et al. 2000; Blas and Limbambala 2001), local responsibility for cost recovery creates a disincentive for granting much-needed exemptions, which means that the poor are left without necessary health care. Thus, decentralization can have very negative consequences for equity both within and between communities (Collins and Green 1994).

Finally, the argument that participation will improve as a consequence of decentralization is also problematic. A study of health care reforms in Zambia confirms that this is not necessarily the case. A major objective of Zambia's national health care reform was to build a system based on self-reliance and participation by individuals, families, and communities. Yet interviews, focus group discussions, and researcher observations determined that community members had a "lack of faith [in the health care system]; they indicated that they had nothing to do with the organization of health care—it was not 'theirs.' " (van der Geest et al. 2000, 60). Moreover, the community members said that they felt betrayed by the changes to the system, which included user fees, not because they objected to paying for care on principle but because they felt that their voluntary labor to help keep their local health facilities running should entitle them to free health care in exchange. When exemptions were not granted on this basis, many people chose to seek health care elsewhere or not at all (van der Geest et al. 2000).

As Collins (1989) argues, the view that decentralization leads ipso facto to improvements in participation is erroneous: "Pious statements about the moral qualities of liberal democracy and its decentralized and participative forms abound in the literature on decentralization and development. However, there is no universal correlation between decentralization and community participation. The relationship will depend basically upon the social, economic, and political setting and the type of decentralization enacted" (170). As we will see, an institutional approach could provide a much more contextualized understanding of policy approaches without recourse to universal solutions. The approach begins with a commitment to the universal *right* to health that states must recognize.

Toward an Institutional Approach to Health

Economic Rights and the Right to Health

A typical definition of economic rights is the following: "[t]he right of access to resources such as land, labor, physical and financial capital that are essential for the creation, legal appropriation and market exchange of goods and services" (Gorga 1999, 89). There are two problems with this definition. First, it equates economic rights only with the right of access, not with the *ability to* access. Second, the focus is on access to resources that are intended for exchange on the market. Here we have economic rights evaluated strictly in terms of their market-focused instrumentality. The definition clearly reflects the narrowing of the economic profession, which has edged toward equating economic rights with economic freedom and even with a larger concept of human freedom that implies the absence of government interference in markets.[20] The view is clearly embedded in de Ferranti's and the Bank's reconstitution of health care policy after 1985, with its emphasis on the allocation of health care goods via markets or market-like conditions. The right to be free from government interference in the health sector thus replaced the universal right to health embedded in the Alma-Ata Declaration. It is time to return to the idea that the right to health is an entitlement that will not magically arise from allocating market-focused economic rights. The remainder of this chapter focuses on how to fulfill the right to basic health in developing countries through the development of the institutional matrix.

Health, Institutions, and the Institutional Matrix

Habits of thought are at the heart of health-related behavior and decision making. The approach discussed above assumes that individuals will make rational health decisions as long as the proper market signals are in place, but most activities that have implications for health have little or nothing to do with markets or prices. They are the products of the complex interaction of psychosocial and economic factors and pressures that are linked to one's surroundings and how they are perceived. As discussed in chapter 5, habits of thought are constructs that are often repetitively invoked in response to contextualized stimuli as perceived by the thought process. The interpretation of the health implications of activities can be mediated to a large extent by mental constructs, in particular, those that are common and socially prescribed.

Take the issue of female genital cutting (FGC), which has been vo-
ciferously opposed both inside and outside of Africa in recent decades.
The practice typically takes one of three forms. "Sunna," the least inva-
sive form, is roughly equivalent to male circumcision but is performed
on the clitoris. Genital excision, or clitoridectomy, removes the entire
clitoris and the labia minora. The most extreme form of FGC is infibula-
tion, which also involves excising the labia majora and sewing together
the raw edges of the vulva so that only a small hole remains. The health
implications, especially those that accompany the more extreme versions,
are well documented. They frequently include shock, bleeding, infection,
painful menstruation and intercourse, and complications during child-
birth. At the United Nations criticism of the practice began in 1964. By
1996 the United States prohibited the practice and made U.S. support for
loans from IFIs contingent on a guarantee from the recipient countries'
governments that they would enact education campaigns to discourage
the practice. During the 1990s virtually every country in which FGC is
practiced has passed a law or adopted a policy against it. Nevertheless,
it is still practiced in twenty-four African countries and by the majority
of families in fourteen of these countries. The World Health Organization estimates that around 130 million women have undergone genital
cutting. In many countries in Africa, not circumcising one's daughters
is considered deviant, despite widespread anti-FGC initiatives. Women
undertaking field work in these countries have often faced ridicule and
disbelief when they confessed that they had not been circumcised.[21] The
desire for continuity is very powerful. Boyle et al. (2002) undertook an extensive survey of 24,976 women with at least one daughter under the age
of eighteen in Egypt, Niger, Sudan, Kenya, and Mali. Nearly all women
(85 percent) who had been subject to FGC had circumcised their daughters or intended to so do.

Other health habits are not as deeply ingrained in the culture but equally
important. Much has been written about the impact of water quality, sanitation, and hygiene on childhood diseases. An estimated six thousand children die every day as a result of diseases related to these issues. In China,
India, and Indonesia, twice as many people die of diarrheal diseases as of
HIV/AIDS (Rosenquist 2005). One study has indicated that improvement
in sanitation and home hygiene can lower diarrhea-related illnesses by
35 percent and 33 percent, respectively (Waterkeyn and Cairncross 2005).
Availability of sanitation has shown little progress in recent years, however. In sub-Saharan Africa in 2002, only 36 percent of the population

had access to "improved sanitation facilities,"[22] a slight improvement over the rate of 32 percent in 1990. The coverage in South Asia also remains at about 35 percent in 2002 (World Bank 2006). Investment in disposal infrastructure is absolutely crucial to moving toward universal coverage. But in the absence of new sanitation facilities, health outcomes can be dramatically altered by new methods of feces disposal if people wash their hands after defecating and before meals and if household members keep separate cups (Waterkeyn and Cairncross 2005). Current habits remain a dramatic challenge. In India, for example, it is estimated that only 2 percent of excrement in rural areas is buried in the ground; most is dumped outside the yards of households or in nearby roadsides (Nath 2003). Historically, people in Africa have had a semi-nomadic existence and do not have much of a tradition of building permanent toilets (Rosenquist 2005). Overcoming these traditions will require developing new norms for transforming health-related activities.

Norms

Recall that norms are socially derived behavioral guidelines concerned with what is expected, required, or accepted. They are important for building professional health services in a manner similar to that discussed in chapters 6 and 7. They also are central to the improvement of health outcomes in developing countries. In developed countries, where scientific results are accepted and rapidly disseminated, health-related norms and behavior change very slowly. For example, witness how many years it has taken for the aversion to smoking to become a generalized societal norm in the United States and for it to translate into a significant reduction in smoking.[23] In the case of developing countries, the barriers to forming some scientifically based health-related norms can be even more significant.

Boyle et al. (2002) examine the potential influence of internationally recognized norms that bar FGC on the practice and on attitudes toward it. As discussed above, the overwhelming factor in predicting women's attitude toward FGC—and whether they subject their daughters to the procedure—is whether the women themselves were subjected to it. The key is to evaluate the routes by which internationally recognized norms can begin to alter behavior that has had such a deleterious impact on women's health. To test this idea, Boyle et al. hold the women's circumcision experience constant while looking for other factors that influence behavior. Using a hierarchical logistic model, they examine the effects of individual characteristics on the likelihood of circumcising daughters and on the attitudes of mother toward the practice. They found that the most important influences on both practice and attitude were years of education, college attendance, radio ownership, working for pay, and Christian or Muslim affiliation.[24]

Working for pay, for instance, decreases the probability that a woman had circumcised or intended to circumcise her daughter by 44 percent and reduces the probability of continuing to support the practice by 33 percent. The authors hypothesize that the five factors act as conduits for the transmission of international norms into practice. For example, Christian women were more likely to be influenced by anticircumcision attitudes arising from their Christian counterparts in developed countries. Although it would have been helpful if the researchers had undertaken more detailed interviews to determine how and why women have altered their views and practices, their work does provide some insight into possible interventions that would assist in altering norms, which could then form new habits of thought. It also points to the need to support new norms with other elements of the institutional matrix. For example, wage employment may be an important route for the influence of new norms, but it also empowers women and generates independent capacities that may alter conditions and allow new norms to influence existing practices. Because all five of the countries studied have anti-FGC laws on their books, the research also exposes the limited influence of focusing on a single element in the institutional matrix when norms and practices are so entrenched.

The importance of taking a multifaceted approach by drawing on interactive elements from the matrix can be seen in the development strategies aimed at improving sanitation and household hygiene and in addressing FGC. Organizations play a key role in institutionalizing new practices and capacities.

Organizations

Recall that organizations are conceptually and often legally recognized entities that combine groups of people with common rules and purposes. They are vessels of containment that are linked spatially and temporally to localized environments but also have their own dynamic. From the perspective of an institutional approach to health, they can provide a protective sphere in which information, ideas, and incentives can combine to generate new norms and mental constructs that lead to correlative behavior that is conducive to improving health.

As discussed above, health outcomes can be dramatically altered by various means such as new methods of feces disposal (cat-style sanitation, or burying feces in a hole) and handwashing. But attempts to simply transmit these ideas without evidence or discussion have had rather limited results. In the 1990s, the Zimbabwean government, with the assistance of donors, developed a toolkit of visual aids and distributed it to eight hundred health technicians responsible for the training of thirty-eight hundred health workers operating in forty-eight of the country's fifty-seven districts. Information was simply presented at standard village meetings. By 2001, there was little evidence of behavioral change, and donors were abandoning the effort (Waterkeyn and Cairncross 2005).

Following this failure, the government proposed a new model of intervention. This one aimed at organizing women's health clubs in each village. The new program, which focused on the women's behavior, was accompanied by new metrics of progress. The key goal was to generate new norms and beliefs aimed at altering group behavior. Each weekly meeting focused on one health topic. Through repeated interaction, strong leaders emerged. Each club was run by an elected executive committee. Health technicians were trained using fourteen sets of illustrated cards to show improved sanitation and hygiene. Each week, members pledged small home improvements, including simple acts such as covering drinking water, using ladles to serve water, constructing garbage pits, and using handwashing facilities. Members would visit each other's homes to monitor progress. Health slogans and songs were devised to emphasize key points. "Certificates of Full Attendance" were awarded in a public ceremony to those who completed all subjects. During the year 2000 they made up 52 percent of the membership in the two districts studied (Waterkeyn and Cairncross 2005).

The authors attempt to quantify the health impact of these new organizational structures on participating households relative to controls in comparable villages without health clubs. They generated twenty hygiene-related indicators in order to analyze the health behavior of 736 club members and compare it to the behavior of a control group of 172 nonmembers. The analysis was based on visits to subjects' homes. In Tsholotsho, the difference in results between members and nonmembers was dramatic and was in fact highly statistically significant for sixteen of twenty indicators (p less than or equal to 0.0001). For example, in 100 percent of members' homes there was no open disposal of feces, compared to 2 percent of homes in the control group. In addition, there were individual cups in 97 percent of members' homes compared to 22 percent of nonmembers' homes and individual plates in 86 percent of members' homes but in 10 percent of nonmembers' homes. Ladles were used in 95 percent of the former and 30 percent of the latter, and the pouring method of handwashing was used in 91 percent of the former and 3 percent of the latter. In Makoni, nine indicators were shown to be statistically significant in favor of the organization members. Most others were higher among members but not to the point of statistical significance. Club members greatly increased their efforts to build latrines and had great success, with 1,200 constructed in Tsholotsho in eighteen months and 2,400 built in Makoni in twenty-four months. This is quite an accomplishment, considering that only 8,083 latrines had been constructed two years earlier for the entire country. Others almost universally practiced cat sanitation (Waterkeyn and Cairncross 2005).

The positive effect of this exercise demonstrates the value of a socially reinforcing environment. Organizations become important entities for protection of ideas, which can germinate new norms by means of education. Those norms can then be internalized via social approbation and other rewards. The risks of altering individual behavior are greatly reduced when they are undertaken within a group. New practices become habituated as new forms of behavior become accepted, required, expected, and ultimately shared within the broader social group. In contrast, merely educating individuals about hygiene is likely to be far less effective in generating new forms of socially prescribed behavior.

Incentives

Incentives are based on the rewards and penalties that arise from different modes of behavior. As demonstrated above and in other chapters, nonpecuniary incentives are very important in transforming institutions. In contrast, the Bank's strategies emphasized altering health care behavior via prices and user fees. More recently, however, new initiatives have been developed to transcend the goals of privatization and the dependence on price signals to incorporate an array of market-related tools to alter health behavior. "Social marketing," or "the use of marketing to design and implement programs to promote socially beneficial behavior change," has been heavily used in the United States to increase consumption of fruit and vegetables, promote breast feeding, increase physical activity, and decrease fat consumption (Grier and Bryant 2005, 319). In developing countries, it has been used to increase access to potable water, eliminate leprosy, improve use of tuberculosis medication, and promote immunization.

In Africa, social marketing has been promoted to increase the availability and use of or insecticide-treated nets (ITNs) in such places as Malawi, Kenya, Uganda, and Tanzania (Kikumbih et al. 2005). Randomized community trials in Africa have demonstrated a 17 percent reduction in mortality and a 50 percent decline in the frequency of clinical malaria cases in children under five where ITNs are used (Mathanga et al. 2006). Social marketing builds on existing commercial networks of net sales to expand their availability and usage to more of the population. Perhaps the biggest player in the social marketing of ITNs has been a Washington-based NGO called Population Services International (PSI), which has been involved with projects in Tanzania (funded by United Kingdom Department for International Development, or DFID, and the Royal Netherlands Embassy), Kenya (supported by DFID), and Malawi (supported by USAID and UNICEF) (Population Services International 2003a).

Beginning in 1998, PSI sold blue nets in Malawi through commercial networks at $6.00 each and green nets for pregnant women through health clinics at $2.00 plus $.20 for a retreatment kit containing insecticide. A cross-sectional survey of 1,852 children and their families in 2002 in a township in Blantyre, where the social marketing took place, revealed limited improvement. Roughly 41.6 percent of the children had used nets the night before the survey took place. But the majority of households (51 percent) had no nets. Of the households with nets, only 17.9 percent had two or more ITNs. A bivariate analysis suggested that greater ownership and use were clearly associated with better material circumstances, more education of the caregiver or parent, electricity in the house, higher-quality housing, and the presence of antimalaria drugs. A multivariate logistic regression using the same variables showed that poor households were 60 percent less likely to have ITNs. Moreover, 90 percent of the households without nets cited cost as the major factor in the decision not to acquire a net (Mathanga et al. 2006). Studies conducted in other African countries have also documented similar percentages of people who cite cost factors in their decision not to purchase nets.[25]

The limited nature of the success in Malawi is linked to the rather misconceptualized nature of incentives embedded in PSI's particular approach to social marketing and to social marketing more generally. To begin with, social marketing has the same microfoundations as neoclassical economic "exchange theory" and holds that individual consumers act "primarily out of self-interest as they seek ways to optimize value by doing what gives them the greatest benefit for the least cost" (Grier and Bryant 2005, 321). Incentives to alter health-related behavior are embedded in the product, price, place, and promotion. According to this theory, it is the product itself that delivers a good or service that will alter health behavior and provide a benefit that consumers will truly value. Price is the cost or sacrifice exchanged for the perceived benefit; it includes not only monetary value but also intangible elements such as the loss of time. In this model, however, prices are always determined from the perspective of consumers, and it is assumed that consumers are willing to pay more for additional perceived value. Products that are priced too low, the theory asserts, may be deemed inferior and thus will not be valued. "Place" refers to the location where goods are purchased and should focus on attractiveness, comfort, accessibility, and convenience to maximize sales. Finally, promotion, which focuses on ways to persuade consumers to purchase products, includes things such as advertising, displays, and public relations.

This focus on the neoclassical economic vision of the market as a medium for behavioral transformation is what limits the impact of efforts by organizations such as PSI. As seen above, the poorest people, those with the greatest need, are the ones with the least access to ITNs. Population Services International is very explicit in its rationale for charging for the nets: "[W]hen products are given away free, the recipient often does not value them or even use them" (Population Services International 2003b, 12). The position is axiomatic; it arises from the neoclassical belief that price reflects utility value to consumers and that a price of zero would leave consumers with the belief that the product has no value. Simple logic would suggest that the value would arise not from the price charged but rather from demonstration of the product's effectiveness. There is ample evidence that free nets can be delivered successfully and inexpensively to vulnerable people such as pregnant women at venues like prenatal clinics (Guyatt et al. 2002). Still, possessing a net does not guarantee that it will be used, whether it is purchased or acquired for free.[26] A shift in capacities is also needed.

Capacities

Recall that to increase capacity is to enhance or transform the ability of actors (individuals, groups, organizations, and countries) to set and achieve their goals in an effective, efficient, and sustainable manner within their accepted norms and rules. On the simplest level, universal ownership of nets is a sine qua non of any ITN strategy. Capacities must go beyond ownership, however, and move toward increasing people's ability to understand the health benefits associated with net use. Skills must also be developed in order to ensure that ITNs are properly used and retreated with insecticide. Education of the type used in Zimbabwe (demonstration cards, local trainers, visits to houses by trained individuals, and so on), delivered in the context of health clubs, could be one approach to increasing ITN capacity.

A similar effort could be undertaken in the school system so that children have information that is symmetric with that of other members of their households. If ITNs are not being used, children should be in a position to ask that they be placed over them before retiring. Shared mental constructs related to the benefits of this request are more likely to lead to a positive outcome. Problems are likely to arise if, for example, children are educated without comparable efforts to inform their parents. Conversely, children are likely to agree to use ITNs if they are fully aware of their health benefits. Peer pressure is also important in such a case. Capacity needs to be extended beyond the household to the broader social setting. Education also needs to focus on the community. Community-wide habits of thought are likely to provide a positive background that offers guidelines regarding what is expected, required, and accepted.

Market promotion and distribution do not guarantee the sustainability of net usage. It will become fully institutionalized when nightly usage becomes a habit of thought for parents and children. Regulations and laws can also have a powerful role in changing health-related behavior and outcomes.

Regulations

Recall that regulations are part of the legal order that defines norms and rules, as well as the system of sanctions that enforces them. They are instrumental in defining, initiating, supporting, and transforming institutions. In the health arena and other contexts, people respond to the guidance of the rule itself, the likely behavior of the regulatory implementing agency, the resources, abilities, and constraints influencing the capacity of individuals to respond to new regulations, and finally the feedback effect of the participant in the process. Additional dimensions are the intrinsic motivation of individuals, groups, or organizations to change their behavior in response to a new regulation, as well as the positive and negative incentives embedded in the regulations to encourage compliance. We saw above that in the anti-FGC laws have little impact in countries where regulations have been seldom enforced and where they are contrary to deeply embedded customs and practices.

Yet regulations and related guidelines and their transformation can have a rapid impact on health care outcomes. Take the case of tuberculosis control measures in Zambia in the 1990s. The National Tuberculosis Program (NTP), established in 1964, was expanded to incorporate leprosy in 1980 and AIDS and STDs in 1993. From 1988 onward, the program was supported by the government of the Netherlands. After the program underwent some changes, the Netherlands agreed to support an action plan to improve district-level TB control. Between 1995 and 1997 the NTP was developed with clear objectives, targets, activities, regulations and guidelines, and budgets to support their implementation. A manual and guide for program staff were published and distributed. Information was gathered and monitored at each district to ensure compliance. All treatment centers received uninterrupted supplies of anti-TB drugs. Semiannual technical review meetings were held to facilitate national evaluations, standardization, and coordination of planning. The result was a highly successful intervention; completion rates for the eight-month course of drugs rose to 70 percent among people enrolled in 1995, compared to 50 percent in previous years.

Yet all this rapidly unraveled as decentralization and deregulation policies were implemented as part of the IFI-inspired health reform packages. In 1995, Zambia passed the National Health Services Act, which created and transferred powers to autonomous district health boards and hospital management boards. This reorganization led to the demise of the National Tuberculosis Program and the expiration of the agreement with the Netherlands in 1997. The responsibility for TB management fell on the district-level boards without the centrally defined regulatory guidelines and practices. Technical capacity was in short supply at the district level, and there was a lack of financial and technical assistance from the national and regional levels. The central government's purchasing of drugs, which had been supported by Dutch aid, was discontinued. The result was disastrous. It led to the breakdown of TB control in the country and an "inevitable" rise in the development and transmission of multi-drug-resistant strains of the disease (Bosman 2000).

In contrast, well-planned legal and regulatory changes can have a powerful and positive effect on health care. Take the example of the introduction of antiretroviral treatment to prevent transmission of AIDS from mother to child in South Africa. In 2001, civil society groups, organized by the Treatment in Action Campaign, sued the South African government. They argued that according to the constitutionally guaranteed right to universal accessibility of health care, the government was obliged to provide universal access of ARVs to HIV-positive mothers in order to help diminish transmission to their children. In July 2002 the Constitutional Court ordered the government to "devise and implement within available resources a comprehensive program on mother-to-child transmission of HIV" (Forman 2003, 10).

By 2006 the program was widely available and had some encouraging effects. The rates of mother-to-child transmission did decline. More than seventy thousand babies annually were still being born HIV-positive, however, which was more than planners had hoped. The universal application of Nevirapine (an ARV) to pregnant mothers should have reduced the number to forty-six thousand, compared to an anticipated ninety-nine without any intervention.[27] The problem was the stigma associated with HIV-positive status and the refusal of thousands of women in South Africa to be tested or to admit they are positive and take the pill (Rosenberg 2006). Although the health care system had the capacities to follow through on the regulations, full institutionalization of the health benefits was not possible due to their inconsistency with norms and other disincentives.

Conclusions

As with other social needs, the World Bank was slow to move into the domain of health care and did not issue its first health care policy report until 1975. This report warned about relying too narrowly on the market and the private sector to deliver health goods because fundamental market failures would prevent effectiveness. These arguments continued throughout the 1970s. The 1980 World Development Report supported food subsidies and warned against introducing user fees for health, education, and water. Neoliberal analysts almost entirely ignored these warnings. In the end, the problems that emerged after market-oriented reforms were implemented in health care looked very much like those predicted by WDR 1980 and the 1975 report. The former and its background paper also supported the 1978 Alma-Ata Declaration. The key to the success of primary health care, it was argued, was to mobilize political support, increase public expenditure, and improve public sector administrative capacities. In response to faltering public support in the wake of funding shortages, and in accordance with the rise of neoliberalism in the 1980s, the Bank began to shift to policies focusing on resource allocation through the market.

Drawing on neoclassical economic theory, the key policy paper "Paying for Health Services" (de Ferranti 1985) inverts the earlier Bank view that the use of prices and market allocation is generally not desirable. The new position is one in which prices and markets are seen as the best means of improving the efficiency of health care. Introducing user fees was supposed to have the triple benefit of augmenting revenues, generating efficiency, and improving equity.

Other parts of the agenda for health care, also developed in the mid-1980s, focus on decentralization, privatization, and insurance for catastrophic illnesses. Decentralization of state services is desirable because it is market-like; services can be best provided by local government "sellers," who sell to local "buyers" via their user fees, which substitute for market prices. This agenda was further refined with WDR 1993. By introducing the concept of disability-adjusted life years (DALYs), the Bank was able to move away from the simple-minded bifurcation of curative and preventive care to begin to concentrate on the optimal allocation of resources, which was accomplished by comparing the cost per DALY of interventions. Yet DALYs are very problematic formulations, based on highly questionable assumptions, and they are certainly not the value-free optimization tool they purport to be.

Review by the Bank's Operations Evaluation Department indicated that after 1985, there was a major shift in Bank support away from technical and infrastructural projects. The new agenda emphasized organizational shifts such as decentralization, and financial reforms such as the introduction of user fees. Programs in these areas did poorly by OED standards. Instead of blaming the design of these projects, however, it doubly faulted the borrowers for incompetent implementation and failing to put in place other Bank reforms related to governance and neoliberalism.

A review of the empirical literature analyzing the Bank reforms indicated problems linked to the faulty premises and designs of the reform program. Contrary to the assertion that user fees would have little impact on the poor, numerous studies indicated that visits by low-income individuals to clinics and hospitals dramatically declined in the face of rising fees. At the same time, delays meant that people arrived at health facilities in worse condition, thereby making their treatment more expensive and less effective. Few additional revenues were generated, and there was little or no evidence of improvement in the quality of facilities.

Privatization and decentralization fared little better. New private health clinics tended to cater to wealthier people in urban areas. Partly because of poor regulations, private health care services were frequently of poor quality. The decentralization of health care led to a shortage of technical staff, an erosion of regulatory guidelines, regional inequities, and little indication of improved participation.

The institutional matrix can be used as a guide for improving health outcomes in a variety of different settings. Habits of thought common to the generality of men and women are at the heart of health-related behavior and decision making. In contrast to the view that individuals make rational health decisions when the proper market signals are in place, most activities with health implications have little or nothing to do with markets or prices. They are the products of the complex interaction of psychosocial and economic factors and pressures that are tied to one's surroundings and how these surroundings are perceived.

The ultimate test of human progress is freedom from disease and the ability to lead a healthy life, not economic freedom unfettered by government intervention. The right to health must transcend the neoclassical view of market rights to one that focuses on universal entitlement to decent health care. If economic policies and structures are incapable of providing viable livelihoods for the population, then they must be changed. People must be given the capacity to fulfill their underlying potential for a quality life. Doing everything possible to improve health conditions for all strata of the population continues to stand as the highest moral imperative.

CHAPTER NINE

Conclusion

Beyond the World Bank Agenda

At the present moment people are unusually expectant of a more fundamental diagnosis. . . . But apart from this contemporary mood, the ideas of economists and political philosophers, both when they are right and when they are wrong, are more powerful than is commonly understood. Indeed the world is ruled by little else. Practical men, who believe themselves to be quite exempt from any intellectual influences, are usually the slaves of some defunct economist. Madmen in authority, who hear voices in the air, are distilling their frenzy from some academic scribbler of a few years back. I am sure that the power of vested interests is vastly exaggerated compared with the gradual encroachment of ideas.—John Maynard Keynes, 1936

Introduction

For most of the postwar period, the institutions designed at the Bretton Woods conference dominated the development agenda. Their power to shape the development discourse reached its apotheosis during the era of neoliberalism. With great power, however, comes great responsibility. The promise of palpable prosperity in exchange for following the Bank's dictates remains elusive and ethereal for millions of the world's most destitute. In this chapter I attempt to sum up the major findings of this volume. In some small way, I hope that this bit of "academic scribbling" will help push the agenda forward, encourage an honest reevaluation of development strategies, and find a path toward a more equitable future.

The Confluence of Ideology, Power, and Theory:
A Historical Summary of the Making of the World Bank Agenda

Chapter 1 presented a brief history of the World Bank and the changes it has undergone from its inception in 1944 to 1979. From the beginning, the United States has played a hegemonic role inside the Bank. This hegemony, it should be recalled, results less from the exercise of naked power than from the institutionalization of rules and procedures that make it appear that decisions are being made objectively and that all parties are treated equally. This internal structure has, in part, helped pave the way for economists to become increasingly dominant in the operational and research domains of the Bank. Mainstream economic theory and policy, with their pretentious claims of scientific objectivity and usage of increasingly obtuse methods and terminology, have provided an important legitimizing veneer for the realization of U.S. priorities inside the World Bank.

The United States has always had a strong role in the World Bank, especially because of its retention of at least 15 percent of the voting power, which, owing to voting rules within the Bank, gives it unilateral veto power over major matters of substance. This power has resulted in the Bank's being used as a vehicle for pursuing American foreign policy objectives. In addition, the United States has always controlled the appointment of the president of the World Bank; there was barely a ripple of disaffection from other Bank members, up to and including the appointment of the neoconservative architect of the Iraq war, Paul Wolfowitz, in 2005 and his eventual replacement by Robert Zoellick, President Bush's former trade representative, in July 2007.

At its inception, the Bank was intended to help European countries rebuild after the devastation of World War II. With the onset of the cold war, however, it quickly became a convenient political tool for financing Western allies. The Bank originally focused on generating a conservative portfolio of loans for infrastructural projects; this interest was due in part to its desire to maintain a good rating for its bond issues, or, in other words, to become a stable and appealing lending institution. The Bank generated much of its revenue from the difference between the interest it charged on loans to member countries and the rate it paid on its bonds. Yet this financing scheme constrained the United States in the pursuit of its interests, which after the war were squarely set on the battle against Soviet influence within developing countries. On the urging of the United

States, the World Bank created a new lending arm, the IDA, for poor countries. It became clear that a new approach to funding was needed to subsidize loans to poor countries. But the opportunity for a fresh start resulted instead in a financing system that opened up yet another avenue of American influence, this time largely due to the need for members of the U.S. Congress to vote every three years on the replenishments on which the IDA relied.

In the 1960s the Bank began to focus its spending more on projects other than infrastructure, including education and agriculture. During the term of Robert McNamara it continued this trend, with infrastructure spending falling to 36 percent of total Bank spending from its previous level of more than 60 percent. McNamara began a push to invigorate rural development and other poverty-focused schemes, but these did poorly by Bank standards.

During that decade economists began to grow in influence within the Bank, largely because of the appointment to the presidency of George Woods, who in turn appointed Ben Friedman, an IMF economist, as his chief economic advisor. The Bank, which had traditionally been dominated by engineers, began to increasingly come under the influence of economists. This made the Bank particularly susceptible to the latest fads in development economics and, more generally, to trends in the discipline of economics as a whole. These trends include the increasing mathematization of the field, a narrowing of ideas and theories, and a growing attack on the basic premises of development economics.

The 1980s proved to have the elements for a "perfect storm" leading to a major agenda shift toward program loans and structural adjustment. The new agenda had a supportive audience among the neoclassically trained economists in the Bank. The rise of conservative regimes in Washington and London and the need to find a mechanism to rapidly disburse loans to deal with oil-related balance-of-payment shocks quickly brought structural adjustment to the fore. To understand the origins of adjustment, however, one needs to examine the history of the IMF.

In Chapter 2 we saw how policy conditionality began at the IMF almost immediately after its inception in 1945. After the demise of the Bretton Woods system of fixed exchange rates, for which it was responsible, the IMF had to invent a new raison d'être, which was found by becoming the world's lender to developing countries. True to its roots, the IMF used the Bretton Woods model of stabilization in its new mission, with an emphasis on austerity and contraction of credit for poor countries. The World Bank, however, was prohibited from making loans for programs except under exceptional circumstances. Its Executive Board ruled that such an "exceptional circumstance" would be an agreement with the IMF. Thus, the IMF became involved in structural adjustment packages, and the Bank and Fund began to work cooperatively toward the institutionalization of the new neoliberal agenda.

Its new agenda was laid out in the Berg Report of 1981 and the 1984 report titled "Toward Sustained Development in Sub-Saharan Africa." In these reports, the Bank's focus was to get prices right by means of deregulation and retraction of the state. Under the tutelage of the dogmatically conservative Anne Krueger, there was a clear shift in the staff toward economists with neoclassical credentials and a strong commitment to neoliberalism. In the process of transforming the structure and ideology of the Bank, the fight against poverty in developing countries was all but forgotten.

The Bank policies described above began to show signs of failure in the late 1980s. Rather than admit that the policies were flawed, it began to search for external reasons for their poor performance. This led the Bank to look into broader issues such as governance and institutions. The Bank also began to rewrite history, claiming that these newly identified issues had prevented its otherwise solid initial policies from working all along. The Bank's reaction had three elements. First, there was unwavering commitment to the core set of adjustment policies, and new elements were used to rationalize their poor performance. Second, each new policy was seen as a complement to adjustment that would enhance or act as a catalyst for reform. Third, the microfoundations of each new element were frequently based on neoclassical economic theory with all its problematic implications. Governance of recipient countries, for example, focused on accountability, transparency, and the rule of law. These factors also have underpinnings in neoclassical economics; accountability and transparency were stressed in order to reduce informational asymmetries and improve transactions in a hypothetical neoclassical world.

The Bank has also undertaken new initiatives such as the poverty reduction strategy papers. The programs they describe are intended to give developing countries ownership of their projects via local consultation and cooperation in the belief that this would somehow make reform programs more acceptable. Yet, as we saw in the case of Tanzania, the programs were less than successful; there was almost no local input, and the policies were nearly identical to those the Bank had been pursuing since the 1980s.

Surveys conducted in other African countries and regions confirm what the Tanzania case suggested: that there was little evidence of a serious shift in agenda and that most participation was perfunctory.

From Theory to Policy

Chapter 3 illustrated the linkage between the economic theories underlying the World Bank's policies of adjustment and the outcomes of these policies. Transformation of economies—in the image of Polak, Swan and Salter, McKinnon and Shaw, and Heckscher, Ohlin, and Samuelson—has engendered widespread economic difficulties precisely because of the weak foundations of the theory. Poorly conceived theory gives rise to policies that give rise to poor economic outcomes. The major theories underlying structural adjustment utilize common microfoundations including *Homo economicus*, rational deductivity, methodological individualism, axiomatic reasoning, and the acceptance of equilibrium as a natural state. These tenets generate six focal points or propositions related to adjustment, including a commitment to the principle of state neutrality or minimalism; preoccupation with static efficiency, a focus on distortions and marginality, a view that changes in relative prices lead to predictable outcomes, and development as a static equilibrium state.

In policy terms, these theories have emphasized strategies based on static comparative advantage, which has encouraged increased specialization and overemphasis on a handful of poorly performing cash crop and resource exports in places such as Africa. Countries pursuing this trade strategy have experienced acute declines in their terms of trade. Other theoretical weaknesses arise from the divergence between the assumed world conceived by proponents of structural adjustment and the reality of the economies of developing countries. States have frequently been emasculated as a consequence of an axiomatic view of the way in which states should operate. At the same time, policies have pushed liberalization in order to get prices right in order to attain presumed gains in static efficiency.

By the World Bank's logic, widespread indications of severe downward trends under the structural adjustment approach do not prove that adjustment is responsible, even if the problems with the theory strongly indicate that this is the case. Therefore the five approaches for statistically testing the relationship between structural adjustment policy and its impact on economies were assessed. There seems to be little consistent evidence that adjustment has improved the targeted economies, and a preponderance of indicators and tests indicate the opposite. Even World Bank studies have frequently shown contrary results; some reports illustrate a worsening of economies as a result of adjustment. Part of the problem is the methodological weakness of the testing, although some have accused the Bank of deliberately designing some studies to show positive results. Partly in reaction, some World Bank economists have tried to offer alternative explanations for the economic decline of countries that are following structural adjustment programs. It is quite clear that the econometrics has at best confused causation with correlation by, for example, associating ethnicity with poor economic growth. The strategy can be interpreted as an attempt to generate auxiliary hypotheses aimed at providing a protective belt around the core axioms at the heart of structural adjustment. The commitment to the core of adjustment has not wavered.

Overall, the poor performance of countries following the dictates of structural adjustment is directly linked to its roots in neoclassical economic theory. Neoclassical economics, with its emphasis on equilibrium, static and narrow notions of human behavior, and misplaced focus on financial variables, is incapable of either assessing the problems of development or presenting a viable strategy for setting development in motion. The key to reversing the economic malaise of regions such as Africa is to consider a broader array of theoretical tools and traditions, including institutional economics. The Bank, too, has discovered institutional economics.

New Institutional Economics and the Theoretical Reconstruction of the Bank Agenda

When drawing on institutional theory, the Bank for the most part applied the new institutional economics, the more neoclassical variant of the institutional school. Although the concept of institutions was discussed in various contexts and often used interchangeably with public sector management or public administration (as discussed in chapter 6), the real focus on institutional economics came after Coase and North received their Nobel prizes. Williamson's 1994 paper was especially important in laying out the relation between his version of NIE and the World Bank agenda.

Bureaucrats in Business, published in 1995, was the first publication to apply Williamson's framework. The report compares state-run and privately run state enterprises to privatized companies by analyzing them as contractual relationships between the government, on one hand, and public and private managers (in the case of state-owned enterprises) or a regulatory contract (in the case of privatized ones) on the other. The report draws on NIE theory largely to confirm the emphasis on the superiority of the private sector and privatization over state-owned and -run enterprises. It argues that information asymmetries create incentives for managers to act opportunistically by negotiating for easily achievable targets. Given that many public managers are political appointees, r there is little incentive for them to comply. Finally, a lack of independent third-party enforcement creates a commitment problem, so there is little reason for parties to the contract to fulfill their obligations.

By contrast, the report insists, success was possible with regulatory contracts because competitive bidding reduced informational asymmetries, regulation of prices would improve performance, and legislatures would pass laws defining procedures for arbitration and appeal of any disputes. Commitment could be more readily achieved. Private managers and owners, unlike their government counterparts, were able to capture the benefits if performance improved because they better responded to incentives and worked harder than government managers (and with better results). The Bank empirically confirmed its argument by carefully redefining the criteria for success and by introducing bias in sample selection. Although the report readily admits that enterprises that were under public management met most of their contractual goals, the criteria of success were redefined with regard to state managers, in order to buttress the report's claims that management by the private sector was superior.

The emphasis on reconstructing and explaining the components of the neoliberal agenda continued in later reports. The tools of NIE were applied to governance, state minimalism, and deregulation. To some degree, the ease with which NIE was used to justify the existing agenda was increased by its utilization of microfoundations similar to those of neoclassical economics. In electing to build on only the aspects of institutional economics that were helpful in supporting the Bank's already firm rhetoric, the Bank missed a valuable opportunity to rethink its policies and to move to make successful changes. An agenda inspired by original institutional economics, in contrast, inspires a rather different emphasis because of its fundamental divergence from neoclassical economics.

Moving beyond the World Bank Agenda:
Institutional Theory and Development

Chapter 5 laid out a new institutional framework with which to view development. In contrast to neoclassical economic theory, Gunnar Myrdal proposes a framework of factors that interact to create a self-supporting and self-reproducing system of circular causation in which induced changes in one factor can alter the direction of other factors, setting off a process of cumulative change. The system has six broad categories—output and income, conditions of production, standard of living, attitudes toward life and work, institutions, and policies—that interact to induce economic development.

Myrdal's theory, although very helpful to advancing the agenda, also has some flaws. He places output and income and the conditions of production on an equal footing with standard of living, attitudes, and institutions. Output and income are flawed measures of well-being for a host of well-known reasons (such as distribution problems), and the conditions of production should be seen as a way to increase capacities and the number of organizations that enable new forms of human interaction. Finally, Myrdal conflates organizations with institutions when, in reality, organizations are institutional constructs.

In contrast, according to Veblen's line of thinking, institutions are habits of thought (not merely habits) common to the generality of men and women. Thought implies process and activity, and it is kinetic. Habits represent potential behavior that can be triggered by stimuli. Habits of thought are not passive entities but are constructs that are continuously and often repetitively invoked in response to contextualized stimuli as perceived by the thought process. They are integral to the human dynamic that connects thought to process and allows people to transform their activities. They are, in other words, the means by which a violin player develops the capacity to play. But institutions are more. Habits of thought must also be socially connected in order for them to be effective. They must be common to the generality of men and women. They must not be idiosyncratic and individualized but rather must be linked to other individuals such that they increase coordination, unity of purpose, and certainty of behavior. Thus, institutions are at the core of a series of institutional constructs whose transformation should be the focal point of any strategy for generating a process of cumulative change to facilitate development.

Institutional constructs are presented in the form of an institutional matrix, which consists of norms, organizations, regulations, capacities, and incentives. Norms dictate guidelines of behavior with regards to what is expected, required, or acceptable. The threat of social disfavor if one does not act in accordance with the norms inspires adherence, as does the reward of approval when norms are followed. Yet in institutional terms, norms are most effective when they are internalized. Because norms are a societal phenomenon, they are not automatically internalized at the individual level. This is where organizations come in. Regulations constitute the legal boundaries that help set the rules of an economy. They buttress norms and rules with a legal system of sanctions and rewards. They are particularly important owing to the comparative speed in which they can be altered compared to other parts of the matrix.

Capacity is defined as an actor's ability to set and achieve goals in an effective, efficient, and sustainable manner, relative to accepted norms and rules. Expanded capacities foster more linkages between entities and in turn increase the diversity of the economic and social activities that are at the heart of development. Finally, institutionalized incentives are the rewards and penalties that arise from different modes of behavior. Response to these incentives involves a high degree of cognition and can therefore be very different for different individuals until via interaction with the other parts of the matrix, the reaction becomes more fully institutionalized.

Institutions are at the center of the matrix. Each component of the matrix affects each other component, as well as institutions themselves. The changes that are made at any level, therefore, have the potential to alter human behavior, which is at the heart of the matrix. Making such changes also implies that a new set of institutions will be created and that they will provide the basis for a new economic and social order. This matrix is then applied in order to understand the state, finance, and health sectors.

World Bank State Reform and the Applications of the Institutional Matrix to the State

Chapter 6 presented the first application of the matrix to the state and to development, focusing in particular on the rather crucial element of civil service reform. Policies aimed at reducing the size and functions of the state began to be implemented in the early 1980s. Under the direction of Anne Krueger, the conservative agenda became the credo, as illustrated by WDR 1983. The report called for curtailing the functions and size of the civil service, reforming and privatizing parastatal entities, decentralizing government, and introducing new sources of financing for public goods such as user fees. Elements of background papers that were consistent with the new conservative agenda were strategically included in the report, whereas other relevant material, including more institutional analysis, was tacitly ignored.

The actual Bank policy concerning the state took two major forms: building up the organizational capacities necessary for implementing structural adjustment policies and reforming the state itself. The former policy was aimed at macroeconomic and financial management, reform of sectors other than the financial sector, and trade and policy administration reform—in a word, *liberalizing* the economy. The latter was aimed at retrenchment and at curtailing the wage bill of the state, all in the effort to minimize the state apparatus to the furthest extent possible.

Overall, many of the civil service reform efforts were poorly envisaged, badly implemented, and for the most part failures, even by the Bank's standards, as set by the Operations Evaluation Department. An initial focus on downsizing the state by laying off large numbers of wage employees, as well as by other means, often led to the departure of the most competent people in government. In addition, contrary to expectations, layoffs rarely generated significant financial savings for the government. There was no evidence that the remaining civil servants operated any more efficiently. In many cases, civil service wages continued to decline in real terms as other elements of adjustment were implemented, including cutbacks in government expenditures and the removal of subsidies for food. Moreover, the social and economic impact of releasing tens of thousands of employees was never actually evaluated; it was simply assumed that these workers would be absorbed by the private sector. Apparently no one had bothered to recognize that the private sector was hardly viable on its own.

The role of the state need not be written off as inherently harmful, and—as the consequences of the Bank's policies demonstrated—it may not be beneficial to restrain it. The institutional perspective provides an alternative vision of the state that focuses on the question of how to internalize development-enhancing behavior using the framework of the institutional matrix. Norms can generate habits of thought, which can be self-reinforcing. If corruption is deemed anathema to the normal operations of the government, it will be disfavored and abnormal. This attitude will elicit corresponding changes in organizational structures, regulations, and so on, which will help lead to lasting institutional change. At the heart of a well-functioning civil service are Weberian bureaucratic norms. States are not really composed of a single organizational entity but rather consist of a cluster of interconnected organizational constructs. Organizations, in turn, are an important vehicle of socialization because they contain the incentives, rules, purposes, and norms that are aimed at transforming behavior. One way to improve organizations in the context of the state is to focus on improving a few units within the government and then allow mimetic isomorphism to spread through the rest of it. In imagining the importance of organizational constructs and their promotion of new norms, the significance of regulations comes to mind.

Regulations are formal guidelines that help institutionalize transformations and priority-setting; they are the most direct way for strategists to purposely elicit change. As part of the legal order, regulations specify the boundaries of organizations, the rules of their operation, and the sanctions and rewards that enforce them. Regulations, therefore, *are defined by* the state and help *define* the state. In contrast to the World Bank's perspective, the institutional viewpoint argues that regulations should be formed according to the needs of the developmental objective and should not be limited by current capacities, which—as would be expected in an underdeveloped state—must be expanded and strengthened.

Capacities are defined in relation to the abilities of civil service members. For the civil service to be successful, it must be able to conscientiously and resolutely achieve its objectives. Accordingly, programs intended to augment state capacities should focus on increasing civil servants' ability to create new capacities; that is, capacity-building must enhance or transform the ability to set and achieve goals in an effective manner, as well as the ability to reinforce the behaviors and processes that lead to success. In a similar vein, incentives relate to the rewards and penalties that arise from different modes of behavior. In the context of states, incentives are important for bolstering the effect of new rules as civil services are transformed. Because they represent an important means by which agents internalize common habits of thought that are at the heart of the effective exercise of state functions, incentives must accompany all other types of institutional change.

Institutional Transformation for Finance and Development

Chapter 7 illustrated the nature and role of the state in the context of building financial systems to facilitate development. It included a critical analysis of the theory and policies underlying the World Bank's approach to financial reform.

Financial repression theory, the main inspiration for the World Bank's financial liberalization policies, relies on a pre-Keynesian notion that prior saving is needed for financial development. This model is subject to several important criticisms. For example, the theory of financial liberalization relies on the textbook world of pure competition. Yet there is a profound difference between the real world and the model; as the imperfect-market theorists have argued, because finance is even more replete with asymmetries of risk and information, it is even less likely to abide by the notion of perfect competition than are other sectors of the economy. It is not surprising, given its faulty premises, that implementation of this model led to a series of financial crises in developing countries during the 1980s.

The Bank used this theory as the basis for the conditions it imposed on the financial sector during the 1980s and early 1990s. With growing evidence that its reforms were provoking financial crises, the Bank went to extraordinary lengths to prove that the two issues were totally unrelated. In typical fashion, by 1993 even its innovative modifications had not halted the failure of its strategies, and the Bank was forced to realize that its reforms had not met expectations. Bank theorists purported to search for reasons that would make sense of the collapse of the strategy, but they continued to dismiss any explanations that would question their underlying theory.

The institutional matrix can be applied to the financial sector to generate alternative strategies. Norms must be developed on two levels: first, banking norms, from codes of conduct to recognition that finance is central to development, are needed. Second, professional standards associated with an employee's line of work must also become norms. Thus, it must be recognized that monetary incentives provide only one dimension of overall incentives. Because humans are social creatures, there are many other ways in which incentives can be generated including promotion, the loss of social esteem, threats of ostracism, appeals to social responsibility, legal repercussions, professionalism, and pride. These social incentives are central to any effort to expand and operate banking systems in developing countries. Both material and nonmaterial rewards are needed to change the goals of banking in order to accommodate development. Incentives must also be designed to buttress other parts of the matrix.

Regulations constitute the legal boundaries that help set the rules of operation in financial systems. A crucial element is a careful specification of the spheres of interaction between the components of the economy, including ownership of the different segments of the financial system and their linkage to industrial, agricultural, and other enterprises in the service sector. An equally significant issue is the promotion of mechanisms that will help institutionalize the legal system and therefore encourage the internalization of the rules of operation. This is, after all, at the heart of a sound regulatory sector.

Capacities are related to the underlying capabilities of the constitutive members (individuals and other subunits) of organizations to operate in an effective manner to achieve their organization's goals within the confines of its norms and rules. In the context of the financial sector, banks and the agencies that regulate them must grow at the same pace as and in line with expanding capabilities. Capacity-building takes time because new skills must be not merely acquired but also internalized. Capacities influence the nature of perceptions, conceptions, and even correlative behavior.

Organizations are the constructs that combine people with structures. In the area of financial liberalization they include state regulatory agencies and financial intermediaries. As intermediaries, countries should focus on creating an assortment of banks to deal with the multi-tiered financial needs of a developing economy (merchant banks, development banks, commercial banks, microfinance banks, local banks, state banks, international banks, cooperative banks, and so on). The orthodox financial liberalization experienced in Nigeria was responsible for generating a major crisis. It could have been averted by taking an institutional approach and looking for alternatives that allowed cooperation and coordination between the state and the financial system.

Institutions, Markets, and Health Policy

Chapter 8 traced the impact of neoclassical economics on the development of health care policy at the Bank. The Bank was slow to commit to supporting health care. Early reports expressed hesitance to intervene in the health sector because it was not an area of expertise for Bank employees.

What little discussion of health care there was focused more on words of caution than on concrete policies. For example, the Bank reports warned about relying too narrowly on the use of prices and markets to allocate health care, because this could worsen inequalities in health care. Moreover, the reports expressed fear that the typical economic method of analyzing human behavior would not be accurate in its predictions, both because consumers were not well qualified to select the best health services (meaning that they would not make their health decisions based on price signals) and because many health choices are made by people other than the recipient of services. By extension, the reports argued, it is essential to recognize the particular nature of health care: disease control and improved health conditions for all have many social benefits that exceed private benefits. Similarly, because health crises are frequently random and catastrophic, individuals cannot budget adequately to prepare for them. This means that good health care requires some risk sharing.

The Bank also supported the 1978 Alma-Ata Declaration, including its commitment to health as a universal human right and to the implementation of a system to deliver primary health care, which aimed to provide a basic level of care to everyone in society. The success of primary health care was contingent on the mobilization of political support, adequate public expenditures, and significant public-sector administrative capacities. After public support faltered in the wake of funding shortages, two approaches were proposed: one aimed at setting priorities according to which primary health care should be applied and one aimed at allocation of resources to the health care sector that would be provided via the market rather than by the state. As the Bank turned to neoliberalism in the early 1980s, it selected the second option.

Once again, the shift in policy focus was buttressed by neoclassical economic theory. The Bank's earlier approaches to health care were dismissed as out of date. In accordance with neoclassical economic principles, the new focus was on improving efficiency in a marginal world by using the principles of affordability and effectiveness.

The concept of affordability utilizes the voluntarism and equilibrium inherent in neoclassical economics. When applied to health care, it signifies that "a health program is affordable if and only if each of the parties that must contribute to financing its operation at its design scale are able and willing to do so" (Prescott and de Ferranti 1985, 1235). From the Bank's perspective, given the looming absence of revenues in sub-Saharan Africa and other regions, the central problem was one of available resources.

Instead of finding ways to mobilize public spending, the Bank emphasized policy adjustments that focused on a "combination of restraint in the size and growth of public sector involvement in the provision of health services together with increased mobilization of non-fiscal resources . . . including the imposition of user fees" (1237).

From the Bank's perspective, introducing user fees would have the triple benefit of augmenting revenues, generating efficiency, and improving equity. In addition to filling revenue gaps, user fees would also help improve allocative efficiency because they would replace the distortionary taxes that had been used to finance public health care. According to the Bank's strategy, where possible, fees were to approach the marginal cost of production in order to maximize efficiency. User fees were also said to be better for the poor because they would provide improvements on the supply side due to increased availability of resources. Concerns about the ability and willingness of poor people to pay user fees were consistently dismissed, either by citing badly flawed studies or by simple assertion unsupported by any data.

According to standard economics, the best solution for health care policy making is to choose health projects that "maximize the health sector contribution to some agreed measure of social welfare." The second-best solution is to "identify through cost-effectiveness analysis those projects which would yield the greatest improvement in health status subject to the resource constraint" (Prescott and de Ferranti 1985, 1238). The suggested approach is to move beyond disease-specific analysis to examining the multipurpose interventions needed to improve overall health and welfare. Yet the tools to do this were unavailable in the 1980s and were not introduced until DALYs were developed in 1993. In lieu of an overall measurement, Bank economists focused on rationally deductive arguments and economic theory to decide where public resources should be used to subsidize user fees.

Two simple categories of health services were proposed: curative treatments and their associated medicines and preventive medicine. According to the neoclassical logic, preventive services that are not patient-related cannot be efficiently priced because they are public goods, meaning that the benefits gained from them cannot be limited to those who have paid. Although externalities may provide some justification for charging fees that are less than the marginal cost for preventive services, curative care must be fully paid. The validation for this conclusion involves the assumption that a rational individual will naturally seek care when he or she is sick or injured. This kind of rational deductive argument draws on the premise that symptoms are universally understood and unambiguous. It omits the consideration that individuals may have to weigh their need to seek medical attention against the potential financial and social burden of doing so and that the burden of the latter may be greater. This is a serious oversight, especially given the vast literature concerning medical anthropology and the related cultural issues within the health care arena. Once again, it is not for lack of relevant information that the strategies are designed the way they are but because they were chosen in accordance with neoclassical theory.

The health care agenda developed in the 1980s recommend that specific reforms be made in order to adhere to the principles outlined above. It focused on user fees, decentralization, privatization, and insurance for catastrophic illnesses. Decentralization of state services is said to be desirable because it is a better substitute for the market. In this analysis, health care is best understood as a commodity with respect to which services can be best provided by local government "sellers," who sell their product to local "buyers" by employing user fees that act as prices. Further refinement of the agenda is developed in WDR 1993. By introducing the concept of DALYs, the Bank was able to move away from the simple-minded bifurcation of curative and preventative care to a new consideration of the optimal allocation of resources, which used DALYs to compare the costs of interventions. However, as we have seen, DALYs are very problematic formulations that are fraught with highly questionable assumptions and they are not free of value judgments.

Reviews by the Bank's Operations Evaluation Department indicated that after 1985 there was a major shift in Bank support away from technical and infrastructural projects. The new agenda emphasized organizational changes such as decentralization and financial reforms such as the introduction of user fees. Programs carried out in these areas did poorly by OED standards.

A review of the empirical literature that analyzed the Bank's reforms indicated problems linked to the faulty premises and designs of the reform program. Contravening assertions that user fees would have little impact on the poor, numerous studies indicated that visits by low-income patients to clinics and hospitals dramatically declined in the face of rising fees. At the same time, delays in seeking care caused people to arrive at health facilities in worse condition than they might have been in if they had sought care immediately. Furthermore, even the initial purpose of collecting revenue failed: few additional revenues were generated, and there was little or no evidence of improvement in the quality of facilities.

Privatization and decentralization fared little better. New private health clinics tended to cater to wealthier people in urban areas. Partly because of poor regulation, private health care services were frequently of poor quality. The decentralization of health care led to a shortage of technical staff, an erosion of regulatory guidelines, regional inequities, and little indication of improved participation.

The institutional matrix can be a guide to improving health outcomes in a variety of settings. Habits of thought are at the heart of health-related behavior and decision making. In spite of the claim that individuals make rational health decisions when the proper market signals are in place, most activities that have implications for health have little or nothing to do with markets or prices. They are, rather, the product of the complex interaction of psychosocial and economic factors, as well as pressures related to one's surroundings.

The starting point of an institutional approach to health care is a commitment to the universal right to health care. An institutional approach, however, does not have a universal policy solution but is foremost a framework aimed at a contextual analysis of the way health institutions can be built to meet the needs of the population. Like other sectors discussed in this book, there is no real alternative to the state; it simply must be at the core of any viable transformation of the health system.

Ultimately, the failure of the World Bank agenda has been a failure of the theory that has generated the agenda. To paraphrase Keynes, the practical people at the helm of the World Bank have been, for far too long, the slaves of defunct economists or—perhaps more accurately—modern *representations* of defunct economists. Let us hope that a gradual encroachment of new ideas will begin to challenge vested interests so that we can move beyond the World Bank agenda of the past toward a better future.

Notes

Chapter One

1. The concept arises from the Treaty of Westphalia of 1648, which recognized state sovereignty in Europe. In international relations, it often signifies international power as a reflection of the sum total of the interests of the constituent states.

2. *Hegemony* derives from the Greek term *egemonia* or *emenon*, meaning "leader or ruler with political dominance." The concept was theoretically developed by Antonio Gramsci. Gramsci was a political activist and social theorist imprisoned by the fascists in Italy from 1929 to 1935. During his incarceration, he focused on the issue of the nature of the "spontaneous consent given by the great masses of the population to the general direction imposed on social life by the dominant fundamental group" (1971, 12). According to his argument, intellectuals play a major role as "deputies" to dominant groups by providing an aura of technocracy that legitimizes hegemony. True control, Gramsci believed, was achieved not by coercion but by gaining the people's approval of such control.

3. See, e.g., the discussion in chapter 2 of governance and the importance to the Bank of maintaining a technical façade around an inherently political issue.

4. A growing literature recognizes the ways in which the Bank and the Fund have been used to promote U.S. interests. For example, Faini and Grilli (2004) examine the pattern of Bank and IMF lending between 1984 and 2001; in their statistical analysis, lending is correlated with U.S. financial and commercial interests. Dreher and Jensen (2004) illustrate the relation between conditionality and UN voting and statistically illustrate a close relation between the number of conditions attached to loans and the alignment between the borrower country and UN voting patterns (fewer conditions are correlated with closer alignment) using fixed-effect poisson regression models. Thacker (1999) also uses UN voting patterns to examine political allegiance and finds that prior to 1990 countries were rewarded with IMF loans if they moved closer to the U.S. voting positions. After 1990, those with most closely aligned patterns were rewarded the most.

5. Path-determinant change (discussed in chapter 5) is an important concept in institutional economics. Although a particular outcome may be a product of a complex confluence of events or a simple accident, it has an impact on the future course of events. Thus, although driving on the left side of the road may have been entirely accidental (no pun intended), it has a dramatic impact on the pattern of traffic, the production of autos, the norms of pedestrians, and so on.

6. *Financial Times,* 27 June 2003.

7. Ibid.

8. In the context of supporting the creation of the Inter-American Development Bank, Eisenhower was quoted as saying: "If this instrument insisted upon social reform as a condition of extending a development credit, it could scarcely be charged with intervention" (quoted in Kapur et al. 1997, 155).

9. To quote a World Bank official working closely with the Treasury, IDA "was not a U.S. affirmative program" but rather was "a desire to assuage Congress" and "to keep off SUNFED" (quoted in Kapur et al. 1997, 155). The latter was the product of pressure from developing countries, which were seeking development assistance in social areas under softer terms. The program was a potential challenge to the domain of the U.S.-dominated Bank.

10. The pressure to remove some health care and primary school user fees, which have been an integral part of structural adjustment from its inception, came not from the Bank's responding to the demands of the poor but from the U.S. Congress. The changes to Bank conditionality exactly match the provisions of the U.S. 2001 Foreign Operations Appropriations Bill, signed into law in November 2000, sec. 596 (cited in Fifty Years Is Enough 2000).

11. Black, however, helped introduce the idea of expanding the Bank's scope to lend to poorer countries on better terms. In 1957 he sent a memo about this issue, written by a Bank official, to Treasury Secretary Anderson. He also pushed the idea in subsequent meetings (Kapur et al. 1997, 154; Oliver 1995, 44–45).

12. This new program was formally introduced at the September 1963 annual meeting (Kapur et al. 1997, 181), bringing IBRD priorities more in line with the new IDA.

13. Eligibility for IDA was set at a per capita annual income of $125.

14. Friedman is quoted as saying that when he tried to recruit an economics staff from people with Ph.D.s in economics working in the Bank, most did not want to be considered economists because they felt that "being an economist in the Bank was the death of a career" (quoted in Oliver 1995, 100).

15. See Oliver 1995, chap. 4 ("The Role of the Economists").

16. Woods supported the candidate owing to his public statements about the need for poverty alleviation and development and because of his "insider" position in the administration, which could help resolve the battles about U.S. support for the second replenishment of IDA. Because of balance of payments problems, the United States wanted a two-tiered payment whereby the U.S. commitment would be tied to IDA-generated exports from the United States (Oliver 1995, 110–44, chap. 8).

17. "Among 38 very poor nations . . . no less than 32 have suffered significant conflicts. . . . As development progresses, security progresses, and when the people of a nation provide themselves with what they need and expect out of life and have learned to compromise peacefully among competing demands in the larger national interest, then their resistance to disorder and violence will enormously increase" (McNamara, May 18, 1966, speech to the American Society of Newspaper editors, Montreal, Canada, quoted in Oliver 1995, 223–24).

18. See McNamara 1981, 233–61.

19. The criterion for failure is an internal rate of return of less than 10 percent on the projects.

20. See Ayres (1983, 112–15) for a discussion of Nigeria and Tanzania.

21. Teleology is based on the principle that the universe has design and purpose. In Aristotelian terms, the explanation of a phenomenon has not only immediate purpose but also a final cause. In Christian theology, the natural order of the universe proves the existence of God.

22. By *dialectics* I mean a pattern of change in which the conflict between a particular state of affairs (a thesis) and its opposite (an antithesis) leads to a new state of affairs (a synthesis). Marx applied the notion from Hegel to explain how stages in history are transcended owing to the contradictions in each phase.

23. Marx's teleological interpretation of history, with its strong Hegelian roots, was never clearer than in his comments about communism in the Philosophical and Economic Manuscripts of 1844. "Communism . . . is the riddle of history solved and knows itself as the solution" (Easton and Guddat 1967, 304).

24. As in the General Theory, fixed investment is the main element of dynamic transformation because it both affects capacity and stimulates aggregate demand, employment, and income. Unemployment will arise because the animal spirits of investment have been sufficiently dimmed. David (1997) also claims that the concept of natural and warranted growth rates was invented by Keynes.

25. Balanced growth strategies (encouraged by Nurkse and Rosenstein-Rodan) focused on promoting multiple related sectors such as leather and shoes; unbalanced growth emphasized a single sector that would stimulate production elsewhere through its linkage effects (proposed by Hirschman).

26. Hirschman's (1973) own contribution to the debate focused on social psychology. Rising inequality can be tolerated if it demonstrates the possibility of upward mobility for those left behind. He refers to this as the tunnel effect (based on the metaphor that in a tunnel, drivers in one lane will be elated if the other lane begins to move).

27. Although the dependency literature grew popular in the 1960s, it has much earlier roots. For an excellent exploration see Palma (1978). By the early 1970s the influence reached beyond Latin America and into other regions. In the African context, see, e.g., Rodney (1972).

28. The right wing has certainly come around to recognizing the centrality of Bauer's contribution. Bauer received the first Cato Institute $500,000 "Friedman

Prize for Liberty" in 2002. To quote the vice president for academic affairs at the Cato Institute, "Today it is not unusual to hear it suggested that the undeveloped world's best hope lies in private property, the market economy, and the rule of law. But a short time ago, that suggestion would have scandalized many audiences. Peter Bauer is a major reason for that shift" (http://www.cato.org/dailys/04-23-02.html).

29. Meliorism, according to Bauer, was "the attitude, belief, or even insistence that we must all work ceaselessly for the improvement of the human condition" (1971, 316). He is critical of meliorist groups in developed countries that feel that needs are universal and knowable and that they can be readily addressed through comprehensive planning and foreign aid in developing countries.

30. Toye (1987) argues that the three major focal points of the Bank agenda by 1985 were countering the overextended public sector, overemphasizing physical capital formation, and addressing market distortions created by state intervention. All three have their roots in the work of Peter Bauer.

31. A revised version of the talk is presented as chapter 1 in Meier and Seers (1984).

32. Anne Krueger's arrival as chief economist in 1982 was an important catalyst. The World Development Report 1983 was the first to be issued under her direction. The report and its background papers draw heavily on these and other conservative authors. See discussion in chapter 6.

33. Note that work on basic needs was done in the mid-1960s in other United Nations agencies by people such as Drewnoski and Scott (1966). They formulated a composite index of basic needs that was called the Level of Living Index.

34. John Fei and Gustav Ranis were coauthors of two of the chapters in Stewart's 1985 volume. Ranis was working on basic needs in the 1990s and gave a paper on the subject at a seminar in 1995 at Hitotsubashi University in Tokyo (I was present).

35. Hirschman (1973) considers Haq (1971) to be a particularly forceful critic of the failure of development economics to deal with the issues of income distribution, employment, and self-reliance. Haq was quite influential with regard to McNamara's new agenda.

36. "The second influence of my work on the book [An American Dilemma] was to make me a fully fledged institutional economist. That there was a close relationship between the economic situation of the Negroes in America and all other conditions of their life, and that of all others, was only too apparent. Nothing of scientific importance could be ascertained except by transgressing the boundaries between our inherited disciplines. In this respect I have adhered to this principle in my later work. I came to see that in reality there are no economic, sociological, psychological problems, just problems, and they are all mixed and composite. In research the only permissible demarcation is between relevant and irrelevant conditions" (Myrdal 1978, 10).

Chapter Two

1. Although the board now consists of twenty-four members, their responsibilities have not changed, nor has the board's selection mechanism.

2. Keynes was concerned that the Fund and the Bank would become political tools. In the inaugural meeting of the Board of Governors of the IBRD and the Fund in Savannah, Georgia, in 1946, he asked the good fairies to look over the "Bretton Woods twins" and hoped that the fairy Carabosse would not be forgotten, because if she were to come uninvited, she would curse the children by saying, "You two brats . . . shall grow up politicians; your every thought and act shall have an arrière-pensée; everything you determine shall not be for its own sake or on its own merits but because of something else." This was spoken with Keynes's usual clairvoyance (quoted in Horsefielde 1969, 1:123).

3. Horsefielde (ibid., 1:67–77) discusses this extensively. Note that Harry Dexter White was not a typical American establishment figure. He was vehemently anti-Nazi and was accused of spying for the Soviet Union during World War II. His support for the IMF's ability to challenge loans could also be interpreted as a way of opposing future fascist regimes. Yet he did not live long enough to see how it was actually operationalized. He died at age fifty-five in 1948. I thank Jomo for raising this point at Cambridge Advanced Program in Rethinking Development Economics session on structural adjustment in July 2006.

4. This includes 125 percent deposited for five years' worth of loans plus 75 percent of their currency as part of their initial deposit in the Fund.

5. Ethiopia and South Africa were the first two African countries to draw from the IMF. Egypt and Liberia were the other African members who were initial members of the Fund.

6. The conditionality of the World Bank was more ad hoc owing to its focus on projects as opposed to program aid. It did attach prerequisites at times, even in the 1940s. For example, in 1948, as a prerequisite for a Bank loan, the Bretton Woods agency demanded that Chile negotiate with the Foreign Bondholders Protective Association to repay what it had borrowed (Oliver 1995, 106). Yet in the early stages it overwhelmingly focused on identifying prospects for repayment of Bank loans, which it felt would be enhanced by related policy matters (Gavin and Rodrik 1995). This was certainly nothing like the pervasive conditionality of the structural adjustment period.

7. In the chapter concerning standby agreements in the official history of the IMF, the author states: "The generally expansionary environment which has prevailed in most parts of the world since World War II has intensified the need for anti-inflationary policies and has encouraged their embodiment in comprehensive stabilization programs. In its work with its members the Fund has devoted much time and thought to fostering such programs" (Spitzer 1969, 468).

8. Special drawing rights, created in 1969, were accounting entries allocated by the Fund to member countries based on their quotas. Approximately $9.5 billion was initially distributed between 1970 and 1972. They could be used to settle debts with other nations or with the IMF. One SDR was equal to a dollar at its inception (or .8861 grams of fine gold), but was eventually tied to a basket of currencies. In February 2007 it was worth approximately $1.49.

9. Created in 1974, the Extended Fund Facility aimed at helping countries with protracted problems with balance of payments. Support was given for up to three years with repayment up to ten years which was a longer term than the more common standby arrangement, which called for repayment in thee to five years. The average EFF repayment was generally between four and one-half years and seven years. The Trust Fund, created by the IMF in 1976 from the sale of gold from its reserves, was used for balance-of-payment support for developing countries.

10. The Oil Facility was created in 1974 to support countries experiencing balance of payments problems owing to rising oil prices. It basically took money from oil-exporting countries and reloaned it to oil-importing countries hurt by price increases.

11. The Compensatory Financing Facility was created in 1963 to help countries experiencing either a sudden loss of exports or a rise in the cost of food imports owing to a sudden fluctuation in commodity prices. The BSFF was introduced by the IMF in 1969. Financing was available for member states involved with international commodity agreements aimed at stabilizing prices.

12. The dispute was focused more on lending terms than on policy, with a particular concern about the sustainability of loan-to-capital ratios and the rising spread between U.S. and World Bank interest rates on bonds (Kapur et al. 1996, 992–997).

13. According to a former colleague in the economics department at the University of Michigan, Berg was very skeptical about planning and state-owned enterprises and considered government failure to be the source of many of Africa's problems. Berg ran the Center for Research on Economic Development (CRED) at the University of Michigan from 1970 to 1977. The center was founded by Samuel P. Hayes, who was an advisor to the Peace Corps during the 1960s and—at the request of President Kennedy—wrote the key background report responsible for the launching of the Peace Corps. The center had a long history of close relations with U.S. agencies. During the 1970s, CRED received significant funding from USAID to research drought in the Sahelian countries of West Africa. Berg likely met Stern at USAID before Stern moved to the Bank in 1972. According to one former CRED economist (now retired), Berg spoke frequently and glowingly of Stern in the 1970s. In 1980, Berg left the University of Michigan for the World Bank to work on the Africa report.

14. Pierre Landell-Mills, telephone interview with the author, August 15, 2005.

15. The quotation is from a memo from Stern to Clausen in December 1983, quoted in Kapur et al. 1997, 732.

16. Ramgopal Agarwala, telephone interview with the author, September 8, 2005.

17. See siteresources.worldbank.org/IDA/Resources/Seminar%20PDFs/deputS.pdf.

18. Agarwala indicated that the European government bureaucracy did not want to reallocate funds away from poor developing countries, so it was easy for Stern to convince them to provide funds to Africa. Agarwala interview.

19. The Japanese saw adjustment as a U.S. priority and supported it in order to promote bilateral relations with the United States (Stein 1998).

20. The World Bank recognized early on the danger of failure of its agenda in Africa. In a briefing given to incoming president Barber Conable (April 23, 1986) it stated, "We must recognize that the role and reputation of the Bank Group is at stake in Africa. . . . We have been telling Africa how to reform, sometimes in terms of great detail. Now a significant number of African countries are beginning to follow the Bank's advice. If these program fail, for whatever reason, our policies will be seen widely to have failed, the ideas themselves will be set back for a long time in Africa and elsewhere" (quoted in Kapur et al. 1997, 730).

21. Krueger's role in reshaping the state reform agenda in the Bank is discussed in detail in chapter 6.

22. Regarding her appointment as the deputy chief of the IMF in 2001, Krueger's colleague at Stanford, a prominent contributor to the neoliberal agenda named Ronald McKinnon, remarked with pride on the way she had shifted the focus at the World Bank: "She changed the whole structure of research there. Before then there had been a terrific interest in central planning models, say, for India, Turkey, and Korea. She scrapped all that and went to what is common practice: trying to make markets work right without having a central allocation of resources." The same SIEPR newsletter noted that she had a long relationship with conservative regimes in Washington. After the election of George W. Bush she was asked to serve on his Council of Economic Advisors. She took the IMF job instead when it became vacant (with the strong approval of the Bush administration) (Stanford Institute for Economic Policy Research 2001, 1–2).

23. The work of economists hired by Chenery, many of whom were on the WDR 1983 team, was closely scrutinized by Krueger. Their chapters were subject to multiple drafts and revisions. In contrast, a chapter written by Helen Hughes (who had also been hired by Krueger) was accepted without revision though it was deemed to be racist in content. It was only altered after the intervention of Ernie Stern. Krueger clearly made life difficult for Chenery's economists, thereby encouraging departures. This information comes from discussions in September 2004 with a member of the WDR 1983 team who prefers to remain anonymous.

24. See Krueger's (1991) study of agriculture for these arguments.

25. "There is no support for the view that adjustment programs generally hurt the poor as a group. The rural poor benefit directly from adjustment programs" (International Monetary Fund 1988, quoted in Kapur et al. 1997 357, n. 111).

26. The Special Office for African Affairs was moved out of Stern's office in 1987 and combined with the East and West Africa regional office into a single unit.

27. To quote Agarwala, "They came down on me like a ton of bricks." He felt that his days as the "blue-eyed wonder were over." Until his retirement in 1996 he spent most of his time working on matters relating to East Asia and China (Agarwala interview). Note that Pierre Landell-Mills has a very different view. He felt he was brought in after the project was languishing. There was no mention of the controversial nature of the content of the first draft (Landell-Mills interview).

28. One senior official, commenting on 1983 progress report, said that "the major cause of the crisis is political not economic and is caused by self-seeking, corrupt politicians, and senior civil servants who really don't care or are not allowed to care about development and their people" (quoted in Kapur et al. 1997, 760). In 1989 politics was creeping into decision making. The Bank suspended disbursements to Benin until the government secured broader support for its adjustment program. Beginning in 1990 the Bank joined donors to press for more political accountability and transparency in Kenya, Malawi, and Tanzania. In November 1990, at a consultative meeting concerning Kenya and chaired by the Bank, aid was made contingent on political reform. Within donor circles, corruption, military spending, human rights, and democracy became acceptable parts of the African agenda (Miller-Adams 1999, 111; Kapur et al. 1997, 761).

29. Agarwala interview.

30. Landell-Mills interview. Historically, there had been others in the Bank who were very interested in governance-related issues. See, e.g., Israel (1987, 1990).

31. The Bank and its officers "shall not interfere with the political affairs of any members, nor shall they be influenced in their decisions by the political character of the member or members concerned" (quoted in Woods 2000, 145).

32. The memo, written by vice president and general counsel Ibrahim Shihata, was titled "Issues of 'Governance' in Borrowing Members: The Extent and Their Relevance Under the Bank's Articles of Agreement," December 21, 1990 (Shihata 1991).

33. There is little doubt that the Bank was quite concerned with maintaining its technical façade. Note that this is perfectly in line with the discussions concerning the procedural dimensions of hegemony in chapter 1. According to the Bank, "It is important to note the underlying motivation behind the restrictions in the Articles of Agreement. These restrictions help to protect the Bank's reputation for technical excellence and objectivity and its status as an international institution that is guided solely by its concerns for economic development and not by any political agenda" (World Bank 1992a, 51).

34. Landell-Mills makes this quite explicit: "I know from conversations with [Larry Summers] that he was much more open to and interested in the PSM/ID/ Governance agenda that we were promoting" than was Anne Krueger. But Stern always remained a skeptic. "I don't think that Larry spent much time persuading Ernie, as it was not high on his agenda either; Ernie simply could not deny the relevance of our arguments, but he never came on board as a supporter. He was simply overruled [by the World Bank president]. Before that, he continued to passively resist and subsequently simply ignored the topic" (Pierre Landell-Mills, emails to author, August 18, 2005).

35. At the time, Serageldin was the director of the African Technical Department. Landell-Mills was a senior policy advisor to the same unit.

36. Landell-Mills recognizes the importance of his contribution. He states: "I wrote a paper (jointly with Serageldin) for a previous Development Economics Conference justifying the Bank's involvement in governance which is often quoted as setting out the case for the Bank's PSM/governance approach" (Pierre Landell-Mills, email to the author, August 17, 2005).

37. As discussed in chapter 6, *Managing Development* was to be the title of the WDR 1983, but was changed by Anne Krueger to *Management in Development* for ideological reasons. Some team members were disgusted by this choice. There is little doubt that the use of this term was deliberate and represents a clear statement by Landell-Mills that he intended to try again to broaden the agenda.

38. The meaning of governance has evolved over time. A recent Bank report about governance cited six dimensions of governance: voice and external accountability, political stability and lack of violence, crime and terrorism, government effectiveness, lack of regulatory burden, and rule of law and corruption (Kaufmann 2003, 5).

39. Despite its flawed conceptualization, the Bank pursued the "rule of law" agenda as part of its battle to improve governance and combat corruption. By 2001 there were seventeen freestanding projects in legal reform and thirteen pending. Legal assistance from the Bank covered forty-five areas in eighty countries (Drake et al. 2003, 9–11).

40. In a precursor of things to come, the Bank justified the new lending not in terms of implementing a wish list of liberalization measures of high priority to the United States and other G8 members, but as a way to reduce poverty. According to the 1999 Annual Report, "Nearly 70% of adjustment lending in FY99 was poverty-focused. . . . The fundamental rationale for Bank involvement in the crisis is to reduce their short- and long-term effects on poverty. This involves support for economic and financial reform . . . aiming to ensure that economic recovery would favor the poor" (World Bank 1999a, 11).

41. Adjustment loans were formally replaced by development policy loans in August 2004, although HIPC-eligible countries had received poverty reduction strategy credits from 2001.

42. The governance guidelines were approved by the Executive Board in July 1997 ("The Role of the Fund in Governance Issues: Guidance Note," www.imf .org).

43. The Fund admits this in the report: "Even before the 1997 report, the Fund's involvement in governance was already considerable. This involvement was often in the form of policy advice and technical assistance that promoted sound public resource management and economic efficiency albeit without an explicit recognition that such activities were related to good governance" (International Monetary Fund 2001, 11). The survey of activities covers the period 1994–1999; this predates the official commitment to governance, which took place in 1997.

44. The list is fairly long and includes the "Code of Good Practices on Fiscal Transparency" (1998); the "Code of Good Practices on Transparency in Monetary and Financial Policies" (1999); and the "General Data Dissemination System" (1997). Only the "Special Data Dissemination Standard" clearly predated the Guidance Note. It was updated in 2000, however (see www.imf.org). These codes involve imposing standards that developed countries never faced, and it is only one of many current examples. For an excellent critical view of the implications of IFI standards and policies for the development process, see Chang (2002b).

45. The public choice theory uses the neoclassical principles of individual decision making to explain the behavior of governments, voters, and politicians. Corruption and rent-seeking occur because *Homo economicus* (rationally calculating individuals attempting to maximize their own utility) are free to pursue their interests without the constraint of markets.

46. The perfect fusion of the property rights and poverty agenda has appeared with the Bank's support of De Soto's Institute for Liberty and Democracy project to provide titling to the poor in Peru. De Soto (2000) argues that poor people have large assets such as housing that they cannot tap because they are not legally recognized. "Dead capital" (De Soto's term for untapped assets) can be turned into "live capital" via titling. This could be accomplished in different ways: the poor can liquidate these assets and supply themselves with cash, or they can use their assets to borrow for collateral, which would allow them to invest in businesses and therefore pull themselves out of poverty. By most accounts, the project has been a disappointment and has not increased the accessibility of credit to the poor. This is perhaps unsurprising: a cursory understanding of the behavior of bankers indicates that they have little interest in foreclosing on properties in general and even less interest in doing so in poor neighborhoods. Lending to poor people is too risky, even with the option to seize their houses. For a discussion of this subject, including a review of the literature about titling in Peru and related matters, see Mitchell 2005. With regard to money supply, one must now add the responsibility of reallocating funds from debt servicing (as a result of HIPC) to education and health spending.

47. See Cramer, Stein, and Weeks (2006) for a more detailed discussion of these.

48. The discussion on Tanzania's PRSPs comes from interviews undertaken by this author in March and April 2002 in Tanzania for a Swedish International Development Agency project concerning ownership (Weeks et al. 2003).

49. Poverty Reduction Budget Support was one of several new bilateral loan mechanisms introduced after the first-generation PRSPs. Donor countries pooled additional resources in support of social spending in recipient countries. As a prerequisite to receiving these funds, poverty assessment frameworks were generated to indicate recipient governments' budget priorities.

Chapter Three

1. In his General Theory, Keynes presents three reasons: holding money for transactions, speculation, and as a precaution.

2. See, e.g., Przeworski and Vreeland (2000); Barro and Lee (2002); Vreeland (2003); Easterly (2005). Easterly, a former Bank economist closely aligned with pro-adjustment forces, is unable to find a positive relationship between growth and IMF conditionality using probit pooled regressions of a large sampling of countries. Under IMF policies there was actually a negative growth rate (–0.5 percent per capita per annum) for a sample of twelve African countries for 72 percent of the time between 1980 and 1999. Only two of the twelve had a per capita growth rate of more than 1 percent.

3. *Structure* refers to the sectoral distribution, the diversity of its activity, the backward, forward, and demand linkages of value-added generating activities, and its depth, as indicated by a number of indices such as financial savings, research and development expenditures relative to GDP, and extent of manufacturing using sophisticated technology. In today's global economy, structural transformation aims to generate new activities that will enhance the competitiveness, economic diversity, economic depth, and economic linkages of an economy. Such a market favors the expansion of manufacturing and industrial economies, not the persistence of economies specializing in unprocessed cash crops. For further discussion, see Stein (1999) and Stein and Nissanke (1999).

4. See the discussion below concerning inconsistencies between equilibrium and other neoclassical microfoundations and developing country conditions.

5. See Simon (1978).

6. See, e.g., the examples provided by Barrows and Roth (1990).

7. Thus, Robert Bates (1991), a prominent rational choice theorist, argues that whereas kinship arises in semiarid regions among cattle owners such as the Luo, where risk diversification is useful, private property and household accumulation occur in low-risk fertile areas, such as the highland regions of Kenya. Pauline Peters, however, asserts that "Bates' propositions are empirically unfounded. . . . In Southern Africa, the high-risk environment produces a range of adaptation among

cattle-keepers, from Heroro with patrilocal homesteads and a social organization where individuals gain rights to pastures . . . to Tswana with their hierarchical kingdoms where access to resources was as much through subordination and servitude as through peer relationship through kin or residential groups. . . . If the different socio-political systems of the Tswana kingdoms or the Nuer or Luo lineage types can be explained as the outcomes of risk avoidance, we have not explained much!" (Peters 1993, 1073).

8. In a 1993 speech Edward Jaycox, the former World Bank vice-president for Africa, admitted that the state retraction strategy simply hadn't worked (Jaycox 1993, 26). The policy had not saved money, nor had the layoffs it mandated led to a stimulation of economic growth. In another Bank document, Dia (1993) argued that retrenchment seriously undermined the already problematic operational capacity of African states. Retrenchment often retired the most experienced personnel, limited the entry of youthfully energetic and inexpensive new recruits, and reduced wages, therefore making the civil service unattractive to the most talented people. Worse still, the layoffs generated enormous apathy and discontent.

9. The reasoning is syllogistic: if undistorted markets are determinants of successful economic growth and development, areas such as East Asia must have been successful developmentally because they did not have distorted markets, or at least because they reversed these distortions at some point. In other words, if this argument is to hold, successful states must have maintained neutrality in the market that allowed them to specialize according to their comparative advantage. This reasoning is embedded in the neoclassical interpretation of Asia, which includes the work of Krueger, Lal, Little, and, to some extent the World Bank's "East Asian Miracle" study. This reasoning has been used by the World Bank to justify the use of structural adjustment in Africa. Yet a significant body of empirical evidence contradicts this assumption. A detailed discussion of these issues can be found in Stein (1995a).

10. By *Popperian falsification* (after the philosopher Karl Popper) I mean the proposition that any theory that is not falsifiable is unscientific.

11. Perhaps the more interesting question is posed by Rosenberg (1994), who asks why economists continue to use such a cognitively weak set of core propositions. He suggests that the reasons are normative (e.g., general equilibrium theory illustrates how self-interest ought to lead to a coherent disposition of resources) and mathematical (e.g., like Euclidian geometry, it provides an axiomatic system that can explain some phenomena for reasons that have little to do with its microfoundations). Rosenberg correctly warns that the current state of economics will create "a vacuum in the foundations of public policy" (1994, 233).

12. The Leontief Paradox refers to the empirical finding that contrary to the prediction of Heckscher-Ohlin, U.S. imports in the 1950s were more capital-intensive

than its exports. Given that the United States was the most highly developed country in the world at the time, the opposite should have been the case if the United States was following its comparative advantage. Most standard trade theory books have lengthy sections intended to explain away the paradox.

13. A good discussion of many of these issues can be found in Hargreaves Heap et al. (1992).

14. For a good discussion of the complications of empirical studies, see Ajayi (1994) and Mosley (1994).

15. To summarize, *Report on Adjustment Lending* (World Bank 1988a) found no significant differences in the rate of growth when comparing recipients and nonrecipients of structural adjustment loans. In 1989, however, by carefully manipulating the data (using 1985 as a date of comparison, classifying countries into three groups, and discounting countries with large external shocks) the Bank argued that strong adjusters did better than weak adjusters and nonadjusters. By switching dates and reclassifying countries, it was able to achieve different results. The Economic Commission for Africa, in what became a rather rancorous debate, accused the Bank of using subjective criteria to classify countries in order to prove the effectiveness of adjustment. By 1992, in a Bank study that controlled for external shocks, the political atmosphere, and the initial conditions and policy stance of the pre-adjustment period, Ibrahim Elbadawi found no statistically significant effect of adjustment on growth rates and no indications of declined investment or savings of early adjusters. By 1994 the Bank's *Adjustment in Africa* study was again claiming positive effects in countries that were undertaking more adjustment. These divergent results reflect differences in classifications, definitions, data, and methods of testing. For a good discussion of some of these issues, see Mosley and Weeks (1993). There have also been many highly critical reviews of the 1994 Bank study of adjustment, including Mosley, Subasat, and Weeks (1995), which provides a very incisive critique of the methods used.

16. See Stein (2000b) for a detailed critique.

17. There are many examples in the literature. Davies et al. (1998) use a CGE that examines the likely impact of trade liberalization on Zimbabwe. They model a variety of features that relax the extreme neoclassical assumptions used by Sahn and others (e.g., by adding unemployment variables). Using a range of reasonable parameter estimates, the authors show that demand will increase, leading to declines in savings, a shift from domestic to imported goods, and an increased trade deficit. These effects are expected; greater availability of imported intermediate goods does not sufficiently stimulate exports to counter increased imports. Moreover, the layoffs in sectors that compete with imports are not offset by an adequate rise in other sectors. This leads to further exacerbation of already high unemployment levels. Whatever the long-term consequences, trade liberalization has clear short-term costs.

18. The authors completely ignore the literature that demonstrates that East Asia did not follow a development path anything like that in the world of structural adjustment. See, e.g., Stein (1995a) for a different perspective on Asian development.

19. There are an estimated 120 to 130 different tribes in Tanzania. Nyerere was from Butiama, near Musoma on Lake Victoria. He was the son of the chief of the tiny Zanaki tribal group, which had a population of roughly sixty-seven thousand in 1987. See "Useful Information About Tribes in Tanzania," http://fizzylogic.com/wasukuma/makabila_tz.html.

20. This is a good example of the absurdity of linear extrapolations from econometric coefficients. In the numbers, the coefficient predicts a 1 percent increase in growth for each 26 percent decrease in inflation. The decline in Brazil's case is from 2,948 percent inflation to 16 percent, a decline of 2,932 percent. This should be divided by 26, which results in the figure 113 percent, and added to the 5 percent growth rate, thereby resulting in a 118 percent rate of growth.

21. The Bank has several divergent understandings of social capital. Definitions range from the "institutions, the relationships, the attitudes and values that govern the interaction among people and contribute to economic and social development" to "the level of mutual trust existing in a group which might be extended to the whole of society." The quotations are from Stein (2002b), which provide a review and critique of the Bank's social capital literature.

22. "Post-Washington consensus" is a term associated with the attempts by Joseph Stiglitz (chief economist at the Bank from 1997 to 2002) to expand the Bank's agenda to include policies that would address market failures such as public goods, monopolies, and externalities. See Stiglitz (1998).

23. In 1995, as part of its conditionality (in spite of strong opposition from the Mozambique government), the World Bank imposed a reduction in cashew nut export taxes on basis of the faulty belief that local processing was too inefficient and farmers would receive higher prices from the shipping of raw exports. The reasoning arose from the neoclassical belief in the perfection of markets: because India produced cashew nuts more efficiently, farmers in Mozambique must be better off shipping unprocessed cashew nuts. The reality was quite different: India was the only buyer of raw cashew nuts, and its processing industry was subsidized by its government. The 1995 policy change in Mozambique resulted in the closing of most of the country's processing factories and the loss of nearly 8,500 jobs. Subsequent studies indicated that Mozambique was losing about $130 per ton by exporting unprocessed cashew nuts rather than processed ones. The export of raw cashew nuts did not lead to higher prices for farmers, although there was some benefit to traders. By January 2001 the export price paid by Indian buyers had fallen to between $355 and $440 per ton, compared to an estimated $660 to $800 per ton on world markets. The government therefore ignored the advice of the World Bank and the IMF and halted the export of raw materials (Hanlon 2000, 2001).

Chapter Four

1. The World Bank considers the ABCDE an opportunity for leading development thinkers to present their ideas to the Bank and to expand the exchange of
ideas among thinkers, practitioners, and policy makers. The conference has been
held annually in Washington since 1988. Since 1999, a second annual conference
has been held in a European capital. See the ABCDE Web site at www.worldbank
.edu.

2. *Network externalities* are the effects on a consumer of others' utilizing an
identical or compatible product or service. *Economies of scope* refers to the cost
reductions associated with expanding a company's range of goods or services.
Complementarities are associated with gains in the economy that arise from the
interaction of institutions or the consumption together of more than one good and
service. Owing to the dependent relationships embedded in economies, institutional change can be difficult or can lead to worse outcomes.

3. For a critique of the urban bias argument, see Stein (2003); Jamal (1995).

4. A good example can be found in the work of Brian Levy, who joined the
Bank in 1989. Levy (1991) argues that because the precontracting costs of transactions in Korea were higher than those in Taiwan, organizational structures were
more hierarchical in that country. Following Williamson (1985), Levy assumes that
postcontract opportunism is high in both countries, but because this occurs at similar levels, the determining factor in the organizational structure is the precontracting cost. Although this research was done by Levy prior to arriving at the Bank
(when he was a professor at Williams College), subsequent work at the Bank relied
heavily on NIE. See, for example, Levy and Spiller (1993), discussed below. One
senior World Bank official indicated in a private conversation that Levy wanted to
publish his NIE-based study of the telecommunications industry as a Bank working
paper. They were so impressed by the work and the theoretical approach, however,
that he was encouraged to publish it as a book (Levy and Spiller 1996). Levy's
work paved the way for *Bureaucrats in Business*, in part by convincing some senior
economists of the utility of NIE.

5. The first annual ABCDE conference in 1989 actually included a paper about
institutions presented by Brian Van Arkadie, an eclectic economist with a long history of working in Africa, and in particular, Tanzania. The paper was also eclectic,
with more discussion of Marxist and structuralist contributions than of NIE, and it
had no lasting impact on the Bank (Van Arkadie 1990).

6. Mancur Olsen's 1965 classic "Logic of Collective Action" applied basic neoclassical economic principles to explain why individuals do not form groups to
deal with collective problems. Among other matters he raised limitations from
free riding, conflict of interest, and coordination problems. For example, oppressed
individuals would prefer to "free ride," letting someone else rebel against the authorities, because they would receive the benefits without the risks. If everyone

tries to free ride, however, no rebellion will occur and the repression will continue.

7. The study has been heavily criticized in the academic literature. See, e.g., Chang and Singh (1997), Jalilan and Weiss (1997), and Fine (1999). Our interest, however, is less in providing a general evaluation than in critically assessing how the report used NIE theory.

8. Firms face behavioral uncertainty because of the opportunism that can arise when information is distorted, disguised, or not disclosed for strategic reasons. This uncertainty is complicated by systemic uncertainty, which is connected to the circumstances of time and place, creating ambiguity of causation, which cannot always readily be resolved through legal action. Behavioral uncertainty is a major source of transaction costs and a challenge in designing governance structures. See Williamson (1985), chap. 2.

9. It seems that in this discussion the World Bank is using the instrumentality of the state to define the nature of the state rather than allowing the nature of the state to determine how that instrumentality will be used. One cannot explain why state-owned enterprises in Singapore work better than they do in Nigeria by resorting to explanations of the design of contracts that better deal with the hazards of omnipresent opportunism. Independent of the theoretically suspect nature of the arguments, the problems are more systemic and cannot readily be altered by a bit of tinkering. These are countries with radically different institutional matrices and different patterns of what constitutes acceptable behavior (I discuss this further below).

10. The study does have a chapter about the politics of reform, which is one aspect of Williamson's concept of remediableness. It discusses the importance of desirability, feasibility, and credibility of reform. The framework is hardly a cogent one, however, and it is largely an endogenously generated choice, theoretically subject to constraints without any discussion of the role of external aid agencies and associated conditionality.

11. Of 183 state divestments that took place in Tanzania through 1998, only 83 were true privatizations. The rest were bankruptcies and liquidations of assets (Gibbon 1999).

12. The information about the controversy comes from an email exchange in September 2004 with someone involved with the writing of *Bureaucrats in Business*. In line with much of the argument in this chapter, the person stated: "Since then the Bank has incorporated institutions into the rhetoric, but has not changed its way of doing business." I respect the wishes of the individual to maintain anonymity, and this person will therefore remain unnamed.

13. Yet Douglass North's first invitation to an event sponsored by the World Bank was in 1987, at a conference on poverty in Mexico. Although he has been invited to a number of different venues, North feels his greatest influence has been through his ex-students at the Bank (conversation with Douglass North at the ISNIE conference, October 2, 2004, in Tucson, Arizona).

14. According to North, the state is an organization with a comparative advantage in violence because "the essence of property rights is the right to exclude, and an organization which has a comparative advantage in violence is in the position to specify and enforce property rights" (North 1981).

15. North's approach is slightly different because he actually refers to informal and formal constraints and emphasizes ways in which formal rules can make informal constraints more effective. See North (1990), in particular chaps. 5 and 6.

16. The literature that critiques these areas is vast. See, e.g., Stein (1995a, 2002); Lall (1996); Chang (1994); Gibbon (1999).

17. It also opened the door for regional departments to explore the implications of NIE for development problems in their area. See, .e.g., Burki and Perry's (1998) study of Latin America and the Caribbean.

18. As Brian Levy recently admitted: "The term 'governance' tends to be very loosely used, with no consistent definition" (Levy 2002, 1). His paper aims to conceptualize governance using NIE tools and to theoretically differentiate institutional from organizational dimensions of governance.

19. Ribot (1999) provides many examples and an extensive literature documenting the rather perverse impact of decentralization on the management of the local environment and natural resources. In Senegal and Niger, for example, decentralization has empowered local chiefs who are accountable to the state but not to the local population.

Chapter Five

1. Data sets formed during the cold war continue to have a powerful impact on studies of institutions and governance. See, e.g., the heavy usage of data from cold war institutions such as Freedom House ("Freedom in the World") and the conservative Heritage Foundation ("Economic Freedom Index") in studies such as Kaufmann et al. (1999), which are aimed at measuring the relation between the quality of governance and growth. A good critique can be found in Khan (2004).

2. Authors such as Edwards (1998), Sachs and Warner (1995, 1997), Dollar (1992), and Wang and Winters (1998) argue that growth in an era of globalization is enhanced by greater openness. Developing countries that follow neoliberal reforms will approach the income levels of developed countries, and those that don't will lag. Sachs and Warner (1995) are unequivocal: "Open economies converge and closed ones don't" (3). In the case of Africa, "poor economic policies have played an especially important role in slow growth, most importantly Africa's lack of openness to international markets" (Sachs and Warner 1997, 335). See below for a discussion of the ways in which these views have permeated the thinking of market players. For a different view of the impact of openness, see Mosley (2000).

3. The *Wall Street Journal,* once the biggest proponent of efficiency market theory, printed an article about the challenge arising from the research of behavioral economists. It quotes Andrew Lo, an economist at MIT who authored a 1999 book titled *A Non-Random Walk down Wall Street.* He confessed that writing the book was extremely difficult because during his education at Harvard University and MIT in the 1980s, "it was drilled into us that markets are efficient." It took him five to ten years to change his views. Quoted in Hilsenrath (2004, A:1).

4. As Myrdal points out, even South Asian professors with strong anti-Western or Marxist views readily adopted the latest economic theories and models coming from Western universities, where they were trained (Myrdal 1968, 1:21). In lectures to university economics departments in such places as Jamaica, Nigeria, and Tanzania, I have been shocked by how much agreement there was with my criticism of the theories underlying structural adjustment, a critique that directly attacks much of their curriculum. After a lecture in September 2002, one economics professor at the University of Ibadan (Nigeria) remarked that he hoped his students would not begin to give him a difficult time after listening to me. The disconnect between what they are teaching and the role of these theories in generating policies that have negatively affected their lives is profound.

5. Value premises are always present in any research and must be made clear and explicit if research is to advance (Myrdal 1968, 1:33).

6. The usage of *structure* in the economic sense in this chapter refers to the sectoral allocation, the backward, forward, and demand linkages, and the depth, according to a number of indices including financial savings, research, and development expenditures relative to GDP and the extent of manufacturing using increasingly sophisticated technology. Globalization can be mediated or filtered into economies at a variety of levels (individual, local, meso, national, regional, and so on) through a variety of organizations, institutions, and policies. The impact of globalization is hardly unidimensional and can be structurally impoverishing or enhancing. Moreover, the ability to respond to the forces of globalization can be circumscribed by the power and rules of international organizations. This ability is affected by the relative power of the mediating units and the extent of concatenation involved in determining what constitutes development-enhancing structural transformation and what policies are needed to access global forces for this positive transformation.

7. One might ask the difference between belief systems and attitudes and how they interact. Belief systems are series of connected ideas organized in the mind that help individuals define the reality around them in a meaningful way. A person's belief systems can be based on religious principles. In Myrdal's world attitudes are inclinations or tendencies that influence the way an individual will respond to particular situations, such as the level of work discipline, punctuality, and orderliness. Attitudes can be connected or unconnected to an individual's belief system. For example, workers might put little effort into their work because they are lazy or because they feel that they are being exploited by their capitalist boss.

8. Hodgson's insistence on using rules, even "embedded social rules," in his view of institutions is perhaps misleading in the context of the organization of institutions for development. As argued in chapter 4, rules can be pro forma. Moreover, Hodgson seems to be privileging rules above all else so that rules transform habits and ultimately behavior by means of reconstitutive downward causation. This ascribes to rules far too much power in determining habits and behavioral outcomes, however, and leaves one wondering how to define embeddedness. An alternative is formulated in the discussion below.

9. Some have argued that Veblen's view of habits of thought reflected the influence of the American pragmatist school, in particular that of John Dewey and Charles Pierce. Pierce focused on the relation between thought and habits of action, not simply action itself. Habits are not mere routines but are formed from deliberate self-reflection and analysis. Habits do not replace thinking but are intellectual and logical constructs that transform and shape the thinking process. They are not simply products of the aggregation of individual previous action; they also designate the principle by which the aggregation took place. Habits are reflective actions that enhance and extend the proficiency of human activities. As Dewey pointed out, how else can one interpret the development of a musician, a surgeon, or a tradesman? There is a strong case that Veblen emphasized habits of thought in order to capture the pragmatist perspective as opposed to the more common view in the social sciences of habits as mindless routine. For an insightful article about Veblen's pragmatism, see Kilpinen (1998).

10. Chapter 9, which concerns norms and networks, should have been the first chapter of WDR 2002 and then could have been systematically incorporated into the rest of the volume. Any serious analysis of institutions in development would recognize the centrality of norms and networks in building economies. The disconnect between the chapter and the rest of the report probably reflects an authorship replete with standard economists who believe that such discussion belongs to the realm of sociology and not their more "rigorous" discipline. Still, the construct largely comes from a view based on NIE, because it aims to constrain opportunism and lower transaction costs. According to the report, "[i]nformal institutions allow those sharing norms or culture to behave predictably and lower the risks in a transaction" (World Bank 2002b, 171).

11. See, e.g., Leonard (2000).

12. I should emphasize that norms are always embedded with power and values. Even accounting standards are neither universal nor value-free; they reflect the interest of hegemonic elements in maintaining the status quo. Generally, the shifting of norms will need to deal with entrenched interests. See, e.g., Dillard et al. (2004); Goddard (2002).

13. Other examples include Taylor (1911); Urwick (1943); Fayol (1949); Brech (1953); Mayo (1945); and McGregor (1960), who give a more human-relations-oriented approach to the single model.

14. The literature about contingent organizations is very extensive if one looks for permutations in structures relative to variations in technology (Woodward 1965; Perrow 1967; Zwerman 1970), size (Hickson et al. 1969; Osborn and Hunt 1974), industry type (Hrebiniak and Snow 1980), strategy (Andrews 1960; Chandler 1962), and dependence on parent organization (Pugh et al. 1968; Child 1972).

15. Until the mid-1970s the bulk of sociological research focused on the reasons why organizations were so different from one another. A series of papers about the similarities of organizations changed that point of view and led to an interpretation more focused on institutions. Zucker (1987) gives an in-depth overview of the theory. There are two predominant views of organizational change: one sees the environment as the source of institutional formation; the other sees the organization as an institution. The former seeks to explain institutionalization in an organization as a process of reproduction, or copying system-wide social facts on the organizational level. This view is seen in the works of authors such as Meyer and Thomas (1984), Meyer and Rowan (1977), and DiMaggio and Powell (1983). The latter view seeks to explain institutionalization as the generation of new cultural elements at the organizational level, where institutional elements arise from within the organization or from the imitation of similar organizations. This view is espoused by, for example, Zucker (1977), Tolbert and Zucker (1983), and Tolbert (1985). One key assumption of this view is that acts and structures embedded in organizations are more readily institutionalized than are those rooted in other informal social coordination structures. Consequently, organizations are important to institutional change because institutional elements are easily transmitted to newcomers and maintained over long periods of time without further justification and are highly resistant to change. The discussion in the text reflects both views of the institutional approach to organizations.

16. See, e.g., Friedman (1969).

17. See, .e.g., Posner (1986).

18. In 1994, for example, two consultancy groups, Research on Poverty Alleviation and the Economic and Social Research Foundation, were organized by two well-known members of the economics department of the University of Dar Es Salaam (Joseph Semboja and Samuel Wangwe). Both have been recipients of large donations, have hired many young economists (in particular the foundation), and have played prominent roles in orienting economics research toward the latest fashions in donors' interests. In March 2002, when I presented a lecture at the University of Dar Es Salaam's economics department, some of my old colleagues and students lamented that there was little or no independent research. The economists who had not already left the university for full-time consulting jobs were using standard neoclassical economic textbooks, not because they agreed with the content but because it was fairly easy to teach, which left them more time to work on donor projects.

19. An institutional conception of the state, the private sector, and the relation between the two is developed in chapter 6. See Mkandawire (2002) for a discussion of the consequences of state retraction for the private sector.

20. The logic of incentives in this neoclassical world is a reflection of the Benthamite view of humanity, wherein "pain and pleasure . . . alone point [to] what we ought to do as well as determine what we shall do" (Bentham 1789, 65–66). Veblen (1919) considered this to be a purely "hedonistic conception of man" as a passive being reacting to outside stimuli and then returning to a steady-state "self-contained globule of desire" (quoted in Kilpinen 1998). Veblen considered humans to be complex and more like *Homo faber*, or the active being.

21. See Krueger (1992).

22. See Summers (1992).

23. Mobutu was able to obtain large sums of money from aid agencies without meeting their conditionality via his use of cold war politics. See Tom Callaghy's (1986) fine exposition of the way in which Mobutu manipulated the World Bank, the IMF, and international creditors.

24. By contrast, in recent years economists have been spending far too much time using increasingly sophisticated techniques to examine data that are available, rather than thinking about new ways to generate more useful information. Some have referred to this as the "looking under the lamppost" syndrome. Even worse, as discussed in chapter 3, the axiomatic nature of neoclassical economics has meant using the data for verification, not falsification. It is no surprise that mainstream economics has had such a paucity of new ideas to offer the developing world.

Chapter Six

1. Myrdal referred to the alternative approach as Democratic Planning. See Myrdal (1968), vol. 2, chap. 18.

2. See, e.g., the discussion of Zambia (World Bank 1981b, 78–79).

3. According to Lance Taylor (who wrote his dissertation with Chenery as his advisor at Harvard University), Hollis Chenery was furious with the changes that Anne Krueger made in the economic research arm of the Bank and very unhappy with the narrowing of the agenda. The 1981 World Development Report was his last. Its seventh chapter contains some rather choice quotations that reflect these concerns, for example, "For developing countries everywhere the exigencies of adjustment over the next five to ten years could undermine the commitment to social programs. . . . Interrupting human development programs may be costly though in ways that may not be immediately obvious" (World Bank 1981, 97). Lance Taylor, interview with the author, July 20, 2005, Cambridge, England.

4. This information comes from a telephone interview conducted on August 15, 2005. Landell-Mills has been a visiting professor at the Institute for International

Policy Analysis at Bath University since September 2000, after his retirement from the World Bank. Unlike a number of other current and retired officials with whom I spoke, he felt comfortable being quoted. All quotations come directly from Landell-Mills.

5. In this conversation, Landell-Mills referred to the Wright Task Force as focusing on the institutional dimension of development. During the late 1970s early 1980s, the Bank used the terms *institution-building, public sector management,* and *public administration* interchangeably. Israel (1987) sees institutions largely as organizational groups that encompass "entities at the local or community level, project management units, parastatals, line agencies in the central government etc." Thus, "institutional development is synonymous with institution building and is defined as the process of improving an institution's ability to make effective use of the human and financial resources available" (11). We can see a clear focus on public sector management issues. According to Landell-Mills, Israel was involved in the first division to deal with institutional development, which it did in 1979–80. This division was eventually folded into the Public Sector Management Unit at the Bank under Mary Shirley in the 1980s.

6. Ramgopal Agarwala, telephone interview with the author, September 8, 2005. Agarwala was part of the WDR 1983 team.

7. Alice Amsden (1989) used the World Bank focus on getting prices right for her famous retort that South Korea was able to develop by the opposite strategy, "getting their relative prices wrong." She used this phrase as a chapter title.

8. Agarwala interview. Pierre Landell-Mills, the head of the team, considered Krueger's management of WDR 1983 to be "one of the scariest moments of my professional life" (Landell-Mills interview) and, according to Agarwala, was very grateful for his contribution. They remained quite close until the controversy over the 1989 Africa report.

9. In the typical neoclassical world, prices would be efficient when the marginal utility or benefit of a good is equal to the marginal cost of the good, with both equal to the price of that good. Prices that are distorted create inefficiencies; because they arise when the wrong incentives have been put in place, they lead to decisions that are not Pareto optimal. Bhagwati and Ramaswami (1963) provide one of the earliest attempts to analyze domestic distortions in a welfare-maximizing framework in which, owing to distortions, the marginal rate of transformation (between goods) is unequal to the marginal rate of substitution (between goods for utility of consumers). In accordance with his overall career, which was aimed at proving the superiority of free trade, one of Bhagwati's first publications argues that if the goal is to counter domestic distortions (from unions or externalities) and to aim at raising welfare, subsidies on goods are superior in all cases to imposing tariffs. Bhagwati's work was quite important in influencing Balassa's analysis of the effect of distortions on incentives, which, in turn, greatly influenced Agarwala's paper. See, e.g., Balassa and Associates (1982), chap. 4, n. 1. The chapter focuses on the effect of distortions and how they can be best remedied.

10. In other words, distortions arise if wages in manufacturing are increasing more rapidly than the general rate of per capita income adjusted for international purchasing power by the terms of trade. Presumably, government intervention in the form of tariffs or wage regulations is the source of the distortions, because otherwise, manufacturing wages would change in tandem with the adjusted incomes.

11. Agarwala, looking back, regretted his work. He is quite aware that his framework, which linked low distortions with higher growth and higher distortions with lower growth had a powerful impact. It led to structural adjustment policies aimed at creating the rather flawed ideal of state retraction to remove all distortions. Independent of the social or political dimensions, he considers adjustment to be a failure purely on economic grounds. It was incapable of generating growth. After watching the results in Africa and working in China in the 1990s as the World Bank's chief economist (1993–96), he came to the position that some distortions were necessary and that growth and development were best generated via public-private partnerships. All information is based on the Agarwala interview.

12. The Bank organized a Public Sector Management Unit in 1983 whose responsibility was to focus on these areas. It was concerned with such things as the management of public spending, civil service reform, and public enterprise reform. As discussed in chapter 2, these were absorbed and reinterpreted in governance terms in 1992. Public enterprise reform is discussed in chapter 4 because it was largely reconstructed theoretically using NIE.

13. In the 1980s most components of structural adjustment were badly eroding the civil service, where wages were seldom increased owing to IMF spending restrictions. Furthermore, deregulation was raising food prices. In Zambia, the cost of a nutritionally adequate food basket went from 39 percent of average earnings in the public sector in 1981 to 159 percent in 1989. Civil service jobs became part-time jobs as workers took on informal-sector activities to survive. Moreover, there was a serious increase in the "corruption of economic necessity." See Chiwele and Colclough (1996).

14. The report is quite clear: "While the internal literature on CSR is replete with prescriptions, it is weak on systematic evaluations of Bank experience. Aside from this OED review and a 1997 self-evaluation by the Poverty Reduction and Management Network (PREM), there has been little by way of a comprehensive, cross-country evaluation of CSR" (Operations Evaluation Department 1999, 2).

15. See "A Third World of Planning" (Myrdal 1968, vol. 2, pt. 4).

16. Johnson is highly dismissive of the Bank's miracle report: "The study does not actually say anything new and is intentionally misleading on fundamentals" (C. Johnson 1999, 35).

17. For example, Calder (1993) argues that private-sector activities, not state strategies, were responsible for postwar success in Japan. Johnson is very critical of the depictions that try to separate the private and public sectors in a manner which reflects the little boxes of American political scientists rather than the reality of Japanese practices. Calder misinterprets the Industrial Bank of Japan as the agent

of corporate-led strategic capitalism. In reality it was a government organ until 1952, when the Allies forced it to privatize, and thereafter it was closely linked to the priorities of the government's industrial policy. A discussion of the quasi-public nature of the long-term industrial bank is presented in Stein (2002a).

18. *Homo faber* is a concept promoted by Max Frisch, a novelist and playwright of Swiss-German origin. It is defined as a person who actively begins to change his environment by means of his tools and creativity. One of his novels is titled *Homo Faber.*

Chapter Seven

1. The "updated" neoclassical version assumes that the expected discount rate must be equal to the ratio between marginal utilities in any two periods in order to generate the first-order condition for intertemporal maximization of utility from consumption (maximizing the utility derived from consumption over time). According to this view, financial liberalization is assumed not only to raise real interest rates but also to give individuals additional access to borrowing. This, in turn, is presumed to lead to an increase in consumption, especially among the young. In a pre-liberalization, credit-constrained world, the marginal utility from present consumption is greater than the marginal utility of consumption in the future. The fall in savings due to increased consumption is seen as ephemeral because individuals alter their consumption over time. An increase in interest rates decreases the incentive to borrow, lowers the utility of consumption, and augments the inducement to save, thereby removing the excess demand for savings. Arguments along these lines can be found in Gersovitz (1988), Bayoumi (1993), and Mavrotas and Kelly (2001).

2. McKinnon (1973) looks at issues related to exchange rates, short-term capital flows, and FDI movements and considers restrictions that might be necessary for governments attempting to align foreign and domestic interest rates. He is confident that "the need for, and desirability of, such extraordinary measures will fade as financial liberalization dampens domestic inflationary expectations, and the domestic nominal rates of interest can be reduced." Weary of the "administrative problems" governments encounter when trying to determine which import credits are "abnormal," he would prefer fewer short-term capital flows just to avoid intervention (169).

3. To McKinnon, an entrepreneur's intertemporal decision making is linked to three issues: the potential quantity of self-deployed capital, his investment opportunities, and options for lending or borrowing in the market. In developing countries' often fragmented markets, these elements are poorly correlated. For example, those with available internal funds might have few profitable opportunities available. Yet progress is possible if the dispersion of rates of return can be re-

duced to a "single allocative mechanism" able to "accurately reflect the prevailing scarcity of capital" (McKinnon 1973, 11–12). Here McKinnon draws on an extreme view of capital theory such as that found in Hirshleifer (1970). The interest rate is not only equal to the return to capital (the opportunity cost of using one's own funds) but is also reflective of the rate of intertemporal preference.

4. The complexity of money as a social construct is well documented in the anthropological literature. See, e.g., Guyer (1995).

5. McKinnon admits, however, that there may be an upper limit on the interest rate. The conduit effect of money might be overwhelmed by the "asset" effect of continuing to hold money rather than using it to finance investment.

6. For optimal results, governments should reduce seigniorage (the net revenue that government gains by issuing money) to zero. McKinnon assumes that this amounts to an "inflation tax," lowering real returns to depositors as well as the incentive to save, with consequences for investment.

7. A simple scan of interest rates on June 7, 2005, in Michigan shows tremendous variations on the returns for the same financial vehicles. For instance, five-year CD rates showed yields of between 2.5 and 4.5 percent, with no apparent logical explanation for the discrepancies (such as variations of risk, convenience, or minimum balances). Five-year Treasury bonds were yielding 3.68 percent on the same day (www.ratepy.com and www.bloomberg.com).

8. Even more favorably inclined writers have noted: "They have put forth a convincing economic philosophy of 'free market for rural finance,' but they have not yet provided a formal and explicit model of financial institutions and financial markets" (Krahnen and Schmidt 1994, 121–22).

9. The list of countries that experienced financial crises includes Uruguay and Chile (1981); Colombia (1982); Philippines (1983); Norway (1987); Senegal and Côte D'Ivoire (1988); Sri Lanka and the Czech Republic (1989); Finland, Hungary, Malaysia, and Sweden (1991); and Japan and the Slovak Republic (1992).

10. Orthodox arguments for financial reform were, however, used in World Bank documents prior to this. See, e.g., World Bank (1983b, 58–59). After the SECALs were introduced, such arguments began to appear in glossy regional reports. See, e.g., World Bank (1989, 171); World Bank (1994b, 114–15).

11. The World Development Report for 1989, the first concerning finance, was inspired by much of the same literature that inspired Gelb and Honohan. This is clear, for instance, in the report's discussion of directed and subsidized credit: "[M]any directed credits have become non-performing loans. The ability to borrow at cheap rates encouraged less productive investment . . . [;] by encouraging firms to borrow from banks, directed credit program have impeded the development of capital markets. . . . It is clear they have damaged financial systems" (World Bank 1989, 60).

12. The OED readily admitted that the OD 8.30 policies were largely in place before 1992: "Although many of the operations included in this review were designed

prior to OD 8.30, the focus on removing distortions and strengthening individual institutions is consistent with the emphasis in OD 8.30" (Operations Evaluation Department 1993, 1:14).

13. "Arm's-length" banking uses indirect means to influence the financial sector. This is accomplished via open-market operations and changes in the discount rate. Bank loans play a minor role in corporate finance. Companies rely heavily on bond and equity markets for financing long-term investments. Regulatory guidelines and a well-entrenched independent central bank are important dimensions of this system. For a critical assessment of this approach and a discussion of the advantage of other financial models, see Stein 2002a.

14. Some Bank studies actually found privatization and other reforms to have negative consequences. In a World Bank policy paper, Cull (1997) uses simple econometrics to analyze the impact of the reforms on financial deepening. Contrary to orthodox expectations, the coefficient for privatization was actually negative, indicating that it significantly lowered financial deepening. Furthermore, reforms aimed at removing distortions were not statistically significant relative to other forms of intervention (36–38). Once again, instead of suggesting there was a need to seriously rethink the strategy, the paper concludes, "[A]s other authors have also suggested, while it may be best to move more aggressively on financial reform when macroeconomic circumstances are favorable, 'visible' reform such as interest rate de-regulation or privatization should be slowed rather than abandoned in less fortunate circumstances" (58).

15. The thesis was named after Federal Reserve Chairman Alan Greenspan and Lawrence Summers, then undersecretary of the Treasury for international affairs. They argued that the cozy links among companies, financial institutions, and the state led to excessive lending, overcapacity, and decreasing profits. Poor corporate governance meant weak internal rules, lax regulatory enforcement, and poor auditing and accounting. The system shielded companies from the discipline of the market. The high debt-to-equity ratios arising from this structure left corporations susceptible to external shocks such as sudden increases in interest rates and rapid currency declines. Companies were weakened by a lack of competition, which was the clear result of granting government-directed and subsidized credit to favored large corporations. To Greenspan and Summers, the Asian crisis demonstrated the clear superiority of American-style free-market capitalism.

16. Glen and Singh (2005) give a detailed critique of the Greenspan-Summers-IMF (GSI) thesis. They argue, for example, that it is implausible that the system responsible for the Asian miracle would suddenly experience a dramatic reversal; it is more likely that something changed. The most significant alteration was the state's withdrawal from the coordination of private-sector investment activity following financial liberalization. The problem was not that there was too much government intervention but rather that there was too little compared to that used in the preceding growth years. Both China and India had far worse fundamentals

than did Indonesia or Thailand, but they largely avoided the crisis by not liberalizing their capital accounts.

17. See World Bank 2002b, 202, n. 32.

18. The Bank study, however, cites none of this evidence. Instead, it includes only Bank-commissioned empirical studies or studies by others that are consistent with the Bank's preconceived positions. In this case it cites an unpublished internal paper by Caprio and Martinez-Peria. The link between liberalization and crisis is explored below.

19. Just for good measure, the Bank throws in more of the agenda of the 1990s by arguing that decentralization may "offset the tendency of central governments to control markets and thwart competition" (World Bank 2002b, 79) and that, of course, "financial development is central to poverty reduction" (75). For a more complicated evaluation of the links between finance and poverty and the problems engendered by the kind of liberalization discussed in this chapter, see Arestis and Caner 2004.

20. Lucy Smy, "Counting out of the Bills and Tightening the Lines of Credit," *Financial Times,* surveys edition, 12 December 2001.

21. *African*, 8 June 2002.

22. Minsky (1957) focuses on the ways in which financial organizations use institutional innovation to respond to attempts by the central bank to tighten monetary policy. Velocity of money increases with interest rates; at the same time, the liquidity of households, firms, and banks declines. Greater debt relative to assets leaves the system financially fragile, susceptible to asset deflation, and in risk of major crisis. A rapid infusion of credit by the central bank as lender of last resort might be necessary to ensure that a financial crisis does not spill into a broader economic crisis.

23. None of the numerous econometric studies conducted in various regions is able to show a positive and significant relation between interest rates and savings. See, e.g., Giovannini (1985); Gupta (1987); Cho and Khatkhate (1989); Gonzalez Arrieta (1988); De Melo and Tybout (1986); Warman and Thirlwall (1994); Oshikoya (1992); Taiwo (1992); Reichel (1991). Some studies, such as Matsheka's (1998) econometric study of savings and interest rates in Botswana, have shown a statistically significant negative relation.

24. See, .e.g., Habibullah (1999), Akinboade (1998), and Sahoo et al. (2001). Even the World Bank (1993), in its study of Asia, found that the causation was growth to savings in five countries (Indonesia, Japan, Korea, Thailand, and Taiwan), was ambiguous in two areas (Hong Kong and Malaysia), and was due to other factors in one other (Singapore relied on a state-sponsored provident fund to finance investment).

25. The Nigerian example is used throughout this chapter primarily because of its familiarity, an important factor in understanding how to transform any institutional matrix. The author made multiple trips to Nigeria to study the banking

system between 1994 and 2002 and included numerous interviews with people in the Ministry of Finance, accounting firms, the central bank, and private banking organizations.

26. Unless otherwise stated, the data come from Stein et al. (2002).

27. Total capital for BIS purposes consists of stock values, retained earnings, loan-loss reserves, and subordinated (unsecured or low-priority) debt.

28. For merchant banks, the initial capital requirement was only 2 million naira, which in 1998 was a mere $240,000 at the parallel rate of exchange (calculated from data in Lewis and Stein 2002).

29. Under the military rule of President Ibrahim Babingida, new bank applications were reviewed by the president's office and by the Federal Executive Council, which was controlled by the military. Retired military officers with no banking experience were instrumental in obtaining banking licenses. Because the aim was to rapidly expand competition, the regime saw an opportunity to reward its constituents. A different strategy built on the institutional foundation already in place at the time could have avoided the problem.

30. Nigeria had a variety of types of foreign exchange, which at times included auctions through banks or direct allocation at fixed rates to priority sectors. Dummy companies would be set up by banks to act as their agents to resell foreign exchange at higher parallel markets for larger profits. Details of the history of the market are presented in Lewis and Stein (2002), table 2.2.

31. It is difficult to calculate the overall cost, which is a combination of paying out NDIC insurance to subscribers, recapitalizing failed banks, paying the high administrative costs of the liquidating and reorganizing banks, and so on. One reliable source indicated in May 1994 that the central bank had submitted a plan to clean up the banking mess for about 86 billion naira. At official exchange rates, this amounted to almost $4 billion, or more than 12 percent of 1993 GDP (World Bank 1995, 166). By 1996 the recapitalization costs of the forty-seven distressed banks already had reached 41.4 billion naira.

32. The CBN wanted to avoid further allocation of credit from the government and to hide the fact that there was another banking crisis brewing. The Big Six agreed to make the loans in return for CBN guarantees. All the information in this section comes from Nigeria Deposit Insurance Corporation (2001) and interviews with banking sector officials in Lagos and Abuja conducted by the author in September 2002.

33. Lewis and Stein (2002), using regression analysis, found that as the number of banks increased, lending to the private sector and the ratio of financial savings to GDP declined (at 5 percent and 1 percent levels of significance, respectively).

34. Advocates of orthodox approaches to finance would argue that government intervention creates rent-seeking and corruption. I argue that corruption is always present, even in the United States, and therefore cannot be unequivocally deemed to be causally related to the actions of the state. Witness, for instance, the scandals

surrounding Enron and other companies. According to the orthodox view, Japan's financial system spawned a crisis in its banking system in the mid-90s. In 1995–96, however, when the author resided in Japan, it seemed clear that the crisis was created not by too much government intervention but by too little. In particular, the real estate bubble was generated by overlending to the building sector. The government realized this and placed restrictions on bank lending to the real estate sector. But it left a loophole that allowed the banks to continue to lend to non-bank financial corporations in the construction sector (*jusen*) that perpetuated the bubble with their loans to the construction industry. Overall, the potential benefits of sharing risk to support private sector initiatives meant to enhance development greatly outweigh the potential rise in corruption. As discussed in chapter 6, there are ways to ensure that this support leads to the desired outcome.

Chapter Eight

1. The link between poverty and poor health is well developed in the literature. See, e.g., McKeown (1988); Leon and Walt (2001); Blakeley et al. (2005); Wagstaff (2002); Whiteside (2002); and Kibirige (1997).

2. See, e.g., Weisbrod et al. (1973); Selowsky and Taylor (1973).

3. The papers influenced the Bank for an additional year. As discussed in chapter 6, WDR 1981 contains a chapter warning of the consequences of adjustment for human development. As indicated in the bibliographic note, it draws almost entirely on WDR 1980 and its associated background papers.

4. The report takes it a step further, calling for "free transport to health clinics" to respond to the evidence that distance from clinics had a negative impact on usage of health care facilities. By 1987, comments such as this would be considered anathema to the Bank.

5. This information is taken from his curriculum vitae, downloaded from www .brookings.edu /scholars /ddferranti.htm.

6. The distinction between willingness and ability to pay, now common among orthodox health economists, is an artificial one arising from a neoclassical economic notion that we all have utility curves, that ability to pay is readily definable, and that there is a measurable maximum price that people are willing to pay for a good or service. In this chimerical world, if a user fee is deemed affordable, people "voluntarily" choose not to attend the clinic because the expected marginal utility gains are less than the price.

7. Balassa, who provided the core work concerning state-created distortions in markets for private goods, expanded his focus to incorporate the distortionary impact of public financing of social spending such as that for health care, which was said to be making labor too costly. He argued that imposing taxes on labor in the interest of financing health care "distort[s] labor markets by raising the cost of

labor, where the extent of the distortions will depend on the ratio of social charges to wage payments" (Balassa 1985, 48). These wage distortions, in combination with government-imposed reductions in the cost of capital, "discourage employment in the formal sector" (55). The influential paper, first published in a journal, was circulated around the Bank in 1985 as no. 406 in the World Bank Reprint Series.

8. For example, the paper suggests that the evidence is found in table 3, which lists the percentage of government health expenditures covered by user fees for a sample of seventeen countries but gives no data about wage levels. There is not a single estimate in the entire paper regarding the level of marginal costs both in absolute and relative to income levels. Table A-1 contains data about public health care expenditures and per capita income. The figures are rather mismatched because per capita income data are from 1981 and the per capita health figures are mostly from 1978. In most African countries, these figures say little about the affordability of user fee charges; because large portions of GNP per capita come from the imputed value of subsistence production, few have much disposable cash income, and the income of the vast majority falls below the average. For these reasons, a fifty-cent user fee per visit (which the author deemed inconsequential) could prove onerous to most families in countries with a $100 per capita yearly income (de Ferranti 1985, 137). As we will see, many people cut back on health care visits when the fees were introduced because they were too much of a burden.

9. De Ferranti cites a study by Akin et al. (1986), originally produced in 1982, to argue that the threshold above which user fees would affect consumption behavior was quite high. But the study suffers from a number of methodological weaknesses that challenge its strong assertions. For example, the initial survey of residents was conducted in 1978 but the evaluation of clinics was undertaken three years later on the assumption that individuals went to the clinics closest to their village. After running probit and other related regressions (tobit and logit), the authors examine the change in the estimated probability of using a service caused by a change (10 percent from the mean) in one variable while holding others constant. For dummy variables, they change the values from 0 to 1 and find that the most consequential element was the perception of the seriousness of the illness, whereas the increases in the economic variables such as price and income (as measured by assets) have no impact. Yet this is a rather problematic way of examining the data because changing a dummy variable is both quantitatively (actually, infinitely!) and qualitatively different than increasing other variables such as price by 10 percent. Moreover, increasing the mean price and income by 10 percent for patients assigned to some hypothetical clinic, using prices prevailing three years after the hypothetical event, can hardly justify the ridiculously strong conclusion that "there is a preponderance of evidence that cost and income are not important to the joint decisions of whether and when to seek care" (768).

10. John Akin, a member of the Health Services Research Center at the University of North Carolina at Chapel Hill, joined de Ferranti between 1985 to 1987

as a senior economist in the Division of Policy and Research in the Department of Health, Nutrition, and Population which was run by Nancy Birdsall. Birdsall was a Yale-trained economist who joined the Bank's Development Economics Department in 1979. Her work, which dealt with the ways in which user fees can improve equity, was produced while she was in the Country Policy Department of the World Bank (1982–84) and was heavily used by de Ferranti in his 1985 paper. There is little doubt that these three authors were on the same wavelength in writing the 1997 Bank policy study about health. This information comes from the authors' curricula vitae and Akin's personal statement, found online at www.unc.edu/~akin/.

11. Economists from other American universities,, including Mead Over and David Dunlop, joined the health team at the Bank after 1987 (Lee and Goodman 2002).

12. To quote John Akin's Web site: "During 1985–87, during a stint at the World Bank, I co-authored that international development organization's official policy on Financing Health Services (*Financing Health Services in Developing Countries: An Agenda for Reform*). That document was approved by the member nations in 1987 and remains the official health care financing policy of the World Bank" (www.unc.edu/~akin/).

13. A number of consultancy firms and universities, including ABT Associates, worked closely with the World Bank and USAID in developing the neoclassical economic approach to health care policy. Lee and Goodman (2002) carefully document the major players associated with health care financing reform during this period. The typical route to the policy elite is a Ph.D. in economics, a faculty position at a prominent (usually American) university, project funding from USAID or the World Bank, and perhaps recruitment by a small number of consultancy companies that work with donor agencies. Lee and Goodman (2002) argue that the result is that "HCF (health care financing) has been fostered by the emergence of a policy elite, rather than a rational convergence of health needs and solutions" (116).

14. For example, in 1987, UNICEF launched the Bamako Initiative, which–among other things–aimed at selling drugs at marked-up prices in the interest of generating a self-sustaining means by which drugs could be supplied to rural communities (Lee and Goodman 2002, 100).

15. A few quotations will illustrate the commitment of WDR 1993 to neoliberalism: "What people do with their lives and those of their children affects their health far more than anything that governments can do" (World Bank 1993b, 37); "[t]he private health sector . . . typically delivers services . . . more responsive to consumer demand than governments" (125); and "government-run health systems in many developing countries are completely overextended and need to be scaled back" (108).

16. This figure is derived from the equation $1.03^{55} = 5.08$ (Anand and Hanson's [1998] calculation).

17. I have excluded three countries from the list–Botswana, Cameroon, and Liberia–that did not undertake adjustment in the 1980s. Cameroon began its first program in 1989. The data from Sahn (1992) cover averages from 1980 to 1983 and from 1987 to 1989. I have assumed a population growth rate of 3 percent or average index growth of 11 percent, so the fraction is $1.11/1.34 = 0.828$. The figure of 1.34 is based on the formula 1.03^{10}. Only four countries had real growth per health expenditure of more than 25 percent, which would cover a 2.3 percent annual population growth rate from 1980 to 1989.

18. I do not review insurance schemes. Although they constitute an additional part of the reform agenda, they have not been implemented nearly as often as the other recommended reforms, nor have they been used very consistently or widely when introduced. This is not terribly surprising: in many developing countries, the majority of the population is too poor to pay monthly insurance rates, even if doing so would help decrease the costs of seeking medical attention on a per-treatment basis. Where insurance schemes have been implemented, they often have not been in force long enough to allow for empirical studies of their impact. This is the case, for example, in the Philippines, where providing insurance to indigents is part of a strategy that was accepted on June 30, 2006 (World Bank Health Systems and Financing Web site, www.worldbank.org).

19. See, e.g., Schuler et al. (2002); Jacobs and Price (2004); Moses et al. (1992); Nyonator and Kutzin (1999); Booth et al. (1995); Blas and Limbambala (2001).

20. To quote the influential conservative economist Milton Friedman: "The essence of human freedom is . . . the freedom of people to make their own decisions so long as they do not prevent anybody else from doing the same thing. That makes clear, l think, why free private markets are so closely related to human freedom. It is the only mechanism that permits a complex interrelated society to be organized from the bottom up rather than the top down. A characteristic feature of a free private market is that all parties to a transaction believe that they are going to be better off by that transaction. It is not a zero sum game in which some can benefit only at the expense of others. It is a situation in which everybody thinks he is going to be better off. . . . In the private economy, so long as we keep a free private market, one party to a deal can only benefit if the other party also benefits. There is no way in which you can satisfy your needs at the expense of somebody else" (Friedman 1991, n.p.).

21. According to Lane and Rubinstein's (1996) interviews with women in rural Egypt, "When they learned that the female researcher was not circumcised their response was disgust mixed with joking laughter. They wonder how she could have thus gotten married and questioned how her mother could have neglected such an important part of her preparation for womanhood. It was clearly unthinkable for a woman not to be circumcised" (quoted in Boyle et al. 2005, 8).

22. The World Bank defines this as "the percentage of the population with access to at least adequate excreta disposal facilities (private or shared, but not pub-

lic) that can effectively prevent human, animal, and insect contact with excreta. Improved facilities range from simple but protected pit latrines to flush toilets with a sewerage connection." See "Definitions for Table 1.3" (World Bank 2006, 31).

23. In 2004, more than 20 percent of the U.S. adult population still smoked. This is extraordinary considering that smoking will be the cause of death for roughly one in every two smokers. There has been only a 50 percent reduction in the rate of smoking since 1964. These data are from www.cdc.gov/tobacco/research_data/adults_prev/prevali.htm.

24. Boyle et al. (2002) discuss how practices vary among Islamic groups. Status within Islam seems to alter the pattern of FGC between groups. For example, in Somalia, the Kenana–who practiced infibulations–were considered to be of higher status due to their close connection to the Islamic world. The Zabarma, on the other hand, who used to undertake a more symbolic form of FGC, worked in a government-organized group with the Kenana, and eventually adopted their more extreme practices (16).

25. In the rural highlands of Kenya, 87 percent of households without ITNs cited cost as the major reason for not purchasing a net. The same study also examined the budgets of poor households (48 percent of the population of Kisii) to see if this was an issue of willingness or ability to pay. The purchase of subsidized nets from Merlin (Medical Emergency Relief International) would cost roughly twice what was spent annually by poor households on health care, and, in turn, would significantly cut into basic needs such as food and education. Ninety-seven percent of the people were willing to pay for ITNs, but the prices they were willing to pay were about one-seventh of the going rate. For what it is worth (hypothetical questions for hypothetical purchases), there were clear constraints on the ability of poor people to pay for ITNs (Guyatt et al. 2002).

26. We can see from the Malawi study that not all owners of nets used them for their children the night before the survey took place. Presumably these nets were obtained from commercial sources.

27. Based on a birth rate of 0.024 and a population of 45.5 million in 2004, a 30.2 percent rate of HIV infection in pregnant women, and an estimated 30 percent transmission rate from mother to child without Nevirapine, there should have been roughly ninety-nine thousand cases of infection. With Nevirapine, which reduced the rate of transmission from mother to child to 14 percent, there should have been about forty-six thousand cases of infection. Thus the figure of seventy thousand is higher than would be expected. World Bank (2006); Rosenberg (2006); http://www.avert.org/safricastats.htm.

Bibliography

Adams, John. 2003. *Review of Mancur Olson and Satu Kahkonen, Editors, A Not-So-Dismal Science: A Broader View of Economies and Societies,* March. http://www.eh.net/bookreviews.

Adelman, Irma, and Morris, Cynthia. 1973. *Economic Growth and Social Equity in Developing Countries.* Palo Alto, CA: Stanford University Press.

Adesida, Olugbenga. 1998. "Creating the African Information and Knowledge Society." *African Development Review* 10, no. 1:239–54.

Adeyemi, K. S. 2002. "The Nigerian Banking System in an Historical Perspective." In *Deregulation and the Banking Crisis in Nigeria: A Comparative Study*, ed. Howard Stein, Olu Ajakaiye, and Peter Lewis. Basingstoke: Palgrave.

Adjibolosoo, Senyo B.-S. K. 1999. *Rethinking Development Theory and Policy.* Westport: Praeger.

Agarwala, Ramgopal. 1983. "Price Distortions and Growth in Developing Countries." World Bank Staff Working Paper no. 575, Washington, DC.

Ajayi, Simeon Ibi. 1994. "The State of Research on the Macroeconomic Effectiveness of Structural Adjustment Programs in Sub-Saharan Africa." In *Structural Adjustment and Beyond in Sub-Saharan Africa*, ed. R. van der Hoeven and F. van der Kraaij, 54–69. Portsmouth, NH: Heinemann.

Akin, John S., Charles C. Griffin, David K. Guilkey, and Barry M. Popkin. 1986. "The Demand for Primary Health Care Services in the Bicol Region of the Philippines." *Economic Development and Cultural Change* 34, no. 4:755–82.

Akinboade, O. A. 1998. "Financial Development and Economic Growth in Botswana: A Test of Causality." *Savings and Development* 22, no. 3:331–48.

Akroyd, H. David. 2003. *Agriculture and Rural Development Planning: A Process in Transition.* Burlington, VT: Ashgate.

Alford, R. R., and R. Friedland. 1986. *Powers of Theory: Capitalism, the State, and Democracy.* New York: Cambridge University Press.

Allotey, Pascale A., and Daniel D. Reidpath. 2002. "Objectivity in Priority Setting Tools in Reproductive Health: Context and the Daly." *Reproductive Health Matters* 10, no. 20:38–46.

Allotey, Pascale, Daniel Reidpath, Aka Kouame, and Robert Cummins. 2003. "The Daly, Context and the Determinants of the Severity of Disease: An

Exploratory Comparison of Paraplegia in Australia and Cameroon." *Social Science and Medicine* 57:949–58.

Alubo, Ogoh. 2001. "The Promise and Limits of Private Medicine: Health Policy Dilemmas in Nigeria." *Health Policy and Planning* 16, no. 3:313–21.

Amsden, Alice. 1989. *Asia's Next Giant: South Korea and Late Industrialization.* New York: Oxford University Press.

Anand, Sudhir, and Kara Hanson. 1998. "Dalys: Efficiency Versus Equity." *World Development* 26, no. 2:307–10.

Andrews, K. R. 1960. *The Concept of Strategy.* Homewood, IL: Irwin.

Arestis, Philip, and Asena Caner. 2004. "Financial Liberalization and Poverty: Channels of Influence." Levy Economics Institute Working Paper no. 411, Annandale-on-Hudson, NY.

Arestis, Philip, and P. Demetriades. 1999. "Financial Liberalization: The Experience of Developing Countries." *Eastern Economic Journal* 25, no. 4:441–57.

Arestis, Philip, P. Demetriades, and B. Fattouh. 2003. "Financial Policies and the Aggregate Productivity of the Capital Stock: Evidence from Developed and Developing Countries." *Eastern Economic Journal* 29, no. 2:219–44.

Arnesen, Trude, and Lydia Kapiriri. 2004. "Can the Value Choices in Dalys Influence Global Priority-Setting?" *Health Policy and Planning* 70:137–49.

Arthur, Gilly, Shrikant M. Bhatt, David Muhidi, Grace A. Achiya, Samuel M. Kariuki, and Charles F. Gilks. 2000. "The Changing Impact of HIV/AIDS on Kenyatta National Hospital, Nairobi from 1988/89 through 1992 to 1997." *AIDS 2000* 14, no. 11: 1625–31.

Ayres, Robert. 1983. *Banking on the Poor: The World Bank and World Poverty.* Washington, DC: Overseas Development Council.

Bagehot, W. 1873. *Lombard Street.* Homewood, IL: Richard D. Irwin.

Balassa, Bela. 1985. "Public Finance and Social Policy—Explanations of Trends and Developments: The Case of Developing Countries." In *Public Finance and Social Policy: Proceedings of the 39th Congress of the International Institute of Public Finance, Budapest, Hungary, 1983,* ed. Guy Terny and A. J. Culyer, 41–58. Detroit: Wayne State University Press.

Balassa, Bela, and Associates. 1982. *Development Strategies in Semi-Industrial Economies.* Baltimore: Johns Hopkins University Press.

Baldwin, Robert. 1971. "Determinants of the Commodity Structure of U.S. Trade." *American Economic Review* 6 (March): 126–46.

Bannaga, Alamedin A. 1990. "Introduction to the Symposium on the State and Economic Development." *Journal of Economic Perspectives* 4, no. 3:3–7.

———. 2002. "The Impact of the Structural Adjustment Policies on Economic Growth in Sudan." Paper presented at the Development Studies Association Conference, University of Greenwich, London.

Barro, Robert, and Jong-wha Lee. 2002. "IMF Lending: Who Is Chosen and What Are the Effects?" NBER Working Paper Series, no. 8951, Cambridge, MA.

Barrows, Richard, and Michael Roth. 1990. "Land Tenure and Investment in African Agriculture: Theory and Evidence." *Journal of Modern African Studies* 28, no. 2:265–97.

Bates, Robert H. 1981. *Markets and States in Tropical Africa: The Political Basis of Agricultural Policies*. Berkeley: University of California Press.

———. 1991. *Beyond the Miracle of Markets: The Political Economy of Agrarian Development in Kenya*. Cambridge: Cambridge University Press.

Bauer, Peter. 1971. *Dissent on Development*. Cambridge: Harvard University Press, 1971.

Baum, Joel A. C., and Christine Oliver. 1991. "Institutional Linkages and Organizational Mortality." *Administrative Sciences Quarterly* 36, no. 2:187–218.

Bayoumi, Tamim. 1993. "Financial Deregulation and Household Saving." *Economic Journal* 103, no. 421:1432–43.

Benson, John S. 2001. "The Impact of Privatization on Access in Tanzania." *Social Science and Medicine* 52:1903–15.

Bentham, Jeremy. 1789. *An Introduction to the Principles of Morals and Legislation*. London: T. Payne.

Bhagwati, J., and Ramaswami, V. K. 1963. "Domestic Distortions, Tariffs, and the Theory of Optimum Subsidy." *Journal of Political Economy* 71, no. 1:44–50.

Blas, Erik, and Me Limbambala. 2001. "User-Payment, Decentralization and Health Service Utilization in Zambia." *Health Policy and Planning* 16, supp. 2: 19–28.

Boas, Morten, and Desmond McNeill. 2003. *Multilateral Institutions: A Critical Introduction*. London: Pluto.

Bonu, Sekhar, Manju Rani, and David Bishai. 2001. "Using Willingness to Pay to Investigate Regressiveness of User Fees in Health Facilities in Tanzania." *Health Policy and Planning* 18, no. 4:370–82.

Booth, D., J. Milimo, G. Bond, and S. Chimuka. 1995. "Coping with Cost Recovery." Report to the Swedish International Development Authority. Development Studies Unit, Department of Social Anthropology, Stockholm University.

Bosman, M. C. J. 2000. "Health Sector Reform and Tuberculosis Control: The Case of Zambia." *International Journal of Tuberculosis and Lung Disease* 4, no. 7:606–14.

Bossert, Thomas. 1998. "Analyzing the Decentralization of Health Systems in Developing Countries: Decision Space, Innovation, and Performance." *Social Science and Medicine* 47, no. 10:1513–27.

Bossert, Thomas, and Joel C. Beauvais. 2002. "Decentralization of Health Systems in Ghana, Zambia, Uganda and the Philippines: A Comparative Analysis of Decision Space." *Health Policy and Planning* 17, no. 1:14–31.

Bossert, Thomas, Moskosha Bona Chitah, and Diana Bowser. 2003. "Decentralization in Zambia: Resource Allocation and District Performance." *Health Policy and Planning* 18, no. 4:357–69.

Boyle, Elizabeth Heger, Barbara J. McMorris, and Mayra Gomez. 2002. "Local Conformity to International Norms: The Case of Female Genital Cutting." *International Sociology* 17, no. 1:5–33.

Brazil, Embassy of. 2004. *Brazil-US Dispute Regarding Cotton Subsidies* [Press Release No. 015]. London. Accessed April 30. http://www.brazil.org.uk/newsandmedia/pressreleases_files/20071015.html.

Brech, E. F. L. 1953. *The Principle and Practice of Management*. London: Long-man.

Brugha, Ruairi, and Anthony Zwi. 2002. "Global Approaches to Private Sector Provision: Where Is the Evidence?" In *Health Policy in a Globalizing World*, ed. Kelley Lee, Kent Buse, and Suzanne Fustukian, 63–78. Cambridge: Cambridge University Press.

Burki, Shahid Javed, and Guillermo Perry. 1998. *Beyond the Washington Consensus: Institutions Matter*. Washington, DC: World Bank.

Burns, John, and Robert W. Scapens. 2000. "Conceptualizing Management Accounting Change: An Institutional Framework." *Management Accounting Research* 11, no. 1:3–25.

Burns, T., and G. M. Stalker. 1961. *The Management of Innovation*. London: Tavistock.

Calder, Kent. 1993. *Strategic Capitalism: Private Business and Public Purpose in Japanese Industrial Finance*. Princeton: Princeton University Press.

Callaghy, Thomas M. 1986. "The Political Economy of African Debt: The Case of Zaire." In *Africa in Economic Crisis*, ed. John Ravenhill, 307–46. New York: Columbia University Press.

Caprio, Gerald, and Daniella Klingebiel. 1999. "Episodes of Systemic and Borderline Financial Crises." World Bank Working Paper.

Chandler, A. 1962. *Strategy and Structure*. Cambridge: MIT Press.

———. 1977. *The Visible Hand: The Managerial Revolution in American Business*. Cambridge: Harvard University Press.

Chang, Ha-Joon. 1994. "State, Institutions and Structural Change." *Structural Change and Economic Dynamics* 5, no. 2:293–313.

———. 1999. "The Economic Theory of the Developmental State." In *The Developmental State*, ed. Meredith Woo-Dummings, 182–99. Ithaca: Cornell University Press.

———. 2002a. "Breaking the Mould: An Institutionalist Political Economy Alternative to the Neo-Liberal Theory of the Market and the State." *Cambridge Journal of Economics* 26, no. 5:539–59.

———. 2002b. *Kicking away the Ladder: Development Strategy in Historical Perspective*. London: Anthem.

———. 2003. "Trade, Industry and Technology Policies in Northeast Asia." In *Comparative Development Experiences of Sub-Saharan Africa and East Asia: An Institutional Approach*, ed. Machiko Nissanke and Ernest Aryeetey, 243–71. Nairobi: African Economic Research Consortium.

Chang, Ha-Joon, Hong-Jae Park, and Chul Gue Yoo. 2002. "Interpreting the Korean Crisis: Financial Liberalization, Industrial Policy and Corporate Governance." In *Deregulation and the Banking Crisis in Nigeria*, ed. Howard Stein, Olu Ajakaiye, and Peter Lewis, 211–24. Basingstoke: Palgrave.

Chang, Ha-Joon, and Ajit Singh. 1997. "Can Large Firms Be Run Efficiently without Being Bureaucratic?" *Journal of International Development* 9, no. 6:865–75.

Chartered Institute of Bankers of Nigeria. 2005. "History." http://www.cibnnigeria.org/corporate/history.htm.

Child, J. 1972. "Organization Structure and Strategies of Control: A Replication of the Aston Study." *Administrative Sciences Quarterly* 17:163–77.

Child, J., and M. Tayeb. 1983. "Theoretical Perspectives in Cross-National Research." *International Studies of Management and Organization* 23, no. 4:32–70.

Chiwele, Dennis, and Christopher Colclough. 1996. "Economic Crisis, Adjustment and the Effectiveness of the Public Sector in Zambia." In *Constraints on the Success of Structural Adjustment Programs in Africa,* ed. Charles Harvey, 192–209. London: Macmillan.

Coase, Ronald. 1937. "The Nature of the Firm." *Economica* 4, no. 16:386–405.

———. 1960. "The Problem of Social Cost." *Journal of Law and Economics* 3, no. 1:1–44.

———. 1992. "The Institutional Structure of Production." *American Economic Review* 82, no. 4:713–17.

Cochrane, Glynn. 1983. "Policies for Strengthening Local Government in Developing Countries." World Bank Staff Working Paper no. 578.

Collier, P., and A. Hoeffler. 1998. "On the Economic Causes of Civil War." *Oxford Economic Papers* 50:563–73.

Collins, Charles. 1989. "Decentralization and the Need for Political and Critical Analysis." *Health Policy and Planning* 4, no. 2:168–71.

Collins, Charles, and Andrew Green. 1994. "Decentralization and Primary Health Care: Some Negative Implications in Developing Countries." *International Journal of Health Serivces* 24, no. 3:459–75.

Collins, D., J. D. Quick, S. N. Musau, D. Kraushaar, and I. M. Hussein. 1996. "The Fall and Rise of Cost Sharing in Kenya: The Impact of Phased Implementation." *Health Policy and Planning* 11, no. 1:52–63.

Corbo, Vittorio, and Patricio Rojas. 1991. "Country Performance and Effectiveness of World Bank-Supported Adjustment Programs." Policy, Research, and External Affairs Working Paper Series, no. 623, World Bank, March.

Cox, Robert, ed. 1997. *The New Realism.* Basingstoke: Macmillan.

Cramer, Chris, Howard Stein, and John Weeks. 2006. "Ownership and Donorship: Analytical Issues and a Tanzanian Case Study." *Journal of Contemporary African Studies* 24, no. 3:414–36.

Cull, Robert. 1997. *Financial Sector Adjustment Lending: A Mid-Course Analysis.* Washington, DC: World Bank.

Czech National Bank. 2005. *Indicators of Monetary and Economic Development.* Prague: Czech National Bank.

Das, D. K. 1998. *Civil Service Reform and Structural Adjustment.* Delhi: Oxford University Press.

David, Wilfred. 1997. *The Conversation of Economic Development, Historical Interpretations, and Reality.* Armonk, NY: Sharpe.

Davies, Robert, Jorn Rattso, and Ragnar Torvik. 1998, "Short Run Consequences of Trade Liberalization: A Computable General Equilibrium Model of Zimbabwe." *Journal of Policy Modeling* 20, no. 3:305–33.

de Ferranti, David. 1985. "Paying for Health Services in Developing Countries: An Overview." World Bank Staff Working Paper, no. 721.

De Maio, Lorenzo, Francis Stewart, and Rolph van der Hoeven. 1999. "Computable General Equilibrium Models, Adjustment and the Poor in Africa." *World Development* 27, no. 3:453–70.

Dembele, Demba Moussa. 2003. *Debt and Destruction in Senegal: A Study of Twenty Years of IMF and World Bank Policies.* London: World Development Movement.

De Melo, J., and J. Tybout. 1986. "The Effects of Financial Liberalization on Savings and Investment in Uruguay." *Economic Development and Cultural Change* 34, no. 3:607–40.

Demirguc-Kunt, Asli, and Enrica Detragiache. 1998. "The Determinants of Banking Crises in Developing and Developed Countries." *IMF Staff Papers* 45: 81–109.

————. 1999. "Financial Liberalization and Financial Fragility." In *Proceedings of the 1998 World Bank Conference on Development Economics*, ed. B. Pleskovic and J. E. Stiglitz, 303–44. Washington, DC: World Bank.

De Soto, Hernando. 2000. *The Mystery of Capital: Why Capitalism Triumphs in the West and Fails Everywhere Else.* New York: Basic.

De Vries, Margaret G. 1986. *The IMF in a Changing World, 1945–85.* Washington, DC: International Monetary Fund.

Dia, Mamadou. 1993. *A Governance Approach to Civil Service Reform in Sub-Saharan Africa.* Washington, DC: World Bank.

Dickinson, Zenas C. 1919. "The Relations of Recent Psychological Developments to Economic Theory." *Quarterly Journal of Economics* 33, no. 3:377–421.

————. 1922. *Economic Motives: A Study in the Psychological Foundations of Economic Theory, with Some Reference to Other Social Sciences.* Cambridge: Harvard University Press.

Dillard, J. F., J. T. Rigsby, and C. Goodman. 2004. "The Making and Remaking of Organization Context: Duality and the Institutionalization Process." *Accounting, Auditing and Accountability Journal* 17, no. 4:506–42.

Dimaggio, P. J., and W. W. Powell. 1983. "The Iron Cage Revisited: Institutional Isomorphism and Collective Rationality in the Organizational Fields." *American Sociological Review* 48, no. 2:147–60.

Dollar, David. 1992, "Outward Oriented Economies Really Do Grow More Rapidly: Evidence from 95 Ldcs, 1976–1985." *Economic Development and Cultural Change* 40, no. 3:523–44.

Domar, Evsey. 1946. "Capital Expansion, Rate of Growth and Employment." *Econometrica* 14:137–47.

Dornbusch, R., and A. Reynoso, eds. 1993. "Financial Factors in Economic Development." In *Policy Making in the Open Economy: Concepts and Case Studies in Economic Performance,* ed R. Dornbusch, 64–90. Oxford: Oxford University Press.

Drake, E., A. Malik, X. Xu, I. Kotsioni, R. El-Habashy, and V. Mistra. 2003. *Good Governance and the World Bank.* Bretton Woods Project Paper. Produced by the Bretton Woods Project (ELDIS). http://www.brettonwoodsproject.org/topic/governance/goodgov/.

Dreher, Axel, and Nathan Jensen. 2004. "Independent Actor or Agent? An Empirical Analysis of the Impact of US's Interests on IMF Conditions." Paper prepared for the Hamburge Institute of International Economics Conference on Public Choice and Development, December 9–10.

Drewnoski, Jan, and Scott Wolf. 1966. *The Level of Living Index*. Geneva: United Nations.

Duncan, Ron, and Steve Pollard. 2002. *A Framework for Establishing Priorities in a Country Poverty Reduction Strategy*. Manila: Asian Development Bank.

Easterly, William. 1997. "The Mystery of Growth: Shocks, Policies and Surprises in Old and New Theories of Economic Growth." *Singapore Economic Review* 40, no. 1:3–23.

———. 2005. "What Did Structural Adjustment Adjust? The Association of Policies and Growth with Repeated IMF and World Bank Adjustment Loans." *Journal of Development Economics* 76:1–22.

Easterly, William, and Ross Levine. 1997. "Africa's Growth Tragedy: Policies and Ethnic Divisions." *Quarterly Journal of Economics* 112, November:1203–50.

Easton, Lloyd, and Kurt Guddat. 1967. *Writings of the Young Marx on Philosophy and Society*. Garden City, NY: Anchor.

Edwards, Sebastian. 1998. "Openness, Productivity and Growth: What Do We Really Know?" *Economic Journal* 108, no. 447:383–98.

Elbadawi, Ibrahim. 1992. "Have World Bank-Supported Adjustment Programs Improved Economic Performance in Sub-Saharan Africa?" World Bank Working Paper Series, no. 1002.

Englebert, Pierre. 2000. *State Legitimacy and Development in Africa*. Boulder: Rienner.

Ensminger, Jean. 1992. *Making a Market: The Institutional Transformation of an African Society*. Cambridge: Cambridge University Press.

Etzioni, Amitai. 2000. "Social Norms: Internalization, Persuasion and History." *Law and Society* 34, no. 1:157–78.

Evans, Peter. 1995. *Embedded Autonomy: States and Industrial Transformation*. Princeton: Princeton University Press.

Faini, Ricardo, and J. de Melo. 1990. "Adjustment, Investment and the Real Exchange Rate in Developing Countries." World Bank Policy Research Paper Series, no. 473.

Faini, Ricardo, and Enzo Grilli. 2004. "Who Runs the IFIs?" Centro Studi Luca D'Agliano Development Studies Working Paper Series.

Fayol, H. 1949. *General and Industrial Management*. New York: Pitman.

Fehr, Ernst, and Armin Falk. 2002. "Psychological Foundations of Incentives." *European Economic Review* 46:687–724.

Ferguson, Tyronne. 1988. *The Third World and Decision Making in the International Monetary Fund*. London: Pinter.

Fifty Years Is Enough. 2000. "Congress Requires US Oppositon to Health and School User Fees." http://www.50years.org/updates/userfee.

Fine, Ben. 1999. "The Development State Is Dead—Long Live Social Capital." *Development and Change* 30, no. 1:1–19.

Fishlow, Albert. 1972. "Brazilian Size Distribution of Income." *American Economic Review* 62, no. 2:391–402.

Forman, Lisa. 2003. "The Imperative to Treat: The South African State's Constitutional Obligations to Provide Antiretroviral Medicines." *Health Law Institute* 12, no. 1:9–15.

Franke, Dirk. 2003, "Banking Markets in Central and Eastern Europe (IV): Czech Republic—the Late Starter." *Die Bank* (June), 2–3.

Friedman, A. F. 1977. *Industry and Labour*. London: Macmillan.

Friedman, Lawrence. 1969. "Legal Culture and Social Development." *Law and Society Review* 4, no. 1:29–44.

Friedman, Milton. 1953. *The Methodology of Positive Economics*. Essays in Positive Economics. Chicago: University of Chicago Press.

———. 1962. *Capitalism and Freedom*. Chicago: University of Chicago Press.

———. 1991. "Economic Freedom, Human Freedom, Political Freedon," address to the College of Business and Economics, California State University, East Bay, November 1. www.cbe.csueastbay.edu/~besc/frlect.html.

Fukuda-Parr, Sakiko, Carlos Lopes, and Khalid Malik. 2002. *Capacity for Development: New Solutions to Old Problems*. New York: Earthscan/United Nations Development Programme.

Gavin, Michael, and Dani Rodrik. 1995. "The World Bank in Historical Perspective." *American Economic Review* 85, no. 2:329–34.

Gelb, A., and P. Honohan. 1989. "Financial Sector Reforms in Adjustment Programs." World Bank Policy, Research and External Affairs Working Paper no. 169.

Gersovitz, M. 1988. "Savings and Development." In *Handbook of Development Economics*, ed. H. Chenery and S. Srinivasan. Amsterdam: North-Holland.

Gibbon, Peter. 1999. "Privatisation and Foreign Direct Investment in Mainland Tanzania, 1992–98." Centre for Development Research Working Paper Subseries no. 4, 99.1, March.

Ginsburg, Tom. 2000. "Does Law Matter for Economic Development? Evidence from East Asia." *Law and Society* 34, no. 3:829–56.

Giovannini, Alberto. 1985. "Savings and Real Interest Rates in Ldcs." *Journal of Development Economics* 18, nos. 2–3:197–217.

Glen, Jack, and Ajit Singh. 2005. "Corporate Governance, Competition and Finance: Re-Thinking Lessons from the Asian Crisis." *Eastern Economic Journal* 31 (Spring): 219–43.

Goddard, Andrew. 2002. "Development of the Accounting Profession and Practices in the Public Sector: A Hegemonic Analysis." *Accounting, Auditing and Accountability Journal* 15, no. 2:655–88.

Golladay, Fredrick, and Bernhard Liese. 1980. "Health Problems and Policies in the Developing Countries." World Bank Staff Working Paper no. 412. International Bank for Reconstruction and Development, Washington, DC.

Gonzales Arrieta, Gerardo M. 1988. "Interest Rates, Savings and Growth in Ldcs: An Assessment of Recent Empirical Research." *World Development* 16, no. 5: 589–605.

Goodman, Roger. 1999. "Culture as Ideology: Explanations for the Development of the Japanese Economic Miracle." In *Culture and Global Change*, ed. Tracey Skelton and Tim Allen, 127–36. New York: Routledge.

Gorga, Carmine. 1999. "Toward the Definition of Economic Rights." *Journal of Markets and Morality* 2, no. 1:88–101.

Gould, David, and Jose Amaro-Reyes. 1983. *The Effects of Corruption on Administrative Performance: Illustrations from Developing Countries*. Washington, DC: World Bank.

Government of Tanzania. 2001. *Poverty Reduction Strategy Paper*. Dar es Salaam: Government of Tanzania.

Gowland, David. 1990. *The Regulation of Financial Markets in the 1990's*. Brookfield, VT: Gower.

Grabel, I. 1995. "Speculation-Led Economic Development: A Post-Keynesian Interpretation of Financial Liberalization Programs." *International Review of Applied Economics* 9, no. 2:127–49.

Gramsci, Antonio. 1971. *Selections from the Prison Notebooks*. New York: International.

Grier, Sonya, and Carol A. Bryant. 2005. "Social Marketing in Public Health." *Annual Review of Public Health* (2005): 19–339.

Griffin, K., and J. Enos. 1970. "Foreign Assistance, Objectives and Consequences." *Economic Development and Cultural Change* 18:313–27,

Gruening, G. 2001. "Origin and Theoretical Basis of New Public Management." *International Public Management Journal* 4, no. 1:1–25.

Gupta, Kanhaya L. 1987, "Aggregate Savings, Financial Intermediation and Interest Rates." *Review of Economics and Statistics* 69, no. 2:303–11.

Guyatt, Helen L., Marinus H. Gotink, Sam A. Ochola, and Robert W. Snow. 2002. "Free Bednets to Pregnant Women through Antenatal Clinics in Kenya: A Cheap, Simple, and Equitable Approach to Delivery." *Tropical Medicine and International Health* 7, no. 5:409–20.

Guyatt, Helen L., Sam A. Ochola, and Robert W. Snow. 2002. "Too Poor to Pay: Charging for Insecticide-Treated Bednets in Highland Kenya." *Tropical Medicine and International Health* 7, no. 10:846–50.

Guyer, Jane, ed. 1995. *Money Matters: Instability, Values and Social Payments in the Modern History of West African Communities*. Portsmouth, NH: Heinneman.

Gwin, Catherine. 1994. *US Relations with the World Bank, 1945–92*. Washington, DC: Brookings Institution.

Habibullah, M. S. 1999. "Financial Development and Economic Growth in Asian Countries: Testing the Financial-Led Growth Hypothesis." *Savings and Development* 23, no. 3:279–90.

Hage, Jerald, and Kurt Finsterbusch. 1987. *Organizational Change as a Development Strategy: Models and Tactics for Improving Third World Organizations*. Boulder: Rienner.

Hagen, Everett. 1963. *Planning Economic Development*. Homewood, IL: Irwin.

Hahn, Frank. 1982. "The Neo-Ricardians." *Cambridge Journal of Economics* 6, no. 4:353–74.

Hands, D. Wade. 1993. "Popper and Lakatos in Economic Methodology." In *Rationality, Institutions and Economic Methodology*, ed. Uskali Maki, Bo Gustafsson, and Christian Knudsen, 61–75. London: Routledge.

Hanlon, Joseph. 2000. "Power without Responsibility: The World Bank and Mozambique Cashew Nuts." *Review of African Political Economy* 83:29–45.

———. 2001. "Mozambique Wins Long Battles over Cashew Nuts and Sugar." Jubilee 2000 Coalition. http://www.jubileeresearch.org/jubilee2000/news/mozamb020201.html.

Haq, Mahbub ul. 1971. "Employment and Income Distribution in the 1970's: A New Perspective." *Development Digest* no. 7 (October):3–8.

Harbison, Frederick, and Charles Myers. 1959. *Management in the Industrial World*. New York: McGraw-Hill.

Hargreaves Heap, Shaun, Martin Hollis, Bruce Lyons, Robert Sugden, and Albert Weale. 1992. *The Theory of Choice: A Critical Guide*. Oxford: Blackwell.

Harper, David A. 1998. "Institutional Conditions for Entrepreneurship." *Advances in Austrian Economics* 5:241–75.

Harrison, Graham. 2004. *The World Bank and Africa: The Construction of Governance States*. London: Routledge.

Harrod, Roy. 1939. "An Essay on Dynamic Theory." *Economic Journal* 49:14–33.

Hartmann, Jeanette. 1994. "The State in Tanzania: Yesterday, Today and Tomorrow." In *African Perspectives on Development: Controversies, Dilemmas and Openings*, ed. Ulf Himmelstrand, Kabiru Kinyanjui, and Edward Mburugu, 218–33. New York: St. Martin's.

Hausman, Daniel. 1994. "Kuhn, Lakatos and the Character of Economics." In *New Directions in Economic Methodology*, ed. Roger Blackhouse. London: Routledge.

Haynes, Jeff. 1999. "Religion and Political Transformation." In *Culture and Global Change*, ed. Tracey Skelton and Tim Allen, 223–31. New York: Routledge.

Heller, Peter, and Alan Tait. 1983. *Government Employment and Pay: Some International Comparisons*. Washington, DC: International Monetary Fund.

Helliwell, John F. 1996. "Economic Growth and Social Capital in Asia." NBER Working Paper, Cambridge, MA.

Hickson, D.J., D. S. Pugh, and Diana C. Pheysey. 1969. "Operations Technology and Organization Structure: An Empirical Reappraisal." *Administrative Sciences Quarterly* 14, no. 1:378–97.

Higgins, B. H. 1959. *Economic Development: Principles, Problems and Policies*. London: Constable.

Hilsenrath, Jon E. 2004. "Stock Characters: As Two Economists Debate Markets, the Tide Shifts." *Wall Street Journal*, October 18.

Hirschman, Albert. 1973. "The Changing Tolerance for Income Inequality in the Course of Economic Development." *Quarterly Journal of Economics* 87:1–32.

———. 1981. *Essays in Trespassing*. New York: Cambridge University Press.

Hirshleifer, Jack. 1970. *Investment, Interest and Capital*. Englewood Cliffs, NJ: Prentice-Hall.

Hodgson, Geoffrey M. 2004. "Reclaiming Habit for Institutional Economics." *Journal of Economic Psychology* 25:651–60.

Honohan, Patrick, and Daniela Klingebiel. 2000. "Controlling the Fiscal Costs of Banking Crises." World Bank Policy Research Working Paper Series no. 2441.

Horsefielde, J. Keith. 1969. *The International Monetary Fund, 1945–1965: Twenty Years of International Monetary Cooperation.* 3 vols. Washington, DC: International Monetary Fund.

Hrebiniak, L. G., and C. C. Snow. 1980. "Strategy, Distinctive Competence, and Organizational Performance." *Administrative Sciences Quarterly* 25, no. 2:317–36.

Hu, T. L. 1984, *My Mother-in-Law's Village: Rural Industrialization and Change in Taiwan.* Taipei: Academia Sinica, Institute of Ethnology.

Inglehart, Ronald. 1997. *Modernization and Postmodernization: Cultural, Economics and Political Change in 43 Societies.* Princeton: Princeton University Press.

International Labor Organization. 1976. *Employment, Growth, and Basic Needs.* Geneva: International Labor Organization.

International Monetary Fund. 1997a. *Good Governance: The IMF's Role.* Washington, DC: International Monetary Fund.

———. 1997b. *World Economic Outlook.* Washington, DC: International Monetary Fund.

———.2001. *Review of the Fund's Experience in Governance Issues.* Washington, DC: International Monetary Fund.

Israel, Arturo. 1987. *Institutional Development: Incentives to Performance.* Baltimore:Johns Hopkins University Press for the World Bank.

———. 1990. *The Changing Role of the State: Institutional Dimensions.* Washington, DC: World Bank.

Jacobs, Bart, and Neil Price. 2004. "The Impact of the Introduction of User Fees at a District Hospital in Cambodia." *Health Policy and Planning* 19, no. 5: 310–21.

Jalilian, Hossein, and John Weiss. 1997. "Bureaucrats, Business and Economic Growth." *Journal of International Development* 9, no. 6:877–85.

Jamal, Vali, ed. 1995. *Structural Adjustment and Rural Labour Markets in Africa.* Houndmills, UK: Macmillan.

James, Chris, Saul S. Morris, Regina Keith, and Anna Taylor. 2005. "Impact on Child Mortality of Removing User Fees: Simulation Model." *British Medical Journal* 331:747–65.

James, William. 1893. *The Principles of Psychology.* New York: Holt.

Jaycox, Edward. 1993. "Capacity Building: The Missing Link in African Development." Transcript of address to the African American Institute Conference "African Capacity Building: Effective and Enduring Partnerships," Reston, VA, May 20.

Jedlicka, Allen. 1987. *Organizational Change and the Third World: Designs for the Twenty-First Century.* New York: Praeger.

Johnson, Chalmers. 1982. *MITI and the Japanese Miracle: Growth of Industrial Policy, 1925–1975.* Palo Alto, CA: Stanford University Press.

————. 1999. "The Developmental State: Odyssey of a Concept." In *The Developmental State*, ed. Meredith Woo-Cumings. Ithaca: Cornell University Press.

Johnson, Susan. 2004. " 'Milking the Elephant': Financial Markets as Real Markets in Kenya." *Development and Change* 35, no. 2:247–74.

Kalipeni, Ezekiel. 2000. "Health and Disease in Southern Africa: A Comparative and Vulnerabilty Perspective." *Social Science and Medicine* 50:965–83.

Kapur, Devesh, John P. Lewis, and Richard Webb, eds. 1997. *The World Bank: Its First Half Century*. Washington, DC: Brookings Institution.

Kaufmann, Daniel. 2003. *Rethinking Governance: Empirical Lessons Challenge Orthodoxy*. Washington, DC: World Bank.

Kaufmann, Daniel, Art Kraay, and Pablo Zoido-Lobaton. 1999. "Governance Matters." World Bank Policy Research Working Paper.

Kenny, Charles, and David Williams. 2001. "What Do We Know about Economic Growth? Or, Why Don't We Know Very Much?" *World Development* 29, no. 1: 1–22.

Keohane, Robert. 1986. *Neorealism and Its Critics*. New York: Columbia University Press.

Keynes, J. M. 1936. *The General Theory of Employment, Interest, and Money*. New York: Harvest/Harcourt Brace Jovanovich.

Khan, Mushtaq. 2004. "State Failure in Developing Countries and Institutional Reform Strategies." 5th Annual World Bank Conference on Development Economics, Europe. Paris: World Bank/Oxford University Press, 165–95.

Kifle, Henock. 1998. "Capacity Building in Africa—the Role of Multi-Lateral Financial Institutions." In *Institution Building and Leadership in Africa*, ed. Jerker Carlsson, Henock Kifle, and Lennart Wohlgemuth, 79–90. Uppsala: Nordiska Afrikainstitutet.

Kikumbih, Nassor, Kara Hanson, Anne Mills, Hadji Mponda, and Joanna Armstrong Schellenberg. 2005. "The Economics of Social Marketing: The Case of Mosquito Nets in Tanzania." *Social Science and Medicine* 60, no. 2:369–81.

Killick, Tony. 1980. "Trend in Development Economics and Their Relevance to Africa." *Journal of Modern African Studies* 18, no. 3:367–86.

Kleemeier, Lizz. 1984. "Integrated Rural Development in Tanzania: The Role of Foreign Assistance, 1972–1982." PhD diss., University of California, Berkeley.

Knack, Stephen, and Philip Keefer. 1997. "Does Social Capital Have an Economic Payoff? A Cross-Country Investigation." *Quarterly Journal of Economics* 112:1251–88.

Knudsen, Christian. 1993. "Equilibrium, Perfect Rationality and the Problem of Self-Reference in Economics." In *Rationality, Institutions and Economic Methodology*, ed. Uskali Maki, Bo Gustafsson, and Christian Knudsen, 133–70. London: Routledge.

Krahnen, Jan Pieter, and Reinhard H. Schmidt. 1994. *Development Finance as Institution Building: A New Approach to Poverty Oriented Banking*. Boulder: Westview.

Krueger, Anne. 1974. "The Political Economy of the Rent-Seeking Society." *American Economic Review* 64, no. 3:291–303.

————. 1992. "Institutions for the New Private Sector." In *The Emergence of Market Economies in Eastern Europe*, ed. C. and G. Rausser Clague. Cambridge, MA: Blackwell.

Krueger, Anne, Maurice schiff, and Alberto Valdes. 1991. *The Political Economy of Agricultural Pricing*. Baltimore: Johns Hopkins University Press.

Lal, Deepak. 1983. *The Poverty of Development Economics*. London: Institute of Economic Affairs.

Lall, Sanjaya. 1996. *Learning from the Asian Tigers: Studies in Technology and Industrial Policy*. London: Macmillan.

Landell-Mills, Pierre, and Ismail Serageldin. 1991. "Governance and the External Factor." In *Annual Bank Conference on Development Economics 1991*, ed. World Bank, 303–24. Washington, DC: World Bank.

La Porta, Raphael, Florencio Lopez de Silane, Andrei Schleifer, and Robert W. Vishny. 1997. "Trust in Large Organizations." *American Economic Review* 87, no. 2:333–38.

Laurell, Asa Cristina, and Oliva Lopez Arellano. 1996. "Market Commodities and Poor Relief: The World Bank Proposal for Health." *International Journal of Health Serivces* 26, no. 1:1–18.

Lawrence, Paul, and Jay W. Lorsch. 1967. *Organization and Environment: Managing Differentiation and Integration*. Boston: Harvard Business School Press.

Lawson, Colin, and Douglas K. Saltmarshe. 2002. "The Psychology of Economic Transformation: The Impact of the Market on Social Institutions, Status and Values in a Northern Albanian Village." *Journal of Economic Psychology* 23, no. 4:487–500.

Lee, Kelley, and Hilary Goodman. 2002. "Global Policy Networks: The Propagation of Health Care Financing Reforms since the 1980s." In *Health Policy in a Globalizing World*, ed. Kelley Kent Buse and Suzanne Fustukian Lee, 97–119. Cambridge: Cambridge University Press.

Leonard, M. 2000. "Coping Strategies in Developed and Developing Societies: The Workings of the Informal Economy." *Journal of International Development* 12:1069–1085.

Levy, Brian, and P. Spiller. 1993. *Regulation, Institutions, and Commitment in Telecommunications: A Comparative Analysis of Five Country Studies*. Washington, DC: World Bank.

————. 1994. "The Institutional Foundations of Regulatory Commitment: A Comparative Analysis of Telecommunications Regulation." *Journal of Law, Economics, and Organization* 10, no. 2:201–46.

————, eds. 1996. *Regulations, Institutions, and Commitment: Comparative Studies of Telecommunications*. Cambridge: Cambridge University Press.

Levy, Brian. 1991. "Transactions Costs, the Size of Firms, and Industrial Policy: Lessons from a Comparative Case Study of the Footwear Industry in Korean and Taiwan." *Journal of Development Economics* 34:151–78.

————. 1997. "How Can States Foster Markets?" *Finance and Development* 34, no. 3:21–23.

———. 1998, "Credible Regulatory Policy: Options and Evaluation," in *Evaluation and Development: The Institutional Dimension*, ed. R. Picciotto and E. Wiesner, 178–89. New Brunswick: Transaction.

———. 2002. "Patterns of Governance in Africa." World Bank African Region Working Paper Series, no. 36.

Lewis, P., and Stein, H. 2002. "The Political Economy of Financial Liberalization in Nigeria." In *Deregulation and the Banking Crisis in Nigeria: A Comparative Study*, ed. O. Ajakaiye, P. Lewis, and H. Stein, 21–52. Basingstroke: Palgrave.

Leys, Colin. 1969. *Politics and Change in Developing Countries: Studies in the Theory and Practice of Development*. Cambridge: Cambridge University Press.

———. 1996. *The Rise and Fall of Development Theory*. London: Currey.

Lienert, Ian, and Jitendra Modi. 1997. *A Decade of Civil Service Reform in Sub-Saharan Africa*. Washington, DC: International Monetary Fund.

Lindgreen, C-J., G. Garcia, and I. S. Saal. 1996. *Bank Soundness and Macroeconomic Policy*. Washington, DC: International Monetary Fund.

Little, Ian D. 1982. *Economic Development: Theory, Policy and International Relations*. New York: Basic.

Lopes, Carlos, and Thomas Theison. 2004. *Ownership, Leadership and Transformation: Can We Do Better for Capacity Development?* New York: Earthscan/United Nations Development Programme.

Malik, Khalid. 2002. "Towards a Normative Framework: Technical Cooperation, Capacities and Development." In *Capacity for Development: New Solutions to Old Problems*, ed. Sakiko Fukuda-Parr, Carlos Lopes, and Khalid Malik, 23–42. London: Earthscan.

Mason, Edward, and Robert Asher. 1973. *The World Bank since Bretton Woods*. Washington, DC: Brookings Institution.

Mathanga, Don P., Carl H. Campbell, Terrie E. Taylor, Robin Barlow, and Mark L. Wilson. 2006. "Socially-Marketed Insecticide-Treated Nets Effectively Reduce *Plasmodium* Infection and Anemia among Children in Urban Malawi." *Tropical Medicine and International Health* 11, no. 9:1367–74.

Matsheka, T. C. 1998. "Interest Rates and the Saving-Investment Process in Botswana." *African Review of Money, Finance and Banking* 1, no. 2: 5–23.

Mavrotas, G., and R. Kelly. 2001. "Savings Mobilization and Financial Sector Development: The Nexus." *Savings and Development* 25, no. 1:33–64.

Mayo, E. 1945. *The Social Problems of an Industrial Organization*. Andover, MA: Andover.

McGregor, D. 1960. *The Human State of Enterprise*. New York: McGraw Hill, 1960.

McIntyre, D., D. Muirhead, and L. Gilson. 2002. "Geographic Patterns of Deprivation in South Africa: Informing Health Equity Analyses and Public Resource Allocation Strategies." *Health Policy and Planning* 17, supp. 1:30–39.

McKinnon, Ronald. 1973. *Money and Capital in Economic Development*. Washington, DC: Brookings Institution.

———. 1993. *The Order of Financial Liberalization*. Baltimore: Johns Hopkins University Press.

McNamara, Robert S. 1981. *The McNamara Years at the World Bank: Major Policy Addresses of Robert S. McNamara, 1968–1981*. Baltimore: World Bank, 1981.

Mehmet, Ozay. 1978. *Economic Planning and Social Justice in Developing Countries*. London: Croom Helm.

Meier, Gerald, and Dudley Seers, eds. 1984. *Pioneers in Development*. Oxford: Oxford University Pres.

Messer, Norman, and Philip Townsley. 2003. *Local Institutions and Livelihoods: Guidelines for Analysis*. Rome: Rural Development Division, Food and Agriculture Organization of the United Nations.

Meuwissen, Liesbeth Emm. 2002. "Problems of Cost Recovery Implementation in District Health Care: A Case Study from Niger." *Health Policy and Planning* 17, no. 3:304–13.

Meyer, John, and Brian Rowan. 1977. "Institutionalized Organizations: Formal Structure as Myth and Ceremony." *American Journal of Sociology* 83, no. 2: 340–63.

Meyer, John, and George Thomas. 1984. "The Expansion of the State." *Annual Review of Sociology* 10:461–82.

Mihevc, John. 1995. *The Market Tells Them So: The World Bank and Economic Fundamentalism in Africa*. London: Third World Network and ZED Books.

Miller-Adams, Michelle. 1999. *The World Bank: The New Agenda*. London: Routledge.

Minsky, Hyman P. 1957. "Central Banking and Money Market Changes." *Quarterly Journal of Economics* 71, no. 2:171–87.

———. 1984. *Can "It" Happen Again? Essays on Instability and Finance*. Armonk, NY: Sharpe.

Mitchell, Timothy. 2005. "The Work of Economics: How a Discipline Makes Its World." *European Journal of Sociology* 47, no. 2:297–320.

Mkandawire, Thandika. 2002. "Incentives, Governance and Capacity Development in Africa." In *Capacity for Development: New Solutions to Old Problems*, ed. Sakiko Fukuda-Parr, Carlos Lopes, and Khalid Malik, 147–68. London: Earthscan.

Mohamed, Elsaudi. 1993. "Sub-Saharan African Debt and IMF Programs: A Critical Evaluation." PhD diss., Colorado State University.

Moses, Stephen, Firoze Manji, Janet E. Bradley, Nico J. D. Nagelkerke, Matthew A. Malisa, and Francis A. Plummer. 1992. "Impact of User Fees on Attendance at a Referral Centre for Sexually Transmitted Diseases in Kenya." *Lancet* 340:463–66.

Mosley, Paul. 1994. "Decomposing the Effects of Structural Adjustment." In *Structural Adjustment and Beyond in Sub-Saharan Africa*, ed. R. van der Hoeven and F. van der Kraaij, 70–98. Portsmouth, NH: Heinemann.

———. 2000. "Globalisation, Economic Policy and Convergence." *World Economy* 23, no. 5:613–34.

Mosley, Paul, and John Weeks. 1993. "Has the Recovery Begun? Africa's Adjustment in the 1980s Revisited." *World Development* 21, no. 10:1583–1606.

Mosley, Paul, Jane Harrigan, and John Toye. 1991. *Aid and Power: The World Bank and Policy Based Lending*. London: Routledge.

Mosley, Paul, Turan Subasat, and John Weeks. 1995. "Assessing Adjustment in Africa." *World Development* 23, no. 9:1459–73.

Murray, Christopher J. L., and Arnab K. Acharya. 1996. "Understanding Dalys." Harvard Center for Population and Development Studies.

Myrdal, Gunnar. 1957. *Economic Theory and Under-Developed Nations*. London: Duckworth.

———. 1968. *Asian Drama: An Inquiry into the Poverty of Nations*. London: Harmondworth.

———. 1978. *Need for Reforms in Underdeveloped Countries*. Institute for International Economic Studies: Stockholm.

Nabyonga, J., M. Desmet, H. Karamagi, P. Y. Kadama, F. G. Omaswa, and O. Walker. 2005. "Abolition of Cost-Sharing Is Pro-Poor: Evidence from Uganda." *Health Policy and Planning* 20, no. 2:100–108.

Nath, K. J. 2003. "Home Hygiene and Environmental Sanitation: A Country Situation Analysis for India." *International Journal of Environmental Health Research* 13:S19–S28.

Nigeria Deposit Insurance Corporation, ed. 2001. "Nigeria Deposit Insurance Corporation 2001 Annual Report." http://www.ndic-ng.com/pdf/ndicar2001.pdf.

North, Douglass. 1981. *Structure and Change in Economic History*. New York: Norton.

———. 1990. *Institutions, Institutional Change and Economic Performance*. Cambridge: Cambridge University Press.

———. 1995. "The New Institutional Economics and Third World Development." In *The New Institutional Economics and Third World Development*, ed. John Harriss, Janet Hunter, and Colin M. Lewis, 17–26. London: Routledge.

Nunberg, Barbara. 1988. *Public Sector Pay and Employment Reform*. Washington, DC: World Bank.

———. 1990. *Public Sector Management Issues in Structural Adjustment Lending*. Washington, DC: World Bank.

———. 1999. "Rethinking Civil Service Reform." *Poverty Reduction and Economic Management Notes* 31, October 31 (newsletter). Washington, DC: World Bank.

Nunberg, Barbara, and John Nellis. 1995. *Civil Service Reform and the World Bank*. Washington, DC: World Bank.

Nurkse, Ranar. 1953. *Problems of Capital Formation in Underdeveloped Countries*. Oxford: Oxford University Press.

Nyonator, Frank, and Joseph Kutzin. 1999. "Health for Some? The Effects of User Fees in the Volta Region of Ghana." *Health Policy and Planning* 14, no. 4: 329–41.

Oliver, Robert. 1995. *George Woods and the World Bank*. Boulder: Reinner.

Operations Evaluation Department of the World Bank. 1993. "Performance Audit Report: Kenya—Financial Sector Adjustment Credit." Washington, DC: World Bank.

———. 1998. "Financial Sector Reform: A Review of World Bank Assistance." Report no. 17454 Washington, DC: World Bank.

———. 1999. *Civil Service Reform: A Review of World Bank Assistance*. Washington, DC: World Bank.

Orru, Marco, Nicole Woolsey Biggart, and Gary G. Hamilton. 1997. *The Economic Organization of East Asian Capitalism*. London: Sage.

Osborn, R. N., and J. C. Hunt. 1974. "Environmental and Organizational Effectiveness." *Administrative Sciences Quarterly* 19:231–46.

Oshikoya, T. W. 1992. "Interest Rate Liberalization, Savings, Investment and Growth: The Case of Kenya." *Savings and Development* 16:305–21.

Oxfam and Action Aid UK. 2004. *To Lend or Grant? A Critical View of the IMF and the World Bank's Proposed Approach to Debt Sustainability: Analyses for Low-Income Countries*. London: Oxfam.

Ozgediz, S. 1983. "Managing the Public Service in Developing Countries: Issues and Prospects." Washington, DC: World Bank.

Palma, Gabriel. 1978. "Dependency: A Formal Theory of Underdevelopment or a Methodology for the Analysis of Concrete Situations of Underdevelopment?" *World Development* 6, no. 7–8:881–924.

Pasekova, Marie, and Eva Hyblova. 2003. "The Financial Management of Small and Medium-Sized Enterprises." Tomas Bata University, Czech Republic.

Patrick, Hugh. 1966. "Financial Development and Economic Growth in Developing Countries." *Economic Development and Cultural Change* 14, no. 2: 174–89.

Perrow, Charles. 1967. *A Framework for the Comparative Analysis of Organizations*. Indianapolis: Bobbs-Merrill.

Peters, Pauline. 1993. "Is Rational Choice the Best Choice for Robert Bates? An Anthropologist's Reading of Bates' Work." *World Development* 21, no. 6: 1063–76.

Picciotto, Robert, and Eduardo Weisner, eds. 1988, *Evaluation and Development: The Institutional Dimension*. Washington, DC: World Bank.

Piore, Michael. 1972. *Upward Mobility, Job Monotony, and Labor Market Structure*. Cambridge: MIT Press.

Polak, Jacques. 1957. *Monetary Analysis of Income Formation and Payments Problems*. International Monetary Fund Staff Papers, 6:1–50.

Polanyi, Karl. 1957. *The Great Transformation*. Boston: Beacon.

———. 1977. *The Livelihood of Man*, ed. Harry Pearson. New York: Academic.

Population Services International. 2003a. "Keeping Malaria at Bay: Mosquito Nets Treated with Insecticide Are Inexpensive, Effective." *Profile: Social Marketing and Communications for Health* (January):1–4

———. 2003b. "What Is Social Marketing?" *Profile: Social Marketing and Communications for Health* (Winter–Spring):1–4

Porter, Michael E. 1980. *Competitive Strategy: Techniques for Analyzing Industries and Competitors*. New York: Free Press.

Posner, Richard. 1986. *The Economic Analysis of Law*. 3d ed. Boston: Little, Brown.

Prescott, Nicholas, and David de Ferranti. 1985. "The Analysis and Assessment of Health Programs." *Social Science and Medicine* 20, no. 12:1235–40.

Przeworski, Adam, and James Raymond Vreeland. 2000. "The Effect of IMF Programs on Economic Growth." *Journal of Development Economics* 62:385–421.

Pugh, D. S., D. J. Hickson, C. R. Hinings, and C. Turner. 1968. "Dimensions of Organization Structure." *Administrative Sciences Quarterly* 13, no. 1:: 65–105.

Rabin, Matthew. 1998. "Psychology and Economics." *Journal of Economic Literature* 36:: 11–46.

Ranis, Gustav. 1982. "Basic Needs, Distribution and Growth: The Beginnings of a Framework." In *Trade, Stability, Technology, and Equity in Latin America*, ed. Moshe and Simon Teitel Syrquin, 373–96. New York: Academic.

Redding, S. Gordon, and Simon Tam. 1995. "Colonialism and Entrepreneurship in Hong Kong and Africa: A Comparative Perspective." In *Asian Industrialization and Africa: Studies in Policy Alternatives to Structural Adjustment*, ed. Howard Stein,183–204. New York: St. Martin's.

Reichel, R. 1991. "The Macroeconomic Impact of Negative Real Interest Rates in Nigeria: Some Econometric Evidence." *Savings and Development* 15:273–83.

Reinert, Erik S. 2000. "Full Circle: Economics from Scholasticism to Scholasticism." *Journal of Economic Studies* 27, nos. 4–5:364–76.

Ribot, Jesse. 1999. "Decentralization, Participation and Accountability in Sahelian Forestry: Legal Instruments of Political-Administrative Control." *Africa* 69, no. 1: 23–65.

Robinson, J. 1952. "The Generalization of the General Theory." In *The Rate of Interest and Other Essays*, ed. J. Robinson, 67–142. London: Macmillan.

Rodney, Walter. 1972. *How Europe Underdeveloped Africa*. Dar es Salaam: Tanzania Publishing.

Roemer, Michael. 1976. "Planning by Revealed Preference, an Improvement upon the Traditional Method." *World Development* 4, no. 9:775–83.

Rosenberg, Alexander. 1994. "What Is the Cognitive Status of Economic Theory?" In *New Directions in Economic Methodology*, ed. Roger Blackhouse, 216–35. London: Routledge.

Rosenberg, Tina. 2006. "When a Pill Is Not Enough." *New York Times*, 6 August.

Rosenquist, Louise Emilia Dellstrom. 2005. "A Psychosocial Analysis of the Human-Sanitation Nexus." *Journal of Environmental Psychology* 25:335–46.

Rostow, Walter. 1960. *The Stages of Economic Growth: A Non-Communist Manifesto*. Cambridge: Cambridge University Press.

Ruderman, A. Peter. 1990. "Economic Adjustment and the Future of Health Services in the Third World." *Journal of Public Health Policy* 11, no. 4:481–90.

Ruger, Jennifer Prah. 2005. "The Changing Role of the World Bank in Global Health." *American Journal of Public Health* 95, no. 1:60–70.

Russell, Steven. 1996. "Ability to Pay for Health Care: Concepts and Evidence." *Health Policy and Planning* 11, no. 3:219–37.

Russell, Steven, and Lucy Gilson. 1997. "User Fee Policies to Promote Health Service Access for the Poor: A Wolf in Sheep's Clothing?" *International Journal of Health Serivces* 27, no. 2:359–79.

Rutherford, Malcolm. 1996. *Institutions in Economics: Historical Perspectives on Modern Economics*. New York: Cambridge University Press.

Sachs, Jeffrey, and Andrew Warner. 1995. "Globalisation and Economic Reform in Developing Countries." Brookings Papers on Economic Activity, no. 1.

———. 1997. "Sources of Slow Growth in African Economies." *Journal of African Economies* 6, no. 3:335–76.

Sahn, David E. 1992. "Public Expenditures in Sub-Saharan Africa During a Period of Economic Reforms." *World Development* 20, no. 5:673–93.

Sahn, David, Paul A. Dorosh, and Stephen D. Younger. 1998. *Structural Adjustment Reconsidered: Economic Policy and Poverty*. Cambridge: Cambridge University Press.

Sahoo, P. Geethanjali Nataraj, and B. Kamaiah. 2001. "Savings and Economic Growth in India: The Long-Run Nexus." *Savings and Development* 25, no. 1:66–80.

Salter, W. E. G. 1959. "Internal and External Balance: The Role of Price and Expenditure Effects." *Economic Record* 35:226–38.

Santiso, Carlos. 2002. *Governance Conditionality and the Reform of Multilateral Development Finance: The Role of the Group of Eight*. Toronto: University of Toronto Press.

Sappington, David. 1994. "Designing Incentive Regulation." *Review of Industrial Organization* 9:245–72.

Schuler, Sidney Ruth, Lisa Bates, and Khairul Islam. 2002. "Reconciling Cost Recovery with Health Equity Concerns in a Context of Gender Inequality and Poverty: Findings from a New Family Health Initiative in Bangladesh." *International Family Planning Perspectives* 28, no. 4:196–204.

Schumpeter, Joseph. 1912. *The Theory of Economic Development*. Leipzig: Dunker and Humblot, 1912.

Seers, Dudley. 1972. "What Are We Trying to Measure?" *Journal of Development Studies* 8, no. 3:21–36.

Seidman, Ann, and Robert B. Seidman. 1994. *State and Law in the Development Process: Problem-Solving and Institutional Change in the Third World*. New York: St. Martin's.

———. 1999. "Using Reason and Experience to Draft Country Specific Laws." In *Making Development Work: Legislative Reform for Institutional Transformation and Good Governance*, ed. Ann Seidman, Robert B. Seidman, and T. W. Waelde, 249–84. Boston: Kluwer Law International.

Selowski, Marcel. and Taylor, Lance. 1973. "The Economics of Malnourished Children: An Example of Disinvestment in Human Capital." *Economic Development and Cultural Change* 7, no. 2:17–30.

Shaw, Edward. 1973. *Financial Deepening in Economic Development*. New York: Oxford University Press.

Shihata, Ibrahim. 1991. *The World Bank in a Changing World: Selected Essays*. Dordrecht: Nijhoff.

Shirley, Mary. 1998. "Performance Contracts: A Tool for Improving Public Services," in *Evaluation and Development: The Institutional Dimension*, ed. R. Picciotto and E. Wiesner, 132–47. New Brunswick, NJ: Transaction.

Silin, R. H. 1976. *Leadership and Values: The Organization of Larger Taiwanese Enterprises*. Cambridge: Harvard University Press.

Simon, Herbert. 1978. "Rationality as a Process and a Product of Thought." *American Economic Review* 68:1–16.

Singh, Ajit, Jack Glen, Ann Zammit, Rafael De-Hoyos, Alaka Singh, and Bruce
    Weisse. 2005. "Shareholder Value Maximisation, Stock Market and New Tech-
    nology: Should the US Corporate Model Be the Universal Standard?" *Interna-
    tional Review of Applied Economics* 19, no. 4:419–37.
Sjostrand, Sven-Erik. 1995. "Towards a Theory of Institutional Change." In *On
    Economic Institutions: Theory and Applications*, ed. Christos Pitelis, Sven-Erik
    Sjostrand, and John Groenewegen, 19–44. Aldershot, UK: Elgar.
Smyth, Russell. 1998. "New Institutional Economics in the Post-Socialist Transfor-
    mation Debate." *Journal of Economic Surveys* 12, no. 4:361–98.
Solow, Robert. 1956. "A Contribution to the Theory of Economic Growth." *Quar-
    terly Journal of Economics* 70:60–94.
Spitzer, Emil. 1969. "Standby Arrangements: Purposes and Form." In *The Inter-
    national Monetary Fund, 1945–1965: Twenty Years of International Monetary
    Cooperation*, ed. J. Keith Horsefielde, 2:469–91. Washington, DC: International
    Monetary Fund.
Stanford Institute for Economic Policy Research. 2001. "Anne Krueger Leaves
    Stanford to Join International Monetary Fund." *SIEPR Perspectives*, Fall
    [newsletter]. http://siepr.stanford.edu/.
Stein, Howard. 1992. "Deindustrialization, Adjustment, the World Bank and the
    IMF in Africa." *World Development* 20, no. 1:83–95.
————, ed. 1995a. *Asian Industrialization and Africa: Studies in Policy Alternatives
    to Structural Adjustment*. Basingstoke: Palgrave.
————. 1995b. "Institutional Theories and Structural Adjustment in Africa." In
    The New Institutional Economics and Third World Development, ed. Janet
    Hunter, Colin M. Lewis, and J. Harriss, 109–32. London: Routledge.
————. 1998. "Japanese Aid to Africa: Patterns, Motivation and the Role of Struc-
    tural Adjustment." *Journal of Development Studies* 35, no. 2:27–53.
————. 2000a. "The Development of the Developmental State in Africa: A Theo-
    retical Inquiry." University of Copenhangen, Centre of African Studies Occa-
    sional Paper Series.
————. 2000b. "Review of David Sahn et al., "Structural Adjustment Reconsid-
    ered, Economic Policy and Poverty." *Economic Development and Cultural
    Change* 48, no. 5:213–33.
————. 2002a. "The Nigerian Banking Crisis and Japanese Financial Develop-
    ment: In Search of Lessons." In *Deregulation and the Banking Crisis in Nigeria*,
    ed. H. Stein, O. Ajakaiye, and P. Lewis, 225–45. Basingstoke: Palgrave.
————. 2002b. "Institutions, Institutional Theory, and Institutional Development:
    Filling the Black Box of Social Capital," paper presented at the conference
    "Social Capital in the Theory and Practice of Development," University of Co-
    penhagen, March 2.
————. 2003. "Rethinking African Development." In *Rethinking Development
    Economics*, ed. Ha-Joon Chang, 153–78. London: Anthem.
Stein, Howard, Olu Ajakaiye, and Peter Lewis, eds. 2002. *Deregulation and the
    Banking Crisis in Nigeria: A Comparative Study*. Basingstoke: Palgrave.
Stein, Howard, and E. W. Nafziger. 1991. "Structural Adjustment, Human Needs, and
    the World Bank Agenda." *Journal of Modern African Studies* 29, no. 1:173–89.

Stein, Howard, and Machiko Nissanke. 1999. "Structural Adjustment and the African Crisis: A Theoretical Appraisal." *Eastern Economic Journal* 25, no. 4: 399–420.

Stewart, Frances. 1985. *Planning to Meet Basic Needs.* London: Macmillan.

———. 1995. *Adjustment and Poverty: Options and Choices.* London: Routledge.

Stewart, Frances, and Michael Wang. 2003. "Do PRSPs Empower Countries and Disempower the World Bank or Is It the Other Way Around?" Queen Elizabeth House Working Paper Series, Oxford University.

Stiglitz, J. 1989. "Financial Markets and Development." *Oxford Review of Economic Policy* 5, no. 4:55–68.

———. 1994. "The Role of the State in Financial Markets." In *Proceedings of the Annual Bank Conference on Development Economics, 1993,* 19–62. Washington, DC: World Bank.

———. 1998. "More Instruments and Broader Goals: Moving Toward the Post-Washington Consensus," lecture given at the annual World Institute for Development Economics Research Conference, Helsinki, Finland, January 7. http://www.wider.unu.edu.

Streeten, Paul. 1979. "A Basic-Needs Approach to Economic Development." In *Directions in Economic Development,* ed. K. Jameson and C. Wilber, 73–129. Notre Dame: Notre Dame University Press.

———. 1981. *First Things First—Meeting Basic Human Needs in the Developing Countries.* Oxford: Oxford University Press.

Summers, Lawrence. 1991. "Knowledge for Effective Action." In *Proceedings of the Annual Bank Conference on Development Economics Conference,* ed. Lawrence Summers and Shekhar Shah Summers, 7–14. Washington, DC: World Bank.

———. 1992. "The Next Decade in Central and Eastern Europe." In *The Emergence of Markets in Eastern Europe,* ed. Christopher Clague and Gordon Rausser, 25–34. Oxford: Blackwell.

Swan, T. W. 1960. "Economic Control in a Dependent Economy." *Economic Record* 36:51–66.

Taiwo, I. O. 1992. "A Flow-of-Funds Approach to Savings Mobilization Using Nigerian Data." *Savings and Development* 16, no. 2:168–82.

Tarp, Finn. 1993. *Stabilization and Structural Adjustment: Macroeconomic Frameworks for Analysing the Crisis in Sub-Saharan Africa.* London: Routledge.

Tayeb, Monir H. 1988, *Organizations and National Culture.* London: Sage.

Taylor, Frederick. 1911. *The Principles of Scientific Management.* New York: Harper.

Temple, Jonathan, and Paul Johnson. 1998. "Social Capability and Economic Growth." *Quarterly Journal of Economics* 113, no. 3:965–90.

Thacker, Strom C. 1999. "The High Politics of IMF Lending." *World Politics* 52, no. 1:38–75.

Thaler, Richard. 1980. "Toward a Positive Theory of Consumer Choice." *Journal of Economic Behavior and Organization* 1, no. 1:39–60.

Tolbert, Pamela. 1985. "Institutional Environments and Resource Dependence: Sources of Administrative Structure in Institutions of Higher Education." *Administrative Sciences Quarterly* 30, no. 1:1–30.

Tolbert, Pamela, and Lynne Zucker. 1983. "Institutional Sources of Change in the Formal Structure of Organizations: The Diffusion of Civil Service Reform, 1880–1935." *Administrative Sciences Quarterly* 28, no. 1:22–39.

Tool, Mark. 1995. *Pricing, Valuation and Systems: Essays in Neoinstitutional Economics*. Aldershot, UK: Elgar.

Toye, John. 1987. *Dilemmas of Development: Reflections on the Counter-Revolution in Development Theory and Policy*. Oxford: Blackwell.

Underhill, G., ed. 1997. *The New World Order in International Finance*. Basingstoke: Macmillan.

United Nations Conference on Trade and Development. 2004. *The Least Developed Countries Report 2004*. Geneva: United Nations Conference on Trade and Development.

United Nations Development Programme. 1992. *Human Development Report 1992*. Geneva: United Nations.

———. 2005. *Human Development Report*. Oxford: Oxford University Press.

Urwick, L. 1943. *The Elements of Administration*. New York: Harper and Row.

Van Arkadie, Brian. 1990. "The Role of Institutions in Development." In *Proceedings of the First Annual World Conference on Development Economics*, 153–75. Washington, DC: World Bank.

van der Geest, M. Macwan'gi, J. Kamwanga, D. Mulikelela, A. Mozimba, and M. Mwangelwa. 2000. "User Fees and Drugs: What Did the Health Reforms in Zambia Achieve?" *Health Policy and Planning* 15, no. 1:59–65.

Veblen, Thorstein. 1919. *The Place of Science in Modern Civilization and Other Essays*. New York: Huebsch.

Vreeland, James Vernon. 2003. *The IMF and Economic Development*. Cambridge: Cambridge University Press.

Wade, Robert. 1997. "Greening the World Bank: The Struggle over the Environment." In *The World Bank: Its First Half Century*, ed. Devesh Kapur, John P. Lewis, and Richard Webb, 611–734. Washington, DC: Brookings Institution.

———. 2002. "US Hegemony and the World Bank: The Fight over People and Ideas." *Review of International Political Economy* 9, no. 2:215–43.

Wang, Zhen Kun, and L. Alan Winters. 1998. "Africa's Role in Multilateral Trade Negotiations: Past and Present." *Journal of African Economies* 7:37–69.

Warman, F., and A. P. Thirlwall. 1994. "Interest Rates, Savings, Investment and Growth in Mexico 1960–90: Test of the Financial Liberalization Hypothesis." *Journal of Development Studies* 30, no. 3:629–49.

Waterkeyn, Juliet, and Sandy Cairncross. 2005. "Creating Demand for Sanitation and Hygiene through Community Health Clubs: A Cost-Effective Intervention in Two Districts in Zimbabwe." *Social Science and Medicine* 61:1959–70.

Waterston, Albert. 1972. "An Operational Approach to Development Planning." In *Crisis in Planning*, ed. D. Seers and M. Faber, 1:81–104. London: Chatto and Windus for Sussex University Press.

Weber, Max. 1968. *Theory of Social and Economic Organization*. New York: Oxford University Press.

Weeks, John, David Anderson, Chris Cramer, Alemayehu Geda, Degol Hailu, Frank Muhereza, Matteo Rizzo, Eric Ronge, and Howard Stein. 2003. *Supporting Ownership: Swedish Development Cooperation with Kenya, Tanzania and Uganda*. Stockholm: Swedish International Development Cooperation Agency.

Weintraub, Eric. 1985. *General Equilibrium Analysis*. Cambridge: Cambridge University Press.

Weisbrod, B., R. Andreano, R. Baldwin, E. Epstein, and A. Kelley. 1973. *Disease and Economic Development: The Impact of Parasitic Diseases in St. Lucia*. Madison: University of Wisconsin Press.

Weller, C. 2001. "Financial Crises and Financial Liberalization: Exceptional Circumstances or Structural Weaknesses?" *Journal of Development Studies* 38, no. 1:98–127.

Wiesner, Eduardo. 1998. "Transaction Cost Economics and Public Sector Rent-Seeking in Developing Countries: Toward a Theory of Government Failure." In *Evaluation and Development: The Institutional Dimension*, ed. Robert Picciotto and Eduardo Wiesner, 108–131. New Brunswick, NJ: Transaction.

Williamson, Oliver. 1985. *The Economic Institutions of Capitalism: Firms, Markets, Relational Contracting*. New York: Free Press.

———. 1994. "The Institutions and Governance of Economic Development and Reform." In *Proceedings of the World Bank Annual Conference on Development Economics 1994*, 171–208. Washington, DC: World Bank.

Wilson, John Oliver. 1991. "Human Values and Economic Behavior: A Model of Moral Economy." In *Socio-Economics: Toward a New Synthesis*, ed. Amitai Etzioni and Paul R. Lawrence, 233–62. London: Sharpe.

Wohlgemuth, Lennart. 1998. "Administering and Leading a University." In *Institution Building and Leadership in Africa*, ed. Jerker Carlsson, Henock Kifle, and Lennart Wohlgemuth, 123–36. Uppsala: Nordiska Afrikainstitutet.

Wolfensohn, James. 1998. "Letter." In *Evaluation and Development: The Institutional Dimension*, ed. Robert Picciotto and Eduardo Wiesner, ix–x. New Brunswick, NJ: Transaction.

Woods, Ngaire. 2000. "The Challenges of Multilateralism and Governance." In *The World Bank: Structure and Policies*, ed. Christopher Gilbert and David Vines, 132–58. Cambridge: Cambridge University Press, 2000.

Woodward, Joan. 1965. *Management and Technology*. Oxford: Oxford University Press.

World Bank. 1975. *Health Sector Policy Paper*. Washington, DC: World Bank.

———. 1980. *World Development Report*. Washington, DC: World Bank.

———. 1981a. *Accelerated Development in Sub-Saharan Africa*. Washington, DC: World Bank.

———. 1981b. *World Development Report 1981*. Washington, DC: World Bank.

———. 1983a. *Financial Intermediation in Nigeria*. Washington, DC: World Bank.

———. 1983b. *World Development Report*. Washington, DC: World Bank.

———. 1984. *Towards Sustained Development in Sub-Saharan Africa*. Washington, DC: World Bank.

———. 1987. *Financing Health Services in Developing Countries*. Washington, DC: World Bank.

———. 1988a. *Report on Adjustment Lending* (Document R88–199). Washington, DC: World Bank.

———. 1988b. *Rural Development, World Bank Experience, 1965–86*. Washington, DC: World Bank.

———. 1989. *From Crisis to Sustainable Growth: A Long Term Perspective Study*. Washington, DC: World Bank.

———. 1990a. *Annual Report, 1990*. Washington, DC: World Bank.

———. 1990b. *Report on Adjustment Lending II: Policies for the Recovery of Growth*. Washington, DC: World Bank.

———. 1992a. *Governance and Development*. Washington, DC: World Bank.

———. 1992b. *Adjustment Lending and the Mobilisation of Public and Private Resources for Growth*. Washington, DC: World Bank.

———. 1993a. *The East Asian Miracle: Economic Growth and Public Policy*. Washington, DC: World Bank.

———. 1993b. *World Development Report 1993*. Washington, DC: World Bank.

———. 1994a. *Governance: The World Bank Experience*. Washington, DC: World Bank.

———. 1994b. *Adjustment in Africa: Reforms, Results and the Road Ahead*. Oxford: Oxford University Press.

———. 1995. *A Continent in Transition: Sub-Saharan Africa in the Mid-1990s*. Washington, DC: World Bank.

———. 1997. *World Development Report 1997: The State in a Changing World*. Washington, DC: World Bank.

———. 1988a. *Lessons from Experience in HNP*. Washington, DC: World Bank.

———. 1988b. *The Initiative on Defining, Monitoring and Measuring Social Capital: Overview and Program Description*. Washington, DC: World Bank.

———. 1999a. *Annual Report, 1999*. Washington, DC: World Bank.

———. 1999b. *World Bank Lending by Sector, 1990–99*. Washington, DC: World Bank.

———. 2000. *Can Africa Claim the 21st Century?* Washington, DC: World Bank.

———. 2001. *Annual Report, 2001*. Washington, DC: World Bank.

———. 2002a. *Annual Report, 2002*. Washington, DC: World Bank.

———. 2002b. *World Development Report 2002: Building Institutions for Markets*. Washington, DC: World Bank.

———. 2003. *African Development Indicators, 2003*. Washington, DC: World Bank.

———. 2004a. *African Development Indicators, 2004*. Washington, DC: World Bank.

———. 2004b. *Adjustment Lending*. Washington, DC: World Bank.

———. 2005a. *World Development Indicators*. Washington, DC: World Bank.

———. 2005b. *African Development Indicators*. Washington, DC: World Bank.

———. 2006. *World Development Indicators*. Washington, DC: World Bank.

———. 2007. *IBRD Votes and Subscriptions*. Washington, DC: World Bank.

World Health Organization. 2003. *World Health Report 2003*. Geneva: World Health Organization.

Wray, L. R. 1990. *Money and Credit in Capitalist Economies: The Endogenous Money Approach*. Cheltenham, UK: Elgar.

Zucker, Lynne. 1977. "The Role of Institutionalization in Cultural Persistence." *American Sociological Review* 42, no. 5:726–43.

———. 1987. "Institutional Theories of Organization." *Annual Review of Sociology* 13:443–64.

Zwerman, W. 1970. *New Perspectives on Organization Theory*. Westport: Greenwood.

Index